Camden History
Journal of the Camden Historical Society Inc

Vol 4, No. 1, March 2016
To
Vol 4, No. 10, September 2020.

Editor
Dr Ian Willis, OAM.

Published by
Camden Historical Society Inc
40 John Street,
Camden. NSW. 2570.

Published by Camden Historical Society Inc.
40 John Street, Camden, NSW 2570
(SAN: 908 3002)

www.camdenhistory.com.au

© 2022 by the Camden Historical Society Inc.

All rights reserved. No part of this publication may be used or reproduced in any manner whatsoever without written permission, except in the case of brief quotations in critical articles and reviews. Contact the Camden Historical Society PO Box 566 Camden NSW 2570 Australia for more information. (secretary@camdenhistory.org.au)

All photographs in the publication are part of the Camden Historical Society's collection or are used with the permission acknowledged in the text.

First published in 2022

1st Edition

ISBN: 978-0-6485894-5-7

Front cover: Peter Watson standing in front of a fire fighting engine used by the Camden Fire and Rescue Brigade. c.2016 (L. Stratton) – reproduced from Volume 4 Issue 1.

Back cover: Camden Museum Holden Motor Car lent by Max Boardman – Australian Day Parade 2017 (L. Stratton).

Introduction

Camden History is the Journal of the Camden Historical Society. It is published twice yearly and contains a wide range of articles and other local history items about the Camden District.

This book is a reproduction of all issues in Volume 4. It spans the period from March 2016 to September 2020.

Individual issues are reproduced from the original text submitted to the printers and contain the errors and omissions in the actual issues. Unlike the original, colour version of illustrations and photographs are used where available.

The page numbers are as printed in the original. They do not correspond to the page numbers in this book.

Page numbers start from 1 in March 2016 and should increment across the issues, finishing at 454 in September 2020. There are discrepancies with the numbers as there are omissions and overlaps at the start and end of the issues.

Following is a table of contents by the author, reproduced from the Society's website. Again, the page numbers refer to the original issue's page numbers.

Each issue starts on a right-hand (recto) page.

Contents

Volume 4, Nos 1-10.
March 2016 – September 2020

Ahmad, Rizwana, and Patricia Johnson, Olive McAleer, Shirley Rorke, Nola Tegel, John Wrigley OAM. 'Alan Baker Art Classes'. p.248

Aulsebrook, Laura Jane, 'A Picture Tells a Thousand Words. Fashion Speaks Just as Loud!'. p.316

Aulsebrook, Laura Jane, 'A vintage girl in a modern world, why a 21st-century girl loves living a 1950s life', p.226

Aulsebrook, Laura Jane, 'Unlocking Camden's History with the Camden Council Heritage Advisory Committee'. p.436

Bearup, Wayne, 'Memories of Pansy, The Camden Tram'. p.142

Bearup, Wayne, 'Pansy, The Camden - Campbelltown Train, Photographs by Wayne Bearup'. p.91

Dodds, Sandra, 'Lively exhibition for the Centenary of Australian Federation'. p.159

Dodds, Sandra, 'Sculptures, Monuments and Outdoor Cultural Material project'. p.203

Downing, Pauline, 'Ghosts and Shadows at Macaria'. p.107

Eagleton, Tara, 'A Personal Reflection on Local History Studies at the University of New England'. p.100

Egan-Burt, Laura, 'An Arts and Crafts house in Menangle'. p.120

Egan-Burt, Laura, 'Menangle Community Association Inc'. p.125

Fisher, Stephen, 'Memories of growing up in Camden'. p.25

Heath, Lenore, 'The Heath Years at Windamere, Cobbitty'. p.204
Hill, Trish and Allen Seymour, 'Digitizing The Roy Dowle Photographic Collection'. p.431
Hokin, Lauren, 'Anzacs of Macarthur'. p.177

Johnson, Janice, 'Ghosts and Shadows At Macaria, A Reply'. p.145

Kramer, Betty, 'Memories of growing up in Camden'. p.1

Latham, Mark, 'Horse History in Western Sydney: Kirkham Stud'. p.60
Lester, Bob, 'President's Report 2015 – 2016'. p.86
Lester, Kathy, 'Changing environments for small charitable organisations'. p.282
Lowry, Genevieve, 'COVID has grounded my travel plans for now'. p. 426
Lundy, Andrew, 'Archaeology and Elderslie Railway Station',. p.232

Matterson, Dianne, 'A Familiar Face: Tildsley's Butchery'. p.441
Matterson, Dianne, 'Camden Museum Volunteer Project',. p.298
Matterson, Dianne, 'Disastrous Theatre Fire',. p 327
Matterson, Dianne, 'The Quiet Achiever: Camden Post Office'. p. 380

McCall, Peter, 'The Abusive Mr Chisholm (Part 3)', p 363
McCall, Peter, 'The Abusive Mr Chisholm (Part Two)', p.299
McCall, Peter, 'The Abusive Mr Chisholm, Part One'.. p.258
McIntosh, Anne, 'Memories of Rob Shumack', p 367
McIntosh, Anne, 'William Macarthur and the Empire of Science, presentation by Dr Julie McIntyre at State Library of NSW. From notes taken by Anne McIntosh'. p321
McIntosh, Anne, 'A 1930 road trip from Sydney'. p.193
McIntosh, Anne, 'A visitor to Camden'. p.199
McIntosh, Anne, 'Australia Day 2017'. p.136
McIntosh, Anne, 'Making the Most of MOSAiC'. p.171
McIntosh, Anne, 'Memories of Ron Davies: Abbotsford'. p.350
McIntosh, Anne, 'Mother's Day at Belgenny Farm 2017'. p.198
McIntosh, Anne, 'Please 'shed' light on Matavai'. p.267
McIntosh, Anne, 'Recollections of Burnham Grove from Virginia Ghezzi'. p.371
McIntosh, Anne, 'St Johns GFS celebrates 50 Years'. p. 393
McIntosh, Anne, 'The Camden Museum Collection - Understanding Its Significance'. p.132
Memories of Milton and Elaine Ray. Gail Carroll (nee Ray). p.274
Mulley, Sophie, 'Dairy Farmer to Young Local Historian'. p.67

O'Brien, Jo, 'Camden's Heritage and the Impact of the 2020 Pandemic'. p. 417
O'Brien, Jo, 'An Independent Woman',. p 336
O'Brien, Jo, 'The Connections Between Local History and Family History'. p. 388
O'Farrell, Brendan, 'Loyal Orange Lodges'. p 332

Peacock, Sue and Brian, 'Stories from The Menangle News'. p.111

Peacock, Sue, 'The story of The Menangle News'. p.117

Pesic, Kathryn, 'Camden Item of Significance'. p.284

Possum, Venessa, 'Baragal Ngurra darami - Budbury and a paddock long ago',. p.307

Riley, Joy, 'Growing up in Camden'. p.81

Rusgrove, Kaleigh, 'U.S. Artist Exploring Seeds at the PlantBank', p 344

Schofield, Ron, 'Memories of the Burragorang Valley'. p.190

Scoufis, Christos, 'Camden Arcade 25th Anniversary Address'. p.97

Sidgreaves, Peter, 'Community Recognition Statement given to the NSW Parliament by Peter Sidgreaves MP, Member for Camden, on 6 August 2020'. p. 440

Smith, Col, 'Memories of Barbering'. p.50

Smith, Tricia, and Frances Warner, Trish Clark, Margaret Wheeler, 'Some Nursing Memories'. p.290

Souter, Tony, 'John and Nona Souter, the story'. p.235

Stait-Gardner, Harry, 'Commander Frank Gardner RAN 1841-1927'. p.185

Styles, Lynette, 'Camden and Wollondilly LGA Rivalry, a view'. p.242

Thornell, Mark and Trish, 'Immigrant Child'. p.140

van Nunen, Linda and David, 'Brian Stratton - the story of a local artist'. p.40

Warne, Catherine, 'Book Launch, Pictorial History of Camden & District'. p.27

Wheeler, Margaret, 'Textiles, History and Smoking Caps', p 342
Wheeler, Robert, 'My memory of my first jobs in 1965 and 1966'. p.195
Wheeler, Robert, 'The Rewards of Volunteering at Camden Museum'. p.157
Willis, Ian and John Wrigley, 'Dr Peter Mylrea OAM'. p.215
Willis, Ian, 'Alan Baker, the artist'. p.242
Willis, Ian, 'Camden Covid Comments'. p. 424
Willis, Ian, 'Camden: The role of heritage in the making of place in a New South Wales country town'. p.31
Willis, Ian, 'Covid19 and the 1919 Spanish Influenza pandemic'. p.421
Willis, Ian, 'Echoes of the Appin Massacre 1816'. p.76
Willis, Ian, 'From the Editors Desk'. p. 415
Willis, Ian, 'Old Photographs'.. p. 431
Willis, Ian, 'President Annual Report 2017-2018'.. p.278
Willis, Ian, 'President's Annual Report 2018-2019',. p 361
Willis, Ian, 'President's Report 2016 – 2017'. p.167
Willis, Ian, 'Ria and the story of the song, Camden'.. p.270
Willis, Ian, 'Sixty Years of Local History, 1957-2017'. p.151
Willis, Ian, 'The Camden District Hospital Nurses' Home',. p.286
Willis, Ian, 'Trainee teachers Camden camp in 1924'..p. 400
Willis, Marilyn, 'A notable scientist from Camden'. p.276
Wrigley John, 'The Rise and Rise of the Camden Museum, Celebrating Fifty Years!'. p. 405
Wrigley, John, 'Janice Johnson'. p.222
Wrigley, Julie and Anne McIntosh, Margaret Wheeler. 'The McMinn Royal Black Sash - Item No. 2017.73.4', p 333

Yewen, Betty, 'My Story: The Tandem Team Launch Tourism, 1978-1988, Macarthur Country'. p.314

CAMDEN HISTORY

Journal of the Camden Historical Society

March 2016 Volume 4 Number 1

CAMDEN HISTORY
Journal of the Camden Historical Society Inc.
ISSN 1445-1549
Editor: Dr Ian Willis

Management Committee
President: Bob Lester
Vice Presidents: Ian Willis, Rene Rem
Secretary: Lee Stratton
Treasurer: Dawn Williams
Immediate Past President: John Wrigley OAM
General Committee: Sharon Greene Stephanie Trenfield
  Roslyn Tildsley Rene Rem
  Cathey Shepherd Robert Wheeler
  Julie Wrigley
Honorary Auditor:
Honorary Solicitors: Vince Barrett

Society contact:
P.O. Box 566, Camden, NSW 2570. Online <http://www.camdenhistory.org.au>

Meetings
Meetings are held at 7.30 p.m. on the second Wednesday of the month except in January. They are held in the Museum. Visitors are always welcome.

Museum
The Museum is located at 40 John Street, Camden, phone 4655 3400 or 46559210. It is open Thursday to Sunday 11 a.m. to 4 p.m., except at Christmas. Visits by schools and groups are encouraged. Please contact the Museum to make arrangements. Entry is free.

Camden History, Journal of the Camden Historical Society Inc
The Journal is published in March and September each year. The Editor would be pleased to receive articles broadly covering the history of the Camden district . Correspondence can be sent to the Society's postal address. The Society takes no responsibility for the contents of articles published in the Journal.

Donations
Donations made to the Society are tax deductible. The accredited value of objects donated to the Society are eligible for tax deduction.

Front Cover: Peter Watson standing in front of a fire fighting engine used by the Camden Fire and Rescue Brigade. c.2016 (L. Stratton)

CAMDEN HISTORY
Journal of the Camden Historical Society Inc.

Contents

Memories of growing up in Camden   1
Betty Kramer

Memories of growing up in Camden   25
Stephen Fisher

Book Launch   27
Pictorial History of Camden & District
Catherine Warne

Camden: The role of heritage in the making of place in a   31
New South Wales country town
Ian Willis

Memories of growing up in Camden

Betty Kramer

My father, Harold Powe was born at Waverley on 5 October 1895. He came to Camden 1912 and was employed as a farm hand on a property at Brownlow Hill.

My mother, Olive Biffin was born at Camden on 24 August 1895 to parents Alf and Jane Biffin who were at that time living and farming on the Camden Park Estate. In 1912 they purchased the property now known as "Woodburn" on Biffin's Road Mount Hunter. Biffins still own the property and run it as a dairy farm. The story is told that Harold walked from the property where he was employed at Brownlow Hill to the Biffin property at Mount Hunter to visit Olive. Visits were restricted and her father always wound the clock at 10pm giving the signal for any visitors to leave!

"Woodburn" Home of W.A.E.(Alf) and Jane Biffin Mount Hunter, Camden

Harold joined the Australian Imperial Force 1st Reinforcements 12th light Horse Regiment on 5 January 1915 aged 19 years and three months. He departed for Anzac Cove on 25 June 1915. On 18 September 1915 he was admitted to 1st Australian Casualty Clearing Station at Anzac Cove suffering from dysentery. He was subsequently transferred to Cairo where on 9 February 1916 he was transferred back to Australia and discharged as medically unfit on 15 July 1916. He received a pension of £3 per fortnight from 16 July 1916.

Olive Powe, Wife of Harold Powe,
Married 14th April 1917

Harold Richard Powe
Australian Imperial Expeditionary Forces -15th January 1916

Olive had worked as sales assistant in Camden Drapers and Clothiers and was given a reference on 12 July 1916. She then obtained a position at Sydney Snow Ltd. A department Store on the corner of Pitt and Liverpool Streets, Sydney in the ribbon department. She remained employed there until 20 March 1917.

On 14 April 1917 Harold and Olive were married at St. Johns Church in Camden by Reverend John Kittell. During the first few years of their marriage Harold was in poor health. He took up a job as a traveling salesman. My mother had to learn to drive their car at this time because dad often became ill while visiting outback properties. They had a farm at Castlereagh, a grocery shop in Penshurst, in partnership with Olive's brother Rupert. They then moved back to Camden where Harold took up a job with The Fresh Food and Ice Company where he stayed until 1925. He then joined the Harris and Ramsay business and became an agent for the Atlantic Union Oil Company in 1927.

His first business was in Murray Street Camden. He built the Camden Filling Station in Argyle Street opposite the milk depot in 1928. My father expanded

Camden Filling Station
26th May 1929

his business to become an agent for the sale of many products. These included Schweppes drinks, Smiths crisps, H.V.MacKay farm machinery, washing machines and sometimes clothing. He had enjoyed his traveling salesman days and always took any opportunity to supply goods to his customers when he visited remote places to deliver petrol and fuel to keep the machinery running.

Harold retired in 1951 and the business was carried on by his son, Bill, until March 1980 when it was sold to Teraco Petroleum – Mr. Rob Godson. Bill described the business as the only floating service station in Australia! He was referring to the fact that whenever the Nepean River flooded so did the service station.

My parents had lost two children prior to the birth of my brother in 1920, so my safe arrival must have been a great joy and surprise to them after such a long period of time. Little did they know that ten years later my sister Wilma would become a very welcome addition to our family.

My recollections of living in the house beside the Camden Filling Station are very slight but I do remember my brother running across the road to jump on to "Pansy" the Camden train as it slowly went past the Milk Depot. This

In 1980 Bill Powe retired and sold the business to Mr. Rob Godson of Teraco Petroleum. By 1983 the old Service station, Workshop and house were demolished and a new "Self Serve" service station built. The poplar trees in the background remain.

would happen if he was late running across the paddock to the Camden Railway Station to begin his journey to Parramatta High School each morning.

In 1934 my parents built a very modern home at 40 Broughton Street Camden. This had electric lights, a telephone and a gas stove and hot water system!! At this time some houses in Camden still had gas lights and the gas-producing works were still operating. We relied on a sanitary service for out-

In about 1933 the House beside the Service Station was built.

40 Broughton Street, Camden.

side lavatories, later a septic system was installed with a filter system near the front gate. The Camden sewerage system became operational in 1939.

In 1936 I began attending Camden Public School where the headmaster was Mr Barnes and my kindergarten teacher Miss Bridge. The headmaster's cottage was located on a corner of the school land. The kindergarten room and wood-working room were next door. I remember there was a wonderful shady tree outside, and we sat under it at lunch time but there were lots of furry grubs falling down on us. In winter Miss Bridge would light the fire in the classroom and we sat in front of it learning to sew patterns with coloured wool on sewing cards. Some other teachers I remember: headmasters Mr Holden and Mr Callinan and class teachers Mr Bowen, Mr Cowley, Mrs Young.

On Sunday mornings I attended Sunday School at the St Johns Church parish hall. This was situated in the grounds of the church at the top of Hill Street. Most Sundays I walked through Macarthur Park, through a gate in our back fence to the hall and then after Sunday School I walked up to the church to join the junior choir. We climbed up the steep stairs to the organ loft where Mrs Brien played the magnificent organ. The robes for the choir were kept up there. We wore veils over our heads, of course all girls and ladies were expected to wear hats to Church at this time, and then down the stairs to lead the procession of the senior Choir and clergy down the aisle to our seats in the front row under the pulpit. I also attended music lessons with Mrs Brien on one day a week after school, but I am afraid I was not very talented. Reverand Paul conducted the services at the church. During Lent a service was held at St. Johns each morning before school. Captain Fisk, who assisted Reverand Paul, rented a room in the house next door to ours and he would accompany me to the Church each morning. It was well attended by children and we would run down the hill to school to be ready for classes to begin at 9.30am.

There were lots of other after school activities. I attended ballet and tap dancing lessons with Miss Dethlefs and Miss Stroud from 1939 to 1941. They also taught elocution, speech training and physical culture. These lessons were conducted in the town hall. A concert was presented at the end of each year at the Paramount Theatre. Parents were expected to provide our costumes. My mother, of course, made all outfits for me and also sometimes for other students. The local library was situated in the town hall building. I remember climbing the stairs to borrow my favourite books, the Anne of Green Gables series from the librarian Miss Freestone. The cost was one penny per book. I joined the Junior Red Cross at Camden School when it was re-established in 1938. My mother had joined the Camden Red Cross as a foundation member when it was formed on 11 August 1914, so volunteer work for this organization was very important to our family. My mother was also an enthusiastic member of the Country Women's Association and served as secretary for some years. The CWA rooms in Murray Street were constructed during her term of office.

Members of the Red Cross and Country Women's Association held street stalls each week in Argyle Street. Cakes, jams, sweets, flowers and vegetables and second hand books were sold. Morning tea, lunch and afternoon tea were served at the specially built canteen at the Camden sale yards near the railway station on sale days. There were often auction sales at local farms and the ladies would provide refreshments for sale on these occasions.

Fundraising was a very important part of life in Camden. Each year the hospital auxiliary, the church, the Country Women's Association and the Camden Show Society held a ball in the Agricultural Horticultural and Industrial Society Hall at the entrance to the showground. These were very grand occasions. For weeks before the event children gathered at the hall after school to practise marching and to learn ballroom dancing. Mrs Kelloway would play the piano and Mrs Huthnance and Mrs Coates would provide guidance

At the Floral Ball - A.H.& I. Society Hall Camden 1937

for these activities. Mr Garnet Rofe and his band would provide music on the night. Supper was provided for the children in the supper room while parents enjoyed some dancing. I suppose they took us home after that. In later years dancing was held in the army hut and upstairs in the Green Room.

Mr Jack Fox operated the Paramount Picture Theatre in Edward Street, near the entrance to the railway station. Two films were shown, together with advertisements, cartoons and shorts for forthcoming films. I attended sessions on Saturday afternoons. The cost was sixpence for front stalls and ninepence for back stalls. I was allowed threepence to spend on an ice cream at interval.

The Camden Show was held every year about two weeks before the Royal Easter Show in Sydney. This gave the local farmers an opportunity to show off their produce and prepare animals for exhibition. The Camden Horse Trotting Society provided exciting races. These were very often won by my Uncle, Bill Biffin, with his horse Prince Billy. Art and crafts, and flower arrangements were located in the hall. There were ring events including show jumping, horse riding and of course the grand parade when all competitors would lead their animals around the ring to show off their awards. Children's rides and sideshows contributed to the noise and entertainment, and fireworks always concluded the evening.

On 4 September 1939 the Second World War was declared and this changed our way of life in Camden. Red Cross ladies knitted socks for the soldiers. Sea boot stockings were knitted for the sailors. Camouflage nets were constructed in the CWA Hall. Royal Air Force personnel were stationed at Camden Airport. An air raid warning siren was installed on the hill in Macarthur Park behind our house. The shelter shed there also served as a spotting station for any unidentified aircraft. Air raid trenches were built in the grounds of Camden Public School and weekly air raid drills conducted. First aid classes were held and we all had first aid kits to wear. School children acted as casualties in the field for adult first aid training in the rectory paddock. Some people had personal air raid shelters built in their back yards. Houses were required to black out windows at night. Blackout lights were installed on all cars. Gas producers were installed on cars, with gas bags on the roof, and land army girl units were formed. Petrol rationing coupons had to be applied for. I remember helping my father count these and put them in bundles so that he could buy bulk petrol for our service station. Ration books were issued and coupons had to be used for all clothing, sugar, butter and meat. Barbed wire fences were erected on Sydney and Wollongong beaches.

Our family always spent some time camping at Stuart Park, Wollongong, during the summer Christmas school holidays. Many families from Camden gathered at Stuart Park. The coal truck drivers who brought coal from the mines at Nattai to Camden during the week, cleaned up the trucks and fitted them out with camping requirements for their Christmas New Year holidays. Lights were set up and community singing held around the camp fires. The Open Air Campaigners regularly called at the Camping Ground to entertain us with songs and Bible stories. Submarine barriers were placed in Sydney Harbour, but one did get through and destroyed ships. I remember the siren going off in Camden and everyone rushing outside to see what was going on. Just as well no gunfire came in our direction. My father and I always enjoyed our holidays at the beach. He taught me to swim and surf at Wollongong but Mum loved the mountains so we went there in winter. These holidays were usually spent at Katoomba. At that time there were many large accommodation houses in the town. Some that come to mind were The Carrington, Holmesdale, Palais Royale, Sans Souci and The California. These had large ballrooms and music for dancing was very popular. We stayed at Hampden Villa a smaller establishment on the corner of Katoomba and Waratah Streets. I never dreamed that in 1955 The California would become our home for 17 years. The new owners changed the name to the Mountain Heritage Retreat. The Sans Souci was also purchased by my husband's brother John. He continued to operate the business as a guest house, but later converted it to a nursing home.

Our house in Broughton Street was divided into two flats which were rented out to wives of Air Force officers serving at Camden Airport, and we moved to a flat behind the office of our Camden Filling Station business. Our delivery trucks were required to help build the airstrip at The Oaks. My brother, Bill, was granted special permission to drive one of these trucks and so was not called to join the armed forces. On 18 February 1941 Wilma was born while we were living in the flat behind the Camden Filling Station.

By 1942 my brother decided to join the Royal Australian Air Force and was to be sent to England on active service. Before he left he married Beryl Rofe on 27 February 1943 and we arranged to move back into the Broughton Street House. Beryl lived in the front flat and when Bill returned from England after the war ended in 1945 they built and moved into their own house. The dividing walls in the Broughton Street house were removed and it was now our family home again. When we moved back into the Broughton Street house my parents purchased a bicycle for me to ride to school. I rode this down Broughton Street, along Murray Street and around the corner into Argyle Street. As I rode around this corner it reminded me of the story my mother told of the day she fell from her horse when riding in to town from their Woodburn property at Mount Hunter. One of the horses used on the property was shared by Mum and her sister, Lillian, when they needed to come to town. Evidently Lillian had a friend who worked at Mr Poole's blacksmith business on the corner opposite the entrance to the Camden show ground and she often called in there to see him. Mum did not know this and one day she was riding the horse in to town and it suddenly turned into the blacksmith shop. Of course this took Mum completely by surprise and she was thrown to the ground. Fortunately she was not badly hurt.

By the end of 1942 I had finished primary school in Camden and it was time to consider high school. It was decided that, rather than travel to Parramatta on Pansy the local train from Camden to Campbelltown, and then on to Parramatta as my brother had done, I should go to boarding school. So at the beginning of 1943 the Sydney Church of England Grammar School at Moss Vale was chosen and my teenage life had begun. I often wonder if the fact that the war was fast approaching Australian shores had anything to do with this decision.

The School was situated on a working farm property, one and a half miles from the town of Moss Vale. The five hundred acre school property had dairy cattle as well as sheep. Vegetables were grown and there was an orchard. At this time there were about 80 pupils boarding at the school and some day girls attended each day from Moss Vale. I completed my Intermediate Certificate at the School and continued to the end of the next year, but did not sit for the Leaving Certificate. At this time some Italian Prisoners-of-

Sydney Church of England Grammar School, Moss Vale.

War were employed on the school property to help with the farming activities. I remember they wore bright red uniforms and we were warned to stay well away from them.

I returned to Camden and, in 1947, once again my mother had to contend with a child catching the early morning Pansy train from Camden Station to Campbelltown. I then caught the train on to Sydney to attend the Metropolitan Business College. The train left Camden Station at 7am and I must admit that some mornings I was late and Mum and I chased the train in the car to Narellan Station. I returned home again at 7pm and of course was picked up again at the station.

In 1955 it came time for my sister, Wilma, to attend high school. It was decided that she should follow in my brother's footsteps and attend Parramatta High School. So, again, Mum found herself driving a child to catch Pansy at 7am in the morning.

At the end of 1947, I obtained a position in the office of Camden solicitor, Mr RAC Adams. Mr Philip Higgs visited from Campbelltown and the business became known as RAC Adams and Higgs and later Higgs and Bowring I worked in their office until my marriage in 1952. I am sure this is where I became interested in local history. Most land transfers were under the Old System and deeds and Registration Copies had to be typed by hand. All letters had to have three copies using two sheets of carbon paper. One original, one blue copy for the client's file and one pink copy for the office records.

All copies of documents had to be checked for accuracy and certified by another member of staff. At this time there were only two girls on the staff. I worked for Mr Adams and Anne worked for Mr. Higgs in the Campbelltown Office. Mr Higgs came to Camden on Tuesdays and visited Picton on Fridays, so Anne was in the Camden office on Tuesdays and Fridays. At this time we also worked for half a day on Saturday mornings. There were no photocopiers in offices at that time. In 1951 Mr Higgs purchased a "tape recorder" and was able to dictate his letters at home. He brought it back to the office and I listened to the tapes through headphones to type them the next day. I remember this machine being about 18 inches long, 6 inches high and 12 inches wide with two 6 inch rolls of recording tape threaded through heads with an on – off switch. I had a foot pedal to control the movement of the tape, so that I could listen and stop depending on the speed of my typing. When I was married at St. John's Church Camden in 1952 Mr Higgs set up this recorder in the organ loft and recorded the service and music. This was transferred from the tape to two records.

At this time my Mother owned and operated a small shop called The Lad and Lass in Argyle Street where she sold children's clothes and baby goods.

In 1949 I joined the 1A Camden Girl Guides. The captain was Mrs King. The commissioner was Miss Freestone. I became lieutenant. Meetings were held in the Scout Hall in View Street and later in the CWA rooms in Murray Street. Activities included hikes in the rectory paddock and in the paddocks beside the Camden showground.

I joined the Country Women's Association Younger Set. The Young Anglican's Group held meetings in the parish hall where we played table tennis. Dances were held most Friday nights, and of course movies were shown at the Paramount Theatre on Saturday nights. Advance bookings could be made at Dunks fruit shop. I met Leo Kramer at the 1950 CWA annual ball at the AH&I Hall. The members of the Younger Set presented a fashion parade and I was one of the models. We became engaged on 9 September 1951 and were married at St Johns Church Camden on 26 April 1952 by Reverend Kirk. Our wedding reception was held in the large dining-lounge room of our 40 Broughton Street home. The carpet was rolled up, Mrs. Kelloway came to play our piano for dancing. Mr Higgs was our very capable master of ceremonies. The room had been very well used during the previous few weeks. As was the custom at this time, a kitchen tea and showing of the items collected in the bride's glory box had to be arranged. Many of her friends attended and of course had to be served supper. It also happened that my 21st Birthday occurred on the 22 April and naturally a party had to be held. More food was prepared by my mother. On the day after our wedding Leo and I flew off to Tasmania to spend two weeks there for our honeymoon.

Members of 1A Camden Girl Guides 1951
Edna Dominish, Heather Marshall, Dawn McCarthy, Pam Chisholm, Judith Dewar, Delma Clinton, Janice Rickets, Jillian Palmer, Margaret Adams, Janice Mitchell, Margery Ferguson, Wendy Hodgson, Jennifer Sidman Betty Collins, Barbara Rix, Barbara Peat, Sylvia Green

A CWA fete at the Murray Street rooms in the early 1950s.

Mum and Dad breathed a sigh of relief and prepared for a well earned rest. However Leo and I became homesick and arrived back in 10 days.

Leo lived in Burragorang Valley. His father and mother, Karl and Anna and their three sons John, Frank and Leo had come from Yugoslavia to Australia in 1928. Leo was then 4 years old. They lived on a farm at Colyton. Mr Kramer had owned his own furniture manufacturing business before coming to Australia, so he decided to begin a furniture manufacturing business in Sydney. In 1942, after being requested to make ammunition boxes for the war effort, they decided to purchase the Burragorang House guest accommodation in Burragorang Valley. Here they provided rest and recreation accommodation for army personnel. The house was beside the

Leo Kramer
Married
Betty Powe
at
St. John's Church Camden
on
26th April 1952

Wollondilly River and provided swimming, horse riding, bush walking and tennis activities.

Buses transport visitors to the numerous Burragorang Valley guest houses, and the local folk to work or shopping in Camden. George Higlett started his bus service in 1945. I used this bus service when I visited Leo prior to our marriage. Bede Daley was the driver. Many and varied are the stories of the bus drivers and their exploits up and down the treacherous mountain pass, One driver was reported to always stop at the hotel at The Oaks before he attempted the drive down the mountain. The mail car brings the mail, and delivers bread and meat to the local folk each morning and will take mail back to Camden to be posted. Sometimes it picks up passengers from the Valley to Camden.

After the end of the second World War in September 1945 the accommodation business began to decline and the family had to consider alternative business opportunities. Also in 1926 the Nepean Times newspaper had mentioned that the Sydney Water Board intended to build a Dam at Warragamba and the Burragorang Valley would be flooded.

All trees and undergrowth had to be cleared along the Wollondilly River and up the sides of the Burragorang Valley to a certain height. The Kramer family saw the need for a sawmill to be set up in the valley and proceeded to do just that. Folk who had lived in the valley for many years were offered only a small Valuer General's figure for their land and knew the Water Board would clear the land below the water level. Private land owners were looking for ways to get rid of the timber on their property before the Water Board took over, so the idea of a sawmill grew. There was another one, Gardner Bros, out at Coolong Swamp.

The sawmill was built in about 1948. It consisted of one big unenclosed shed with timber supports and iron roof. All machinery was set in concrete mixed by motor mixer on the site. Cement trenches were beneath the saws to collect sawdust on a conveyor belt. The mill was powered by a Crossley 4 cylinder Air Starter Diesel Engine. Cooling water was piped from the Wollondilly River. Diesel was supplied by Mr HR Powe of Camden. Firewood from offcuts collected and sold. Sawdust was collected by conveyor belt was dumped and burnt.

All rolling and loading in the mill was done by hand with cant hooks. No winches or other machinery was used in the mill. All loading of sawn timber and firewood was done by hand. Telegraph poles and mine props were also delivered on the trailer.

Burragorang House, Burragorang Valley near Camden Home of the Kramer Family from 1942 to 1955. The House was demolished to make way for the Warragamba Dam.

Burragorang House was built on the banks of the Wollondilly River near the junction of the Nattai River.

The mill was primarily a family concern with Leo working in the bush, cutting, snigging and delivering logs. He also worked as tailerout on the machines and helped with the loading and did all the deliveries. Frank looked after the office work and at this time was also able to help with some driving and loading. He was however disabled with polio from the age of about five years old.

The Kramer family also sponsored folk from Yugoslavia to come to Australia and some of these worked in the mill and guest house until they were able to find work elsewhere in Australia. The timber for the mill was also supplied by contractors and owners of private properties in the valley. Mel Catt and the Houlahans were some of these suppliers.
Timber came from Penny' Ridge, Blattmans, Mangans, the Burragorang House property and various other places. A small amount of

Karl and Anna Kramer with their three sons, John, Leo and Frank at Burragorang House Burragorang Valley about 1950

Kramer Sawmill Mill
Equipment

- 25ft girth Frame Saw
- No.1 Bench - 4 man circular saw for building material, palings and tomato stakes
- No.2 Bench - Canadian Breakingdown saw for Mine Baulks.
- A 4 header for weatherboards and flooring
- Swing docking saw for cutting specific lengths.
- Gulleting machine for sharpening saws.

Vehicles

- G.M.C. (army disposal) 6x6 prime mover with bogie trailer
- G.M.C. Prime mover and bogie trailer
- G.M.C. 6x6 snigging truck for snigging, loading in the bush and loading the log ramps for the frame saw. This truck was equipped with winches and a "jib" designed and built for the purpose.
- FORD V8 for deliveries - tabletop with removable sides designed and built for delivering fire wood. All trucks were loaded and unloaded by hand ! No pallets or fork lifts back then

Employees

- Mr. Frank Johnstone, Sawyer,
- Mr. Alf Reilly from The Oaks, Sawyer,
- Jimmy Wallace, a deaf mute boy employed for many years by the Kramer family,
- Brian Simic, Doug,
- Sep - engineer from Berghouse Engineering
- Barney Coil
- Mr and Mrs Laurie

timber was supplied by the Water Board as they gradually took over the properties.

Some special purpose timber was cut for: the top of the water reservoir on top of Burragorang near the lookout; planks for the Mount Hunter bridge and special orders for the Cement Mine at Maldon. Usual orders were for building materials. Fence palings, rails and posts. Tomato stakes, Flooring boards, weatherboards, pit props, telephone poles, mine baulks. All these were loaded and unloaded by hand. No pallets or cranes then. The Kramer family also secured the contract to build the Nattai Community Hall. This was completed and officially opened on 9 October 1954.

Loading logs at Penny's Ridge

Karl Kramer's son John left the valley in about 1947 to open his own Furniture Manufacturing business at Arncliffe.

Leo and the boys loading timber at Penny's Ridge for the Sawmill at Burragorang Valley, 1950

Camden Flood 18th June 1949 - view towards bridge - train line and road.

The diesel to run the sawmill operated by the Kramer family in Burragorang valley was supplied by my father. One evening Leo arrived at my home dressed in his shirt and underwear with his good trousers over his arm. It was Saturday night and we were to attend the movies at the Paramount Theatre. He said "I have come through 'flood and high water' to visit you" ! He neglected to mention that he had driven his truck up to ask my father if he could pick up a couple of drums from Camden Filling Station next morning. Needless to say the request was granted and Leo stayed the night at our house, collected the diesel on the Sunday morning and returned home.

After our marriage in 1952 Leo and we lived in Krazy Kottage a small house situated on a block of land between the Burragorang House and the sawmill. The house was by then only open for guests on holiday weekends and school holidays. Casual staff would be hired for these occasions. University students from Sydney usually filled these positions and Leo would drive to Sydney to bring them to The Valley and deliver them back at the end of their employment. During our courting days these trips would be our special outing after the Easter weekend holiday. Leo would pick me up in Camden on his

The aftermath of the 1949 flood, showing highwater mark

way to Sydney with the girls. After dropping them at their destination we would continue on to the evening session of the Royal Easter Show. He then drove back to Burragorang after leaving me at my parents home in Camden. Leo drove his truck to Sydney markets to pick up supplies for the guest house. These were stored in the cool room. There were no deep freeze facilities then. The kitchen and guest dining room were located on the second floor of the house. All cooking was done on a large four oven fuel stove, so all firewood and provisions had to be carried up the stairs by hand. Electricity was supplied to the kitchen and dining room via a private line from the mines. A generator was used to provide lights for all guest bedrooms.

A mail car from Camden would arrive each day. It delivered bread and meat from Camden and returned each evening. A passenger bus took workers from the coal mine at Nattai to Camden each day. Gradually the valley was cleared of timber and the Water Board took over all properties and the buildings were burnt. Our beautiful fertile valley, which had been supporting farming families for many years, was drowned by the water stored behind the Warragamba Dam wall.

In 1955 our son, Carl, was born and the Kramer family purchased the California private hotel at Katoomba. This building had been taken over by the navy during the Second World War and used as accommodation for navy

"KRAZY COTTAGE"
Burragorang Valley
first home of Betty and Leo Kramer

wives and children. The building was in very bad condition, in urgent need of repair. It was auctioned for sale. The family put in a low bid, not expecting it to be accepted. It was and we were obliged to move in and begin restoration work. The furniture contained in The California was not as good as the furniture in Burragorang House so we decided to exchange it. I carried our baby on a pillow on my knee in our Ford truck as we negotiated the rough and winding roads between Burragorang Valley and Katoomba. There were no seat belts or baby capsules required in vehicles at that time. Almost the first word Carl spoke was buckets because our trips between The Valley and Katoomba were very frequent and we always traveled under the ropeway carrying buckets of cement to the Warragamba Dam Wall construction site.

Of course, as well as moving furniture from the Valley to Katoomba, the sawmill had to be demolished and the machinery sold and removed. This took approximately two years to accomplish. At the time the machinery and equipment was valued at about £10,000. The Crossley 4 Cylinder Engine which, I believe, weighed about 8 tons was sold and had to be delivered to the Ulladulla area. It was loaded on to our Ford truck and Leo and I and our son Carl, now aged about two years set off to deliver it. All went well until we were traveling down Mount Ousley Road into Wollongong when the brakes failed. Fortunately we were on a fairly level part of the road with a slight incline into the bush at the side. We were able to stop unhurt. There were, of course, no mobile phones available then. We managed to flag down a passing motorist who took Carl and me in to Wollongong to find a service station. The mechanic took us back to our vehicle, did some repairs to the brakes and Leo was able to drive the load back to his workshop. I telephoned my parents in Camden and they drove down to pick us up. Needless to say they insisted on caring for Carl at Camden, when, in about two weeks time, Leo and I drove back down to pick up the repaired truck and continue the delivery.

In 1966 our daughter, Sue, was born at Katoomba. In June 2011 we visited the picnic area overlooking the site of our Burragorang House and sawmill. I remembered the happy, hard working days when our family lived in the Valley and I am sure there are many people who remember spending happy holidays in this beautiful valley.

Demolition of "Burragorang House" prior to the flooding of Burragorang Valley to make way for the Warragamba Dam

"The California" Private Hotel - (named "The Naval Guest House) purchased at Auction by K. Kramer and Sons (Karl and Anna Kramer and Sons, Frank and Leo) in 1955.

Betty Kramer and her daughter Sue Reynoldson overlooking Lake Burragorang at Warragamba Dam in 2013.

Camden Fire Brigade Presentation Camden Historical Society 10 February 2016

Ian Willis

At the February meeting Joel Kursawe, the Deputy Captain of the Camden Fire Brigade, Station 248, gave a very informative talk on the history of the brigade. In the audience was Peter Watson, 94 years old, a retired fireman from the brigade who told funny stories of his time in the brigade and his love for the job. Peter contributed to the story of the brigade by Peter Mylrea published in Camden History in 2009.

This year is the centenary of the opening of the Camden Fire Station at 38 John Street, Camden. The brigade was formed up in 1900. The brigade moved into the new premises after the NSW Fire Brigade purchased the Temperance Hall for over £300, and spent another £300 on improvements. The new station was opened in January 1916.

Joel presented a time-line of events from the brigade's foundation in 1900 to the present day and outlined the types of fire events that the brigades has attended over the years. In recent years the firies have added snake catching to their repertoire.

The original brigade was formed up on military lines with officers holding rank. The Occurrence Books give the detailed activity of the brigade. In the 1920s and 1930s the brigade was called out to between 1-5 fires each year, which increased in the 1950s to around 30 per year and in last decade between 200-400 calls. The Camden brigade was originally founded with 15 volunteers, and now has 17 on-call officers.
The fire fighting capacity of the district was increased in 1999 when the Narellan Fire Station was opened which handles over 800 calls a year.

Camden Fire & Rescue NSW are planning a bigger event in April to celebrate 100 years of the Fire Service in Camden and we will advise further details at a later date.

Camden Fire & Rescue NSW Brigade crew stationed at Elderslie with Peter Watson and society president Bob Lester. (L Stratton)

Peter Watson chatting to John Wrigley and Roslyn Tildsley after the society February meeting with Joel Kursawe (L Stratton)

My Life as a Nasho

Stephen Fisher R.A.E.M.E Craftsman 2801168

Presented to the Historical Society meeting in September 2015 by Frances Warner, Stephen's foster sister, during a show and tell session on family and war. The story, as told by Francis, is presented in the first person by Stephen.

I was sitting on a beach on a small island (Rocky Island) just off Seaforth, north of Mackay, QLD, listening to the ABC on my transistor radio. They were reading out the dates from the latest National Service call up ballot. It was 2 April 1972 just 2 days after my 20th birthday. My birth date was one of the dates selected. Myself and good mate of mine had been living on this tropical island for the past 3 months after completing my trade apprenticeship.

But alas it was time to head home and do my patriotic chore. I worked for a few months before I had to show up for my medical examinations and finally present for enlistment at Marrickville. We then were sent off by bus up the Putty Rd to Singleton with all my other long hair and somewhat bewildered enlistees. As we drove through the main gate at Singleton Army Barracks, I was thinking to myself how wonderful and clean this place was and how did they keep it so tidy. I soon found out.

This was the longest day of my young life. We went from one hall to another, receiving all sort of kits and uniforms, bedding, needles, filling out numerous forms. From arriving in the late afternoon to finally getting to our allocated huts with all our bedding, myself and the rest of the 600 recruits finally got to bed at 2am only to be awoken at 6am in the morning for more of the same the following day. After a day of hard training, marching, exercising, more marching, class rooms lectures, more marching, swimming, eating, running, marching and numerous movies all relating to discipline. Zulu was one, a movie of bees, this showed us the chain of command and how everybody had their job and how well they worked as a team. There were also talks by teams of dentists on how to look after your teeth.

After 4 weeks they opened the bar. It was the longest queue I had ever seen. Along with the opening of the bar came the fights, not too many though. Then after 8 weeks we were allowed to go home for a four day break, but before we were allowed to leave we had to watch a 2 hour documentary on what happens to a human body in car crashes, 2 hours of blood, brains and guts. I will never forget that movie.

After 3 months of basic training, we had our passing out parade. I have never been so proud of all these men and the honour it is to wear the slouch hat (which I still have). It was about 3 days before we were to leave Singleton to head off for corps training that a Federal election was held and Mr Whitlam was voted in. It was a sad day for me and a happy day for others who were able to leave the army within one week.

I elected to stay in and complete my time serving in the army. I was posted to Bandiana near Albury for my 3 month corps training and up to Holsworthy for the next year where I served with 1 company workshop R.A.M.E.M.E. We were a field unit and spent most of the time on exercises in outback NSW and up and down the east coast.

I made lots of good mates, most were regulars and most were Vietnam Vets. I look back at my Military career with great memories and pride. Anyone who has not done military service has missed out on an adventure and I will always cherish these precious memories.

Book Launch
Pictorial History of Camden & District

Catherine Warne
Kingsclear Books
4 December 2015
At the Camden Musuem

Good evening Ladies and Gentlemen

My name is Catherine Warne and I am the publisher at Kingsclear Books. Kingsclear Books has been publishing pictorial histories of Sydney local government areas for over 30 years, since 1983. You can see them displayed in the room. It was with great pleasure that I finally decided to do a book on Camden. I met Ian Willis at a history conference in March 2014 and discussed writing the book. He got to work on it in late 2014.

With his published work available in part on the internet, his blog, his writing for the District Reporter and his work editing and writing for the Camden Historical Society Journal, he rivals Alan Atkinson as Mr Camden. He was the perfect choice for the Pictorial History Camden and District. Ian's thesis on the Camden Women's Voluntary Services was completed in 2004, and his Masters Degree in 1996 was on the Camden Red Cross. Detailed articles can be found on the internet and make for good reading and clarification of the growth of this district from the occupation of the Dharawal, the colonial times through to this time of urban sprawl.

Catherine Warne (Brett Atkins)

I would like to quote from Dr Ian Willis's article on Oran Park which I think summarises the changes in Camden district:
Oran Park and other colonial estates like it, were part of the spatial pattern and economic structure of the Cumberland Plain established by a powerful colonial elite by 1840. They built themselves impressive homes, and in the

Cowpastures their ilk included John Macarthur's Camden Park, George Macleay's Brownlow Hill, John Oxley's Kirkham and Elderslie, Alexander Riley's Raby, Edward Lord's Orielton, William Howe's Glenlee, Thomas Hassall's Denbigh and Garnham Blaxcell's Curtis Park. This set, who modeled themselves on the British elite, established a social and economic hegemony over the region that persisted into the twentieth century.

Ian Willis signing books at launch (Brett Atkins)

He continues, discussing more recent years:

The commodification of the rural setting, and local history, are constant themes for land releases in the Camden local government area. The Dart West website claimed in 2009 that their development is located in the historic and beautiful Camden district, combining the best of Camden country living. New residents houses, the developer maintained, will be set in rolling paddocks and bushland ridges and valleys in a beautiful rural environment. These values are at the heart of the existing community's sense of place and identity, and attract the new suburbanites. The new arrivals come looking for a place where the country looks like the country[1]. Yet the paradox of the whole situation is, that in time, they will convert the area into something that they are trying to escape, Sydney's urban sprawl.

On my first day in Camden this year, when I came to the museum to begin scanning images for the book, I first visited the Camden markets at the bottom of John Street. Here the flooded paddock glittered behind the post and rail fence. Frogs were loudly croaking and the stalls were full of fruit, vegetables, including giant cauliflowers, eggs, honey, flowers and other delights. The growers were locals. On my last day in Camden, last Thursday when I was selling the books, it was 40 degrees. I drove through to Oran Park, a treeless estate, a landscape of swirling red dust, skeletal houses which were just timber frames and in the dead centre of it all was a giant Woolworths, car park and pharmacy. So much for the rural idyll. Gone were the days of thousands of ducks, giant green frogs, tortoises and an abundance of other birds in the Cumberland woodlands.

To conclude I would like to mention that the main source of local images was the Camden Historical Society which is run with the untiring voluntary efforts of its members. I spent many happy days scanning images from their files, using the Camden Images website as a guide. I found all the members and volunteers I met to be delightful, helpful and interested. In all the years Kingsclear Books has been publishing local history and all the historical societies we have worked with, Camden can take a special little prize for competence, intelligence and organisation. And very pleasant company. An essential ingredient in any project. I would like to also thank the Oaks Heritage Centre for use of their images and their hospitality.

MC for launch John Wrigley (Brett Atkins)

John and Julie Wrigley guided me closely and helped with proofreading and final corrections but my thanks go to all of you for your warmth and your help. And thank you all for organising tonight.

I would like to thank my technical and design assistant Paul Taylder of Xigrafix who works with care, commitment and integrity on all of the pictorial histories. Some of you may have met him at the scanning workshop. To all others who helped, I refer you to the acknowledgements in the book to see the contribution of members of the society and others in the community.

To conclude, Camden has its own distinctive history and the area is loved by people who grew up here. This book gives local people a written and photographic record of the district and how it has changed. There is and will be a nostalgia for the good old days and this book has captured that in Ian's words and the collection of images. Thank you all for coming and enjoy the rest of the evening. It gives me great pleasure to launch the book.

Happy customers at launch (Brett Atkins)

Camden: The role of heritage in the making of place in a New South Wales country town

Ian Willis

In June 2008 the headline on the front page of the *Camden Advertiser* announced in shrill tones, 'Heritage Under Threat'. The report warned that 'Camden's rich history is under threat after proposed changes to planning laws passed through NSW Parliament last week'. The quote illustrated the contentious nature of some of the issues surrounding the meaning and use of the term heritage and at the same time it also shows how its use is sometimes confused with history. Yet, while heritage acknowledges the value of things from the past, it can also help define and reinforce a sense of place and community identity, according to some like the History Council of New South Wales.

Camden is a community whose identity and sense of place is based on its past, and particularly its colonial origins, cultural background, social structures and geography. It was once a small dairying town surrounded by the estates of the landed gentry on the banks of the Nepean River. Like other country towns across Australia, it was a closed community that was socially conservative, Anglo-centric and had social interactions based on class, gender expectations, localism and rural ideology. In the last 50 years urbanisation has progressively re-shaped the town's rurality until today it is one largely based on mythology and nostalgia. The past has been used to create a point of difference from the rest of Sydney around a 'country town idyll'. In the process heritage concerns have been used as a political weapon, tourist promotion, saviour of business, moral shield, promoter of local history and a panacea for a host of other causes that revolved around 'community obligations' and 'private rights'. This is the proposition that is examined in this paper.

The meaning of heritage
Initially the first question that should be asked in this discussion is: What is the background to heritage? Geographers, Graham, Ashworth and Tunbridge, take a broad view and see the development of the idea of heritage (or concern for the past) as part of modernity and locate it with the development of nationalism (or national heritage) and the deification of nature in the nineteenth century. On the local front one of the most useful examinations of the meaning of heritage in Australia has been undertaken by Graeme Davison, where he discusses how it has evolved from a narrow literal interpretation of something that has been or may be inherited to a wider usage where it covers 'inherited customs, beliefs and institutions held in common by a nation or community' and more recently has expanded to include 'natural' and 'built landscapes, buildings and environments'. Writers like David Lowenthal maintain that supporters of heritage view the past as a 'foreign country', where it is treated as 'an artefact of the present', and there is a sense of separateness and an urge to commodify the past for the consumption of tourists and others.

St John's Church, Camden. (I Willis)

The use of heritage in Camden has elements of each of these interpretations. Members of Camden's European community have used the past as a way of protecting themselves from the present and the processes of urbanisation that accompany it. So where did the interest in Camden's past stem from?

Changing interest in Camden's past (its heritage)

Interest in Camden's colonial past (mainly its built heritage) has only been evident from the 1920s. It parallels efforts by others in this area, for example the foundation of the Royal Australian Historical Society in 1901 and its Victorian equivalent in 1909, along with work done by people like William Hardy Wilson, an architect, who wrote *The Cow Pasture Road* (1920) where he detailed the 'charming old homesteads' of the Camden area. Stories of the area's gentry pioneers started to appear in the 1930s with the influence of the Sesqui-Centenary (1938), articles in the journal of the Royal Australian Historical Society (1928,1929, 1934) and the golden jubilee of the foundation of the Municipality of Camden (1889). Local Camden journalists, George Sidman and Arthur Gibson, each separately marked the golden jubilee of the foundation of the Municipality of Camden (1889). Sidman, the owner of the *Camden News*, published the memoirs of JB Martin in a series of newspaper columns. While Gibson, the owner of the *Camden Advertiser*, commissioned James Jervis from the RAHS to write *The Story of Camden*. These eulogised the role of John Macarthur and other colonial gentry, and would now fit the mythology of John Hirst's 'pioneer legend'. The pioneer story was repeated in later publications, for example, the Camden entry in the first edition of the Australian Encyclopaedia in 1958, and contributed to the foundation of the Camden Historical Society (1957), one of the community guardians of Camden's heritage.

The 'invention' of Australian heritage in the 1970s contributed to a shift in the emphasis of the Camden story away from the pioneer, with the foundation of organisations like the Camden Residents Action Group (1974), another of the community guardians of Camden's heritage and, the influence of the Bi-Centennial and the publication of Alan Atkinson's *Camden*. Around this time CRAG sponsored a heritage review of the town and the St John's church precinct was officially recognised for its cultural importance for the first time. For many in the local community this was the first time that heritage issues had been taken seriously in the town. This position has been strengthened by historical research on 20th century Camden and the development of a heritage plan by the local council for the central town area.

Heritage, place making and a sense of place

While an understanding of Camden's past is needed it is equally important to see the significance of the many questions heritage raises about the meaning of place' and the importance of emotions and beliefs in the process. While researchers like David Turton have asked: Where does the power of place come from? What makes it? The answer lies in the view of some that the 'sense of belonging to place… is fundamental to identity' and that representations of the past are an important part to the meaning, purpose and value of that identity. One of the most useful discussions on the meaning of place and identity in Australia has been conducted by Peter Read.

Rural scene on the approaches to Camden along Camden Valley Way. (I Willis)

For Memmont and Long the making of place involves creating bonds between people and their environment and in Camden emotional links between the community and the environment are represented by local stories from the past. They are an integral part of an emotional attachment to the landscape and posses universal truths about local identities, community celebrations, local folklore and a host of other cultural elements. The stories are found in local histories, memoirs, local newspapers, personal recollections, diaries, letters and a host of other memorabilia and ephemera. These stories are both complex and multi-layered. They are not immediately obvious to the casual observer and are bound up in class, conservatism, gender expectations, localism, and rural ideology. They are the basis of the community's sense of place and help construct a sense of who they are; their sense of identity, 'their heritage'. The complexities of these stories create a position where there are multiple identities and a variety of interpretations of place (landscape).

The contested nature of place making and heritage in Camden

Place making and the construction of identity in Camden is built around difference. The meaning of place is contested in terms of insiders (those who own the dominant story) and those who are not part of it; the notion of Otherness. Each of these opposing perspectives competes with each other and often have conflicting beliefs, values and aspirations. People on different side of the divide have different interpretations, different perceptions, different use of language, different emotional attachment to place and different traditions of heritage. This dichotomy has a number of connotations and can be expressed as: town/country; Indigenous peoples/European settlers (settler society); British/non-British (Asian – Chinese); Catholics/Protestants; developers/conservationists; locals/outsiders; male/female; public/private; townies/farmers; gentry/smallholders; middle class/working class; local/outsiders; wartime homefront/wartime battlefront; patriotic/unpatriotic; or just winners/losers. The dichotomous nature of these relationships are not mutually exclusive, and they can co-exist with each other and create parallel paths. Two brief examples illustrate this point.

One example of place making revolves around the local geography of the river, the floodplain and the town within this landscape and is constructed around two societies: settlers and indigenous people. The European settlers created place in Camden through their economic and cultural activities and their land management practices altered the landscape around their need to mould the land to suit their economic purposes and scientific interest. The settlers cleared the land, farmed it and in the process created a cultural environment (landscape) that was characterised by progress and development. They created an ordered landscape in a unruly wilderness that was made up of a patchwork of rural properties including the estates of the landed gentry and a number of smallholders. It was typified by farm houses, out buildings, haysheds, machinery sheds, dairy buildings, the pattern of areas under cultivation, farm windbreaks, tracks and roads, the pattern of boundary fences, hedgerows and a the patchwork nature of land clearing. The settlers tried to re-create 'a little England' in Camden. This was further reflected in local placenames and other Eurocentric practices. Most recently these practices have been documented in a register of significant trees in Camden, particularly exotics.

The settlers created a landscape based on their view of the world unlike the indigenous Dharawal people who had managed the local environment for their traditional purposes, and kept the Nepean River floodplain covered in grassy flats and free from undergrowth. When the first Europeans arrived they viewed this landscape with different eyes, in terms of an economic imperative and aesthetic notions of landscape. The Dharawal view of the landscape was based on people-environment relations with traditional models of ownership of places and territories, customary religious and ceremonial practice. According to Memmont and Long the concepts of 'people' and 'environment' overlapped whereas in Western thought they are classified separately. In traditional cultures there were strong emotional attachments to place as the focus of class identities and the relations between humans and nature is an interactive process, unlike Western approaches which are anthropocentric in nature and attempt to manipulate the environment to the needs of people.

A second example involving locals and outsiders illustrates the co-existence of opposites and shows how they can work against each other. The Camden community (who are the locals) perceives themselves to be different from 'others' (outsiders or anyone else) and their sense of worth is based on the interrelationship of place and heritage. Members of the local community have, over many decades, seen Camden as 'something special'. They have a degree of aloofness, or separateness, that contributes to their identity. The origins of this notion are found in the rural ethos that is drawn from within the nineteenth century rural traditions brought from Great

Britain, where there was a romantic view of the country and has been variously described as 'countrymindedness', 'rural ideology', 'rural ethos', 'ruralism', and a 'rural idyll'. Within this tradition there is an Arcadian notion of a romantic view of rural life where there is a distinction drawn between the metropolis and the village and has been expressed in works like Ray William's *The Country and the City*. This was the essence of pre-war Camden (a town of around 2000) where rural culture provided the stability of a closed community which was suspicious of outsiders, especially those from the city, with life ordered by social rank, personal contacts and familial links. It was confined by conservatism, patriarchy and an Anglo-centric view of the world. The 1960s might have seen permanent economic changes to the country town, but not to people's emotional attachment to it. The contemporary manifestation of this process is the 'country town idyll', which is really a spatial metaphor for keeping 'others' at bay. Sociologist Gabrielle Gwyther has identified this identity of difference in her examination of the master plan estates in the Camden area.

The spatial metaphor of a 'country town idyll'

Camden's sense of place and identity are based on a deeply embedded cultural mythology around the notion of the country town. Heritage and place have combined in the form of an imagined rural arcadia; a 'country town idyll'.

The sense of place is expressed in the language supporters of the idyll use to describe it. They express the heritage values that the local community are trying to protect. They talk about the retention of Camden's 'country town atmosphere', or retaining 'Camden's country charm', or 'country town character'. They describe the town as being 'picturesque', or having 'charming cottages'. To them Camden is 'a working country town', or is simply 'my country town'. These elements are evocative of an emotional attachment to a place that existed in the past, when Camden was a small quiet country town that relied on farming for its existence. It is a form of idyllic rural place making.

The idyll is a metaphor for Otherness and provides a safe haven where the community can retreat from reality of Sydney's encroachment on the town, away from a sense of anxiety caused by the evils of the city. It provides a sense of security in a fast changing world. But is is more than that. It also represents: the rural/urban divide and the dislike of 'outsiders'; resistance to change and fear of difference; Camden's Britishness (or British heritage); a desire by some for no development in the area in the face of Sydney's urbanisation; and the retention of traditional country values, which include their connectedness, their moral order, their Christian religiosity, their conservatism and their parochialism.

The metaphor is representative of the dislike of the social costs that accompany urbanisation, particularly, increased congestion, crime, loss of open space, increased population density, the invasion of suburbia, the loss of identity and a sense of place.

The spatial context of the metaphor is expressed by the river, the floodplain and the rural vistas that these create with the township. The most striking is the vista of the township across the floodplain, with the spire of the church on the hill dominating the

Camden Show (Camden Images)

town area. The townscape provides a cultural landscape which is indicative of the 1930s country town that was dominated by the dairy industry. The height and setback of the buildings in central Camden has changed in little in 70 years, and gives the visitor the impression that the town has changed little in that time. The land use in the town area still reflects the mix of the country town of the 1930 with retailing, commercial, light industrial, residential, open space, education and churches. The grid patterns of the streets is still intact from the 1840s and the major 19th century public buildings are largely unaltered. The railway has been removed from the northern entry to the town, but the 1920s milk factory is still intact as are two service stations. The townscape underpins the sense of place and the community identity is drawn from people's emotional attachment to it.

The origins of this cultural myth surrounding the idyll are located in the town's past and is defined as an idealised version of a country town from an imagined past which uses history to construct imagery based on Camden's heritage buildings and other material fabric. At the heart of the idyll is the view that Camden should retain its iconic imagery of a picturesque country town with the church on the hill, surrounded by a rustic rural landscape made up of the landed estates of the colonial gentry. The idyll has been created by its supporters in an attempt to isolate Camden, like an island, in the sea of urbanisation and development that has enveloped the town. The imagery is firmly located in 'the country' that Kerrie-Elizabeth Allen maintains is a location of nostalgia where one can experience an idyllic existence. Central to this notion is a nostalgia for the past and an escape from the present, where rural life was associated with an uncomplicated, innocent, genuine society in which traditional values persisted, and a place where lives were real and relationships were seen as honest and authentic.

The construction of the mythology associated with the metaphor is complex. It is drawn from the rural idyll, one of the main components of which is the rural and city divide, which dates from 19th century England. Here the city is seen as all things that are evil and the rural country is the source of real wealth and moral development of the community resided. Camden's British heritage means that the community thinks of itself as an English rural village, with church on the hill. St John's church is the moral heart of the metaphor.

The moral imperative of the church on the hill that is St Johns underpins the values of the idyll and the development of the romantic notions surrounding the town and its past. The church is on the highest point in the town and completely dominates the town. The church was strongly supported by the Macarthur family who regarded the town as part of their fiefdom. They ensured the moral tone of the town by endowing the church, providing public parks that carried their name and providing patronage to local Protestant organisations.

The geography of the Nepean River floodplain creates a sense of openness around the town, or ruralness, that engenders a 'country' mindset of those who live, or would like to live, in the local area. One of the sites in Camden that celebrates the idyll each year is the Camden Showground when thousands of 'outsiders' come to the annual show to participate in the mythology surrounding the metaphor.

Tourist promotions draw on the historic nature of the town and the vistas of the floodplain and the values of the idyll in brochures, promotions and the internet. Camden Council has embraced the mythology in their planning and policy documents and the idyll has been harnessed to oppose a number of development proposals for the town and immediate area surrounding it. (multi-storey carpark in central Camden, a McDonalds outlet at South Camden, an Islamic school on the outskirts of the town, and a shopping mall).

Conclusion
To sum up, the country town idyll is one mechanism that harnesses heritage to construct a sense of place and identity within the Camden community. So what of the future? There are early signs that the impact of the idyll is being diluted (or overwhelmed) by the new arrivals, who are predicted to number over 250,000 in the next 25 years.

Notes
Originally presented at the Australian Historical Association Conference at the University of Melbourne in 2008. Footnotes have been removed from this paper. For a complete paper contact the author <chn@live.com.au>

Camden signage at the entry to the town area (I Willis)

CAMDEN HISTORY

Journal of the Camden Historical Society

September 2016 Volume 4 Number 2

CAMDEN HISTORY
Journal of the Camden Historical Society Inc.
ISSN 1445-1549
Editor: Dr Ian Willis

Management Committee
President: Dr Ian Willis
Vice Presidents: John Wrigley OAM, Cathey Shepherd
Secretary: Lee Stratton
Treasurer: Dawn Williams
Immediate Past President: Bob Lester
General Committee: Sharon Greene   Rene Rem
                      Roslyn Tildsley   Julie Wrigley
                      Robert Wheeler   Stephanie Trenfield

Honorary Solicitors: Vince Barrett

Society contact:
P.O. Box 566, Camden, NSW 2570.   Online <http://www.camdenhistory.org.au>

Meetings
Meetings are held at 7.30 p.m. on the second Wednesday of the month except in January. They are held in the Museum. Visitors are always welcome.

Museum
The Museum is located at 40 John Street, Camden, phone 4655 3400 or 46559210. It is open Thursday to Sunday 11 a.m. to 4 p.m., except at Christmas. Visits by schools and groups are encouraged. Please contact the Museum to make arrangements. Entry is free.

Camden History, Journal of the Camden Historical Society Inc
The Journal is published in March and September each year. The Editor would be pleased to receive articles broadly covering the history of the Camden district . Correspondence can be sent to the Society's postal address. The Society takes no responsibility for the contents of articles published in the Journal.

Donations
Donations made to the Society are tax deductible. The accredited value of objects donated to the Society are eligible for tax deduction.

Front Cover Image: Camden Arcade 25th Anniversary (I Willis)
Inside Back Cover: Stables Camden Park Open Day 2016 (A McIntosh)
Back Cover Image: Camden Park East Lawn Open Day 2016 (A McIntosh)

CAMDEN HISTORY
Journal of the Camden Historical Society Inc.

Contents

Brian Stratton - the story of a local artist Linda and David van Nunen	40
Memories of Barbering Col Smith	50
Horse History in Western Sydney: Kirkham Stud Mark Latham	60
Dairy Farmer to Young Local Historian Sophie Mulley	67
Echoes of the Appin Massacre 1816 Ian Willis	76
Growing up in Camden Joy Riley	81
President's Report 2015 – 2016 Bob Lester	86
Pansy, The Camden - Campbelltown Train Photographs by Wayne Bearup	91
Camden Arcade 25th Anniversary Address Christos Scoufis	97
A Personal Reflection on Local History Studies at the University of New England Tara Eagleton	100
Ghosts and Shadows at Macaria Pauline Downing	107

Brian Stratton - the story of a local artist

Linda and David van Nunen

Brian Stratton writes:
I have been a Camden ratepayer since 1972 when I purchased a 30 acre block of land in the then sleepy hollow of Bringelly. The land was part of a grant of 1500 acres made in 1815 by Governor Macquarie to the magistrate Robert Lowe. Bringelly has been my home, my studio and my refuge for nearly 43 years but this is coming to an end. With the Southwest Sydney Growth Centre all will change. My block will be in Lowes Creek. The rural aspects will disappear as the land has been designated for industrial and residential uses.'

Born in Sydney on 23 May 1936 to Allan Thomas Stratton and Edna Mavis Lynch, Brian Stratton was the only member of the Australian Watercolour Institute to twice preside as president. Stratton's father, like many of his generation, was profoundly affected by the Great Depression of the 1930s and consequently devoted his life's energies to the union movement. A bookbinder by trade, Allan Stratton was to hold numerous positions in the Amalgamated Printing Trades Union, being a vigorous campaigner in the industrial fight for the 40-hour week, which was formally approved by the Commonwealth Arbitration Court on 8 September 1947 to take effect from 1 January 1948. He became Head Teacher of Bookbinding with the New South Wales Department of Technical Education, relinquishing his union position but remaining for many years their Returning Officer. However, his unremitting union activism took a heavy toll on the family, culminating in a marriage breakdown with the result that, for most of his life, Brian Stratton has had a close association with his mother and her relations.

At the outbreak of World War II, Stratton was a child of three but he distinctly recalls that his first intimation of its gravity was two years later, following the Japanese attack on Pearl Harbor in December 1941, when his teacher, Mr Farrell, announced to the class at Punchbowl Primary School, 'Boys, we are saved. I got down on my knees last night and thanked God that America is in the War.'

He would witness the radical changes war wreaked on the home front. There were blackouts in cities and coastal areas and, due to petrol shortages, charcoal burners propelled cars while trucks and public buses were fuelled by massive bags of gas that was a by-product of iron manufacturing. With the entry of Japan into the war and the attacks on Darwin, women and children

Brian with his entry in the 2010 in Quanhua Watercolour Gallery Zhujiajiao at Shanghai in China at which Brian won at award. (L & B Stratton)

were evacuated from northern Australia. The widespread fear that this country would be invaded was somewhat attenuated by the influx of thousands of American soldiers. Holes were dug in backyards with galvanised sheeting for roofs as improvised air raid shelters but, when it rained, they flooded with water. Shop windows were boarded up and stringent rationing was in force for essential items such as food, fuel, clothing and footwear. Stratton remembers walking to school barefoot during winter frosts, wearing short pants mended with a succession of patches, always carrying with him a small drawstring bag containing cotton wool and an eraser. The cotton wool was intended to serve as earplugs while the eraser was to be clamped between one's teeth in the event of bombing raids.

In his last year at Punchbowl Primary School, Stratton's teacher, Mr Rufus, suggested that their classroom would benefit from some adornment on its barren walls. Money was collected and two reproductions were hung -- Hans Heysen's virtuosic 1909 watercolour, *Summer*, and Robert Johnson's bucolic *Burragorang Valley*, the original oil painting having been a finalist in the 1939 Wynne Prize at the Art Gallery of New South Wales. These two images were Stratton's first visual experience of Australian art.

After obtaining his Intermediate Certificate, he commenced work in the printing industry, initially as a halftone, and then colour, etcher at the leading photoengraving company, Hartland and Hyde. Associated with Hartland and Hyde at that time was the renowned modernist photographer, Max Dupain. As the junior member of staff, one of Stratton's tasks was to buy the lunches so that there were times he would be in the dark room with Dupain and his assistants, among whom was Kerry Dundas, son of the artist Douglas Dundas MBE, who played an important role in his future career. Dupain would use an early oil painting by Stratton in the background of one of his commercial projects.

Following a five-year apprenticeship at the School of Printing (later Graphic Arts), Stratton was awarded the Bronze Medallion by the Premier of New South Wales, Joseph Cahill, at Sydney Town Hall as 'Most Outstanding Apprentice of the Year' in his trade. Continuing his studies at night, he subsequently obtained the Higher Trades Certificate.

In 1952, at the age of 15, he commenced part time studies in drawing and composition at North Sydney Technical College two nights a week under the tutelage of John Godson (a member of the Australian Watercolour Institute from 1934-50). On one occasion, Godson showed the class some of his unframed watercolours, which were the first original landscapes Stratton had seen. By far the youngest member of the group, Stratton was confident that his drawing was solid but felt his compositional skills were lacking. One of the guest lecturers in composition was the newly appointed teacher, Peter Laverty, who would be appointed as State Supervisor of Art for New South Wales prior to serving as Director of the Art Gallery of New South Wales from 1971 to 1977 and, subsequently, as vice president of the Australian Watercolour Institute.

An influential figure in Stratton's career was his teacher of life drawing, Douglas Dundas MBE, President of the Society of Artists and a trustee of the Art Gallery of NSW. During model breaks, his insights into art societies and galleries, as well as his informed responses to questions about artists and paintings, was an education in itself for Stratton. A member of the selection committee for full-time teachers of art, Dundas would be Stratton's first Head of School in TAFE. In 1970, Stratton interviewed Dundas in his studio, recording eighteen hours of tape concerning his life and career, which culminated, in 1974, in an edited, print version entitled, *Douglas Dundas Remembers*, copies of which are retained in State galleries and libraries throughout Australia. The original tapes were forwarded to the National Library in Canberra only to be destroyed when the delivery van burnt out. Stratton subse-

Brian at the 2010 Inaugural Shanghai Zhujiajiao International Watercolour Biennial Exhibition Opening Ceremony in China at which he was a finalist. (L & B Stratton)

quently completed a 90-minute follow up interview, which he presented to the library.

The following year, Stratton began working in watercolour, assiduously producing three full-sheet paintings per day during his holidays from work. In 1954, he joined the Tuesday night 'Still Life Wash' class taught by New Zealand-born, realist painter, Alfred Cook, Head Teacher of Commercial Illustration and Commercial Art, who had a life-long passion for watercolour, working almost exclusively in that medium. His watercolour demonstrations were revelatory for Stratton, who cites Cook as the most important influence of his career in his approach to painting. By his third year in that class, he was doing as much teaching and demonstrating as Cook was, with his encouragement. Consequently, in 1959, upon the recommendation of Alfred Cook, L. Roy Davies, Head of National Art School, invited Stratton to take this class. For the next few years, he worked in the printing industry by day and was involved in Technical Education most nights of the week, teaching in the Art School and studying at the School of Printing.

In 1962, he was appointed a full-time teacher of Art in the New South Wales Department of Technical Education, which came as a surprise to Stratton, who had foreseen the possibility of a teaching position within the School of Printing but a vacancy never occurred. However, after five weeks in the Art School, the Head of the School of Printing approached him to transfer to his staff. Stratton declined the offer and retired nearly thirty years later as Senior Head Teacher of Art and Design at Liverpool College of TAFE.

At the age of twenty, in 1957, Stratton won his first art award, the South Strathfield Watercolour Prize, adjudicated by Sir Erik Langker and watercolourists, G.K. Townshend (AWI) and Rufus Morris. On the advice of Alfred Cook, he had made a minor adjustment to the work, a holiday painting from Kurrajong, after which Cook announced prophetically, 'This looks like a prize-winner to me'. After the award presentation ceremony, G.K. Townshend commented to Stratton, 'This will not be your last prize,' a prognostication that proved correct. To date, Stratton has won more than 280 art prizes, culminating in two prestigious international awards at the 2010 *Shanghai Zhujiajiao International Biennial Watercolour Exhibition* at Quanhua Watercolour Art Gallery, Zhujiajiao, and the 2013 *Shenzhen International Watercolour Biennial*, in Shenzhen. The subject of both winning entries was one of Stratton's preferred painting locations, the north face of Crookhaven Heads on the south coast of New South Wales. Like Cézanne's Mont Sainte-Victoire and Arthur Boyd's Pulpit Rock, Crookhaven Heads has been a recurrent motif in Stratton's *oeuvre*, the artist having painted, since 1985, in excess of 200 works at this site. Invariably, his watercolours are technically proficient, closely observed and masterfully rendered both in their realism and depth of illusion.

Following the *Shanghai Zhujiajiao International Watercolour Biennial*, Stratton was invited to hold a solo exhibition, *Sand, Sticks and Stones*, the first in the *International Watercolour Masters* series at the Quanhua Watercolour Art Gallery, with the production of a book-quality catalogue containing 30 full-page reproductions. The most touching moment of his career, Stratton says, was during the opening in Zhujiajiao when his interpreter, Jo Jo Chen, daughter of Quanhua Watercolour Art Gallery Director and eminent watercolourist, Xidan Chen, introduced two Chinese artists who had travelled 3,000 kilometres to view his exhibition and to meet him.

It was as a foundation member of the Ryde Art Society (later City of Ryde Art Society), in 1959, that Stratton initially learned the dynamics of societies, presiding as President from 1962 to 1969 and becoming a Life Member in 1968. During his tenure as president, he organised exhibitions and annual awards, attracting art luminaries as guest speakers, such as Douglas Dundas,

Brian with David Napthine and his winning painting in 2014 (L & B Statton)

John Coburn, Peter Laverty, Elwyn Lynn, Alfred Cook and Henry Hanke, among others. He also liaised with Drummoyne Council for the establishment of a new society and strongly supported the Drummoyne Art Society in its formative years. At the opening of the Ryde Art Society's 50th Annual Art Award in 2010, Stratton delivered an address, being the only exhibitor in the first and fiftieth exhibition. Since 1958, he has also been a member of the Royal Art Society, being elected a fellow in 1964.

When Stratton was nineteen years of age, Alfred Cook encouraged him to submit a work for the Australian Watercolour Institute's annual exhibition, which was accepted for hanging. Douglas Stewart, noted poet, art critic for the *Bulletin* and husband of artist Margaret Coen, commented favourably on his work in his review of that 1955 exhibition. As an exhibitor in the next two AWI annual exhibitions, Stratton's work was hung next to those by Kenneth Macqueen. Inevitably, lessons were learnt about being overshadowed by the power of Macqueen's paintings. After exhibiting with the AWI for six years, Stratton was invited to membership, together with Elaine Haxton, in 1961, and served on the AWI Executive Committee from 1962-63. During that time, membership was extremely difficult to obtain, as the Institute was split on ideological grounds between traditional and modernist painters, and a two-thirds majority vote of the members was required. Through a later amendment to the Constitution, a 50% majority vote is now the requirement.

Upon George Duncan's resignation of the AWI presidency in 1964, he approached Stratton to succeed him in that role. Thus, Stratton was nominated for the office, as was Alfred Cook, his mentor. To Stratton's astonishment, Cook accepted the nomination, presenting Stratton with the immediate dilemma of whether to withdraw or go to a ballot. He has never comprehended why Cook stood, being certain that he voted for him. In what was perhaps the most bittersweet event of his life, Stratton was elected, with Alfred Cook and George Duncan serving as vice presidents. His saddest duty as president was writing a letter of condolence to Cook's widow in 1970. An initial difficulty he faced was filling the position of AWI Secretary. As no member was prepared to assume that role, Stratton's then wife, Adrienne (neé Moore), supported him and the Institute with distinction as secretary throughout his presidency. One of Stratton's initial undertakings in his role as president was to draft letters to the Art Gallery of New South Wales requesting a comprehensive exhibition of watercolours and to Douglas Dundas, then Head of the National Art School, pointing out the lack of watercolour instruction given to painting diploma students. The AWI annual exhibitions were timed to coincide with Stratton's TAFE vacation to allow for his manning of the shows.

George Duncan was also Director of the David Jones Art Gallery (1953-1963), located in the Elizabeth Street store, where the AWI had held its annual exhibition for a number of years. The loss of this central, well-patronised venue, due to Duncan's retirement from the directorship of the David Jones Art Gallery, would affect the fortunes of artists and societies for years to come, presenting a particular problem for the AWI in siting its annual exhibitions.

At the beginning of the decade, there were five major art societies in New South Wales – the Royal Art Society, the Society of Artists, the Contemporary Art Society, the Australian Watercolour Institute and the Australian Art Society -- but only one gallery available to stage their exhibitions, notably the space on the top floor of the Education Department building in Bridge Street, Sydney. This space was *in extremis* satisfactory, although ill lit and in a state of disrepair. To redress this situation, Erik Langker, President of Royal Art Society, Lloyd Rees, President of Society of Artists, Jack Santry, Secretary of the Society of Artists, Guy Warren, Contemporary Art Society and Stratton

Brian and two of his new friends at the Shanghai Museum in 2010 that are over 1000 years old. (L & B Stratton)

collectively met with the then Minister for Education, the Hon. Frank Wetherall, with the objective of securing improvements to the venue. Unfortunately, their deputation was to no avail. In a few years, the Society of Artists and Contemporary Art Society, together with the Australian Art Society, were no longer existent but, interestingly, Lloyd Rees, John Santry and Guy Warren would subsequently become members of the AWI.

Among the reasons for the demise of these societies was the proliferation of art galleries, which meant that established artists were disinclined to belong to a group when their professional needs were being met by private dealers. Another factor was the aforementioned absence of a suitable space that could accommodate a large number of works. Also, there was a change in the purchasing policies of State galleries, particularly the Art Gallery of New South Wales. Prior to this change in the purchasing policy, a quorum of trustees of the Art Gallery of New South Wales, as well as Directors of other State galleries, would visit exhibitions on the preview day and have first pick of the works displayed to acquire for their respective collections. This ensured that, by the time the public attended, the exhibition was off to a successful start with sales well underway. Stratton recalls an occasion when, just before the policy was abandoned, Hector Gilliland had three works purchased from one show by three State Galleries. This trifecta not only added greatly to the artist's reputation but also increased the status of the Institute and the annual exhibition.

From 1965-66 and 1969-71, Stratton replaced Rah Fizelle as representative of the Australian Watercolour Institute on the Australian National Advisory Committee for UNESCO (Visual Arts), which generally met in Canberra under the auspices of the Commonwealth Government. That committee comprised such luminaries as Sir Erik Langker (artist, art administrator, Trustee of the Art Gallery of NSW, President of the Royal Art Society and pioneer of the Sydney Opera house), Eric Westbrook (artist, Head of Victoria's Ministry of the Arts and influential director of the National Gallery of Victoria), Alan McCulloch (art critic, art historian, curator, gallery director and publisher of *The Encyclopaedia of Australian Art*), Ronald Appleyard (art administrator, curator and writer) and Professor Sir Joseph Burke (who was educated at King's College, the Courtauld Institute and Yale University before arriving in Australia in 1946 to take up his appointment as the Herald Chair of Fine Arts at Melbourne University). Stratton found him the most compelling among the participants. After one meeting, Sir Erik Langker exasperatedly remarked to him in the lift, 'They can talk, can't they!' Stratton shared the same view that, in the main, it was indeed a talkfest, as he cannot recall that committee achieving anything of significance.

After a period of 32 years, having been made an AWI Life Member in 1989, Stratton re-joined the Executive Committee in 2004 purely to make up numbers. In 2005, he opened the *82nd Annual AWI Exhibition* at Gosford Regional Gallery, which marked his fiftieth consecutive year of exhibiting with the Institute and, in 2011, he joined the elite group of artists who have held membership in the AWI for fifty years or more, notably Margaret Coen, Hector Gilliland, Jean Isherwood, Kenneth Jack, Ronald Steuart and Max Angus, who was made an Honorary Life Member in 2004.

The year 2006 was an unusual one in the history of the AWI, with all senior members of the AWI Executive Committee stepping down. Stratton stepped into the breach and was elected for a second term as president with a new team of officers and committee, the major priority on the agenda being a book, *The Australian Watercolour Institute: A Gallery of Australias Finest Watrcolours*, which the Book Committee did an admirable job in producing, with a print run of 4000 copies. After three years in office, with confidence that the group had the ability to serve the Institute well, Stratton stood down in 2009. He remains an honorary member of the AWI Executive Committee and a valued advisor.

Stratton's work has been exhibited in the United States, New Zealand, Mexico, Canada, Korea, Hong Kong and China, and he has been invited to judge over 100 art awards. He is represented in numerous public and private collections in Australia and overseas, including the Art Gallery of Western Australia and Art Bank.

In 2006, Brian Stratton was awarded the Medal of the Order of Australia for service to art as a painter and educator, and to professional organisations, including the Australian Watercolour Institute.

1. van Nunen, Linda, *Brought to Light II: Contemporary Australian Art 1966-2006*, Queensland Art Gallery, 2007, pp. 33-34.
2. Ibid
3. Smith, Bernard, Smith, Terry and Heathcoate, Christopher, *Australian Painting 1788-2000*, Fourth Edition, Oxford University Press, Melbourne, 2001, p. 433.
4. Eagle, Mary and Jones, John, *A Story of Australian Painting*, Macmillan, Sydney, 1996, p. 266.

Reproduced with permission of the copyright owners from **Brushes with History: Masters of Watercolour** by Linda and David van Nunen (2015), ISBN: 9780646909455, © Linda and David van Nunen 2015. Further reproduction prohibited without permission.

Memories of Barbering
Col Smith

I remember it well.

It was the beginning of April 1956 I had just turned 15 years old and my parents, myself and my brother and sister sat down for our evening meal.

My mother said, 'Your father and I have made a decision about your future. You are not doing so good at school so we think it's about time you went out to work and learnt a trade'

Mum said a friend's son had just left a barber shop where he worked and got a job on board a ship. In those days it was a very good job to see the world. The barber shop where he worked was looking for an apprentice barber. I went for an interview with the manager Ray Holmes. He said he would give me a three month probation period to see it I liked the idea of learning the trade.

The shop was owned by the Thorburn family who had two ladies salons and one barber shop in Forest Road Hurstville. There were seven barbers chairs downstairs and three chairs upstairs. Upstairs was called the Space Ship Salon and it was used to cut kids hair, especially when the kids were screaming.
My job naturally was to sweep the floor and refill the Brylcream Jars for the seven barbers who were constantly cutting. Non stop. There was a waiting area for about 20 people

A young Col at Punchbowl (C Smith)

Beige, Col and Rachel at Col's Clip Joint in Camden (C Smith)

which was pretty busy all day. Each barber was on a bonus system. He had to cut 130 clients before he got onto the bonus which was sixpence per head over the 130. The barbers were so busy trying their hardest to make a big bonus at the end of the week, that none of them had time to teach me any of the skills involved in cutting hair and using the clippers.

So I had to be content to stand behind the barbers and watch how it was done and now and then, ask questions. A barber back in those days could do up to six haircuts an hour. So you can understand why they did not have time for me and that included the manager Ray. But I guess I expected too much too soon.

At the end of the three month period I made up my mind that becoming a gents hairdresser was the way to go. Men and boys would require regular haircuts and my parents kept saying you will have a job for life.

Leaving Belmore Boys High School in Second Year was the right choice because I was not very academic. My parents made the decision for me. Not that I agree with parents choosing their children's occupation.

When my three months was up, Mrs Thorburn was the only person that could

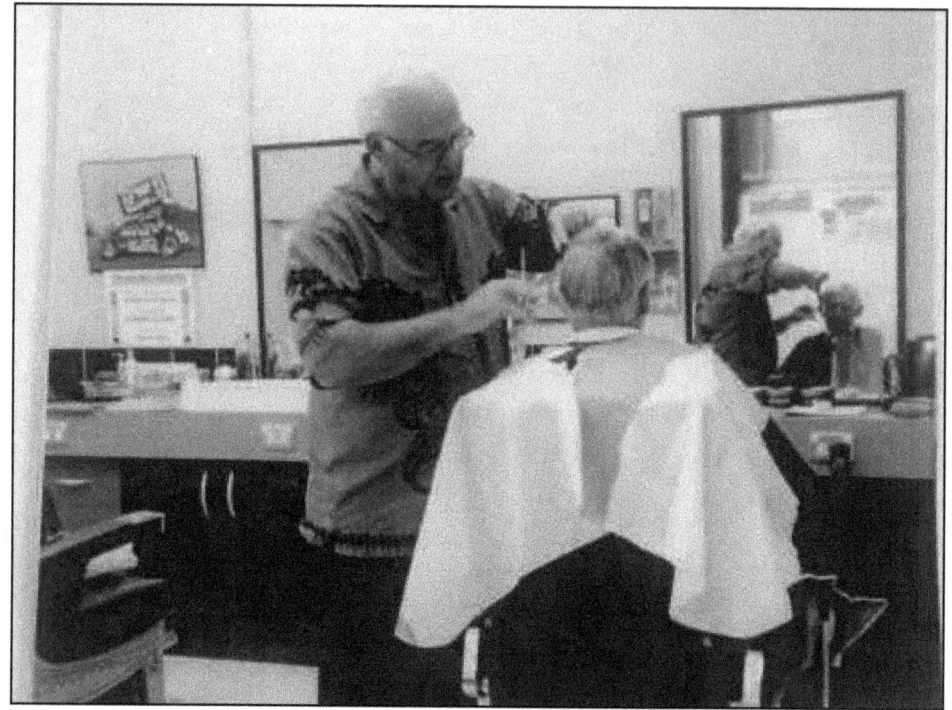

Col clipping John Southwell his Camden barber shop (C Smith)

sign my apprenticeship papers. But she had gone for a holiday to the USA for a couple of months with her daughter.

I complained to my Dad who used to go to a barber in Punchbowl. His name was Fred Tozer. When Fred heard about me he came to see me. He said, 'If you want to come and work with me at my shop, do the right thing with your present employer by giving them plenty of notice. You have served your three months with them already and I will sign your apprenticeship papers.' I always remember when I left (Thorburns) because of my love for music; it was the week that Elvis Presley's song (Heartbreak Hotel) became number one on the hit parade.

I worked in Punchbowl for five years and in that time I formed a friendship with well-known radio personality John Burgess. He was one of our gang in those days. We were known as the Punchbowl Bogies. No! We did not look for trouble. We just went to stadium shows in Sydney and the usual rock 'n' roll parties etc.

I was not happy with my boss at Punchbowl John Frolich even though he was a better cutter than Fred Tozer. John had purchased the barber shop from Fred two years after I started which was 1958. At the beginning of 1962 I told my Dad that 'I was not happy working there anymore,' so my Dad said, 'Well, you have got your licence now, so maybe it's time to move on'.

Back in the 1960s there was always plenty of work for barbers. I remember ringing up for a job in Marrickville. The owner of the shop said 'If you can't do seven haircuts in one hour on a Saturday morning for four hours don't bother coming for a trial'. I told the owner of the barber shop that I could do six in an hour and he said 'Don't bother coming for a trial'. To think that my ex-boss John Frolich was happy with my six an hour back in Punchbowl.

I then saw an ad for a barber in Kingsgrove at Jack Meads barber shop. I went for a trial at Jack's shop and got the job. I lived in Belmore South in those days which was only minutes down the road from Kingsgrove. At the end of the first week on pay day Nancy, the boss's wife came up to me with my pay. She said Jack was happy with the way I worked. I said to her with a smile, 'Would you believe Nancy that when I was a boy I used to regularly have my haircut here after school. Little did I know that one day I would learn the trade and end up working for Jack'. I also told Nancy that when I was 12 years old I was selling newspapers at the entrance to Kingsgrove Station. When I was 13 years old I became a telegram boy after school and Saturday mornings.

Jack owned the barber shop and the residence upstairs. I envied Jack's setup and I told him so. He said, 'Follow your dream boy, you will get there'. Unfortunately by the time I opened my barber shop in Camden in the late 1960's I got the news that Jack had passed away through cancer. I wanted so much to tell him I had a barber shop. I know he would have been happy for me.

Jack had two barber shops in Kingsgrove, the one that he owned and lived in plus one next to Kingsgrove Railway Station which he rented. I became the go between barber, meaning when the shop near the station got busy I had to race up there help them and get back to the other shop. After 12 months of this I got tired. I decided to leave at the beginning of 1963.

I remember the barber shops in the 1950s and the 1960s. Especially the 1950s, if you owned a barber shop and you were a good cutter ,you had a licence to print money.

Brylcreem, Vaseline and Spruso hair cream were very popular in the 50s and 60s, and also very messy. If some clients used too much of the product on their hair it caused problems with our equipment. When we cut their hair it would keep sticking to our combs and between the blades of clippers. This caused jamming of our clipper blades although it was the only product to be used at the time.

I always remember one day when business was a bit quiet I said to Jack and his other barbers, 'You know boys we have the flat tops, the crewcuts and Tony Curtis haircuts but the day will come men and boys will grow their hair long'. Of course they laughed at me. I just did not realise how true that statement was.

Flat tops and crewcuts became very popular in the 1950s and early 60s and styles like these required regular cutting to keep them well groomed.

Shortly after James Dean died in that tragic car crash teenagers would bring photos in for me to cut their hair like James Dean. James was my idol. He starred in three movies, *East of Eden*, *Rebel Without a Cause* and *Giant*. It was quite common for young clients to bring in photos of their famous movie stars to have their cut the same.

There was no price cutting in those days because the price of haircuts was controlled by the Barbers Union. If you were found charging more or less than the price which was set by the union you would be fined! In other words you won business by good cutting not price cutting!

In those days a barber could support a wife and children without his wife going out to work.

At the finish of my apprenticeship I got my licence to become a barber. I saw an ad in the paper for a barber in Aware Street, Fairfield which was owned by Geoff Smee. The year was 1963. I got the job after the interview with Geoff on Saturday morning. I arrived for work on the Monday morning Geoff ran his shop like Thorburns did in Hurstville. You had to get a number off the wall before you sat down in the waiting area otherwise you lost your turn. The barbers were on a bonus system similar to the Thorburns - where - you had to do 130 haircuts before you got one "bob" per head .

I remember the first day. One of the barbers, Don Young, came up to me and said, 'Do yourself a favour, don't work fast this week because Geoff is not a barber. He depends on the manager of the barbers section Allan who will watch you closely the first week. If he sees that you are quick, he won't hire you because are on trial the first week'. I went slow the first week. On payday Geoff asked Allan 'Does Col get the job?' Allan said 'Yes' Then Don

Col's Clip Joint celebrates 41 years of continuous service to the Camden community after being established in 1969 (C Smith)

said to me after work on the Saturday, 'You are now hired and you can pick up your speed because he can't go back on his word'.

I spent six enjoyable years at Geoff Smee's barber shop. One of my clients Brocka Cortess was a wrestler from the Sydney stadium. I used to go and see the wrestling on a Friday night. I asked, 'It's all an act isn't it?' He kept saying, 'It's real'. I said, 'How come I have not seen you win a match?' He would say, 'I guess I'm not good enough'. I knew better so I never challenged him again.

About the first week in March 1969 the apprentice David Banks came to me and said, 'Where's Camden, Col?' He was holding *The Liverpool Leader* in his hand. He went on to say that there was a barber shop in an arcade in Camden that had to be closed down by the owner through bad health. The barber's name was Jim Flockart. My Dad and I went to his house in Campbelltown to find out how much he wanted for it seeing it had been closed for 8 weeks. We did a deal and both parties were quite happy with it. On 16 March 1969 I opened 'Col's Clip Joint'.

I remember the Saturday before I opened the shop. My wife and I had a counter lunch at The Plough and Harrow Hotel. The owner of the hotel back then was John Kennedy a friend of my parents for many years. It was Saturday after lunch when John stood on the bar and said to all the drinkers in the pub "Could I have your attention please. This gentleman sitting here is Colin Smith. He is a friend of mine and he is opening a barber shop on Monday in the arcade." John went on to say, with a smile on his face, "If you don't give him a go I will shut the beer off". Naturally they all laughed and booed him.

I always remember the first week in business. A man walked in, jumped into the chair and introduced himself as the Mayor of Camden, Bruce Ferguson. He welcomed me into Camden and said "You will do alright son, this town is a wealthy place to have a business". I soon found this out when you consider how strong the coal mines were doing and dairy farms also were very big. Ferguson said that he was known as "Mr Finance" amongst the business people of Camden. If any of the business people in Camden need financial help he would be there for them at a very low interest rate.

About a month later on a Saturday morning I had just closed my shop at 12 noon. All shops back then ceased trading at 12 pm and did not open again till Monday morning at 9 am. Back in those days if you worked from Monday to Friday you had plenty of family time because only two types of businesses were open on weekends: convenience stores and milk bars.

Anyhow back to my story about this particular Saturday morning. A gentleman wearing a white shirt and white pants knocked on the door. I opened the door, the man put his hand out to shake my hand and said "I am Albert Baker, the barber from down the other end of town. Welcome to Camden Col, I hope you do well." I said "Thank you Albert"!" I said to Albert, "I guess you play cricket?" he said, "No! I play Lawn Bowls" and the rest is history. I have now played lawn bowls for 45 years. Albert was my first coach and was a great bowler himself.

The first Crop The Cop fundraiser in Camden. Col Smith in blue shirt in centre. (C Smith)

I knew from that moment that I had chosen a great town to open a business. Back then there was no Macarthur Bridge and only five shops in Narellan. There were only five shops in Tahmoor which meant that Camden was the closest place to shop. It was quite common for semi-trailers and coal trucks passing through the town. People going to Melbourne and Canberra had to pass through Camden. The passing trade in the town was quite good.

About six months later just before Christmas 1969 a man walked in sat down whilst I was cutting someone's hair. I noticed that he was watching me carefully, the way that I was cutting. When he got into my chair he told me his name was Mick Prior, a barber from Picton.

I had cut Mick's hair a number of times. At the beginning of the 1970's Mick Prior said to me while I was cutting his hair one day, 'I am thinking of retiring and selling my two shops and residence in the main street of Picton. Col I would love to see you in Picton'. Mick said that the shop next to his barber shop was being rented to a nursery by him for $11.00 a week. 'Don't forget that this was the beginning of 1970 and I was paying $22 a week for my shop', he said.

To think that Mick was asking $18,500 for the lot. I said to Mick, "If I had not taken up a loan 12 months ago to buy my first home in Campbelltown which I had to borrow $10,000 to build, I would have purchased it for sure". As I continued to roll through the 1970's I did not realise what famous people's hair I was cutting. For example, I cut the hair of the late 'Gary Dowling' who played for Oakdale Workers Club. He played for the Canterbury Bulldogs as a fullback at the beginning of 1971. He ended up playing for Australia on the wing. I also cut the hair of John Fahey who was our local accountant and ended up being Premier of NSW.

Gary McCoy, Matt Mladin, Anthony Gobert were also clients of mine who went on to be champion motor bike riders. Each one signed their pictures which were hung on the wall of my shop for many years. Now the pictures hang on the wall of my "man cave" at home. One day in the shop Darren Britt, who played for Canterbury in the late 1920's gave me a signed jumper which read, "Thanks for the Bulldog haircuts".

The 70's became a cruel period for barber shops as men and boys started growing their hair long. I remember seeing write ups in the Sydney newspapers about how the long hair fashion had a bad effect on the barbering industry. There were even photos of barbers standing in their doorways hoping that the fashion would not last long. It ended up lasting about 15 years. In that time we started losing business to ladies hairdressers who were slowly taking our young boys which were our future trade.

Gone were the days when mothers would drop off their sons for a haircut and they would go to their ladies hairdresser for their cuts. So the Unisex Salons were created and slowly men and boys were drifting away from barber shops. What really affected after school trade was that the mothers would make an appointment for their sons so they did not have to waste time sitting in a barber shop. It became quite a disaster in most barber shops in the 1970's and 1980's.

I even noticed some of my solicitor clients, doctors and dentists disappear because they were making appointments in the salons. They did this because they shut their doors between 1pm and 2pm which was the only time they had for a haircut.

In conclusion I must confess that if I had the time over again I would not change a thing. I enjoyed 56 years working as a barber. I met a lot of nice people and made a lot of friends.

The biggest award that I received in 2011 was being named the 2011 business man of the year. This trophy sits in my 'man cave' at home. Every time I

Col clipping Steve Austin for cancer fundraising in 1996 (C Smith)

look at it I remember all the business people cheering me as I went up on stage. I am a very emotional person and I was fighting back tears as I received my award. I look at it now as a reward for coming to this lovely country town of Camden and opening my barber shop named 'Col's Clip Joint'.

Horse History in Western Sydney: Kirkham Stud

Mark Latham

Every weekday morning, in driving my children to school, I pass by a local landmark in the suburb of Kirkham, near Camden in southwest Sydney.

It's a set of horse stables, brightly white in colour and featuring a series of ornate-looking arches.

The surrounding yards hold a few horses – perhaps an agistment facility for jumpers or recreational riders.

It's one of those places that's still ticking over but also gives the impression that it was much grander and significant in its heyday.

Earlier this year, I decided to do something about my daily curiosity and research the story of the white stables.

My morning friend has quite a history.

It's the Kirkham Stud, established in 1816 by the surveyor-explorer John Oxley (1785-1828), as part of extensive land grants he received in the Camden and Cobbitty districts from Governor Macquarie.

The stud was named after Oxley's birthplace: Kirkham Abbey in Yorkshire, England. Its heritage-listed stables are believed to be the oldest structure of their kind surviving in NSW.

In 1830, following Oxley's death, his business partner, former Navy Captain John Coghill, managed the farm. Coghill imported the British thoroughbred stallion, Bachelor (1926), to stand at Kirkham.

In 1845, John Oxley Jnr took over the property, aged just 21, but failed to advance the family's racing interests.

The golden era at Kirkham occurred during the last three decades of the 1800s, following the farm's purchase by James White (1828-1890) – a wealthy pastoralist, a NSW parliamentarian (in the Legislative Assembly 1864-68 and Legislative Council 1874-1890) and long-serving member of

Kirkham Stables constructed around 1816 is the oldest farm building in Australia. It is a landmark building in a rural setting relatively intact from colonial times(Camden Images)

the AJC committee, including two terms as AJC Chairman (1880 and 1883-90).

White was one of Australia's greatest-ever owners of racehorses, also establishing commercial farms in the Hunter Valley including the famous Segenhoe Stud.

In 1878 he purchased the Newmarket stables at Randwick, where he is thought to have been responsible for building, or at least lavishly enlarging, the historic Big Stable. Today Newmarket houses the Inglis auctioneers and sale-yards.

Among the sires White stood at Kirkham were the Melbourne Cup winners Chester (1874, Yattendon x Lady Chester by Stockwell) and Martini Henry (1880, Musket x Sylvia ex Juliet). He purchased Chester as a two-year-old from his breeder Edward King Cox of the Fernhill Stud at Mulgoa, near

Penrith, the horse having won the AJC Sires Produce Stakes.

Chester went on to win the Victorian Derby/Melbourne Cup double in 1877 (trained by the legendary Etienne De Mestre), a feat repeated by Martini Henry six years later. White reputedly won enough money backing the Chester double to fund the establishment of his Kirkham breeding operation. He also heavily backed the Martini Henry double in 1883, winning 25,000 pounds – millions in today's money.

Most horse owners dream of winning either the Cup or the Derby during the Melbourne Spring Carnival, yet White was able to win the double twice.

Chester is buried in the southwestern corner of the Kirkham property, his tombstone reading, rather plainly: Chester, Died 21st November 1891. He was a highly successful stallion with his best son being Abercorn (1884, ex Cinnamon by Goldsbrough – another son of Sylvia). Raced by White, Abercorn won the 1887 AJC Derby and 17 other stakes races. He is best remembered for defeating the mighty Carbine three times at weight-for-age.

Chester sired a total of 26 stakes-winners (for 104 stakes-wins) and was Australia's leading sire on four occasions. Martini Henry sired 15 stakes-winners. These are tremendous achievements but only one part of James White's dominance of racing during this period.

It is inconceivable in the modern era that any Australian owner could match White's record of major winners between 1877 and 1890, each carrying his renowned pale blue and white silks: two Melbourne Cups, six Victorian Derbies, three VRC Oaks, six VRC St Leger Stakes, three Caulfield Guineas, four Australian Cups, five AJC Derbies, three AJC Metropolitans, five AJC Sires Produce Stakes and four AJC Champagne Stakes.

In his masterful book *Horsemen of the First Frontier (1788-1900)*, Keith Binney chronicles the full extent of White's triumphs, writing of how, "At the Victorian autumn meeting of 1888, (he) had nine winners, which took out every important race on the card. In 1889 at the Randwick carnival, White's horses won the AJC Derby, the Oaks, the Spring Stakes, the Randwick and Craven Plates, the Second Foal and the Mycomb Stakes, as well as the Metropolitan."

In total, White raced 66 winning horses, which won a total of 252 races and more than 120,000 pounds in prizemoney. Remarkably, his stable rider Tom Hales rode 302 races for him and won 137 of them. As owners, what any of us would give for a single day at Randwick or Flemington standing

View of the grave of racehorse 'Chester' winner of the 1877 Melbourne Cup with Kirkham Stables in the distance c.1997 (Camden Images/J Kooyman)

in the shoes of the Honourable James White.

Not content with his Australian achievements, White embarked on a special breeding project: an audacious bid to win the English Derby. He bred the colts Kirkham (1887, Chester x La Princesse) and Narellan (1887, Chester x Princess Maud) to English time and transported them to the old country.

Unfortunately Narellan broke down in training. But Kirkham made it into the 1990 Derby field, the first Australian-bred horse to run in the classic. He finished sixth to the great Sainfoin (1887, Springfield x Sanda) – a permanent influence in modern pedigrees as the dam-sire of Phalaris (1913).

Today we have another reason for remembering White's legacy. At Kirkham, the prolific Canadian-born colonial architect John Horbury Hunt built two houses for him. One of them, the towering, Gothic-style Camelot, features as the homestead for the Australian television drama *A Place to Call Home*.

It was also part of the 2008 Baz Luhrmann film *Australia*, starring Nicole Kidman and Hugh Jackman. Camelot was built on the site of John Oxley's Kirkham Mill and partly on its foundations.

Following White's death from heart disease in 1890, most of his racing stock was dispersed. Kirkham passed into the hands of his wife, Emily *nee* Arndell, who continued to import stallions and breed thoroughbreds there until 1896. Then she remarried and moved overseas, passing away in Scotland in October 1897.

The Whites had no children to carry on their racing interests at Kirkham. With his passing, James White's business partnership with his brothers Francis and Henry was dissolved. In the resulting restructure, the four youngest of Francis White's six sons took over the vast Belltrees property on Gundy Road, Scone in the Upper Hunter. This was the boyhood home of the celebrated Australian author Patrick White, James White's great-nephew.

Founded by Oxley and expanded by White, Kirkham experienced its third incarnation under the ownership of Sir Fred Sutton in the 1960s and 70s – he the founder of the car retailer Suttons Motors.

As an owner, Sutton raced numerous good horses out of Tommy Smith's stable, including Flying Fable (1965, Snark x Miss Pilot), winner of the VRC Sires' Produce Stakes, AJC Oaks, AJC Flight Stakes and third in the 1968 Golden Slipper. But his biggest contribution to the industry was the restoration of Kirkham Stud, which had declined in the first half of the 20th century.

Sutton stood several imported sires at Kirkham, including the English stayer Proper Pride (1959, Prince Chevalier x No Pretender) and the Irish 2000 Guineas place-getter Kingfisher (1964, Alcide x Warspite). By far his best stallion was Agricola (1956, Precipitation x Aurora, ex Rose Red), which sired 31 stakes-winners, including the outstanding General Command (1963) and Roman Consul (1964). In May 1973, Agricola was transferred from Kirkham to the Kelly family's Newhaven Park Stud near Yass.

A schoolmate of TJ Smith, Sutton followed the master's advice: that a successful breeding operation relies on the purchase of the best fillies and

Chester, winner of the 1877 Melbourne Cup c.1874 (cc Wikimedia/Turf Cavalcade)

mares on the market. Thus Sutton acquired the 1962 Golden Slipper winner Birthday Card (1959, Edmundo x Magnificent Lady) for Kirkham – one of many high-quality broodmares on the property. Another was Better Gleam (1968, Better Boy x Silkes), winner of the 1971 Flight Stakes and dam (by Showdown) of the very good mare Kapalaran (1975).

Fred Sutton passed away in December 2004, aged 89. Kirkham has stayed in the family's hands: not as a horse breeding enterprise, but as a small working farm, running mainly cattle. Camelot is now owned and maintained by the Powers family. In contrast to the Suttons, they are very active in the local community, telling people about the heritage of their amazing home.

The Kirkham story is a powerful reminder of the role of the County of Cumberland as Sydney's thoroughbred nursery during much of the 19th and 20th centuries. With urban sprawl now touching the city's outer limits, it's hard to visualise Western Sydney as top-class horse country. But in colonial times, it was as important as the Hunter Valley is today – the go-to location for the very best thoroughbred breeders.

Hopefully, ongoing urbanisation will not mean the loss of iconic sites such as Kirkham Stud. What else will I have to daydream about at the end of my morning drive?

Chester, Martini Henry and Abercorn, through to Agricola and Birthday Card – they are more than just names in the Stud Book, they're the memories, the romanticised Australian legends that make our racing industry unique. To love the thoroughbred, as we all do, means honoring the memory of places like Kirkham.

In an inspiring pattern of endurance and rejuvenation, Oxley's stables have now reached their bicentennial year. High on their gable, a painting of the head of Chester remains – surveying what was once his breeding kingdom.

Below Chester's portrait is the inscription: Kirkham Stud 1816, Metam Tetigit. This is Latin for "The post, he touched it", or in its racing sense, "First at the Winning Post".

In the glory days, indeed they were.

First published in *Thoroughbred History*, 1 April 2016.

Dairy Farmer to Young Local Historian

Sophie Mulley

Since the professionalization of history in western society, a debate has turned between "amateur" local history writers and academic historians.[1] The academics questioned the depth of the writers historical understanding, they saw no importance in covering the history of small town or people, and quite often questioned the methods and approaches of these writers and whether their findings were of "historical truth."[2] Now we can see in Australia, local histories of township and family have become increasingly popular in communities such as our own, and the debate between amateur and academic has continued.[3] Frank Furedi, a sociologist and former professor at the University of Kent, argues that the practice of local history leads to "the destruction of historical thinking."[4] Through engaging with the local

Sophie Mulley with her grandparents - Nan and Pop - Ian and Dawn Mulley. (S Mulley)

community and Camden Historical Society I have found this statement to be a narrow judgement of local history, as I have found local history acknowledges the interests of 'ordinary people'. Anna Clark describes this type of history as "familiar, experiential, and tactile", being that it is "deeply connected to people's families and communities."[5]

My name is Sophie Mulley and generations of my family have lived in Camden since the year 1907. [6] As I am currently majoring in history at the Australian Catholic University and researching my family history with the Camden Historical Society, I have been given the opportunity to view this historical debate from both sides and evaluate how public and family history is approached, and discover what value history holds in the community. Overall, I have observed that historians play a role in shaping local history and therefore should frame their approaches and methods accordingly to help shape the future of a community and its view on the past, present and future.

As a volunteer researcher at the Camden Historical Society, I was given the task to research my family history since their arrival in Camden, 1907. I have conducted my research through a family tree, through the Trove digital database of newspapers and articles[7], scholarly books on Camden, and conducting oral interviews with my family. Throughout this project, as a historian I adopted various methodologies and approaches, which did not come without there peculiarities.

"It used to be said that facts speak for themselves. This is, of course, untrue. The facts speak only when the historian calls on them: it is he who decides to which facts to give the floor, and in what order or context." [8] – E. H. Carr (1964).

Carr's above statement has resonated throughout my engagement with the Camden Historical Society. Through the practice of genealogy, it was imperative to be mindful of the facts being drawn on and why these facts were being selected over others. For instance, when searching the Trove digital database, I would use search terms that I later realised had been developed by my own pre-existing knowledge of my family. I had always been told my family were dairy farmers on the old Camden Park Estate. Soon I realised searching 'Dairy, Farm, Camden, Mulley,' would only draw upon the evidence that upholds local and national discourses of Camden heritage, colonialism and agriculture. In fact, Bottero's research also found "dominant discourses" gave shape to the way the family historian selects their facts.[9] Furthermore, Carr states "the historian is of his own age, and is bound to it by the conditions of human existence. The very words which he uses ... have current connotations from which he cannot divorce them."[10]

It is not fair to say that local history is destructive due to the fact the amateur history writer is inescapable from the existing discourses that shape their life. What I have found is that for the participant, discourses create a bridge between the past and the present, allowing the participant to connect themselves with their ancestors in their present day understanding. If this is a common process of the family historian, then this is a valuable contribution to the community as it allows ordinary citizens to feel connected to the past and allows future historians to later examine the discourses that exist within a group of people.

"Genealogists not only trace ancestors but also find out about their lives and generate 'storied' narratives of connection through time."[11] The Camden Historical Society, not only asked me to research my family history, but also to also reflect on these findings through my own experience of growing up in the Camden community. This meant bringing the past and present, into the future. My approach to my family history was inspired by David Walker and his book, 'Not Dark Yet – A Personal History'[12]. Instead of choosing to write about national events, Walker chose to write about the ordinary events that revolved around his family and their community. Walker believes, "Small events also have their place in determining who we are and what we value as individuals and as a community."[13]

The Mulley family were early colonial settlers, who moved from Junee to Camden in New South Wales in search of land and work. The reality is my family did not own a great colonial estate like Camden Park, or Brownlow Hill, and they didn't serve in the war. In interviews I felt my family had to explain away this 'ordinariness' of our family history. The truth is that there is a story to be told. Because our story does not align to popular national discourses, of war heroes and prominent colonial families, it does not make it any less important.

My approach was to discover 'history from below' which came out of social history. Edward P. Thompson chose to not write a history of the 'winners', but rather write a history on "the poor stockinger, the Luddite cropper, the 'obsolete' hand-loom weaver, the 'utopian' artisan, and even the deluded follower of Joanna Southcott," and rescue them "from the enormous condescension of posterity."[14]

My own family were from a class of tenant farmers who worked on the Camden Park Estate in Cawdor that was owned by the well-known Macarthur family.[15] Through interviews with my relatives, and research into the dairy industry in Australia, I discovered that the commercialisation of dairy farming in Camden meant that small dairy farms like my own family's, struggled to compete in the market and keep up with the changing dairy board standards.[16] This eventually led to the closing down of my great grandfather's dairy practice and the search for a new job outside of his known trade. As a member of the Camden community, I know this is not the type of story you would often hear about Camden's agricultural past. Through discovery of 'history from below' I found I was able to recognise those who had not been spoken for before. This historical approach is valuable to the community as it empowers ordinary people, while providing future generations with a 'realistic' history on an often idealised past.

One of the difficulties of writing about my family was that there is only so far you can write when only using snippets from news articles, and details found on birth and death certificates. In keeping with the movement of 'history from below', I turned to my family to learn their oral history. I believe that this is where academic historians begin to criticize the practice of family history, as oral interviews can be seen as "unreliable and tainted by personal subjectivity" due to its reliance on memories.[17]

Oral histories may be problematic with family history, as the interviewee may wish to withhold information about their family, or fabricate the family history for their own purposes. However, through reflection on my interviews, I discovered that this risk did not outweigh the potential to gain valuable memories of my family's past.

Three family members were interviewed over the course of my project. Each interview gave me a deeper insight into what life was like growing up and working in the Camden community and various other details about family life. What I observed was that the memories of my family did not provide specific dates of events, rather, each interview seemed to contain structured narratives of the family's past.

My Pop spoke of the hardship of living on the farm. There seemed to be a common theme of family struggles and how they got through them.

It was a hard time during the war and I remember you couldn't buy much. You couldn't buy chewing gum ... I know that ... and dad and mum didn't do too easy either I don't think, only that we were on the farm, you know, there was a lot of milk, things to eat, you know, mum would make rice things and all that with milk. And we lived on that and we lived on rabbits ... rabbits and hares ... they were a delicacy![18]

Historians refer to this as "the way individuals constructed their life histories, to create a usable past," which makes the individual feel at ease with the past.[19]

Original Mulley Farm house in Cawdor. Still standing today. C. 1988. (S Mulley)

Oral history is now recognised as a credible source for interpretation. Within family history, it allows the historian to analyse the family in terms of gender roles, traditions and belief systems, and the overall structure of the family and how this has changed over time. Passerini states, "all autobiographical memory is true; it is up to the interpreter to discover in which sense, where, for which purpose."[20] Oral histories, not only serve the historian, but also the interviewee.

My Nan and Pop were so happy to talk to me about their past, and appreciated being listened to and having their memories recorded. This is a unique method of history, as it allows ordinary people to be heard and they are given the opportunity to inform future generations of their past.

The practice of family history was valuable to my family and myself as it developed a deeper understanding of my identity and my family's identity within the Camden community. Boretto expresses a similar sentiment, "Remembering the past is 'crucial for our sense of identity' with this 'situating of self' occurring through 'the development of a self-narrative that starts, not at one's birth, but with one's forebears'."[21] Family histories are

Mulley Family. Top Row – Gertrude Mulley, Charles Reginald Mulley, Mabel Mulley. Middle Row – Charles Mulley, Mary Anne Mulley, Alice Mulley. Bottom Row – Claude James Mulley and William Cecil Mulley (S Mulley)

also valuable to the community as they have the ability to challenge "social dislocation," strengthen family ties, and discover family likeness in times of change.[22]

This project was valuable to the Camden Historical Society, as it 'filled in the gap' of my family's local history as well as providing a new perspective on Camden's past and present. It is important that young community members are involved with their local history, as they can offer new perspectives and approaches to history. For example, through conducting oral history interviews, I was able to approach the article as a 'history from below', telling the stories of ordinary people within our community.

Clark, states "rather than historians and politicians trying to overcome a perceived historical ignorance in the broader community, these participants might teach us a thing or two about how to make, write and do the sort of history that widely engages 'ordinary people'." This statement highlights the importance of the historian engaging with the community. I am truly grateful for the opportunity to work with my local historical society, as it has brought me closer to the Camden community, to my family, and overall has developed my historical understanding and the type of historian I would like to be in the future.

Notes
1. Georg G. Iggers, "The Professionalization of Historical Studies and the Guiding Assumptions of Modern Historical Thought", *A Companion to Western Historical Thought*, Lloyd Kramer and Sarah Maza (eds), Blackwell Publishing (2006): Introduction, doi: 10.1111/b.9781405149617.2006.00014.x; John Beckett, *Writing Local History*, Manchester: Manchester University Press (2007): 140.
2. ibid; Edward H. Carr, *What Is History?*, (Harmondsworth: Penguin, 1964):
3. Anna Clark, *Private Lives, Public History* (Melbourne: Melbourne University Press, 2016): 5-7; Wendy Bottero, "Practising family history: 'identity' as a category of social practice," *British Journal of Sociology 66, 3* (2015): 534, doi: 10.1111/1468-4446.12133.
4. "About." Frank Ferudi. May 2016. http://www.frankfuredi.com/about; Beckett, *Writing Local History*, 140.
5. Clark, *Private Lives, Public History*, 7.
6. 1936 "Death of Mr. Jas. Mulley", Camden News (NSW: 1895 - 1954): 18 June, 1. Retrieved from: http://nla.gov.au/nla.news-article140597603
7. "Trove," *National Library of Australia*, http://trove.nla.gov.au/
8. Carr, *What Is History?*, 11.
9. Bottero, "Practising family history: 'identity' as a category of social practice," 539.
10. Carr, *What is History?*, 24-25
11. ibid, 537.
12. David Walker, *Not Dark Yet – A Personal History*, (Sydney: Giramondo Publishing, 2011).
13. David Walker, *Not Dark Yet – A Personal History*, 25.
14. Edward P. Thompson, *The Making of the English Working Class* (New York: Vintage Books, 1964): 12.

15. Alan Atkinson, Camden (Melbourne: Oxford University Press, 1988): 68.
16. "The Australian Dairy Industry." Australian Bureau of Statistics. http://www.abs.gov.au/Ausstats/abs@.nsf/0/B006A83A9127B0F5CA256DEA00053965?Open; James Ian Mulley, Interview with Sophie Mulley (Sydney, 27th May, 2016).
17. Anna Green and Kathleen Troup, *The Houses of History: A Critical Reader in Twentieth-century History and Theory* (Manchester: Manchester University Press, 1999): 230.
18. James Ian Mulley, Interview with Sophie Mulley (Sydney, 27th May, 2016).
19. Anna Green and Kathleen Troup, *The Houses of History: A Critical Reader in Twentieth-century History and Theory*, 234.
20. ibid, 236.
21. Bottero, "Practising family history: 'identity' as a category of social practice," 539.
22. ibid, 535 – 536.
23. Anna Clark, *Private Lives, Public History* (Melbourne: Melbourne University Press, 2016): 145.

Bibliography

"Death of Mr. Jas. Mulley." *Camden News*. NSW: 1895 – 1954. 18 June, 1936.
    Retrieved from: http://nla.gov.au/nla.news-article140597603
Atkinson, Alan. *Camden*. Melbourne: Oxford University Press, 1988.
"The Australian Dairy Industry." Australian Bureau of Statistics. http://www.abs.gov.au/Ausstats/abs@.nsf/0/B006A83A9127B0F5CA256D EA00053965?Open
Beckett, John. *Writing Local History*. Manchester: Manchester University Press, 2007.
Bottero, Wendy. "Practising family history: 'identity' as a category of social practice."
    British Journal of Sociology 66, 3 (2015): 535 – 556, doi: 10.1111/14684446.12133.
Carr, Edward Hallett. *What Is History?* Harmondsworth: Penguin, 1964.
Clark, Anna, and Ashton, Paul. *Australian History Now*. Sydney: NewSouth, 2013.
Clark, Anna. *Private Lives, Public History*. Melbourne: Melbourne University Press, 2016.
Green, Anna, and Troup, Kathleen. *The Houses of History: A Critical Reader in Twentieth
    Century History and Theory*. Manchester: Manchester University Press, 1999.
Hughes-Warrington, Marnie. *Fifty Key Thinkers on History*. 2nd ed. Routledge Key Guides.
    Hoboken: Taylor and Francis, 2007.
Iggers, Georg G. "The Professionalization of Historical Studies and the Guiding Assumptions of Modern Historical Thought." *A Companion to Western Historical Thought*.
Kramer, Lloyd and Sarah Maza (eds). Blackwell Publishing (2006): Introduction, doi: 10.1111/b.9781405149617.2006.00014.x
James Ian Mulley, Interview with Sophie Mulley (Sydney, 27th May, 2016).
"Trove." National Library of Australia. http://trove.nla.gov.au/
Thompson, Edward P. *The Making of the English Working Class*. New York: Vintage Books, 1964.
Walker, David. *Not Dark Yet – A Personal History*. Sydney: Giramondo Publishing, 2011.

Editor's note
Sophie's story has had an influence beyond her university project. Oral history, as Sophie mentions, can be more of a narrative than time, dates and places for some folk. Stories provide markers in peoples lives around family traditions, commemorations and celebrations.

After reading Sophie's story **Roslyn Tildsley** in a conversation with **Anne McIntosh** recalled fondly bonfire nights at Cawdor on the Mulley's property.

Dad was great friends with the Mulley's (they used to go away for weekends/weeks shooting at Oberon) so we often spent time together. However cracker night on the Queen's Birthday weekend in June was what we looked forward to most.

We would save up and buy crackers and then keep them in our shoebox in our bedroom. My brother Wayne, sister Susan and myself each had our own shoe box full of fun.

On the night we would rug up and drive out with Mum (Margaret) and Dad (Frank) in Dad's Holden station wagon. Having packed the car with the necessities –including our tin mugs and plates, parkas, beanies, scarves and 2 camping seats (little fold up metal stools with a red seat cover – no armrests or cup holders in those days!) we knew we were headed for a great night with friends.

There would always be a huge bonfire to sit around and we would toast bread , marshmallows and boil water on the bonfire ready for the tea, coffee and hot chocolate.

However the highlight of the night for us kids was the fireball soccer game. It took Cec Biffin and family many days to make the ball as it entailed sewing rags together around and around into a tight ball and then leaving it to soak in kerosene for days. On the night we would then spend a wonderful time kicking and watching this lit ball fly through the air. The big boys especially liked aiming their kick at each other. We never did get burnt or burn our clothes and initially I was scared to play but as each year passed I enjoyed it more and more.

It is a very fond memory I have of my childhood - Bonfire night with the Mulleys and Biffins.

Echoes of the Appin Massacre 1816

Ian Willis

This year is the bicentenary of the Appin Massacre when Governor Macquarie's troops clashed with the Dharawal people south of the village of Appin.

From 1813 Europeans had begun to move into Dharawal land after having established farms in the area. Between 1814 and 1816 relations between Europeans and Dharawal deteriorated, exacerbated by a severe drought. Members of the Gundagurra, from the Blue Mountains, attacked settlers and Governor Macquarie ordered out the troops with disastrous results.

This incident illustrates that the colonial frontier in settler societies like New South Wales was a violent place when there was dispossession of land from indigenous people.

This year there have been a number of commemorative events and Camden folk band Stringline performed a music piece to add to the commemorations. A poem written by Pat Took was put to music by Paul Malia a member of Stringline. The first public performance of the piece occurred at the Camden Sports Club in July this year at CK's Open Mike Night.

Wiritjiribin...Lyrebird Spirit
P Took

Chorus.
Spirits in this Pass shimmer
the water - stir the bones.
Hear lyrebird scream out...
don't be in that gorge alone.

Rocky cliffs, cool green gorge
Lyrebird sang this place.
Dreaming fire- straight past.
……..Dharawal space.

Whites fella came with fence
strange animals came.
Land of drought/ short of food
……..payback game.

Stringline Folk Band performing *Wiritjiribin...Lyrebird Spirit* at Camden Sports Club on 2 July 2016. The line up in Stringline - on lute is Kris Took, fiddle Paula Holstein and on mandolin Paul Malia. (I Willis)

CHORUS.

Macquarie ordered violence
to quell the area's feud.
Elders shot - hung - displayed
……..heads removed.

To Gov't House – sugar bag
full of trophied heads.
White fellas, know they're safe
……..in their beds.

CHORUS

Riding locals found the tribe
Women/ children – meeting place.
Horses' hooves on skin and bone
……..bloodied disgrace.

Those not trampled up above
sent to the river, alive.
Herded off the cliff
……..how many died?

CHORUS

Bones in the river gravel
sandstone leaches blood.
No need for Kadaicha Man
……..death, in the mud.

CHORUS.

Go to the Pass today
plaque speaks of the bones.
Hear lyrebird scream out
don't be near the plaque… alone.
Don't be near the plaque… alone
Don't be in that gorge alone.

The words of the song are published here for the first time.

For the full story of the massacre see Carol Liston, *Campbelltown, The Bicentennial History* (1988) and the Dictionary of Sydney http://dictionaryofsydney.org/entry/appin_massacre

Show and Tell Night at the Museum
History Week 2016

Ian Willis

At the September meeting of the society a number of members spoke about cooking, cook books and their favourite recipes, as part of the 2016 History Week program in Camden. Cooking brings families, friends and communities together. It builds resilience and sustainability, and neatly fitted history week's theme of neighbours.

Stories of cooking and recipes were presented by society members Leonie Jackson, Marjorie White, Frances Warner, Joy Riley, Julie Wrigley, Gordon Bird, Warren Sims, and Betty Yewen. This turned out to be a very popular segment and many people were amused by the tall tales and yarns about favourite recipes. Members produced battered cook books that had been used to death. One cook book called 'Camden Town Cook Book' was put together as a fundraiser by the Camden Pre-School Kindergarten in the late 1970s. Betty Yewen's 'Xmas Fruit Cake Recipe' produced a laugh amongst the audience of 38 members. (see overleaf)

It must be noted that he society library has a number of cook books from earlier eras. Several of the presenters showed that they were good cooks as well as being story tellers. There were samples for tasting at supper time after the presentations. The goods quickly disappeared. The society has some hidden talent amongst its membership if their cooking talent is anything to go by.

One story presented by Marjorie involved 'Aunty Jean's Plain Sponge' which was given to Marjorie by her mother in 1958 in Moss Vale. She said, 'It is a simple foolproof recipe'. Aunty Jean was her mother's aunt and gave it to her many years ago. Marjorie thinks that the recipe is probably of Scottish origins.

Aunty Jean's Plain Sponge
4 eggs, 6 oz sugar, 5 1/2oz self raising flour, 4 tablespoons hot water, 1 teaspoon butter, 2 teaspoon vanilla essence.
Beat egg whites until very stiff, add sugar gradually, whisk until sugar is all dissolved. Add egg yokes one at a time and add vanilla essence. Fold in sifted flour with a wooden spoon. Quickly stir in hot water and melted butter. Bake in an oven over 400°F for 20 minutes.
For additional advice, see Marjorie.

The 2016 Camden History Week program included the NSW Family History Conference called 'Cowpastures and Beyond' (350 participants), a tour of St Paul's Anglican Church Cemetery at Cobbitty (43), the mini-discoverers cooking adventures (40) and a photographic exhibition called 'Camden then and now'. The Camden programme was a joint event between Camden Council Library Service, Camden Historical Society and the Camden Area Family History Society.

Xmas Fruit Cake Recipe

~ Ingredients ~

1 cup butter
4 large eggs
1 cup diced fruit
1 tablespoon nuts
1 teaspoon baking soda
1 cup brown sugar
1 tablespoon lemon juice
1 bottle whisky

Method ~

1. Sample whisky to check for quality.
2. Take large bowl. Check the whisky again to be sure it is of the highest quality. Poor one level cup and drink. Repeat.
3. Turn on electric mixer, beat one cup of butter in a large fluffy bowl, add one spoontea of sugar and beat again.
4. Make sure the whisky is sill OK. Cry another tup.
5. Turn off the mixer. Break two leggs and add to the bowl and chuck in the cup of dried fruit. Mix on the turner. If the fruit gets stuck in the beaters, pry it loose with a drewscriver. Sample the whisky again to check for tonsisticity.
6. Next, sift 2 cups salt. Or something - who cares? Check the whisky.
7. Now sift the lemon juice and strain your nuts. Add one ballspoon of brown sugar, or whatever colour you can find. Wix mel. Grease the oven. Turn the cake pan to 350 gredees.
8. Don't forget to beat off the turner. Throw the bowl out the window. Check the whisky again and go to bed.

Growing up in Camden

Joy Riley

I was born Lorna Joy Dunk on 1 February 1938 at Nurse Taplin's maternity home in Oxley Street, 'Welborn'. I was always called Joy, which was a bit confusing as I have to use Lorna on any medical or legal matters. My sister Doreen was seven years older than I was and was born in our home at 66 John Street.

My father Jack Dunk was born at Orangeville on 1 March 1908. He attended Camden Public School but left at age twelve. In the late 1920s he opened a garage with his brother Cliff at 126 Argyle Street, opposite the Post Office, doing mechanical work, and operating a tow truck, car hire and car sales business.

He owned a motor garage in Picton before World War Two but it had to be sold as staff and parts were hard to get. He enlisted in World War Two in 1940, returning in 1942. He served in the 9th Battalion in the Middle East and was one of the Rats of Tobruk. After the war he did many things including having a market garden at 'Little Sandy' Chellaston Street, helping Chinese market gardeners by ploughing Miss Davies' area near Macquarie Grove, carting cement from Berrima, selling rotary hoes, tractors and farm machinery, and carting wheat at Grenfell. From 1949 until 1960 he owned a fruit and vegetable shop at 152 Argyle Street Camden (at the time between Wrench's store and Furner Brothers, and now Blooms chemist).

My mother Laura May Rix was born at Bowral in 1908. Her father Albert worked for Sam Horden at Bowral then moved to Camden. The family worked on a dairy on Werombi Road, 'Fairview', owned by the Watsons. Mum and her mother milked cows and lifted the heavy cans onto the milk stand for the milk truck to pick up. Mum and her sister, Dorothy (later Baxter) walked to Camden Public School over the head of the Carrington Dam and across the paddocks. After school they milked cows again. Their brother Allan was able to ride a horse to school.

The Rix family moved to Camden and lived in a house, owned by Camden Park, on the corner of the Hume Highway and Macquarie Avenue. Mum worked at the Model Dairy No 2 at Camden Park. She married Jack Dunk in 1929, and had two children. During the war Mum took in married couples from the air force stationed at The Grove. I used to go to Macarthur Park with the wives when they were aircraft spotting, I still look up when a plane goes over. I spent a lot of time playing on the guns in the park with Laurence and Mary Rolfe who lived a few doors down from us. Doreen and I both went to Camden Public School. On leaving school Doreen worked at Frank Whiteman's shop.

In 1949 Mum and Dad purchased from Fred Betts a fruit and vegetable mixed business with a milk bar at 152 Argyle Street. I left school in 1952 and went to work at the fruit shop and Doreen worked there too. Trading was 7 days a week from 9 a.m. to 10 p.m. On Sundays we had a lot of passing trade as the highway went through the town. Sir William McKell was Governor General and would call on his way to Yarralumla in Canberra. He said one of the attractions was the delicious milkshakes served at the shop. He called Yarralumla 'Frog Hollow'. He was first cousin to my grandfather, Albert Rix.

In later years we closed at lunch time on Saturday and all day Sunday. So Dad and I were able to become members of the local car club, and the Peugeot Car Club, participating in many car trials and other events.

Every morning the first job was to sweep the footpath. This happened at Wrench's Shoe Shop, Furner Bros, Mrs Kelly's Dress Shop, and Mrs Powe's

Camden Airfield (Joy Riley)

Baby Shop. It was great in the winter as you got warmed up – no air conditioning in those days. Dad went to the markets twice a week in Sydney (Paddy's Markets now). We had a large cool-room and were able to keep food fresh. A lot of local vegetables were purchased from the Chinese market gardeners. Dad was great friends with the Chinese and when there were floods they would wait for Dad or the Bond Bros to come and move them before the water rose. Fruit was purchased from the orchard at Camden Park, where Charley Barrett was the manager. Dad went to school with him at Camden Public School. Dad would take the truck to Yetholme near Bathurst to get Delicious Apples and was able to store them in the cool room.

Belgenny (Joy Riley)

We had a fruit and vegetable run to Cobbitty where there were a few guesthouses and private homes. On Saturdays we also went to Mount Hunter and Spring Creek. I would go on the run with Dad and be back in time to go to the matinee at the pictures. We also took the bookings for the pictures on Saturday nights. In the eleven years working for our family we got to know most of our customers very well, including Miss Faithfull Anderson from 'Camelot'. At Christmas Dad would make up a fruit and vegetable box for all her employees and deliver them. When Miss Faithfull-Anderson attended Queen Elizabeth's Coronation she brought back gifts for each of our family.

We made many life-long friends with people from other businesses. Doreen married Col Shepard, the barber across the road; Joan Howlett from the hamburger shop was her bridesmaid; Joan married Les Tildsley from the butcher shop; my friend Dawn Howlett married Ron Shoesmith from the cake shop. Everybody knew everybody else. Due to Dad's ill health the shop was sold in 1960. Dad passed away in 1962, aged 54. Mum passed away in 1976.

After the shop was sold I went to work for Coles Grocery (formerly Haffendens) opposite the Crown Hotel. I worked there for 6 years to 1966. I transferred to Coles New World Supermarket and altogether I worked for 17 years for Coles in many positions, including store openings and supervision.

I married Bruce Riley in 1976 and left work in 1977. Bruce was a deputy in the coal mines. We moved to Elderslie in 1977. Unfortunately Bruce passed away suddenly in 1990.

Dad was president of the RSL for a few years in the late 1940s and was instrumental in acquiring the mess hall from the army camp at Narellan to be moved to Oxley Street. Many weddings, birthday parties, Friday night dances, deb balls, Slim Dusty Concerts, Maloney's mannequin parade, and other celebrations were held at the hall which is now the site of the Civic Centre.

I remember in Third Class our teacher Mrs Howe had a very broad Scottish accent. I still blame her for my not being able to spell. At a school reunion in 2009 for Sixth Class in 1950, a lot of the students mentioned Mrs Howe, though the boys seemed to like her more than the girls.

We didn't have excursions in our days at school but looked forward to bus trips for sports days to Picton, Moss Vale, or Campbelltown, if you played netball for girls or football for boys.

Doreen and I spent a lot of time with our mother's parents, Albert and Ellen Rix. Grandfather was head stockman and horse studmaster at Camden Park and lived in Belgenny Cottage in the 1940s and 1950s. One highlight of his work was in January 1947.

The Camden News wrote, *"When reckoned in years Albert Rix, Camden Park Studmaster, is by no means a young man. The years however, have certainly not affected his capacity for direct action. His masterly riding and experience of cattle enabled him to win the Camp Draft event at the last Camden Show. Then last week, after arrangements by Edward Macarthur Onslow and J.S. Haddin* [Camden Park General Manager], *Albert arrived at Macquarie Grove Flying School at 4 a.m. and boarded one of the school's aircraft. Two and a half hours later he was two hundred miles south and making a very successful cattle deal for Camden Park. Not bad for a man of sixty-four."*

Grandmother was a great cook and won many prizes at the local show. She was a member of St John's Mothers' Union Hospital Auxiliary and CWA. She drove a 1927 Pontiac - you had to keep clear of her because she would do a u-turn in front of you without any signal. She tipped the car over on the bridge over the creek into Camden Park and broke her collar bone, but she was still able to drive into Camden. On Tuesdays, together with Mrs Rita Tucker, they cooked and served at the saleyards canteen. They raised money for the CWA Rooms in Murray Street, where the Baby Health Centre functioned.

My mother's parents purchased the house next door to us at 64 John Street from Dad's parents, William and Jemima Dunk. William died in 1930. Jemima moved to Regents Park to live with her daughter Vera and family. Jemima passed away in 1943, six months after Dad returned from the war. The John Street house was rented out until Grandfather Rix retired from Camden Park.

When I was growing up we went for holidays to Stuart Park Wollongong. We had a caravan that Dad had built before the war. Stuart Park was 'little Camden' as most local people went there for their holidays. The coal truck drivers were able to take their trucks loaded with camping gear and bikes. We swam and paddled in the lagoon and played in the park on the swings and seesaws, and playing equipment.

Looking back at my early years in Camden I think I have had a pretty good life so far actually.

Camden Historical Society Inc
President's Report 2015 – 2016
Robert Lester

It is with pleasure that I present my report for the year 2015 to 2016 as it has been a busy and fulfilling one. Through the reading of this report I hope you gain an understanding of the society's activities, the operation of the Camden Museum over the past twelve months and the involvement of the society's committee members and volunteers who really make things happen.

The relevance of the historical society within Camden is shown through its involvement with the community and value given to our local heritage and history by community members. The society over the past twelve months has continued to be active in keeping the stories of Camden alive and raising the interest in local history especially amongst the younger and newer members of our community

Within The Community
The society has been active within the wider community through attendance at community events including: Camden Show; Camden Antique Fair; Belgenny Farm Family History Day; Catherine Park House – ANZAC remembrance; The Oaks Heritage Centre book launches; Australia Day Parade; Camden Fire Service – celebration of 100 years in Camden; and the Narellan Rhythms Festival.

These events are an opportunity to provide people with information, showcase publications available for purchase and display photographs and information from our museum collection. They bring additional visitors to the museum and give support to other local organisations.

With ongoing community concern regarding the works taking place in the main street of Camden and future proposals for developments within the township, the society has worked closely with other like-minded groups to voice its opinion on what is occurring. Meetings have been held with council staff to keep abreast of the changes to the Argyle Street streetscape and it is encouraging to see some of our ideas being implemented, for example, retention of street furniture colour scheme of a heritage green flavour and breaking up of the predominately grey pavers with earthy pavers and sandstone. The society needs to remain vigilant to ensure it has input into any future works undertaken by council in order to preserve the heritage of our town.

There were also discussions with staff on the proposals to review the planning guidelines for the township and future development, stressing the need for proper and full community consultation. Council has appointed consultants to undertake this review over the next twelve months and the society looks forward to being a significant participant in this process.

The society made comments on two contentious development applications that we considered would have significant impact on the heritage of Camden, namely the decked parking station for Oxley Street and changes and additions to the Old Milk Depot in Argyle Street. Whilst council approved the parking station without any changes put forward by the community, it is still to formally consider the other development applications. Hopefully the community anger with this proposal will see it either changed to an appropriate scale or withdrawn by the applicants.

Society Meetings
Whilst the purpose of our monthly meetings is to conduct the affairs of the society they are also important in providing its members and the general public with information and knowledge on local history. Again guest speakers have made presentations at our meetings on a wide and interesting range of topics:

   Joel Kursawe – 100 yrs of Camden Fire Service
   Cameron Archer – Belgenny Farm development
   Brian Stratton – History through the eyes of an artist
   History Week Show and Tell – Treasures from my back yard
   John and Julie Wrigley – The Chinese Market Garden project
   Robert Wheeler – Major Thomas Mitchell
   John and Edwina Macarthur Stanham – The renovation of the stables at
      Camden Park
   Society members – My family and war
   Pauline Downing and Peter Hayward – The Camden School of Arts

Attendance at meetings has been steady with a number of visitors coming along for specific speakers. Thanks to our volunteers Joy, Jo and Frances they are always assured of a great supper afterwards. The committee of the society meets before some of the general meetings and quarterly on a Saturday afternoon to undertake the administrative requirements of the society, look at proposals to develop new projects and museum displays and ensure everything is operating for the benefit of our members and the community.

Volunteers
Our volunteers remain the backbone of both the society and the museum without whom we would not be able to operate at the level we currently do.

Work on our photographic collection, improving our research files, operation of the website, exhibition formation and collection conservation are some of the many roles volunteers undertake behind the scenes. Rene Rem our Volunteers Coordinator keeps the number of volunteers high to meet all our shifts and ensure new volunteers are made welcome and aware of their duties.

The society committee has approved the design of a shirt for volunteers. Grey and white in colour, it is a way of promoting the society and making our volunteers recognisable at the museum and community events.

Museum operations
The Camden Museum is the main venue within Camden that people come seeking history related information and to look at the wonderful displays. Many overseas visitors are recorded in our visitors' book along with a growing number of people from the newly developed areas of Camden. Schools continue to visit the museum as part of the students' learning curriculum along with organised groups and those on a bus trip around the area.

The society needs to encourage more of our new local community members to come along to the museum and learn about what will become their local history in years to come. Our highly successful Facebook page hopefully is reaching many of these households.

Exhibitions presented over the past twelve months have kept a focus on the First World War. A new display highlighting schools has received positive response from visitors as has the expanded photo display on the Camden Fire Station. In the past few weeks a major upgrade has occurred in the upstairs Dick Nixon Room with the purchase and installation of new display cabinets. When the work is completed they will make a very fine improvement to the room.

We continue to gather more photographs from local residents with many included in our online collection in partnership with Camden Library. New items have been included in our growing collection both from our members and members of the public. This support is greatly appreciated.

A significant event during the year was the publication of a new book featuring photographs from our collection and text by Ian Willis – *Camden and District*. It was successfully launched by its publisher Catherine Warne of Kingsclear Books at a function in November 2015 in the galleria of the library, attended by many society members and guests. This publication has been highly successful with many copies being sold by the Society and local retail outlets. I congratulate Ian and Catherine on a job well done.

Partnership with Council

The society participates with council and the Camden Family History Society in a partnership to cooperatively work together. Activities around Heritage Festival in April-May and History Week in September are undertaken and the photographic collection on-line is a joint project between Camden Library and the society.

The society has submitted recommendations for street names and parks for new housing developments that reflect the names of past residents and historical events. Many more names are required into the future as new estates are planned and a list of over 450 names have been given to council for such use.

After much to-ing and fro-ing the Oxley anchor was finally moved by Council to its new site next to the Camden Visitors Centre. In addition Council placed a metal portrait of John Oxley on the wall of the cottage. An interpretation board will be erected in coming months telling the history of John Oxley in the area and the significance of the Anchor. This will be paid for from a generous donation by an Oxley descendant.

Council continues to support the society through a yearly subsidy that covers our insurance, the provision of two storage units at Narellan for our "excess items" and for the maintenance of the museum itself. The society appreciates this especially with all the issues we have had with water leaks in the building.

Communication

The society's twice yearly journals were published through the efforts of Ian Willis including stories on local identities, historical places and events. Lee Stratton produces a number of newsletters displaying many photos of society activities over the year. This year Lee organised printing of them in colour for which we thank our local Federal Member's office. I thank our former member Russell Matheson for his support of the society over the years and look forward to working with our new member Angus Taylor who we have already gotten to know.

A Facebook page post by Brett Atkins of a photo of a line of coal trucks received a mammoth number of hits with over 18,000 people having a look at it and, hopefully other stories on our page. We even had a truck driver bring his big blue truck to the museum (well he parked it outside) to show the picture to his young son.

Society members continue to contribute stories to the well read Back Then page of The District Reporter. The society thanks its editor Lee Abrahams for her ongoing support of local history and the museum.

Financial Assistance
Last year the society received a $5,000 community grant that will led to the production of a DVD on the Chinese marker gardeners who lived and worked along the Nepean River and elsewhere in Camden. This grant has been fully expended and through the process a host of information was obtained on the Chinese people who lived, worked and often died here. The Chinese display in the Museum will reflect this new information when completed. We express our thanks to John and Julie Wrigley for undertaking what, at times, has been a challenging project.

The society continues to receive financial support for its overall operations through donations from members, local residents and visitors to the museum. The Camden Show Society recently gave us a donation of $1,000 from the proceeds of the Camden Show to help maintain its collection housed in the museum. This support, membership fees and sales of our various publications enables the society to cover its yearly operational costs. The society remains in a very healthy financial situation and I thank our treasurer Dawn Williams for the work she does maintaining our financial records and meeting our legal obligations.

In conclusion I wish to thank everyone on the committee and all society members for their support over the four years that I have been president. I have been honoured to be able to serve in this position of what is a highly regarded community organisation. I wish the incoming committee all the best for the coming year and encourage all members to continue to play an active role in the society whether as volunteers or by attending our monthly meetings and activities.

August 2016

Pansy, The Camden - Campbelltown Train
Photographs by Wayne Bearup

Text: Ian Willis
Images: Editing - A McIntosh, Scanning - R Rem

Pansy, the Camden train, never fails to raise vivid memories for anyone with an interest in steam. The train chugged and coughed its way between Camden and Campbelltown railway stations several times a day over many decades. It is now a nostalgic memory from the past.

Wayne Bearup from Manilla, NSW, has recently made a generous donation of a collection of photographs and ephemera concerning Pansy, the Camden train. The photographs illustrate many aspects of Pansy and its movements between Camden and Campbelltown.

Wayne is a keen railway and tram enthusiast and said, 'I have had a life-long interest in railways and tramways'. Wayne says that his photographs of Pansy were taken between 1960 and 1962. He has written a short history of the locomotive for the Bush Telegraph (Tamworth) which will be published later this year.

The Camden train storming the grade out of Campbelltown towards Maryfield on one of the last runs. (W Bearup)

Wayne writes that the Pansy DVD 'brought back many happy memories and some that had faded from my memory'. He recalls when he lived at Lane Cove he was one of the keen tram enthusiasts who were able to ride on the last tram: on Sydney's North Shore in 1958; from Martin Place to La Perouse in 1961; and down George Street in 1959.

At the Camden terminus Camden Railway Station on the last service (W Bearup)

Camden Railway Station on the last day of service (W Bearup)

S Class Locomotive 3077 near Narellan Station c.1961 (W Bearup)

On the branch line heading to Camden c1961 (W Bearup)

S Class Locomotive 3140 heading towards Camden c.1961 (W Bearup)

S Class Locomotive 3140 with carriages bound for Camden (W Bearup)

Liverpool Campbelltown passenger service c.1961 (W Bearup)

Narellan Railway Station on one of the last runs (W Bearup)

Camden Railway Station c1961 (W Bearup)

Camden Arcade 25th Anniversary Address
Christos Scoufis, Arcade Owner
23 September 2016

Ladies and Gentlemen

Thank you for joining us today to celebrate Camden Arcade's 25th Birthday. Twenty-five years is a special milestone for us, as we look back on how the arcade has taken its place, as a prominent part of the Camden shopping precinct.

Today we have a vibrant mix of retailers, who each contribute to the arcade's bright future, ready for the next 25 years.

This year we are playing our part in keeping Camden's history alive for the next generation. As you can see around you, we are showcasing Camden's rich history with our photographic collage. It will be on display throughout the coming months.

We are very proud of the things we have done over the years, and of our contribution to the Camden community, including our instigation, electrical design, and supervision of the Light Up Camden 2000 project, in conjunction with Camden Council and the Camden Chamber of Commerce.

This popular annual event will continue to grow and draw people to Camden well into the future. Today I pledge the sum of $5,000 to the chamber to improve the lighting on the trees.

Camden, we have the name, we have the history and no one can this from us. Camden is positioning itself as a major tourist destination and take its business houses will grow and prosper with this and the added influx of the many new people currently moving into the area.

I would like to thank all the shops that make up this wonderful Camden Arcade community. You have put on a great spread for us this afternoon. Thank you.

Special thanks to Trevor and Sue Robinson from The Strictly Limited Company who have presented this outstanding collection of images from the Camden Museum and to John Wrigley who helped access the museum archives.

And finally to our customers. It is through your continued support over the many years that we can celebrate today. Thank you.

Our birthday is your celebration. Please enjoy the afternoon.

Camden Arcade owner Christos Scoufis (I Willis)

A Personal Reflection on Local History Studies at the University of New England

Tara Eagleton

My name is Tara Eagleton. I am currently studying a Bachelor of Arts (History) at the University of New England, Armidale. I study via distance education to allow myself the flexibility to look after my family, work and pursue my interests while attempting to keep up with the demands of coursework. My historical interests are varied but recently I was introduced to local histories and community studies that led to my joining the Camden Historical Society.

The unit mainly looked at different ways historians analyse and interpret local histories through a variety of primary and secondary sources. The unit also examined the different approaches and forms of presenting local and community history. My first assignment was to produce an annotated bibliography of four primary sources and two secondary sources that focused on the history of a specific locality or community. As I have an interest in the history of child welfare I decided to focus on childhood in Camden from the mid to late 1800s. This presented some challenges as a large portion of Camden's history centres on the Macarthurs and the settlement of Camden town and surrounds. Sources pertaining to the everyday lives of common people in this period are difficult to come by and sources relating to the lives of children are even more challenging.

I analysed a variety of different primary sources that could provide a glimpse into the past lives of different Camden childhoods – a photograph, newspaper clipping, painting, and a short biography. Atkinson's book provided some contextual background into the roles of women, family life, and schooling while Gorton and Ramsland revealed the employment of child convict labourers by the Macarthurs. [1]

I happily received a Distinction for this assignment and the unit overall. However, aside from the grades, I have maintained an interest in the local and social history of places. I have joined the Camden Historical Society to gain knowledge of Camden's local history beyond the textbooks. Camden still has much to share of its past.

A Camden Childhood 1840 to 1900.

Locality
Camden is a semi-rural town situated about seventy kilometres south west of Sydney, New South Wales. To the north and east of the town lies the Nepean River and to the south and west rises the Burragorang Ranges and Razorback Mountain. The town has a unique presence in history of colonial New South Wales, renown for the establishment of quality merino sheep farming by John and Elizabeth Macarthur in 1805.[2] However, the making of Camden as a village and farming community was founded by their son, James Macarthur. From the 1830s to the 1850s, Camden settled into its own local identity and sense of place. To this day, the Macarthur estate and farm is operational and descendants of the Macarthurs still reside on the premises. The town is also still home to descendants of other prosperous land owners of the 1800s. The original layout of the town centre is still intact and three of the original hotels are still operational under their original names.

Focus
The following annotated sources focus on the childhood experience of the 1830s to early 1900s in the rural colonial village of Camden, NSW. Most of Camden's history is based around the Macarthurs' and other prosperous land owners. Less is known of the illiterate poor or other minority groups, including children.[3] There is no standard childhood experience. Childhood in Camden during this era largely depended on status, family management and other conditions of life.

Sources

Alan Atkinson, *Camden, Farm and Village Life in Early New South Wales*, Melbourne, Oxford University Press, 1988.

Secondary source #1
This book provides a rich history of the making of Camden as a community from the 1830s to the late 1890s. It steps away from the dominantly Macarthur history of agricultural and economic development and instead focuses on the people who lived and worked in the locality, their daily lives, relationships, families, faiths and neighbours. Atkinson accounts for the religious fervour of the Primitive Methodists who recruited children into the 'Band of Hope', who in its second year had children parade down the main street singing songs of 'total abstinence'.[4] Apart from religion, the book observes the changing roles of women and household management of large families.[5] This in turn impacts on the lives of children - increasing health and mortality rates, labour and family responsibilities, and schooling opportunities, albeit

dependent on the families' economic situation.[6]

Alan Atkinson is a well known authority on colonial Australian history. The book includes photographs, sketches, and maps throughout. Atkinson has included family trees and an appendix listing immigrant arrivals to Camden. There are extensive notes at the end of the book and a large bibliography that includes references to primary manuscripts and documents along with secondary sources. Also included is a number of unpublished works of an autobiographical nature. The book provides a thorough background for the observance of childhood experiences in this time.

Kerin Gorton and John Ramsland, Prison playground? Child convict labour and vocational training in New South Wales, 1788-1849, *Journal of Educational Administration and History***, Vol. 34, No. 1, 2002, pp. 51-62.**

Secondary Source #2

This article examines the lives of convict children during the early colonial period of 1788-1849. Gorton and Ramsland declare that the scarcity of written documentation on the lives of colonial children makes it challenging to provide a complete picture of their childhood experience. The authors investigate the use of convict children for labour in public and private enterprise, their deplorable working wages and conditions and the idea of convict children as independent adults.[7] The Macarthurs of Camden are referred to as a private employer of convict children. Stating further that John Macarthur preferred to employ convict children over adult convicts because they complained less. This reference illustrates a different Camden childhood experience from the Atkinson source.

John Ramsland is a skilled historian and author of numerous books, articles, and conference papers including a vast amount of research in child welfare history. He was a professor at the University of Newcastle when this article was written.[8] Kerin Gorton co-authored the article and was a PhD student at University of Newcastle in at the time. Although this source can only indicate the situations child convicts were placed in, rather than their actual accounts of life as a convict child, it does assist to expose the absence of childhood and family for convict children. With limited information available on children in colonial times and an even greater shortage of documentation for convict children, this article is an important secondary source. The bibliography provides access to further information into the colonial child of New South Wales.

Elsie to Dear Dorothy, published letter, 13 June 1895, Camden News, NSW, Trove, http://trove.nla.gov.au/newspaper/article/133282218?searchTerm=camden%20news%20children%27s%20corner&searchLimits=l-title=638 **accessed 2 March 2016.**

Primary Source #1
This is a children's column called "Children's Corner' published in the Camden News in 1895. Australian newspapers had begun to address children as readers in the late 19th century.[9] American newspapers had encouraged young readers to write letters to the newspaper since the 1840s. Letters were addressed to an 'uncle' or 'aunt' that could provide advice on all manner of topics. The idea was replicated in Australian newspapers with 'Uncle Harry' in the *Adelaide Observer* and later 'Aunt Dorothy' in South Australia's *Advertiser*. Many country newspapers in South Australia and other states started to publish children's columns[10] and in the *Camden News*, 'Aunt Dorothy' received the children's letters.

Children's Corner gives an insight into the daily lives of local children. The letter from Elsie states that another local newspaper, the *Camden Times*, is publishing a fashion plate every week. Elsie and her sister are very receptive to this idea and suggest the *Camden News* might do something similar----. They are also pleased with the prospect of reading material for children each week. Elsie's style of writing and use of grammar show that she is a receiving an education from school and being taught the skills of dressmaking by her mother at home. Her older sister is already adept at this. This suggests that dressmaking was a skill taught to children from their mothers, likely to daughters. It is not certain why she does not want her name revealed. Further research is needed to place the location of Stump Farm. From this information in may be possible to trace who Elsie's family are.

William Russell "Werriberrie", *My Recollections*, **Glebe, 1914.**

Primary source #2
William Russell was born on the banks of the Werri-berri creek located in The Oaks, near Camden, in 1830. Russell is believed to be one of the last of his people and at the time of his autobiography, by far the eldest Indigenous man in the area.[11] The book is an oral history as told to grazier Alfred Leonard Bennett (1877-1942). The Gundungurra (Gandangara) group lived in south west Sydney, an area which includes the Burragorang Valley near Camden.[12] William recollects his childhood as a young Aboriginal boy living through rapid changes to the land and society around him as the Camden town grew. He describes different locations, but mainly recollects all the different people, both white and indigenous, that he grew up knowing or knowing of.

This is a short booklet of 31 pages. It includes a portrait photograph of William Russell, some information on Gundungurra language and two maps showing the locations Russell describes in his recollections. It is a useful primary source as it creates a visual image of early times in Camden from the perspective of an Indigenous person and particularly important in its descriptions of childhood from the first person perspective. Taking into consideration that memories are highly subjective and typically non-chronological, personal accounts provide an opportunity to access firsthand experience of events and times in history albeit from one individuals perspective.[13]

Emily Macarthur, *Old schoolhouse at Camden by lower garden 1850s*, painting, National Library of Australia, 1850-1859.

Primary source #3
1850 - 1859
By Macarthur, Emily. Contributed by National Library of Australia [nla.pic-an11461090]

Emily Macarthur was a female colonial artist of the Macarthur family of Camden Park. This watercolour painting is part of a collection called Album of Emily Macarthur. The handwriting in the lower centre reads 'now pulled down 1928'. The title suggests that this schoolhouse was built on the Macarthur estate as it refers to 'the lower garden'. A schoolhouse on the estate indicates there were enough children on the estate to justify the building. Previous sources also indicate that the children in the painting would not be convict labourers or Indigenous children. The children depicted are dressed in bright colours suggesting their parents have affordable means and the children are not required elsewhere. The different ranges in height indicate the children range in ages.

The trees painted in the background are non-native; they resemble the evergreens and firs of the English countryside. It would require considerable time for such trees to grow to this height and considering the date of the painting, this would not be possible. Therefore, perhaps Emily Macarthur is reminiscing of home. Considering this, the painting may not reflect the actual landscape at the time. Landscapes of England may have been popular at the time or the artist was fusing the old environment with the new. A painting is very much open to interpretation but is a valued part of material culture that can enrich documentary research.

Primary source #4
Large collections of photographs can assist in the reconstruction of a place,

time or family.[14] This photograph is part of a collection of photographs of the Boardman family. It is portraiture of four of the Boardman children although their identities and familial relations are unknown; the photo suggests they are siblings. Portraiture would require the children to dress in their best clothing. It is difficult to ascertain whether this is a popular style of the time and to what status the children belong without referring to more photographs of children in the same time frame. The serious demeanour and lack of emotion implies a middle or higher class status. The children's gaze is directed at the same place implying that there is something or someone in the background.

The photograph enriches the examination of children's lives in early Camden however more companion photos would allow greater perspective on the children's identity, status and a better understanding on the character of typical family portraits.

Boardman family, photograph, 1896, Camden Libraries, Camden Images Ref. CHS2473, http://catalogue.library.camden.nsw.gov.au/cgi-bin/spydus.exe/SET/ARCIMG/ARCENQ/1640026/5140830? NREC=10&NAVDIR=-1 accessed 20 March 2016.

Notes
1. Alan Atkinson, *Camden, Farm and Village Life in Early New South Wales*, Melbourne, 1988; Kerin Gorton and John Ramsland, Prison playground? Child convict labour and vocational training in New South Wales, 1788-1849, *Journal of Educational Administration and History*, Vol. 43, No. 1, 2002, pp. 51-53.
2. John Wrigley, A History of Camden, extract, Camden, 2001. http://www.camdenhistory.org.au/chhistoryofcamden.html accessed 1 March 2016.
3. Alan Atkinson, *Camden, Farm and Village Life in Early New South Wales*, Melbourne, 1988, p. 206-207.
4. Atkinson, *Camden,* p 181-182.
5. *Ibid.*, p. 196.
6. *Ibid.*, 143.
7. Kerin Gorton and John Ramsland, Prison playground? Child convict labour and vocational training in New South Wales, 1788-1849, *Journal of Educational Administration and History*, Vol. 43, No. 1, 2002, pp. 51-53.
8. Anon. *John Ramsland*, Authors Unlimited, Australian Society of Authors, 2016, https://authors-unlimited.org/memberportfolios/john-ramsland
9. Leonie Rutherford, Forgotten histories: ephemeral culture for children and the digital archive, *Media International Australia, Incorporating Culture and Policy*, No. 150, p.67.
10. State Library of South Australia, *SA Newspapers: Children's columns*, http://www.samemory.sa.gov.au/site/page.cfm?u=1470 accessed 23 March 2016.

11. William Russell "Werriberrie", *My Recollections*, Glebe, 1914, p. 5.
12. Jim Smith, New Insights into Gundungurra place naming, in *Aboriginal Placenames*, Harold Koch & Luise Hercus (ed.), Canberra, ANU Press and Aboriginal History Incorporated, 2009, p.87.
13. Beverly Mack, 'Personal Accounts', World History Sources, http://chnm.gmu.edu/worldhistorysources/unpacking/acctsmain.html accessed 23 March 2016.
14. Robin Lenman and Angela Nicholson, *The Oxford Companion to the Photograph*, Online, 2005, DOI: 10.1093/acref/9780198662716.001.0001 accessed 15 March 2016.

References
Primary
Boardman family, photograph, 1896, Camden Libraries, Camden Images Ref. CHS2473, http://catalogue.library.camden.nsw.gov.au/cgi-bin/spydus.exe/SET/ARCIMG/ARCENQ/1640026/5140830?NREC=10&NAVDIR=-1 accessed 20 March 2016.
Elsie to Dear Dorothy, published letter, 13 June 1895, Camden News, NSW, Trove, http://trove.nla.gov.au/newspaper/article/133282218?searchTerm=camden%20news%20children%27s%20corner&searchLimits=l-title=638 accessed 2 March 2016.
Macarthur, Emily, *Old schoolhouse at Camden by lower garden 1850s*, painting, National Library of Australia, 1850-1859.
Russell, W., *My Recollections*, Glebe, 1914.

Secondary
Anon. *John Ramsland*, Authors Unlimited, Australian Society of Authors, 2016, https://authors-unlimited.org/memberportfolios/john-ramsland
Atkinson, Alan, *Camden, Farm and Village Life in Early New South Wales,* Melbourne, Oxford University Press, 1988.
Gorton, K. and Ramsland, J., Prison playground? Child convict labour and vocational training in New South Wales, 1788-1849, *Journal of Educational Administration and History*, Vol. 43, No. 1, 2002.
Mack, Beverly, 'Personal Accounts', World History Sources, http://chnm.gmu.edu/worldhistorysources/unpacking/acctsmain.html accessed 23 March 2016.
Rutherford, L., Forgotten histories: ephemeral culture for children and the digital archive, *Media International Australia, Incorporating Culture and Policy*, No. 150, pp. 66-71.
Smith, J., New Insights into Gundungurra place naming, in *Aboriginal Placenames*, Harold Koch & Luise Hercus (ed.), Canberra, ANU Press and Aboriginal History Incorporated, 2009, pp. 87-114.
State Library of South Australia, *SA Newspapers: Children's columns*, http://www.samemory.sa.gov.au/site/page.cfm?u=1470 accessed 23 March 2016.
Wrigley, J., *A History of Camden*, extract, Camden, 2001, http://www.camdenhistory.org.au/chhistoryofcamden.html accessed 1 March 2016

Ghosts and Shadows at Macaria

Pauline Downing

If a man is killed before his life span is completed, his vital spirit is not yet exhausted and may survive for a while as a ghost -   Chu Hsi (Chinese philosopher) 5th century AD

For a house of this scale, Macaria is among the best picturesque Gothic houses in Australia. This, when combined with its importance to Camden, makes it a building of great significance. (National Estate Database) The building is part of the John Street group.

Macaria is a fine early townhouse of distinctive and interesting architectural quality, associated with an important figure of the town's early years. (NSW Heritage)

Macaria at 37 John Street Camden has always fascinated me. Macaria translates from the Latin and Greek to mean either *Happiness* or *Blessed*.

It is a beautiful mansion built in 1859-60 in the Victorian Italianate style (tending towards Victorian Gothic) for Henry Thompson, the local miller in Camden, who tragically was killed before his grand home was completed. The Thompson family sold the house to Mr Milford who did not survive long before passing it as inheritance to his daughter Sarah.

Not many years later Sarah Milford made, it seems, an unfortunate marriage to a farmer named James Tiffin who struggled with Sarah's determination for the house, Macaria, and its land to be left in her name and the rights not pass to him upon marriage.

Within several months Sarah became very ill and passed away. Convenient for Tiffin? Many consider the Victorian Era as the Golden Age of Poisoning. Poisoning was an easy form of murder to get away with because it could be done in secrecy. Moreover, the proof necessary to convict someone in a court of law in that time tended to rely on circumstantial evidence.

James sold the house and moved away from Camden and the district. Sarah, or her 'presence', is supposed to be unable to leave the house her father bought. Taken from life so early it seems as though she stays about the old place, happy and content, causing no problems.

My own childhood was shaped by my grandmother who cared for me until adulthood. An incredibly superstitious woman, as were most people born in the late 19th century and who lived into the mid 20th century, her superstitions come back to me frequently. They were an everyday part of my childhood.

She would cover all the mirrors and silverware in a thunderstorm; not put new shoes on a table; if we spilt salt it was vital to throw a pinch over your left shoulder; if someone sneezed it was thrown over your right shoulder; spilling sugar meant joy; a whistling woman was bad luck … and so on. You will surely have heard some of these old beliefs from your own grandmother.

So I believed there are ghosts sharing this mortal coil with us. I was told so as a child, and today I cannot shake that lingering belief. I remember waking one night as a child and looking at a figure dressed in shining white standing at the bottom of my bed. Unbidden, although I know their worth, they still reside in my psyche. There are too many inexplicable reasons why spirits, or souls, could be stuck between here and there.

In 1880 the Camden Grammar School was established in Macaria. The students experienced strange noises at midnight, furniture moving and the sounds of broken crockery. (Was it simply hungry boarders pillaging the larders?)

By 1900 the school had moved to Narellan. Ghostly beings awaited them at the new site of their school at Studley Park, itself imbued with stories of strange happenings, albeit these paranormals were happier beings. *"A cheerful, childlike presence"* was the reference.

A dentist established a practice in Macaria, but lost a patient in the chair when an oval section of the ceiling fell on the unfortunate patient. (Was this a result of a water damaged ceiling? An oval shaped puddle formed by a leaking roof?)

Dr. Lumley had his home and surgery there. Returning late after a house call he was thrown around his bedroom. Relatives of Mrs. Lumley (who lived in Larkins Cottage – also built by Henry Thompson) avowed there was *'something'* in that house.

There is another entity, *'Bill'*, who causes problems at Macaria. Mrs. Farquar, who left the employ of Camden Council in 2008, was adamant there was *'something'* as there were experiences of an un-sourced feeling of coldness that signaled *Bill's* presence.

The late Derrick Thorn, one of Council's long time past employees, held Mrs. Farquar in great esteem as did the rest of the council staff. He had heard the stories and added another about a very level-headed staff member, who, working upstairs writing a report one night at 9.30pm, was spooked by the sound of footfalls on the stairs. There was nothing there. He decided not to work any later that night.

Common sense tell us not to forget the old house is very tall with an incredibly high, but beautifully pitched iron roof. Metal does shrink and contract with temperature changes. Wood does move and creak. Old sailors were only comfortable sailing a wooden ship that *'talked'*. The ceilings of Macaria are up to four metres high. Derrick suggested the chimneys attached to the outside walls could be sounding chambers for the breezes from particular directions.

So? Is it just the old girl stretching her old bones, or is it old bones stretching their attachment to the old house?

Thankfully, today Macaria is an integral part of our valued heritage architecture because of Miss Llewella Davies (1901 -2000). Camden was her town and she knew or wanted to know **everything** that was going on in her town.

The story goes that Macaria was to be demolished and the building behind, previously occupied by Council, be brought forward in its place. Miss Davies swung into action and Macaria still stands in John Street today.

References:
Dominic McNamara, Paranormal Investigators.
Derek Thorn, Pers Comm.
Back Then, *The District Reporter*
Mark Powell.
The Ghost Guide to Australia, Richard David 1998.
www.geocities.com.au.
Camden Crier July 1992,
Melissa Denford,
http://camdenhistorynotes.blogspot.com.au/2015/12/macaria-camden-heritage-icon.html

CAMDEN HISTORY

Journal of the Camden Historical Society

March 2017 Volume 4 Number 3

CAMDEN HISTORY
Journal of the Camden Historical Society Inc.
ISSN 1445-1549
Editor: Dr Ian Willis

Management Committee
President: Dr Ian Willis
Vice Presidents: John Wrigley OAM, Cathey Shepherd
Secretary: Lee Stratton
Treasurer: Dawn Williams
Immediate Past President: Bob Lester
General Committee:　　Sharon Greene　　Rene Rem
　　　　　　　　　　　Roslyn Tildsley　　Julie Wrigley
　　　　　　　　　　　Robert Wheeler　　Stephanie Trenfield

Honorary Solicitors: Vince Barrett

Society contact:
P.O. Box 566, Camden, NSW 2570.   Online <http://www.camdenhistory.org.au>

Meetings
Meetings are held at 7.30 p.m. on the second Wednesday of the month except in January. They are held in the Museum. Visitors are always welcome.

Museum
The Museum is located at 40 John Street, Camden, phone 4655 3400 or 46559210. It is open Thursday to Sunday 11 a.m. to 4 p.m., except at Christmas. Visits by schools and groups are encouraged. Please contact the Museum to make arrangements. Entry is free.

Camden History, Journal of the Camden Historical Society Inc
The Journal is published in March and September each year. The Editor would be pleased to receive articles broadly covering the history of the Camden district . Correspondence can be sent to the Society's postal address. The Society takes no responsibility for the contents of articles published in the Journal.

Donations
Donations made to the Society are tax deductible. The accredited value of objects donated to the Society are eligible for tax deduction.

Cover: 2017 Australia Day Parade (A McIntosh)

CAMDEN HISTORY
Journal of the Camden Historical Society Inc.

Contents

Stories from *The Menangle News*	111
The story of *The Menangle News* Sue Peacock	117
An Arts and Crafts house in Menangle Laura Egan-Burt	120
Menangle Community Association Inc Laura Egan-Burt	125
The Camden Museum Collection - Understanding Its Significance Anne McIntosh	132
Australia Day 2017 Anne McIntosh	136
Immigrant Child Mark and Trish Thornell	140
Memories Of Pansy, The Camden Tram Wayne Bearup	142
Ghosts And Shadows At Macaria, A Reply Janice Johnson	145

Stories from *The Menangle News*

Ian Willis writes:
The Menangle News is a small community monthly newssheet that has circulated in the Menangle village for many years. It has been the baby of Susan and Brian Peacock who have guided its birth, growth and maturity over many decades. It has carried village news, community news, advertisements, yarns and tall tales and village doings. It really has been a village crier in the best sense of the term. Here are some of these stories.

How's Zat (1980)
Tom Curry writes:
Whilst watching the galaxy of star batsmen on the tele in recent weeks, dressed as though they were about to take part in a sword duelling contest, my thoughts went back to an amusing incident which happened many decades ago.

One annual cricket match which created great interest and prestige in the district was the one when the Macarthur Onslows were hosts to the team of class cricketers from Sydney to play a specially selected Camden District team on the beautiful cricket oval on Camden Park.

Amongst the employees of Camden Park were quite a few very fine cricketers, descendants of whom are playing cricket in the district today. One such employee was always assured of the honour of being selected to play as wicket keeper. He was Jim English, affectionately known to one and all as "Grandfather English". He was a very robust man, with large hands often referred to as big as a No 8 shovel. In those days Jim's wife made all his cricketing trousers, mainly because he needed extra-large pockets, and Jim preferred front pockets to side pockets.

During this particular match one city batsman was giving the locals a real leather hunting. Captain Onslow had tried all his best bowlers without success, so in desperation he gave one of the non-bowlers of his team a turn at the bowling crease. Old Jim English seized the opportunity to give the batsman some information about the new bowler. He told him "This bloke thinks he can bowl, but he's all skite. I'd like to see you teach him a lesson. Hop out and hit him for six."

Down came the first ball which the batsman missed, and the ball slipped through Old Jim's gloves and disappeared. Jim turned and faced the long stop fieldsman. The batsman assumed the ball had gone for byes and started to run. Old Jim quickly removed his glove and retrieved the ball from his huge trouser pocket and knocked the bails off! The batsman was halfway down the pitch when he realised he was out.

This was a true story told to me by an old gentleman who was a member of the local team at this particular match. His veracity in such matters is beyond reproach.

Boxing Day (1980)
Tom Curry writes:
It is strange but very true how some little remark or event will spark off a train of thoughts that leads one away down memory lane. Such a thing happened to me on Boxing Day just passed.

Nell and I and our family from the Crookwell District had partaken of a sumptuous luncheon and our ever exuberant grandchildren were champing at the bit to get going to spend a promised poolside afternoon party with their uncles, aunts and cousins at Douglas Park.

It was then my thoughts wandered back some sixty odd years. Boxing Day on those far off days was always picnic day at the river for all the residents of Menangle. With hampers packed full to the brim with all the goodies of Christmas fare, and the old black billy, one of the most important items to take along, groups of families would parade off, some to the front river with its beautiful swimming pool and sandy beach, others would make for the back river and the grassy plateau leading to Archie's Crossing, while others would go to the black hole to spread their picnic rugs down beyond the big steam boiler which supplied the steam for the pumps that supplied the water for the butter factory and Gilbulla.

As the sun began to set in the west, the surface of the river would come alive with countless thousands of fish, just as though a hail storm was hitting the water.

They were such happy joyous days in my childhood one could never forget the pleasure of living in such a pantisocracy and of such propinquity as was Menangle when I was a boy.

Tribute to Tom Curry (1981)
By way of tribute to Mr Tom Curry who died earlier this month (July 1981) two of his closest friends, Mrs Beryl McGrath and Mrs Nea Templeman have written down some memories for our paper.

Nea Templeman writes:
Tom Curry, or Ronald Ralf were one and the same; a friend to those who knew him. Going back thirty years or more Tom's interest in horses with his knowledge and experience was invaluable to my husband Noel and brother Ken. His visits were looked forward to – even if it was to listen to stories of those who had passed on.

Tom rode a dark chestnut horse called Freddy to round up the cattle on killing day for the meat for the family butchery. During the Depression our family seemed to live on sausages, there is no doubt a couple extra were edged into the parcel. My mother who lived at the old post office often passed the remark, "I heard Tom go through the Catholic church to work at 3am again this morning." This was his short cut to the store where Tom managed the butcher shop.

The local kids (me being one of them) dearly loved to stand just inside the door to see the sausages being made.

When Tom was courting the one and only Nell, he had a single seater silver grey Ford car, all the kids would ache for a ride in the dickey seat.
I feel we have lost a real friend, I am proud to have had him as a friend and confidante. Up until the 1940s we all seemed one big family in Menangle, sharing good times and bad.

I am happy to say Nell accepted what eventuated and seems to be her smart, quiet, smiling self. She has accepted her years to come with her three wonderful children and her grandchildren.

Thank you for asking me to think up past tales, it was a pleasure, remember I was talking mostly as things were in my teens.

Beryl McGrath writes:
God-given peace came to the life of our town's most loved and respected citizen Ronald Ralph Curry always known affectionately as Tom throughout his 72 years in Menangle. At the time of his birth Tommy Burns was at the peak of his boxing career and the new baby was given the nickname of Young Tom.

His entire life has been spent in the village, with his family attending school and Sunday School, and then in adult life he was our butcher at the shop run by his parents G. Curry and Sons for 25 years.

It was a sad day when the business passed out of their hands 33 years ago and they purchased a property in the Crookwell district and branches of the family moved away. Over the past few years Tom and Nell have been the sole remaining Curry family to stay in the town.

There are still a few remaining senior citizens in the town who have journeyed down the years and watched Tom's life unfold. Firstly his romance with Nell Dowle, one of six young eligible daughters of Mr and Mrs Alf Dowle, also life-long residents, was watched with interest as it blossomed, and finally the wedding. Then came the births of their children Elaine, Warren and Claire and they were all permanent residents until Elaine married Austin Ryder and lived at Douglas Park. Warren married Mar Dawson of Mount Hunter and settled on the property at Bertalba and Claire married Bill Glenn and went to Douglas Park to live.

For many years Tom commuted between their respective homes and the property spending the working week on the land and the weekends at home. Then as the years and failing health finally caught up Tom retired from physical work. Through his later life came much suffering and trips to hospital, but it was with a smile and a happy memory of past incidents that he loved to recall that he greeted everyone. Tom's happiest hours were spent at the numerous "Back to Menangle" celebrations that have been organised over the years reminiscing with friends who had spent their childhood in the village. Amongst my personal memories I will always recall the evening the people of Menangle organised a kitchen tea for my future husband and I in the local hall. Tom was asked to present us with the gifts and as he spoke he broke down and cried, and I did likewise. And of course we always wondered if it was because he was sorry for us or if he was crying with happiness for us. But all who have known him realise just how deeply he felt for everyone he knew, he was not afraid to show his emotions.

St James Menangle, the church he has attended all his life, was filled to capacity on 9 June when his funeral service was held and was a tribute to both Tom and all his family when so many gathered to show their esteem. Sincere sympathy is extended to the family and we know that his suffering has ended. Some happy memories will linger with us all.

The School Of Arts
Vera Hawkey writes:
In the early 1920s Menangle was a very conservative place where you minded your "Ps and Qs" in fear of what the neighbours might say.

Many happy functions were held, none the less, in the old School of Arts. The dances were a delight with good country music, a lively M.C. and an air of great festivity. The chaperones sat on one side of the hall, the girls on the other, and the boys grouped around the door. As the music struck up, the

M.C. called "Select your partners for the Old Time Waltz."

The lads broke free and made for a girl of their choice who was looking shy, coy and hopeful. After a bright medley of dances a huge supper would be served and the young couples would walk sedately home behind their chaperones.

Times are a-changing

Vera Hawkey writes:

In 1837 the highest paid price for newly purchased land was 18/- per acre.

The first mention of dairying on Camden Park was in 1826 when John Macarthur is reported to have taken 14 female convicts with the hope of turning them into dairy maids. However only when wool and wheat went west did cattle come to the fore.

In the 1890s milk, butter and cheese were taken by road from Menangle Factory to Sydney. Menangle became the chief receiving depot. Pigs were raised on skim milk from the butter factory, which, produced the Estate's own "Laurel" brand butter.

Keep Smiling
A Menangle local writes:

Another resident of the village who wishes to remain anonymous has written some snippets which might spark some memories amongst the long-time residents of Menangle.

Early in my teens this rumour or story went the rounds. To begin with there were two middle aged brothers living with their aged mother and rarely mixing with the locals except in their work. One night a spinster cried, "Peeping Tom", and as usual a search was made but no culprit was found.

The following day one of the brothers related this story: 'Me and my brother rushed down and hid in the Camden Road Creek – we were sure we would be blamed."

To my knowledge they had some strange ideas but were never in trouble in this district. Strange how our minds work when in a panic!'

I wonder how many remember these old names: Bill Calvert; Charlie Cox (do we remember?) if only that he was said to be one of the best wicket keepers in the district.

Once, playing cricket in the factory paddock, now the rotolactor yards he was wicket keeping against the mighty Donald Bradman. Other personalities included Scotty Creighton, Jordy and Freddy Cotterill who was a valet, come man servant, to Captain and Mrs Rex Smart, who lived in the home now occupied by Mr and Mrs Halfpenny.

Also these old men mostly carried a sugar bag – goodness knows the contents – but during the 1930s and 40s the bogey man was well instilled in the kids' minds. Thank goodness he seems to have died a natural death and kids today don't have to go through that harassment.

The Nepean. (1980)
Nea Templeman writes:
One of the strong influences on life in Menangle, from the very earliest days of the colony, has been the Nepean River. In the earliest days the river was the boundary for the colony. Visits from Governor Hunter and Matthew Flinders to the area, and the subsequent allotment of small holdings along the river account for much of the early development.

The supply of fresh water to the early pioneers was essential, a thing which has remained essential to this day and for time to come. More recently the river has supplied the sand for the construction of the Sydney Harbour Bridge. The river sand was the best quality sand available, and a special railway line was built from the Menangle railway bridge to the river for its transport.

One historic point on the river is Bird's Eye Crossing or "Archie's Crossing" as it became known. Archie Tulloh had a cart run across the river at this point, a short cut between Appin and Menangle which he used for many years. This was also the point where Hume and Hovell crossed the Nepean in 1824.

Erratum
Camden History Sept 2016
Pp 50-59 Memories of Barbering Col Smith, Nick Prior should be Mick Prior

The story of *The Menangle News*

Sue Peacock

Brian and I moved to our little cottage in Station Street Menangle from Liverpool in May 1977. The Nepean was in flood so we came the long way round via Camden! We were warmly welcomed by our neighbours - other young couples who were also buying their first homes as the workers' cottages from Camden Park were sold off. As we settled in and began our family, we realised that many of the older Menangle residents had lived here all their lives and had some wonderful stories to tell.

As well as St James Anglican and St Patricks Catholic Churches, and the fire brigade the first Menangle playgroup started up about that time. I decided it would be good to have a way to collect the news from these community groups and publish it. I had recently been through a significant epiphany with an encounter with Jesus, who had healed me instantly of post-natal depression, and given me hope and joy. I wanted to share this with my friends and neighbours too!

Another secret of the success of *The Menangle News* was the centralised post office where each household had a mail box, and Margaret Ritchie our post mistress, was very happy to have the "News" on her counter for all to receive. The very first issue of *The Menangle News* was typed up on *gestetner* stencils and duplicated at St John's Church Office in October 1980.

In the early years we had some Menangle celebrities like Tom Curry and Nea Templeman as our story writers – "Menangle As I Remember It" was very popular. (One of Tom's stories is earlier) Our local gossip column "Mayne Lines" was penned by Sue Mayne, who with her husband Dave were proprietors of the Menangle Store, and kept us up to date with births, deaths and marriages etc.

Many community activities took place at the Menangle School of Arts in its day – it was a wonderful centre for dances, trivia nights, playgroups, and elections. Every election would find trestle tables out the front laden with homemade cakes for a fundraiser of some kind. All these things were promoted through *The Menangle News* of course!

Helen Halfpenny's recipes were always keenly sought after, and we had occasional columns on "healthy eating" from resident nutritionists, and medical advice from local doctors. *The Menangle News* is simply a community newsletter – reports from Durham Green, Men @ Shop, Fire Brigade, Menangle

Community Group, promotion of community events like the Christmas Carols on the Common, annual Australia Day Breakfast (which actually began as an afternoon tea to thank all our contributors and was called "The Menangle News Australia Day Awards". We encouraged Menangleites to nominate neighbours for "awards" and we printed up certificates. Since the School of Arts has not been usable, the fire brigade very kindly allowed us to move down there. They now even take care of all the catering for the breakfast.

Menangle is a wonderful community, and we enjoy contributing with the monthly Menangle News. Originally it was my "baby", providing an outlet for my love for writing when I had the wonderful privilege of being a stay-at-home-mum, but in more recent years Brian had taken on the production role, allowing me to continue writing a column which is really aimed at spiritual edification. For many years now Steve Charles has printed the "News" on the St James photocopier and Kerry Charles then walks around the village posting it in letterboxes.

Brian and I have been married to each other for over 40 years, we have 4 adult offspring and 8 grandchildren about whom we are dotty! We attend St James Church. Brian works as administrator for St James, and does bookkeeping for St Johns in Camden, and keeps the accounts for our Curves business. He is treasurer for many community groups because he is good with numbers and very kind hearted.

The central motivation of my life is my love for God and desire to see His kingdom come on earth as it is in heaven. As well as Sundays at St James I belong to a wonderful interdenominational Christian movement called "Aglow International". I have served as President of Camden Aglow since 2006 and love the opportunities it offers to grow in my own faith and encourage others as well.

A large chunk of my time is invested into running our Curves business – a labour of love! I trained as a PE teacher in the early 1970s, and enjoy providing a gym for women to exercise together and support each other in caring well for their bodies. The Curves circuit of exercise machines is beautifully designed to provide a full body workout in just 30 minutes, which means busy women can fit it into their lifestyle.

The Menangle News Circulation
Circulation: 218. Email distribution: 68. Letterboxed and community distribution: 150.
Distribution sites: Just the village and Durham Green. Copies are also left at the Store & church for people to take.

THE MENANGLE NEWS

VOL 27 NO 1   JANUARY 2017

St James – *the light on the hill*

Photo by Steve Branding

Minister: Rev Chris Moroney
Enquiries: Ph. 4633 8594

SUNDAY CHURCH SERVICES
8.30am: Traditional Service
10am: Family Service and Sunday School

www.menangle.anglican.asn.au

What's on at St James

BELL RINGING PRACTICE
Wednesday evenings from 7 to 8 PM
New members welcome.

MEN @ SHOP
...an opportunity for men to relax, with other men, over a cup of coffee or tea in a friendly atmosphere once a week at 10.30 a.m. on Thursdays at the Menangle Store.
The meetings usually last about an hour.
Contact Chris 4633 8314 / Graham 4633 8810.

St. Patrick's Church

Mass: 1st Sunday of each Month at 6pm

JANUARY BIRTHDAYS
5th   Terry Swanson
7th   Doug McDonald
8th   James Tedesco
16th   Victoria Foulks
19th   Bianca Peretin
20th   Rheannen
21st   Joshua Bond
28th   Paul Thompson

ANNIVERSARIES
29th   Harry & Francis Warner
Add your special dates to our list by sending an email to: byp257@gmail.com

Library
The Wollondilly mobile library visits Menangle every Friday between 11am and 12noon. You will find it parked in St James Ave
AND don't forget the Little Library at 12 Station Street; available whenever you're passing by!

AUSTRALIA DAY BREAKFAST
8AM THURSDAY 26th JANUARY
AT THE FIRE SHED
$5 PER HEAD/$10 PER FAMILY
BACON – EGGS – DAMPER
JUICE – TEA – COFFEE

An Arts and Crafts house in Menangle

Laura Egan-Burt
12 Station St, Menangle

Menangle is a unique, historic village in Wollondilly, New South Wales. Many of the original buildings and cottages survive from the time when the Macarthur family ran the area as part of an English-style feudal village or model town. At least six buildings remain in Menangle that are resonant of William Morris's Arts and Crafts movement. I originally wrote this article as an examination of links to the organisation, however, I have since discovered that Sulman knew Morris! *"Sulman was a student of the Royal Academy and was much among the foremost artists in London [sic] and was well acquainted with William Morris and the leaders of the art revival In England in the seventies."* (Sydney Morning Herald, Monday 20 August 1934)

Is Menangle Australia's example of a homegrown Arts and Crafts enclave?

The St James Church in Menangle is beautiful and unique.

"St James' is situated atop a high hill at the southern end of the village of Menangle and is visible across many miles of rolling hills. The Nave was designed by John Horbury Hunt and constructed in 1876. Sir John Sulman designed the central tower, chancel and apse which were built after the generous benefaction of Mrs Elizabeth Macarthur-Onslow in 1896." [1]

The amazing organ was designed and constructed by Bryceson and Bryceson.[2]

In 2007 I bought a house that no-one else would buy. My house has some of the same brickwork as the St James Church in Menangle. Ever since I purchased the house, I have been flummoxed as to whether it is Victorian, Queen Anne, Federation or Edwardian. I have been combing historic buildings to find likenesses and precedence in styles. It dawned on me today how very unique my house really is.

My house is an Australian example of an Arts and Crafts house.

I have often watched lifestyle shows, envying the Arts and Crafts movement in Britain and North America. However, I recently realised that I, and two of my neighbours reside in three of Australia's answers to these houses.

Egan-Burt Cottage at 12 Station Street Menangle 2017 (L Egan-Burt)

Indulge me as I examine just how viable my theory is, as I draw similarities between the church, the school and the house.

My cottage is hand-hewn, the pitched-roof building is solid, determined to resist change and impervious to all types of weather. The lovingly restored, ten-foot ceilings are made from horsehair; the bricks are of Flemish Bond – which is much more treasured in Perth than Sydney, where heritage listings of similar brickwork have occurred.[3]

The doors are a mix of solid wood and French styling. The verandah harks back to the days where the men would sleep outside due to the weather and their state of cleanliness. There were (and are) no fly-screens, the windows are wide and open outwards, there is always a sense that they should be just that much larger and I am confused as to why the encapsulation of light was not more important to the builder.

The hall is long and luxurious with beautiful original floorboards (alas, these were too damaged in most other rooms to be saved). These floorboards survived due to the four layers of linoleum we stripped away. The other floors were covered in threadbare rugs and shellacked around the perimeter of the rooms. These floorboards have mainly been claimed by rising damp and have needed attention.

The fireplaces light up what could be a drab and grimly practical house. The one in the kitchen would have housed a wood-burning stove. The dining room fire is wide, warm and inviting, the one in the loungeroom is cosy and comforting. I also have a boarded-up fireplace in my bedroom. I will get it working again one day…

I bought the house without a functioning kitchen or bathroom. The bathroom was a revolting lean-to added in the 1930s and distastefully renovated in the late seventies. I presume that in the grimly rustic kitchen, women slaved over the wood stove and perhaps a few bits of furniture provided some comfort during their cooking, The ladies would have been hot in summer and cold in winter, as the double brick walls certainly celebrate and permeate the changes in nature and the seasons.

Another feature of my house that makes no sense is an ornate arch, which will eventually house the doorway to my bathroom. It is strong, solid and handsome. Such a lovingly built arch clashes with the almost puritan feel the other rooms had before I added comforts such as carpets, paints and soft furnishings. The arch would have only served as a thoroughfare from one verandah to another, where the old copper and stand-alone bathtub would have been located.

Would William Morris concur?

I think he would. William Morris would understand that I see the beauty in the hand-hewn, anti-industrial architecture and materials of my house.

The Arts and Crafts movement flourished between 1880-1910, which is when the Macarthur family built Menangle in a feudal-style to house the workers of Camden Park Estate.

I have heard it rumoured that my house was hand-built by the Macarthurs' resident estate carpenter between 1880-1910. My house is one of three facing Station Street and the old creamery and rotolactor. They were the dairy managers cottages. Workers of the estate were housed in mainly weatherboard settlers' huts.

With all this building and construction, and nostalgia and for an 'Olde Eng-

External Brickwork on Cottage at 12 Station Street Menangle 2016 (L Egan-Burt)

land', would a desire for quality not have been encouraged by the Macarthurs and achieved by their trades and artisans? I believe the quality must have been of an extremely high standard. Menangle is a true tribute to this as the buildings have survived since the 1880s, despite various threats of residential and industrial change to the area.

If the Arts and Crafts movement were 'en vogue', why then would these clever craftsmen not have been directly influenced by the projects undertaken by the famous architects Hunt and Sulman who collaborated with the Macarthur family on their public buildings?

The Macarthur family commissioned the building of the historic Menangle school, St James' Church, Gilbulla and many historic houses and cottages nestled within the Camden/Wollondilly landscape. They did not skimp on quantity or quality of their architectural commissions and employed John Horbury Hunt, who designed the church nave, and was recognized as an Arts and Crafts leader in Australia.

"The movement advocated truth to materials and traditional craftsmanship using simple forms and often medieval, romantic or folk styles of decoration. It also proposed economic and social reform and has been seen as essentially anti-industrial."[4]

Interestingly, John Horbury Hunt must have crossed paths with John Sulman in a few locations as both are recorded as designing churches and schools in Armidale and Menangle between the years 1875 -1900.

Unfortunately, there was little camaraderie between the two men and perhaps the clash and mix of styles in my house reflects the public war waging about the clash and mix of architecture in Sydney.

"Hunt, finally welcomed back into the Institute in 1887, continued where he left off. Much of his scorn was directed at the Palladians, a movement led by John Sulman, whose work Hunt (indirectly) described as 'huge in bulk, vile in conception, false and reckless in construction, piles that are revolting to the cultured taste and positively revolting to the public mind'. Sulman and eighteen other members resigned in 1890, decimating the Institute. The press dubbed the remaining body 'The Horbury Hunt Institute' or 'Horbury Hunt's Secret Society'."[5]

Despite factions within architecture, both men are recognized as pioneers of the Arts and Crafts movement in Sydney. Harriet Edquist chronicles this history in her text, Pioneers of Modernism: the Arts and Crafts Movement in Australia.[6]

As my brickwork is exactly the same as Flemish-bond brick in the entryway to the church that these Arts and Crafts giants designed, I am confident in proclaiming that I reside in a unique Arts and Crafts style cottage in Australia.

Notes
1. http://www.menangle.anglican.asn.au/
2. http://www.menangle.anglican.asn.au/
3. http://www.lifeonperth.com/wesleychurch.htm
4. http://en.wikipedia.org/wiki/Arts_and_Crafts_Movement
5. http://www.nswera.net.au/biogs/UNE0216b.htm
6. http://findarticles.com/p/articles/mi_hb4817/is_2_94/ai_n31151655/

Menangle Community Association Inc

Laura Egan-Burt

The Menangle Community Association (MCA) was established when there was a general realisation that assertive community members had been individually fighting battles against a number of development proposals in Menangle.

Since 2004, there had been many different frontiers of engagement, originating with the Menangle Action Group (MAG), led by Trevor Eirth and Kate Terry. MAG had successfully thwarted a development proposal for an enormous Railport between Menangle and Douglas Park. The only development to occur since MAG's inception was the establishment of Durham Green Retirement Village on Menangle Road in 2007.

Station Street Development Proposal

Approximately 30 years ago, Wollondilly Council had passed a small development application for housing blocks to be developed to the north of Station Street. During 2009-10 the blocks were made 'ready to sell', by the installation of electricity supply boxes and leveling earthworks, causing the historic houses on Station Street to be covered with dust and debris for an extended period of time. As at November 2016, these blocks remain un-marketed and unsold. Unfortunately, a more dramatic planning proposal was about to be released.

Menangle Pastoral, a group of local landowners, employed Elton Consulting to draw up plans to develop the Menangle rotalactor paddock and Moreton Park Road. The initial proposal was for an industrial estate that has been subsequently re-defined as a housing estate of some three hundred and fifty dwellings that that will dwarf Menangle![1] The group who would eventually form the Menangle Community Association (MCA) started using the collective wisdom and precedent set by MAG, lodging formal objections to the varying proposals. The plans delivered by Elton Consulting changed each time, depending on objections and planning advice.

The MCA have chosen to take a thoughtful and well-researched approach to their actions providing extensive documentation and genuine objections as to why the planning is not feasible. Menangle Pastoral, however, was displeased with Wollondilly Council's careful reaction to the proposal and lodged a gateway preapproval with the Joint Regional Planning Panel (JRPP). In November 2016, the JRPP was disbanded and responsibilities have been passed

Menangle Community Association Meeting 2016 Maurice Blackwood, Graham Noyes and Lesley Traverso at a Menangle Community Association meeting (L Egan-Burt)

onto the newly formed Greater Sydney Commission. The final view of the JRPP was that there would be development in Menangle, but the size and scope of the development is as yet unconfirmed (November 2016). Menangle is now waiting to see how the GSC will view developments in light of the State Government created 'South West Growth Area' Plans.

School

In Station Street there is an historic school building, built by Camden builders Hindes and Farringdon in 1906,[2] on an earlier school site dating from 1871. Laura Egan-Burt and Jason Burt noticed before Christmas 2007 that a development application had been submitted for the demolition of the school with rezoning for housing.

As the Burts had realised the Flemish Bond brickwork was a similar design to the Menangle Store, Gilbulla, St James Church and 12, 14 and 16 Station Street,[3] it was likely that it would be of historic significance.[4] A protest was held at the school site, which was attended by Robyn Parker, who was then

Banner for Menangle Community Assocation Inc #SAVEMENANGLE Campaign (L Egan-Burt)

the NSW Shadow Minister for the Environment and Heritage. A petition was lodged to state parliament, calling for a moratorium on the demolition and rezoning.[5] After gaining the interest of Alan Jones, radio personality and John Della Bosca, who was the Minister for Education at the time, a moratorium was placed on the demolition of the school.

Maurice Blackwood

Maurice Blackwood, Menangle Rural Fire Service Captain, then stepped in and organised for a land swap to occur between the NSW Department of Education for land at Douglas Park Public School and Wollondilly Council for the land at the Menangle School site.[6] This land swap occurred after much lobbying by Maurice. Once Wollondilly Council took ownership they surrounded the school building with a secure fence. The original weather shed and two toilet blocks remain on the site. The original block has recently been subdivided and one large house is now situated on former school land. Currently, MCA is liaising with Wollondilly Council to establish whether the toilets and weather shed can be refurbished. Unfortunately, the school building itself is now fenced off, awaiting a restoration opportunity.

Maurice was one of the contributors to the original vision document developed by MAG that was used as part of its submissions to both state and local government strategic planning strategies and planning proposals. The documents formed the basis of the community's vision to lobby council for a landscape conservation area for the village of Menangle. This vision was successful.

At the time of the creation of the document, Maurice was a member of MAG and his contribution was focused on identifying the heritage assets in and around the village. Also, other community and MAG members collated information on biodiversity and agricultural assets. MCA has continued to utilise this document and further develop it for subsequent submissions.

Prior the formation of MCA, Jason Burt had been requested by the Wollondilly Mayor, Judy Hannan, to run third on the ticket for East Ward. She suggested to Jason during this time that Menangle should consider some more formal representation to council. Concurrently, albeit separately, Kate Terry organised a meeting for former members of MAG, the Burts, the Anglican Church Ministry and other community members at the only large meeting space available in Menangle – Durham Green Retirement Village. Finally, the formation of the MCA was gathering momentum. Maurice collected names of interested community members at the Menangle Christmas Carols gathering in 2009. Subsequent community meetings became more formal and Maurice was elected chair of the MCA in 2010.

Under Maurice's leadership, community liaison with Wollondilly Council and other stakeholders increased. Maurice achieved many victories, both small and large, amongst which were:

1. Curating a Menangle Heritage Photographic Display and giving related talks to any interested parties. The photographic display is still in the custodianship of the MCA.

2. Lobbying Wollondilly Council for the extension of the existing pathway, - the "path to nowhere" to link residential areas to the railway station. This resulted in Council gaining funds to design a pathway master plan for the village of Menangle, which will go a long way in triggering funding into the future to actually extend the pathway.

3. Making regular submissions to Council and the State Member of Parliament in relation to development applications and rezoning proposals that covered and adjoined Menangle.

4. Liaising with Chris Betteridge, historian for the publication of the land-

Rotolactor Paddock Menangle 2016 (L Egan-Burt)

scape conservation area report.[7]

5. Creation of the Menangle walking tour.[8]

Maurice believed in making personal contact with each of the councillors throughout his leadership of the MCA as he saw engagement as key to ensuring good outcomes. This view was taken up by many of the MCA after Maurice's passing in December 2016. A park bench and plaque reading "In recognition of Maurice Blackwood and his tireless contributions to the Wollondilly Community, Dedicated 4 June 2016" was gifted by council to his memory and stands in Dean McGrath Memorial Park in Station Street.

Maurice's main legacy is organising Wollondilly Council to sell the condemned Menangle School of Arts Hall to the Menangle Community Association, elevating the organisation to an 'incorporated' status.

The Menangle School of Arts hall, on Station Street, had been built from cheap materials in the early 1900s. Many newspaper articles from that time cite the hall as a cultural and social centre. The hall flourished. After the council condemned the hall, there remained funds of twenty five thousand dollars, for hall restoration, to be held. Brian Peacock as treasurer of the disbanded hall committee, agreed to the role of treasurer for the MCA and the new vice chair, Hans-Lothar Huhn is leading liaison with council, planners and architects for the future hall restoration.

Community Engagement and Motivation

Menangle is primarily a village occupied by professionals who commute elsewhere to work. Motivation of busy community members and expectations of them to understand the complexities of planning proposals and lobbying can be challenging. *The Menangle News*, run voluntarily by the Peacocks for over 30 years, the http://www.menangle.com.au website, also run by Brian Peacock, the 'Menangle' Facebook page and signage have all played a part in major campaigns, together with more traditional meetings, door knocking, polling and local media liaison.

MCA is exceptional as it also supports members in local political election campaigns. To date, MCA has actively supported Kate Terry[9] (former president of MAG and MCA member) and Matthew Death [10] (former chair of MCA), successful in his #SAVEMENANGLE marketing campaign, to their successful elections as Wollondilly councillors. Unfortunately, both personalities have had to resign their committee roles, as there is a need for separation between council and the MCA, to avoid conflict of interest. The current MCA chair is Lesley Traverso, vice chair is Hans-Lothar Huhn, the secretary is Laura Egan-Burt and Brian Peacock is treasurer, Sarah Deeth is a long-term committee member.

Acknowledgements
Lesley Traverso, Hans-Lothar Huhn, Brian Peacock, Jason Burt, Kate Terry, Benn Banasik, Matt and Sarah Deeth

Notes

1. Elton Consulting, Final Community Workshop Outcomes Report, Nov 2008, Available online: http://www.planningpanels.nsw.gov.au/Portals/0/RPA/Menangle%20Rezoning/7%20Community%20Workshop%20Outcomes%20Nov%202008.pdf

2 Hawkey, H & Tomkins, W, Menangle School 90th Anniversary Booklet, 1961, available : http://www.menangle.com.au/documents/souvenir-booklet-menangle-school-90th-anniversary.pdf

3 Egan-Burt, Laura, 'Is Menangle Australia's example of a homegrown Arts and Crafts enclave Available online: http://menangle.com.au/?page_id=349

4 Egan-Burt, Laura, speech to Wollondilly Council, 2008, available online: http://menangle.com.au/?page_id=199

5 Legislative Council Hansard, 2008, Available online: https://

www.parliament.nsw.gov.au/Hansard/Pages/HansardResult.aspx#/docid/HANSARD-1820781676-59532

6 NSW Department of Education Sale and acquisition of land, 2004/5 - 2014/15, Available online https://www.det.nsw.edu.au/media/downloads/about-us/statistics-and-research/key-statistics-and-reports/sale_acquisition_land_0405_1415.pdf

7 Betteridge, Chris, Menangle Landscape Conservation Area Report, 2012,Available online: http://menangle.com.au/?page_id=553

8 Menangle Community Association, 'Menangle Walking Tour' Available online: http://www.menangle.com.au/documents/menangle-walking-tours.pdf

9 Locals stand for Council, The Menangle News, Aug 2012, Available: http://www.menangle.com.au/MenangleNewsArchive/1208-aug.pdf

10 Wollondilly Advertiser, Wollondilly Council will see new faces take a seat at the chamber, Sep 2016, Available online: http://www.wollondillyadvertiser.com.au/story/4163050/fresh-face-at-council/

The Camden Museum Collection Understanding Its Significance

Anne McIntosh

There are hundreds of small museums, public and private, scattered across Australia. Camden Museum is one of many. But which items in those museums are significant? And why does it matter? Are any items in the Camden collection significant, and if so, why?

To preserve 'value' within the context of the overall collection, the Camden Museum would like to research and record the 'significance' of every item or group of similar objects. In 2008, John and Julie Wrigley produced a report that considered the significance of the Camden Museum's collection. It lists those items known to be significant within an Australian and NSW context. This report is on file in the Museum.

Background

Camden Museum aims to unfold the history of the town and surrounding district from pre-colonisation through agricultural development and evolution of the community, until today, when the Nepean valley houses (note the pun!) Sydney's fastest growing suburbs (on land where cattle, turf and poultry once grew).

The records and displays reflect the everyday experiences of all communities: joy and grief, drought and flooding rains, recreation and work, caring and learning. As a collection focused on an area, the museum aims to support anyone interested in researching Camden local history and to provide children with an informed sense of 'place' and hopefully, civic pride.

Camden Museum has no paid staff. Membership fees are minimised. Members may come and go, levels of enthusiasm may vary over time. The budget for acquisitions is small – most items have been donated.

For an established collection, curatorial management within limited space becomes increasingly challenging. What donations should be accepted? What items should be retained or have funds invested to preserve them? Who manages 'the vision' for the collection as a whole?

To assess individual items (and even an entire collection), a standardised process has been developed. The Powerhouse Museum and National Library (NLA) provide training, expertise and resources so that individual collectors and small museums can prepare consistent and useful documentation on items in their collection.

The term 'significance' has been used to collectively draw together a description and other information about an object, and then assess why it has value within the context of a collection. To be significant, an item does not have to be rare or of financial value. Identical items in two collections may be significant for different reasons. Context matters when talking about 'significance'.

Templates for reporting on significance may vary, but they all include a description of an object, its physical condition, the owner and/or where and when it was used, and how the museum acquired it. It also records other sites or museums with related themes or similar objects.

An item may have significance through one or more of the following:
1. its story or role at an earlier time or place (history)
2. its design or styling (aesthetic significance)
3. its origins, source and 'individual story' (provenance)
4. its typical features or unique characteristics (representativeness, rarity)
5. its state of repair and completeness (condition)
6. its ability to communicate and educate in the context of the collection (interpretative capacity).

Having assessed an item against each of these criteria, it is not difficult to sum up the reason that an item is worth acquiring or retaining within collection. This summary is the "Statement of Significance".

Do something significant for the Museum - Prepare a statement
Although 24 statements of significance have been completed, only a small

proportion of the items within the Camden Museum collection have been documented in this way.

Julie Wrigley oversees the process (contact Julie via the front desk at the museum) and is always looking for volunteers to investigate an object and prepare a statement. Most of the information will be obtained from the museum, the internet, asking members or by contacting sources gained online.

'Assessing the significance of an object' is an excellent resource that describes how to prepare a statement of significance. Available from http://www.centralnswmuseums.orangemuseum.com.au   The Powerhouse Museum has summary statements of their entire collection online providing professional examples across many classes of objects. See http://www.powerhousemuseum.com/collection/database/

"Why are we hanging onto that rusty old thing? We can do that task so much better today. The item is not rare, couldn't be valuable..."

Camden's Collection of Statements

Any member can read the Statements of Significance – plastic folders are placed in boxes near the map files in the 'Library/Workroom' . Volunteers will discover 'snippets' to communicate to visitors, and should be aware which items in our collection have a well-documented background story.

Images of the objects and those used to illuminate their history and provenance are added to the CHS digitised collection, and can be offered to people approaching the museum for information or publication - with acknowledgement, of course!

As CHS members move away, lose interest or pass away, the context of decision making on acquisitions may be lost. The full Statement of Significance provides more information than the MOSAIC digital database. The consistent format should aid management of the collection and protect against naive or personally-motivated decision making.

List of Statements of Significance

Camden Museum

Box 1

1970.157	Maud Hodge's Wedding Dress	*Julie Wrigley*
1970.195	Tomkison Grand Pianoforte	*Janice Johnson*
1970.240	WWI Spinning Wheel	*Julie Wrigley*
1970.264	Madras Cavalry Uniform	*J Johnson, M Wheeler, J Wrigley*
1980.221	Lassetters' Mantolini Mangle	*Anne McIntosh*
1980.396	Thurn Grape Crusher	*John Wrigley*
1995.423	Teamsters' Wagon	*John Wrigley*
1995.424	Teamsters' Wheel	*John Wrigley*
1996.29	Model of the 'Sirius'	*René Rem*
1996.118	WWI Memorial Plaque of R.E. (Rex) Smith	*Janice Johnson*
1998.216	VAD Uniform	*Anne McIntosh*
1998.249	WWI Memorial Plaque of Hilton Chesham	*Ray Herbert*
1999.121	Ensign Folding Camera	*Robert Wheeler*

Box 2

2003.64	Queen's South Africa Medal	*John Wrigley*
2008.6	Murrandah Breastplate	*Bob Lester*
2008.78	Miss Llewella Davies' Key to the Town	*Betty Yewen*
2008.88	WWI Souvenir Utility Belt	*Janice Johnson*
2009.3	WWI Shell Case	*Chris Hill*
2009.41	Clark WWI Souvenir Belt	*Janice Johnson*
2009.53	WWI British Lusitania Medallion	*Janice Johnson*
2010.22	Tea Service, John Martin Hawkey	*Cathey Shepherd*

Box 3

2012.26	Chinese Market Gardener's Watering Cans	*John Wrigley*
2013.28	Signature Tablecloth from 1902	*Sharon Greene*
2013.71	Murdoch WWI Certificate of Appreciation	*Janice Johnson*

Australia Day 2017

Words and Pictures Anne McIntosh

As is traditional in Camden, after the ceremonies to welcome new Aussie citizens, the community gathered along Argyle Street to watch a parade of community groups and a growing collection of renovated cars.

From Oxley Street to Elizabeth Street crowds were four or five people deep, with children seated on the kerbs sporting colourful home-designer fashions in green and gold or featuring the national flag,

For the seventh year, Steve Wisbey, dressed in military camouflage, provided commentary along with his friend, the 'town crier' dressed in red.

John and Julie Wrigley represented the museum in a pale green Holden ute generously loaned by Max Boardman.

In addition to the huge array of restored vehicles, it was pleasing to see the parade led by the riders representing the 7th Light Horse Regiment. October will be the centenary of the decisive charge on horseback at Beersheba, a victory that was key to the British Allies' ongoing progress in Egypt. One of the Light Horse Brigade's main training depots was near Menangle.

The Rum Corps appeared in their historic, climate-inappropriate uniforms. Another highlight was a costumed family in their historic vehicle, dressed in Victorian attire for picnic.

Australia Day has always been an important day for the Camden Museum. Before and after the parade, crowds mill around the displays, stalls and rides in John Street.

This year, several large display stands were positioned directly in front of the library. This may have prevented some passers-by from realising that the museum was open. However, by the end of the day, more than 120 visitors had passed time in the museum; about one quarter were children.

Additional volunteers were on deck to greet visitors and respond to questions. Volunteer coordinator, Rene Rem, who spoke to almost every group, said, "We had a mix of out-of-towners and locals, but it is always an important day, and many had never been into the museum."

Thank-you to those who helped on the day: Ian Willis, Rene Rem, Lee Stratton, Rob Wheeler, Doug Barratt, Geoff Chegwyn, Maurice & Kay Augustyn and Anne McIntosh.

Wood turning demonstration in John Street at the 2017 Australia Day celebrations in Camden (A McIntosh)

John & Julie Wrigley in Camden Museum Holden Motor Car lent by Max Boardman (L Stratton)

Crowds of enthusiastic onlookers at 2017 Camden Australia Day Parade at the corner John and Argyle Streets.

Volunteer co-ordinator Rene Rem on Australia Day showing the tally sheet of visitors who came into the museum

Immigrant Child

Mark and Trish Thornell

Long term Camden residents Trish and Mark Thornell perform as The Honey Sippers. They wrote the song "Immigrant Child" and performed it for the first time publicly at the 2016-2017 Gulgong Folk Festival.

The song "Immigrant Child " refers to the story of child migrants who came to Australia post-World War II. In 2007, David Hill published a book called "The Forgotten Children" telling of his experiences as one of these children.

In 2009, Prime Minister Kevin Rudd issued an apology to the 'Forgotten Australians', those children who had been in institutional care and suffered abuse, and former child migrants, who were sent to Australia without their consent.

In the post-war years Britain was eager to shed itself of the cost of supporting impoverished families. Australia was keen to gain cheap, malleable migrants from good British stock, to populate its vast empty spaces. In an era of "populate or perish" another common slogan was "the child, the best immigrant".

Some of the these children grew up in the local area. The reality of what these children experienced was far from the promised "Sunshine and Oranges". Mark and Trish expressed their thoughts in words music and this is their song.

Immigrant Child (Song)
Words: Mark and Trish Thornell (2016)

Verse
They promised an adventure with food of every kind,
But hands were rough and harsh as they shoved me into line.
They gave me a case of brand new clothes, the first I'd ever had,
Said I should be grateful, I was a lucky lad.

Chorus
Don't ask me any question, why me and why so far?
For I've never had an answer, no need to tell a child.
No need to tell a child what's what, no need to ease their fears,
No gentle smile to soothe, no touch to calm their tears.

They packed me off like baggage to a strange land far away.
And set me on a farm to work, a man's work without pay.
They taught me how to read and write, do my sums and pray.
And when I reached a certain age they sent me on my way.

I still dream of my mother, her touch, the songs she'd sing.
Small memories so faded now were all that I could bring.
She never saw me grown, never got to hold my child.
I have no tales of her to tell, no history safely filed.

I guess my mother's long gone now, words I won't hear her say.
Did she sometimes think of me half a world away?
Would she be proud of what I've done, proud of the man I am.
I more than paid for what I've got with blood, sweat and pain.

Mark and Trish Thornell performing as the Honey Sippers at the Camden Sports Club at CKs Open Mic Night in 2017 (I Willis)

Memories Of Pansy, The Camden Tram

Wayne Bearup

Being a member of the NSW branch of the Australian Railways Historical Society (ARHS), I was able to travel behind many vintage steam locomotives around NSW, and this included the Campbelltown/Camden branch line.

Liverpool station was the end of the electrified network, and if you wanted to travel to Campbelltown you boarded the local Liverpool/Campbelltown steam service, hauled by a C30 class engine. Also known as the "S" class side tank steam locomotive, hauling vintage end platform cars.

You were not permitted to ride on these end platforms or stick your head out of these open window carriages, but I confess to doing so. That was the terminus for the local, and if you wanted to travel further south, you caught the southern highlands express hauled by a mighty C38 class steam locomotive.

From Campbelltown was the eight mile branch line to Camden that I was fortunate enough to ride on, including the last days.

There was a dock platform for the Camden train, and you would wait at the platform to board your train, which usually was comprised of one carriage and one steam engine, but on occasions there were two engines to haul one carriage. The reason for this was to also haul the milk wagons from Camden and coal wagons from Narellan.

The extra engine was needed to conquer Kenny Hill. Only light weight side tank steam locomotives of the 20 and 30 class were allowed to work the line. Sometimes it was necessary for three engines to be used - two leading and one pushing. This was what was required for the last two days of operation to work the passenger train full of steam enthusiasts.

The last day of service was officially 31 December 1962 and had eight carriages. Permission was granted to run a special train on 1 January 1963 organised by the ARHS. The train ran from Central to Camden and return, and ran with nine carriages.

The last regular train on 31 December 1962, scheduled to leave at 11:58pm, left late from Campbelltown because passengers both on the train and on the platform were singing Auld Lang Syne for the new year of 1963, and so its departure was delayed.

The train was scheduled to leave Camden at 12:30am and arrive at Campbelltown at 1:12am, but this last regular train arrived back well after 1:12am because someone had greased the tracks on Kenny Hill and they had to be cleaned and copious amounts of sand had to be applied to the track to gain traction. The crews were not happy, but we passengers didn't mind.

The last train, 1 January 1963, was scheduled to leave Central at 9:09am.
    Arr. Campbelltown 10:42am
    Dep. Campbelltown 11:02am
    Arr. Camden 12:00pm
    Dep. Camden 2:30pm
    Arr. Campbelltown 3:28pm
    Dep. Campbelltown 3:43pm
    Arr. Central 5:16pm

The last day train ticket 1 January 1963 cost me 14/- .

The photos I took were taken either on the last days or in the weeks prior to closure. A mate of mine borrowed his father's Ford Prefect car to go "Pansy" chasing. The Prefect can be seen on page 94 of your journal (September 2016).

The two carriages used on the regular service between Campbelltown and Camden were known as composite cars, coded as CCA. Each carriage was comprised of a guard compartment and seating for 1st and 2nd class passengers. To work one train required a crew of three – guard, fireman and driver, plus station staff at Narellan and Camden.

In the closing years, light weight diesel locomotives of the 41 & 70 classes were permitted to work the line from Narellan for the coal wagons, but only steam worked into Camden.

As there was no turntable at Camden, only side tank locomotives could be used, but the Camden Historical Society gained special permission to run a 12 class 4-4-0 tender and engine no. 1243.

In this story I have called it the Camden tram because that was what the locals called it, as the line was built to run steam trams on it. The railways and tramways were originally known as the NSW Government Railways and Tramways, and became separate government departments after 1932.

As the Camden line was originally built for the running of steam tram motors, there was no need for a turntable at Camden, because they could work in either direction without turning.

The only passing loop on the single track line was at Narellan, and safe working was conducted using the staff and ticket method, and the line was divided into two sections:- Campbelltown to Narellan; and Narellan to Camden.

Pansy the last ride. This photography was taken by Wayne Bearup on the day of the last Camden train in 1963 (W Bearup)

Ghosts And Shadows At Macaria, A Reply

Janice Johnson

I read with interest the Camden History Journal September 2016 and the article on *Macaria* by Pauline Downing. Unfortunately Pauline, an excellent researcher herself, used as a reference to Sarah Tiffin an article by Melissa Denford that appeared in the Camden Crier 8 July 1992. Denford, a 15 year old high school student from Elderslie, had won the 1992 History Week competition sponsored by Soroptomists International in the Macarthur region and based her entry around *Macaria*. Her story appears to have been based on the article "The Ghost of Macaria" published in the Macarthur Advertiser 22 July 1987. In an interview with John Wrigley on 25 July 1987 Miss Llewella Davies declared the article was *"nonsense"*.

The Macarthur Advertiser story was pure fiction but it provides a warning to us all to check and triple check reference material no matter how plausible it may appear. Failure to properly identify such errors may result in them misleading future researchers such as Denford and Downing, the fiction being perpetuated, posted on the Local Studies website, and accepted as fact.

Any history on *Macaria* would not be complete without the story of Sarah Tiffin. In an endeavour to provide a factual history on *Macaria*, and the "ghosts", I have included Sarah's history and that of her fellow "ghost" William (Bill) Gordon.

Tiffin arrived with James and Emily Macarthur on the "Royal George" on 10 March 1839. Sarah nee Milford had been born in Devon in 1807 the daughter of John Milford. Prior to 1838 she married Robert Tiffin (or Tiffen) but shortly after their marriage Robert was arrested, tried for theft and transported for 7 years on the "Bengal Merchant" arriving 21 July 1838. Employed as a maid to Emily Macarthur (nee Stone), Tiffin may have been hopeful of being reunited with her husband; whether this occurred is unclear. Robert had been assigned originally to Newcastle and later received his Ticket of Leave but this was cancelled due to drunkenness. In the 1840 Census he was living in St. Leonards where he died 1 February 1842. His Certificate of Freedom was granted 25 October 1844 – two years after his death.

Emily Macarthur, in her diaries, referred to Sarah as *"Tiffin my trusty right hand"*; and appointed her as housekeeper at *Camden Park*. The Macarthurs recommended Sarah use an inheritance left by her father to purchase on 6 November 1840 a ½ acre allotment (Section 3 Lot 9) for £36 in John Street

Camden. Sarah had a small Georgian brick cottage (*Camden Cottage*) constructed with a corrugated iron hipped roof, brick chimney and a timber posted verandah. According to Alan Atkinson the cottage had been built within two years after the purchase of the land. Sarah, according to Atkinson, *"secured her property to her own use by deed of settlement"* and left the property to *"her maiden sister in England"*. In doing so she ensured that a husband would not be able to claim her estate and named as her trustees as Rev. Charles Frederick Durham Priddle (rector of St. Luke's Church of England Liverpool) and James Macarthur. In 1844 the cottage was leased, with the assistance of the Macarthurs, to the Court of Petty Sessions for £20 a year. This cottage still stands today and in 2016 was known as the gift store/café *Epicure*.

John Benson Martin, the Clerk of Petty Sessions in Camden, described Sarah's cottage - *"I began my duties in the John Street cottage, there was but little elbow room as the greater part of the house was occupied by Constable Davidson and his bedridden wife. The spectators overflowed into the verandah, the window being kept open for their convenience, for ventilation and perhaps to constitute an open case. In that small room more important business was done than in any since."* Constable John Davidson left Camden after the death of his first wife Ann on 17 May 1855 and moved to Campbelltown.

In 1850 Sarah left *Camden Park*, purchased a house in Palmer Street Woolloomooloo, and married widower Francis Middlehurst (1800-1862) on 20 November 1850 at Christ Church St Lawrence Sydney. Middlehurst, formerly a carpenter from Narellan, his son Francis (1843-1913) and Sarah lived in Woolloomooloo until Sarah's death 14 May 1854. Unfortunately burial records do not give the cause of death but it is understood that she had been ill for some time.

The Woolloomooloo residence was sold in January 1855 by her trustees as part of her estate, but it was not until 20 April 1855 that Henry Thompson purchased the John Street property for £656.5.0 from the trustees. In 1856 Thompson began construction on the picturesque Victorian Gothic building which would be known as *Macaria*. He intended for the building to be used by the Camden Commercial and Classical School under the guidance of headmaster and founder William Gordon.

Gold rush fever delayed construction and on 12 January 1857 Gordon opened his school at *Macquarie Grove* in the house owned by Rowland Hassall. Gordon described himself as a *"Reader at St. Peter's Campbelltown"* and also mentioning that he was the author of three books. This school was both a boarding and day school for boys and continued until its closure in 1866 when he opened the Spring Vale Academy at Campbelltown; this was a day

Macaria in the late 1800s John Street Camden (Camden Images)

school only; by July 1866 the school had changed its name to Campbelltown Classical School. In April 1869 he moved the Camden, Campbelltown Classical School to *Burton Ho*use Narellan (formerly the *Burton Arms Hotel*). Gordon died at *Burton House* 24 October 1877 and was buried St. Thomas' Church of England Narellan.

Henry Thompson died on 29 July 1871, eleven days after being kicked in the head by his horse outside his house and store in Edward Street Camden. He never lived in *Macaria*. His wife Anne, nee Bardwell, moved to "Marama", Burwood where she died 20 February 1912.

The second son of Henry and Anne, Charles Augustus Thompson an Insurance and Property Agent, lived after his marriage in 1887 in Sarah Tiffin's cottage until his death 26 August 1929. Thompson's eldest son William Henry (1846-1923) managed the Thompson properties in Edward, Argyle, Mitchell and John Streets on behalf of his mother.

Macaria remained empty until 1875 when Dr. George Goode purchased the medical practice of Dr. Edwin Chisholm in Argyle Street Camden and leased *Macaria*. He lived there with his family until January 1887 when he moved to Orange. During Goode's tenure there were no known deaths on the premises and no other Sarah's or Bill's known to be associated with the property.

From 1885-1887 the house was leased by Dr. Robert Ettingsall Beattie (1853-1895), before being leased in 1888 to George Bernard Crabbe who opened the Camden Grammar School. It was from this period that the stories of the "ghosts" of *Macaria* began to emerge with the "ghosts" known as "Sarah" and "Bill". The "ghosts" may have been the result of childish pranks by senior students against gullible juniors. Students told of hearing strange noises at midnight, furniture moving and broken crockery; the "ghosts" had awakened! Or were the sounds merely wind in the chimneys and the normal creaking sounds as metal, timber and stone expanded and contracted with temperature changes? Why should Sarah Tiffin and William (Bill) Gordon haunt a house neither of them had lived in? In 1900 the school moved to *Studley Park* which had its own ghost for students to contend with.

According to the Camden Municipal Rate List of 1900 *Macaria* was empty and the owner Mrs. Thompson. From January 1901 the house was leased by Dr. Francis William West who established his residence and practice and then on 5 May 1904 purchased *Macaria* from Ann Thompson, William Henry Thompson and Alfred Thompson (1852-1940). Dr. West remained in the house until his death 20 October 1932.

Dr. Leo Barclay Heath (1893-1959) purchased the house from the Permanent Trustee Company, executors of Dr. West's estate) on 19 May 1936 for £2,000 and sold it on 22 August 1938 for £2,500 to brothers Dr. Robert Elbury Jefferis (1893-1979) and Dr. James Tatham Whittle Jefferis (1895-1972). The brothers had served in the Australian Army Medical Corp during WWI.

The next known report on the "ghosts" was from the time of Dr. George Frederick Lumley (1902-1981) who rented Flat 1 in the house from December 1955 until August 24, 1970. There are reports that after returning to the property after a late a house call he was thrown around his bedroom by "Bill"; Lumley's handwritten history makes no mention of the "ghost" incident.

In October 1965 *Macaria* was purchased by Camden Council who in August 1970 decided to demolish the building and construct a modern two storey office block. Dr. Lumley in Flat 1, and John Thomas Bourke in Flat 2, were given notice to vacate. Miss Llewella Davies and the Camden Historical Society swung into action raising public awareness of the disaster that was about to take place. On 6 November 1970 the National Trust of Australia recommended that *Macaria* be included in the Trust's Register of Historic Buildings. Council bowed to public pressure and decided to retain *Macaria* but demolish the adjoining stables. *Macaria* remains in John Street today as an integral part of our valued heritage architecture.

Have the "ghosts" finally departed *Macaria*'s elegant walls? Former council employees such as Lorna Farquhar argue that there is 'something' in the building as there were experiences of an unsourced feeling of coldness that signaled Bill's presence. The late Derrick Thorn told the story about a very level-headed staff member, who, whilst writing a report in an office one night about 9:30 pm was spooked by the sound of footfalls on the stairs but was unable to find anyone else in the building.

Others who felt the presence of the "ghost" include former Mayor, Liz Kernohan M.P., who whilst attempting to leave a room one evening after a meeting believed she was physically restrained from doing so! Former Mayor, Frank Hulme Brooking is also reported to having heard Sarah *"rattle crockery"* during evenings when he was in his office but did not feel threatened by her presence.

I'll leave it to the reader to make their own decision on *Macaria's* "ghosts".

References
Annette Macarthur-Onslow - Emily Macarthur Diaries
Burial Certificate - Robert Tiffen (Tiffin) 250/18425 V18425250 256B
Burial Certificate - Sarah Middlehurst 591/1854 V18545291 41A
Camden Municipal Council: Municipal List Rates Book 1894-1907
Camden: Farm & Village Life in Early New South Wales – Alan Atkinson
In Memoriam - JBM (John Benson Martin) - Camden News 2 & 23 April 1896
Macaria – Helen White
Marriage Certificate – Middlehurst, Francis/Tiffin, Sarah 3523/1850 V1850353 36B
Petty Session Changes – JBM (John Benson Martin) – Camden News 23 & 31 July 1896
Some Personal Historical Notes – Dr. G.F. Lumley
The Memoirs of Samuel Herbert Thompson – 26 April 1905

2017 Australia Day Parade Camden (A McIntosh)

CAMDEN HISTORY

Journal of the Camden Historical Society

September 2017 Volume 4 Number 4

CAMDEN HISTORY
Journal of the Camden Historical Society Inc.
ISSN 1445-1549
Editor: Dr Ian Willis

Management Committee
President: Dr Ian Willis
Vice Presidents: John Wrigley OAM, Cathey Shepherd
Secretary: Lee Stratton
Treasurer: Dawn Williams
Immediate Past President: Bob Lester
General Committee:	Sharon Greene	Rene Rem
	Julie Wrigley	Robert Wheeler
	Sue Cross	Stephanie Trenfield

Honorary Solicitors: Vince Barrett

Society contact:
P.O. Box 566, Camden, NSW 2570. Online <http://www.camdenhistory.org.au>

Meetings
Meetings are held at 7.30 p.m. on the second Wednesday of the month except in January. They are held in the Museum. Visitors are always welcome.

Museum
The Museum is located at 40 John Street, Camden, phone 4655 3400 or 46559210. It is open Thursday to Sunday 11 a.m. to 4 p.m., except at Christmas. Visits by schools and groups are encouraged. Please contact the Museum to make arrangements. Entry is free.

Camden History, Journal of the Camden Historical Society Inc
The Journal is published in March and September each year. The Editor would be pleased to receive articles broadly covering the history of the Camden district . Correspondence can be sent to the Society's postal address. The views expressed by authors in journal articles are solely those of the authors and not necessarily endoresed by the Camden Historical Society.

Donations
Donations made to the Society are tax deductible. The accredited value of objects donated to the Society are eligible for tax deduction.

Cover: 2017 Mother's Day at Belgenny Farm Camden (A McIntosh)
Back Cover: 2017 Mother's Day at Belgenny Farm Camden (A McIntosh)

CAMDEN HISTORY
Journal of the Camden Historical Society Inc.

Contents

Sixty Years of Local History, 1957-2017 Ian Willis	151
The Rewards of Volunteering at Camden Museum Robert Wheeler	157
Lively exhibition for the Centenary of Australian Federation Sandra Dodds	159
President's Report 2016 – 2017 Ian Willis	167
Making the Most of MOSAiC Anne McIntosh	171
Anzacs of Macarthur Lauren Hokin	177
Commander Frank Gardner RAN 1841-1927 Harry Stait-Gardner	185
Memories of the Burragorang Valley Ron Schofield	190
A 1930 road trip from Sydney Anne McIntosh	193
My memory of my first jobs in 1965 and 1966 Robert Wheeler	195
Mother's Day at Belgenny Farm 2017 Anne McIntosh	198
A visitor to Camden Anne McIntosh	199
Sculptures, Monuments and Outdoor Cultural Material project Sandra Dodds	203
The Heath Years at Windamere, Cobbitty Lenore Heath	204

Sixty Years of Local History, 1957-2017

Ian Willis

Address given at the 60th Anniversary Meeting of the Camden Historical Society on 24 July 2017

Welcome all. First of all I would like to thank the 60th Anniversary Organising Committee for their work in organising this event. (Rene, Cathey, Dawn and Lee).

When I was told that I was presenting the keynote address at this anniversary meeting I was also told that there would be no other speakers. So what to say? The society has had 60 wonderful years since its foundation in 1957.

I want to drill into those 60 years and ask the question: What is the business of the society? What is our mission statement?

I maintain that the role of the Camden History Society is to tell the Camden story. Stories are an integral part of place making and the creation of community identity. They are full of meaning and allow the past to inform the present. They help those in the present to understand why things are as they are.

Stories are about context and help explain where we fit in the big picture of things. And telling the Camden story explains why our community is the way it is today.

Telling the Camden story has led to a number of firsts for the society.

The first history of the society was written by Peter Mylrea in the first journal published by the society, Camden History, in 2001. The upcoming issue of the journal will be part of volume 4.

The first public lecture was presented at the first ordinary meeting of the society in August 1957 by the society's first vice-president Harold Lowe. The talk was called the 'History of Camden Park'. Harold was an interesting local identity, a farmer from Elderslie and good cyclist who competed in the Goulburn-Sydney cycle races. He was an alderman on Camden Municipal Council for many years and in 1925 with Toby Taplin rescued undertaker Percy Peters and his driver George Thurn when their hearse was washed off the Cowpastures Bridge in the flood.

The first lobbying of Camden Council by the society occurred in 1957. The society was concerned about the location of the John Oxley's anchor that the Council had been given in 1929. The British Admiralty had given Australia three commemorative anchors to serve as memorials of the death of John Oxley. The other two are in Wellington and Harrington NSW. The Camden anchor was from the Destroyer Tomahawk. Oxley was a naval officer, the first colonial Surveyor General in NSW and had been assigned the grants of Kirkham and Elderslie. The anchor languished in the council yard for over 25 years all but forgotten. The society lobbied council for six years and in 1963 the anchor was unveiled in Kirkham Lane. The society has recently lobbied council again and in 2015 the anchor was moved to Curry Reserve, along with a sculpture of Oxley's profile.

The first community partnership was with Camden High School on the foundation of the society in 1957. The first meeting was held at the school and chaired by the president of the Camden High School P&C Society. The first president Bill McCulloch was the deputy principal of Camden High School, who was followed by John Brownie, the school principal. Society meetings were held at the school for 42 years. There have been a host of other community partnerships and two of the largest have been with Camden Rotary in the foundation of the museum in 1970, and currently with Camden Council Library and Camden Area Family History Society. Other organisations that have collaborated with the historical society have included Camden Lions, Camden Quota, Camden Show Society, Camden Red Cross, Camden Council, as well as our affiliation with the Royal Australian Historical Society.

Some other firsts for the society include: the first society excursion was a day trip to Yerranderie in March 1958 before the Burragorang Valley was flooded, with the first overnight trip to Canberra in 1964; the first time the society acted as tour guide was the visit of the Catholic Historical Society in September 1958; the first time community speakers were provided was at the Festival of the Golden Fleece in August 1960; the first newsletter was put together in 1970, with a short rebirth in 1985-86 as the 'Camden Historian', and most recently from November 2005; the first radio broadcast was Dick Nixon's 'Know Your Camden' for community radio 2CR in 1978; the first society publication was John Wrigley's, 'A History of Camden' in 1979; the first grant to fund society activities was $150 in 1979 from the state government; the first website for the society appeared in 1997 sponsored by Christine and Steve Robinson and from 2006 the society launched its own website, <camdenhistory.org.au>; and in 2015 the society launched into the social media space with its own Facebook page.

I would argue that probably the most important first for the society was the establishment of the museum.

In 1967, a children's book, EL Konigsburg's 'From the Mixed-Up Files of Mrs Basil E Frankweiler' was published in the USA. The book tells the story of two kids, 12-year-old Claudia and her 9-year-old brother Jamie, who ran away from home to live in the New York's Metropolitan Museum of Art.

Claudia and Jamie have an exciting adventure living in a museum coming to face-to-face with the thrilling mysteries of art history. They immerse themselves in the adventures of learning about everything. The book won numerous awards and is used extensively in schools in the US.

Now, the Camden Museum is not the New York Met. I would hope that visitors to our museum want to learn everything about Camden.

Hopefully a visit to the Camden Museum will allow folk to immerse themselves in the mysteries of the past and be a learning adventure on the way.

A yearning for the past is not new. For some people the past provides security and safety. The Camden Museum provides a safe zone where visitors can immerse themselves in their memories. Nostalgia for the past.

By definition, nostalgia is a yearning for a sentimental rose-coloured view of the past. Recent research has shown that nostalgia can be a positive thing. But it was not always so. In the past nostalgia was considered to be a medical disease and a psychiatric disorder. Hopefully a visit to our museum does not affect visitors this way.

Local museums tell local truths and are trusted sources of local stories and histories. They are honest and straightforward. What you see is what you get. They are not fake news.

The Camden Museum is a mirror to the community where visitors can reflect on their past in the present. The museum displays, collection and archives represent the Camden community to itself. The museum is the custodian of these stories.

The Camden Museum can also provide challenges for visitors who take their time to look for the nuances in our stories. If you drill into the stories of museum objects they touch on deeper social and cultural characteristics of the country town of the past Some of these elements include: class, rural conservatism, gender, intimacy, race, religion, parochialism, localism, rural ideology, city/country divide and a host of other things.

I would argue that the Camden Museum has a critical role in the construction of resilient communities of the present. The museum acts as a site of place making. The continued growth and expansion of the Camden Local Government Area demands sites that contribute to the creation of social connections and facilitates community networks.

The museum provides a space for the creation of social capital through volunteering and philanthropy. Museum volunteers provide a successful model as a centre of active citizenship and volunteering which contributes to the social glue of the community.

The museum helps create a healthy society characterised by trust, reciprocity, support networks and social norms. The museum provides an opportunity for volunteers to actively participate in the social, political and economic life of the Camden LGA. The museum is a centre of local tourism and can play a role in job creation.

So while the Camden Museum may not be the New York Metropolitan Museum of Art, it does provide a meaningful window into our past. Like the story of Claudia and Jamie, the Camden Museum can provide a learning adventure into the thrilling mysteries of our past. Something that we can draw on in the present.

So hopefully the legacy that we are currently leaving might ensure that the Camden Historical Society and the Camden Museum might continue to tell the Camden story for another 60 years and beyond.

Members of the organising committee Lee Stratton, Rene Rem, Dawn Williams (and also MC of the night) and Cathey Shepherd (absent overseas) (B Stratton)

The cutting of the 60th Diamond Anniversary cake by Past Presidents of the Camden Historical Society Bob Lester (L) and John Wrigley (B. Stratton)

The Rewards of Volunteering at Camden Museum

Robert Wheeler

Robert recounts some questions from visitors to volunteers at the museum desk and the discovery trail that followed. (ed)

A week in August provided an amazing range of questions that commenced with a lady from Queanbeyan seeking information on 'Caernarvon' house in Kirkham. Firstly we couldn't find anything as we were looking under 'Carnarvon' and not the Welsh spelling. It was eventually realised, however there was little in the folder, mostly an auction notice dated 2000.

I checked out 'Trove' on the computer and only found an article on the death of T M Sheil who had built 'Carnarvon' (the 1937 paper's spelling) in 1904. Not knowing exactly where 'Caernarvon' was I drove up Macquarie Grove Road and found the house on top of the hill, looking south towards the Nepean River and Camden Valley Way.

I stopped and walked to the front gate for a better look. The owner was feeding her dog and she came to greet me and said "Hello Robert." I was a bit shocked, but then I recognised Jenny, a past tennis partner, along with her husband Ross. They had bought 'Caernarvon' at the 2000 auction.

I explained my visit and Jenny said that a past resident had visited the house in 2010 and Council had taken an oral history from her. Her name was Mary Locke, the granddaughter of T M Sheil. Jo Oliver from the library had done the oral history. The 26 page transcription is now in the Museum's folder. It is a story worth reading.

Next day at the 'Antique Fair' volunteering at the Historical Society's table a lady from Campbelltown was reminiscing about Camden when she talked about getting off at Kirkham railway station and walking up Kirkham Lane to the dairy, which was of course, 'Caernarvon'.

Then the following Thursday I was playing tennis and mentioned my experiences with 'Caernarvon' in the last week with my tennis partner and he told me that he had rewired the house, probably just before the auction in 2000.

However it gets better as the next day at the museum an elderly man walked in asking about 'The Cowpastures', as he was retracing Hume and Hovell's 'Hoddle Track' around Kiama and was seeking to photograph any monuments about the cows.

Then he mentioned that he alone was just completing the retracing of the first white expedition in Australia on foot, which had occurred in 1797. It was from 90 Mile Beach in Victoria to Sydney Cove, about 700kms.

This story is not well known. I only found out about it when I read a new book in the library earlier this year called: 'From The Edge – Australia's Lost Histories' by Mark McKenna. He was surprised that we knew the story and went and got his laptop to show the photographs of his walk which he had started five months earlier.

I only hope the ABC does a documentary on this amazing story of retracing our history.

Volunteering at our great museum certainly provides its own amazing and rewarding encounters.

Editor's Note
The Museum welcomes volunteers in a range of roles. To learn more, contact Rene Rem Ph. 4655 3400. If Rene is not available when you call, speak to one of our volunteers on the phone, and leave your details.

Lively exhibition for the Centenary of Australian Federation

Sandra Dodds

This article outlines the Australian Federation Exhibition mounted by the society in 2000 and curated by Sandra Dodds.

The Camden Museum was the place to be between November 2000 and July 2001 for the exhibition *'Federation – Contemporary Views of Australia'*.

Exhibition highlights:
- Over 800 school students at the Camden museum
- Objects from the time of Federation
- Contemporary artists and performers
- Specially designed and constructed Federation archway for the Museum entranceway
- Camden Museum featured on the cover of the local telephone book.

In a first for the Camden area, contemporary art was a key element within the context of an historical exhibition, making links between the past and contemporary issues. Contemporary artworks featured in the exhibition to en-

Federation Archway at the entrance of the Camden Museum (S Dodds)

Federation archway at the entrance of the Camden Museum. Joyce Dodds and Alan Cortissos study the images on the Federation archway at the Camden Museum on the opening day, November 12, 2001. (S Dodds)

hance the audience's understanding of the effects of Australia's First Nation people's exclusion from the Federation constitution.

Triumphal arches featured throughout all major centres for the inauguration of the Commonwealth of Australia in 1901. And for the Camden centenary exhibition the celebratory structure was built in the Camden Museum entrance. Richard Stringer designed the archway and he was assisted in its installation by Peter Hayward and other members of the Camden Historical Society.

The archway had juxtapositions of images and text from the time of federation and 2001 and proved to be of great interest to all visitors. It was a grand entrance to the exhibition and it was where school students sat for their introductory talk about the education program.

As Julia Doyle stated in *Museum Matters*, October 2001:

…'The arch highlighted notions of continuity and how issues of the past find their repetition and resonances through current issues and debates … The arch began to liberate themes the exhibition hoped to examine such as notions of identity in Australia'.

And so it was, as we entered the museum, we started our journey through the exhibition. Standing under the archway made of four impressive columns covered with an array of images and text, we started to understand the context of the exhibition. Adjacent to the archway, in the display case were an interesting collection of objects from the time of Federation and the present, echoing the juxtapositions found throughout the exhibition.

Some objects from the time of Federation included a book owned by Edmund Barton on Constitutional law, programs for the opening of Parliament in 1901 and commemorative crockery displayed alongside contemporary Aboriginal paintings by Andrew Bell and stone tools.

Further through the exhibition, in another display case, were Aboriginal ceremonial objects, on loan from one of the artists, Jan Shipley. The objects included a didgeridoo and a feather headdress, arm and leg bands, spears, nulla nullas and carved sculptures.

Also included in the exhibition were reproductions of the Barunga Statement (1963), the Yirrkala Petitions (1968), posters and literature from the Reconciliation Council, Amnesty International and the United Nations, a map of Aboriginal Australia, videos: 'A Fair Go: Winning the 1967 Referendum', 'A Sea of Hands', 'From Sand to Celluloid', footage of the opening of Parliament and the Federation celebrations, and other events of 1901.

There were also numerous references including books and catalogues about the artists, International Council of Museums addresses, Barton lectures, the Vincent Lingiari Memorial lecture, 'The past we need to understand', material from Australians for Native Title and Reconciliation and other material.

Artists in the exhibition included Shirley Amos, Bronwyn Bancroft, Andrew Bell, Jonathan Jones, Marlene Cummins, Christine Christopherson, Leonie Dennis, Sally Morgan, Janice Shipley and Harry J. Wedge. The artworks were on loan from: the Boomalli Aboriginal Artists' Cooperative in Sydney; Campbelltown Arts Centre; and private collections and artists.

Jonathan Jones, who last year was the Kaldor Public Art Projects artist with the installation barrangal dyara (skin and bones) at the botanic garden in Sydney, exhibited his work entitled 'Tent Embassy' at the Camden Museum, a sculpture made from

'…corrugated iron sheets curved to resemble a shelter, the sculpture alluded to rudimentary housing, temporary structures, transient places. Inside each curved piece of metal there was a light bulb. Against the grey of the iron, the bright light created a harsh contrast. The sculpture was a metaphor for the

Jonathan Jones, Tent Embassy, 1999. Corrugated iron, marine cable and lights. Boomalli Aboriginal Artists' Cooperative (J Wrigley)

establishment of the tent embassy, the fight for representation and justice. ... [It] was based on the history of the struggle of Aboriginal people to gain land rights. The corrugated iron sheets held together with wire cable and lights suspended inside each iron shape represented hope and containment.[1]

Inside the space where the paintings and prints were displayed, we were met with more powerful works with strong messages. On one wall there were three silkscreen prints by Sally Morgan: *'Citizenship'* (1987), *'Mother and Child'* (1990) and *'Brokenhearted'* (1989). *'Citizenship'* is a representation of how Aboriginal people regarded their citizenship certificates which had to be carried at all times, were conditional upon certain regulations and could easily be revoked.

Aboriginal people who applied for citizenship rights had to promise to give up their traditional ways and live a European lifestyle and keep away from other Aboriginal people. The certificates removed them from the restrictions of State protection laws (Commonwealth Department of Training and Youth Affairs, Discovering Democracy Discussion Paper 6 NSW, Discovering De-

'Federation – Contemporary Views of Australia' exhibition at the Camden Museum. Artworks by Sally Morgan. (S Dodds)

mocracy Professional Development Committee, Sydney, NSW, undated, 10 - 12, p.99, in S.Dodds MA thesis).

The fact that Australia's First Nation people had to apply for citizenship in their own country was a powerful message in the context of Federation and their exclusion from the Constitution. 'While discussions and meetings were taking place to create a federated Australia, Aboriginal and Torres Strait Islander children were being removed from their families'[2]

In 1944, Aborigines were allowed to become 'Australian Citizens'. Aboriginal people called their citizenship papers 'Dog Tags'. We had to be licensed to be called Australian'.[3]

All of the artworks carried political messages about aspects of life from the perspectives of Australia's First Nation people. This gave us insights into how the main artefact of Federation, the Australian Constitution, excluded them.

The exhibition focussed on learning through the arts and drew on learning theories to inform both the content and direction of the education program. It

School children and teachers and parents from Mawarra Public School discussing artworks in the   exhibition, '*Federation – Contemporary Views of Australia*' with Sandra Dodds, exhibition and education (S Dodds)

was extremely well received by teachers and students.

The exhibition and education program was a huge success and school students thoroughly enjoyed all of the art activities as part of their museum visit. The inclusion of contemporary art within the context of a social history museum made the interpretations of social issues accessible through the experiences of the artists.

The artworks lit up the museum space and students were drawn to the works. They were interested in discussing the artworks and they were enthusiastic about creating their own artworks. The juxtapositions of art and historical objects and ideas facilitated understandings of the past in relation to the present.

The exhibition and education program for the Camden Community Federation Education Program was made possible by a Commonwealth grant and was supported by the loan of artworks from the Boomalli Aboriginal Artists' Cooperative, Campbelltown Arts Centre, collectors and artists.

The exhibition and education program involved many people and provided a great resource for schools in the area. The opening day included Aboriginal dance performances, and performances by a children's dance group and a local musical society, demonstrations of wood carving and emu egg carving, a painting workshop and story telling. 'It was a great day, starting with our first Welcome to Country and it was such a thrill to see so many Aboriginal people in the museum grounds, painting, carving wood, dancing and telling stories.

'Members of the Bundabunna Miyumba Indigenous Heritage and Cultural Experience and the Society for Education in Dance and Theatre (EDTA) celebrate the opening of the exhibition 'Federation – Contemporary Views of Australia' at the Camden Museum.

The mayor and the local member of parliament were able to meet many people whom they had not met previously and to chat with them. One outcome was a lovely photo from that day used on the front cover of our local telephone book the following year'.[4]

Notes
1. Sandra Dodds, Representations of history in museums, MA thesis, School of Historical and Philosophical Inquiry, University of Sydney, 2004, pp. 97 -98.
2. Dodds, 2004. Camden Community Federation Education Program, 'Federation – Contemporary Views of Australia' exhibition rationale, in "Representations of history in museums', MA thesis, School of Historical and Philosophical Inquiry, University of Sydney, 2004, appendix.
3. Dodds, 2004. 'Citizenship' text by Sally Morgan quoted in Sandra Dodds 'Representations of history in museums', MA thesis, School of Historical and Philosophical Inquiry, University of Sydney, 2004, p. 98
4. Dodds, 2004. John Wrigley, President Camden Historical Society (2001), Camden, New South Wales Correspondence, January 25, 2004, p. 103.

President's Report 2016 – 2017

Ian Willis

It is with pleasure that I present the annual report of the Camden Historical Society. It has been a busy and fulfilling year with the society and its members fulfilling its aim of the telling the Camden story in a variety of ways and places.

The society and its members continue to take a prominent role in a number of ways in the Camden community. The society continues to contribute a number of roles within the community and they include:
- contributing to the construction of resilient communities by enhancing community networks and social connections
- acting as a centre of volunteering where we build social capital and allows members to contribute to active citizenship
- contributing to the local tourism industry as a major visitor attraction with the Camden Local Government Area.

Advocacy
Part of the role of the society is acting as an advocate for the Camden story and all it stands for including promotion of local history and heritage. The society has contributed to this role on a number of local issues including:
- sale of land at St Johns Church
- the Camden Town Centre Urban Design Framework
- a number of development applications eg, Camden Vale milk depot
- review of Camden Local Environment Plan
- providing suggestions for street names in new suburbs
- Belgenny Trust Strategic Planning Day
- The redevelopment of the old Camden Vale milk depot
- The reduction of the curtilage around Gledswood homestead

Participation in the Community
The Society has been active within the wider community through attendance at community events. They have included:
2016
- Camden Council Volunteers Night Dec 2016
- NSW & ACT Asssociation of Family History Societies' State Conference
- Inspection of Camden Park Stables

- Narellan Rhythms Festival

2017
- Australia Day Parade
- Camden Show
- Camden Antique Fair
- Belgenny Farm Family History Day
- Preview of Baker Collection to go into Macaria

Society Meetings

The society's monthly meetings continue to provide a range of interesting and informative speakers, along with presentations from society members. Individual speakers have included:
- John Macarthur Stanham on the restoration of The Stables at Camden Park
- Maurice Augustyn on Warragamba Dam
- Andrew Allen on Lost Buildings at Campbelltown
- Stephen McMahon on Maryland
- Wen Denaro on her film 'One Hundred Yards of Silk'
- Roger Percy on the development of the art gallery in Macaria
- James Warrand on the grounding of the HM Bark Endeavour in 1770.
- Stephanie Trenfield on her visit to Mongolia.

60th Anniversary Celebrations

One of the highlights of the past year was the society's diamond anniversary. The 60th anniversary was celebrated with an early evening cocktail party which was attended by over 135 people. The event was organised by a small committee consisting of Rene, Dawn, Lee and Cathey. Great job and thanks to all concerned.

Volunteers

Our volunteers remain the backbone of both the society and the museum do a great job in a range of capacities from staffing the front desk, research, attending functions, advocacy and a host of other activities.

The roster at the front desk is ably managed by Volunteer Co-ordinator Rene Rem, who inducts new volunteers and looks after any issues. There are currently 56 volunteers on the roster that provides staff on the front desk.

Volunteers do a range of other activities including research, writing statements of significance, scanning and digitising material, representing the society at community events, and other things.

Volunteer Training
The society offers training opportunities for those who are interested and this helps the society achieve its aims. Some of these have included:
- The society was represented by John at the Metal Conservation Workshop at the Wollondilly Heritage Centre.
- Rene and Anne attended a MOSAiC Training Workshop. MOSAiC is the software package that the society uses to manage the museum collection.
- General training for those who want to be on the volunteer roster.

Museum
The most important activity of the society is managing the Camden Museum and the society's collection of objects and artefacts, as well as the museum's archives. The museum continues to attract over 6500 visitors a year including a number of community and school groups.

The society has purchased new display cabinets for the Chinese exhibits upstairs. There will be the return of the Percival wagon from Macarthur Anglican School where it has been partially restored. Camden Council funded a new kitchen cupboard, sink and hot water service, and the society purchased a new urn.

Education
Society Education Officer Stephanie Trenfield organised the Education Program Redevelopment project and two education workshops in July. Attendees discussed ways the school syllabus could be used with the museum collection.

Policy Matters
The society
- clarified its policy on life membership.
- streamlined its payment systems.
- investigated the matter of increased security for the collection and the building

Community Partnership
The society's community partnership with Camden Library and the Camden Area Family History Society continues to work well for all concerned. Joint activities are conducted as part of Heritage Week in April, History Week in September and the collection of photographs in Camden Images Past and Present.

The society granted Camden Area Family History Society use of the museum for its meetings due to a space issue in the library meeting room.

Communication

The society publishes the journal twice yearly and they have recently been posted online. Lee Stratton produces a number of newsletters and they are printed at the office of the local Federal Member of Parliament, Angus Taylor. The society is grateful for this assistance.

A Facebook page is looked after by Brett Atkins and Rene Rem, who regularly post some old images from the society's photographic collection. There are currently around 900 likes on the Camden Museum Facebook page.

A number of members write historic articles of interest for the Back Then page of *The District Reporter*. The society facilitated the publication of *Camden School of Arts – A History,* a new museum brochure, and a forthcoming book on the Nepean River Council Council.

Financial Assistance

The society has the continued support of Camden Council through a yearly subsidy that covers insurances, the provision of two storage units at Narellan for our "excess items" and the maintenance of the Museum.

The society has received a number of generous donations:
- Vintage Car Club $500
- Camden Show Society $500
- A member $80

Membership

The current paid up membership is 111, and life members 9.

Final Thanks

In conclusion I wish to thank everyone on the committee, volunteers and others who have assisted the society to make the past year a success. I look forward to a successful 2018.

Making the Most of MOSAiC

Anne McIntosh

MOSAiC is a database developed in Australia to assist museums, art galleries and private collectors to record and manage their collections. More than 500 organisations use the software. The name 'MOSAiC' refers to its capability to link objects, books, events, places and people through internal hyperlinks, so that researchers can gain a multi-faceted picture of their subject of interest.

Camden Museum has been using MOSAiC to track acquisitions and donors for eight years. In early June 2017, there were over 3800 items documented in the database, with a brief description and a record of their ID number, and in all but 730 instances, the person who donated the item. Statements of significance have been linked to the 24 items that have one. The Museum would love to have more Statements of Significance in the database – if you are interested in researching any museum object, Julie Wrigley or Anne McIntosh will be happy to assist you with your project.

Having a central record of our collection is important because, over time, different people are more or less actively involved with the museum. The database provides a point of accumulated knowledge about each item, as built up over time. The information can be sourced when those who organised this addition to our collection are no longer involved.

Any museum volunteer can look at the database as a 'Visitor'. You will not be able to see the administrative data, and you cannot make changes, but you can search for items and read about them. It's a 'risk free' exploration! The instructions are clear and easy to follow (See page 173 for instructions), and available to any volunteer on the computer in the Research Room.

In early June, Rene Rem and Anne McIntosh attended MOSAiC training in Manly. Anne's program was focused on searching across multiple fields and the creation of reports about museum items. Rene learnt about curating the collection.

John and Julie Wrigley ensure that all items donated to our Museum have a MOSAiC record and the donors are recorded. The known history of the item is noted at the time that they are donated. (This is why it is important that a donation form is completed for any item offered to the Museum – these can be found in the red folder at the front desk.)

We are working to include pictures of the all items in the the museum collection in the database. So far, about 120 items have a linked image. Many items have multiple images, enabling you to see hidden details that may not be visible on the display. Doug Barratt has photographed a number of objects from the collection which are linked to the items in the database.

Rene has been coordinating Stephanie Trenfield and volunteers to scan the items in the filing cabinets, a process that is likely to be ongoing over several years.

There are many tasks involving MOSAiC for which additional assistance would be welcomed. If you have some spare time and attention to detail, specialist knowledge, an interest in digital still life photography or enjoy computer and administrative tasks, have a chat with Rene or Julie.

Camden Museum has some very special records. MOSAiC will assist us to link the items in the museum (including those in storage) with other items and sources. We already have the files, but effort is needed to improve our database, so that we can produce complex mosaics that will reveal our stories in new ways.

Using the *MOSAiC* Catalogue as a Visitor

To get you started, you need to get a Committee member to log on to the computer and click the *Mosaic* icon - it looks like a Roman temple.

1. **Log on to *Mosaic*.**
2. **Name**: type 'Visitor'. You may need to delete the last name used.
3. **Password**: leave blank. (As a visitor you cannot change any data, so you do not have to worry about losing any data.) Click 'OK.'
4. **Find**. There is a choice of 3: "Find Item" which allows you to search for Objects. "Find Subject" which allow you to search for People or Subjects. "Library" which allows you to search the Reference Library books.
5. Click the one you are interested in searching. (The best one to start with is Find Item.)
6. **Find Items**. On the dark green page [FIND ITEM RECORDS] the 'Item type' is 'OBJECT'. The Accession Identity (if known) is the catalogue number but you do not need to know it.
    (You can also type a year such as '2017' to find the objects accessioned that year.)
7. **Search** by typing in the NAME field, or in the DESCRIPTION field, and click "FETCH ITEMS". (You may need to guess a word for the object's name e.g. 'mangle'.)
8. **Retrieve Records?** When the program finds a possible object it

will ask: "RETRIEVE 1 [or more] ITEM (OBJECT) RECORDS? Click YES.
9. **View Records.** On the turquoise-coloured page [VIEW ITEM RECORDS] you can look at the name, description, significance, location, and possible photographs of the object.
10. Click the file if there are photographs.
11. Click the arrow at the bottom of the page to go forward or backwards to other records.
12. **Close.** Click CLOSE when you have finished that search. Start again if you wish.
13 **Reset.** Click 'Reset Find Criteria' to start a new search.
14 **Exit.** Click EXIT when you have finished all of your searches.

Write a note if you want to suggest any changes.
Julie Wrigley, 2017

Sample searches as a 'Visitor'.

You can see the results of your search as a form (ie. a list) or as a series of individual entries.

FIND items that include the word 'Elderslie' in their description

__SEARCH fetched 9 items__

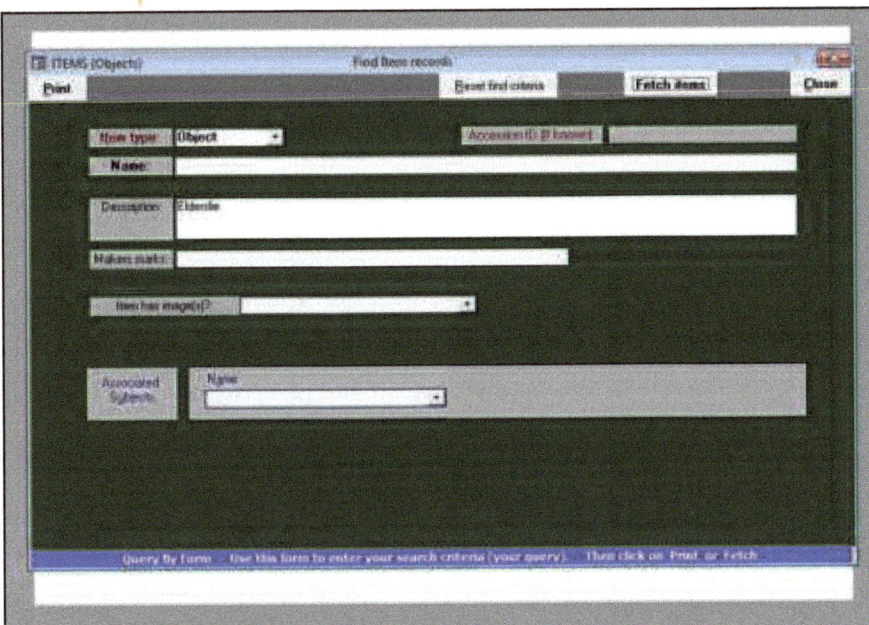

Search Green Screen

- DRESSMAKERS' NAME PLATE
- 2 x INDENTURES (not on display)
- WHIP, SULKY
- TEASPOON, ELDERSLIE HIGH SCHOOL
- BADGE, 'ELDERSLIE HIGH SCHOOL SENATOR'
- WATERING CAN, CHINESE MARKET GARDENER'S
- ST MARKS CHURCH SIGN

FIND items with 'Elderslie' in their description AND an image attached.
SEARCH fetched 1 item

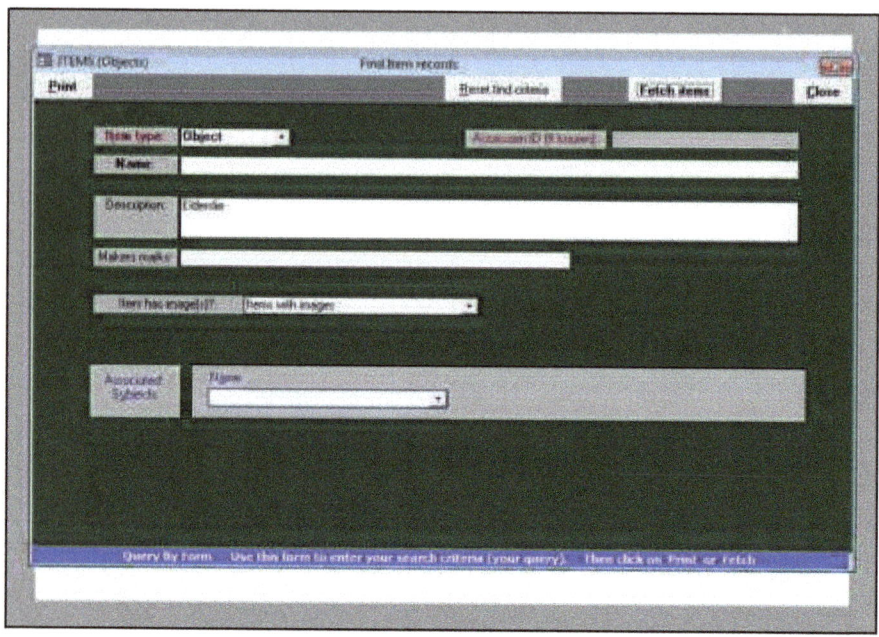

DRESSMAKERS' NAME PLATE

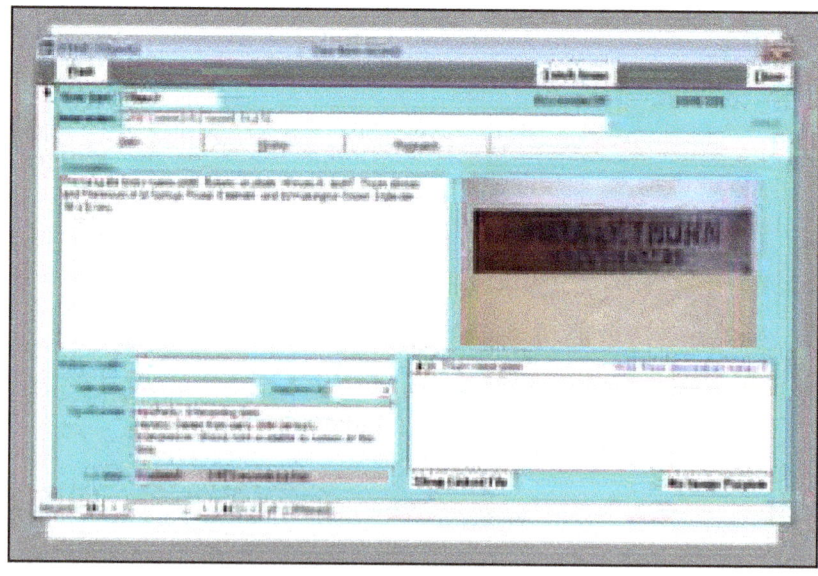

(record screen)

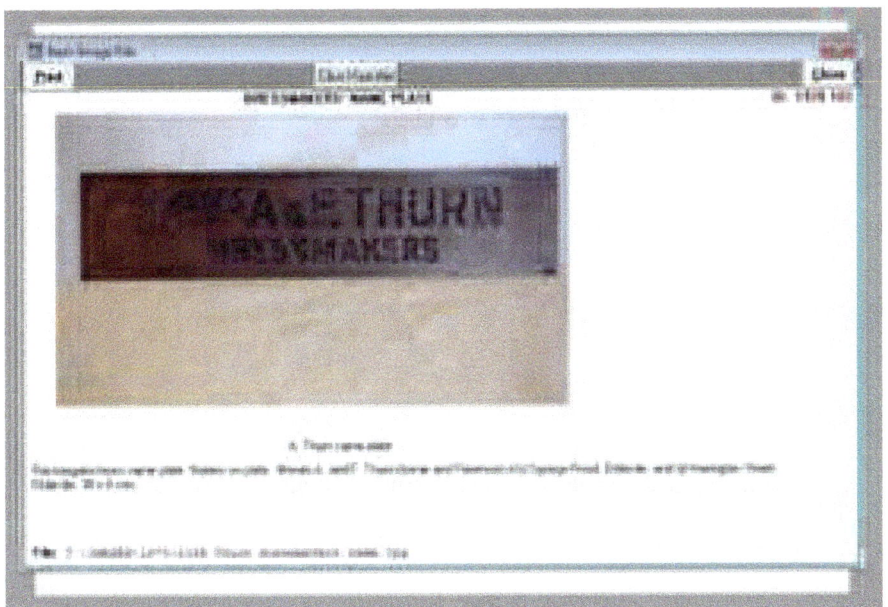

(image screen)

More complex searches are available and can be undertaken using a MOSAiC login.

Speak to Rene.

Anzacs of Macarthur: The Men and Women Who Served in the First World War
A Research and Writing Journey

Lauren Hokin

In 2012, the Federal Government developed an initiative to assist electorates in commemorating their First World War heritage. It was known as the Anzac Centenary Local Grants Program. Late the following year, politicians, RSL Sub-Branch members, and other interested parties from the Macarthur area, were brought together to come up with ideas for the Grants Program. I was approached by the Veterans' Recreation Centre in Campbelltown to develop some plans for their project. I came up with the idea to research and write a book detailing the wartime stories of servicemen and women from the Macarthur area who served in the Great War, and the efforts of those on the home front. The book was approved and as part of the Grant, was to be donated for free to every school, library, RSL, historical group and Government institution. However, as I was handing out the donated copies, many people within the community, especially descendants, were disappointed that they could not have a copy of their own. So at the beginning of 2017, I decided to do a re-print of a 2nd edition to be made available for sale to the public.

The book is an anthology of the 1100 plus soldiers, sailors and nurses who came from Campbelltown, Camden and Picton and their surrounding districts, now suburbs. The purpose behind the book is to provide the community with a resource of their First World War history to be used for commemorative, research and educational objectives. It also serves those interested in family and local history, thus ensuring that the stories of so many of our brave servicemen and women are not lost. I have always had an interest in history, and especially in military

My great uncle Clifford Aubrey Jahns killed in action on the 31st of May 1917. *Tamworth Daily Observer*, 23rd June 1917.

Gravesite of Clifford Jahns located in The Strand Military Cemetery in Ploegsteert, Belgium. Site: Hokin.

matters. My father served in Vietnam, my maternal grandparents both served in the army during the Second World War and I have several great uncles whom fought and died during the First World War. I have completed a Bachelor of Arts (Honours) and a Master of Teaching (Secondary) at Western Sydney University, carrying out a thesis on The Historiography of General Sir Douglas Haig and the Third Battle of Ypres.

The Process
Once the outline of the project had been approved by the Macarthur committee, I got to work. The first thing I had to do was generate a list of service personnel with verifiable connections to the Macarthur Region. This was achieved by going through rolls of honour, local newspaper articles printed during the war, official databases from the Australian War Memorial and the National Archives of Australia, such as embarkation rolls, and other resources including books and journal articles. I then went about researching and writing the book simultaneously, as the research informed the writing and vice versa, emphasising what needed further investigation or background information. The project was so large that understanding how to fit both the research and writing the book within a tight time frame was paramount. This required splitting my time into different tasks, namely research, writing, typing and editing.

The research component entailed by far the largest effort. The main source of material came from military service records, accessed through the National Archives of Australia.[1] Service Records are quite informative. First World War Army Records are divided into three sections, first the Attestation Papers including details such as age, employment, next-of-kin, previous military experience, to specific details such as height, weight and hair colour. Next is the Service/Casualty Forms, describing their training, departure overseas and war service. However, because of security and army standard operating procedures, these forms do not go into detail about where a serviceman was placed in the trenches or what battles they fought in. They simply say 'in the field.' So in order to make sense of a soldier, sailor or nurse's particular movements, you must read extensively about the development of battles, rest stations, hospitals and military organisational structure.

Lastly, and sometimes, most interestingly, Service Records contain correspondence. This correspondence is either between the military and servicemen or women, usually after the war, or between the military and the next-of-kin. Here, there is a plethora of information available. You can determine address changes, family details, such as marriages, children and siblings, wills, employment, education, and sadly, in too many cases tearful letters from mothers, fathers and wives desperately trying to find any information about their loved ones lost to the battlefields.

The Australian War Memorial provides useful sources concerning photographs, embarkation rolls, awards and recommendation details, rolls of honour, Red Cross files, unit diaries and circulars.[2] Further information about servicemen and women, their families, employment and aspects of their civilian life were found in articles from newspapers printed during the war, specifically the *Camden News* and *Campbelltown Herald,* and within publications such as the Camden Historical Society Journals. These periodicals were especially useful in providing material for what the war was like for those on the home front, such as the development of Recruitment Associations, fundraising for the Red Cross, the War Chest Fund and donating luxuries to the troops, to the throwing of farewell parties and solemn public memorials for those whom were lost.

Between researching, I would start writing the entries for each serviceman and woman's war service, describing their pre-war life, enlistment, proceeding overseas, battles they were involved in, any battle wounds etc. I would spend four days hand-writing the 30-40 entries before typing them up and then going back to researching. The most tedious aspect of the project was the editing. The book consists of half a million words, and required lengthy and laborious proof-reading and fact checking. This necessitated the construction of numerous drafts and correlation with the book design team, concerning editing changes, placement of photos, captions and footnotes. With such extensive use of facts and dates; particulars such as birth, marriage and death details, name spelling and battle and unit details had to be checked against NSW Birth, Marriage and Death indexes and battle and unit histories respectively.

Throughout the project I encountered many problems. The biggest hurdle was the lack of information. As you can imagine the First World War began over a 100 years ago, and much of the memory of those who served and paper documents relating to them have been lost to the passage of time. Conducting research into the lives of those who lived so long ago is made difficult when the information you are after is unavailable. Sourcing newspapers on microfilm was particularly tricky, as there were only four surviving issues of the *Campbelltown Herald* between 1914-1918, and several issues missing from the *Camden News* over the same period. Finding birth, marriage and death details proved to be also problematic. Although a large majority of indexes are available from the NSW Birth, Marriage and Deaths Department, there is a selection of names which do not appear.

Whether this is a result of lost church records, inaccurate spelling or mistakes in uploading digital data is anyone's guess. Another issue was trying to connect servicemen or women to the area. Names appeared in newspapers and on honour rolls of personnel who were not born in Macarthur or according to their service records or embarkation rolls were not living here at time of their enlistment. During the 1800s and early 1900s, many labourers came to the area for work, but whom were not permanent residents. Farmers would often offer seasonal work on their orchards and farms to plant, pick or to drive cattle and sheep. Unfortunately, there are little to no records of these men working or staying in the area.

Other difficulties arose from record inaccuracies. No doubt keeping exact details of almost 400 000 service personnel during the Great War, in an age before computer processing, would have been an insurmountable task. Embarkation rolls and service records were particularly susceptible to accuracy problems. With embarkation rolls, quite often the address of the serviceman or woman was unavailable and it was assumed that they resided with their next-of-kin. Sometimes these addresses were overseas, such as in England, which is, not only, obviously wrong, but also, begs to question where in Australia that particular serviceman or woman was living. Attestation papers of service records were often filled in by military clerical staff, and consequently can be rife with inaccuracies. Names were often spelt wrong, and places of birth were recorded incorrectly or generalised, not to mention those who lied to enlist to conceal their age or criminal history.[3]

Private William F. Moore. Site: R. W. Smith

Regional areas which listed their servicemen and women, either in the newspaper as they joined up or on honour rolls, would frequently use nicknames or other names they were known by. This made finding a service record very challenging, as they would naturally enlist under their full name. An example includes a H. Lancaster. This name appeared on a local list, however, searching through the several hundred possible H. Lancasters, there was none born or living in the Macarthur area. There was a Victor Lancaster listed, who I could find, as he was killed in action, and I assumed this H. Lancaster was related to him but again no matches. While I was researching the correspondence section of Victor's service record, I came across his will. In it I found mention of his brother, a Gordon William Horace Lancaster.[4] I then searched for a service record for Gordon and eureka I found him. The lack of information and inaccuracies in official records made researching especially taxing. The only solution was to keep digging or trying different avenues to find the information, or simply work with what was available.

Another hindrance that plagued the project was the very tight time-frame. The committee wanted to see the book completed by the close of 2015. How-

William and his lovely bride, Emma, in England November 1918. Site: R. W. Smith

ever, during discussions in 2014, the area I was researching was increased to include certain suburbs that were not officially part of the Macarthur electorate, but essentially what is viewed as part of the Macarthur Region. This resulted in an extra 400 service personnel that had to be investigated, written up and slotted in. Thus, this limited how much research time and entry space could be devoted to each serviceman or woman.

Some Interesting Stories

Through the research, I have discovered many sad and inspirational stories of our servicemen and women. Sisters Mary Morton and Rose McAnene trained as nurses and came to the area to work at Camden Hospital, where Mary became Matron.[5] Feeling they could offer their services, they joined the Australian Army Nursing Service. They worked tirelessly to save lives while witnessing the ghastly mutilations that modern weaponry could do, assigned to various hospitals in Egypt, England and France.[6] Menangle born Peter Gallagher was always a good student. Completing various public service exams, he found work as a shorthand reporter for the Supreme Court.[7] Becoming a Lieutenant, he joined his unit at Pozieres, where he was caught in an artillery

Trooper Henry James Moore. Site: R. W. Smith

blast, sending shell fragments into his left hand, arm and side.[8] Unfortunately his arm developed gas gangrene and was amputated. Remarkably, after he recovered, Peter refused to go home, asking to remain and serve. He was able to put his clerical skills to good use in the War Records Section in London.[9]

Brothers William Frederick and Henry James Moore were living on Broughton Rd in Camden when they decided to enlist.[10] The Moore family had developed strong ties to the area, while William and Henry worked as a carter and gardener respectively.[11] William joined the 20th Battalion at Gallipoli in August 1915. Developing dysentery, he was evacuated to Egypt. Shortly after being promoted to Lance Corporal, William was wounded during the Second Battle of Bullecourt, shrapnel slicing his scalp. On the 14th of March 1918, he was wounded again receiving a gun shot wound to his back. Sadly, a few months later, he was wounded a third time, caught in a gas attack.[12]

William was lucky to survive the war, marrying the lovely Miss Emma Elizabeth Buttridge in Shepton Mallot, England, on the 21st of November 1918.

[13] Henry passed his physical in Camden and officially signed up on the 22nd of March 1916.[14] Whilst completing his training, Henry and some other local lads were given a farewell social. Held at Foresters' Hall, Argyle Street, Camden, the boys were congratulated for joining up and presented with wrist watches.[15] Henry soon met his unit in Egypt, serving with the 1st Light Horse Field Ambulance.[16] The Field Ambulances provided forward medical assistance, with sections often patrolling alongside the Light Horse and following them into battle. Henry and his devoted unit helped save the lives of many sick and wounded troops, scared and far from home. Unluckily, Henry contracted malaria in Jericho, and was invalided home in January 1919.[17]

Notes

1. National Archives of Australia: B2455, First Australian Imperial Force Personnel Dossiers, 1914-1920 or A6770, Service Cards for Petty Officers and Men, 1911-1970. Found through www.naa.gov.au.
2. Circulars were a form issued to the next-of-kin of deceased service personnel shortly after the war. They were designed to provide the Government and historians with data concerning their war dead, such as education details, familiar relationships to other servicemen or women, employment and factors surrounding cause of death and gravesites.
3. Often service personnel born or living in Campbelltown, Ingleburn, Minto or Glenfield were emphasized as coming from via Liverpool and those from Cobbitty and Narellan were stated as coming from Camden; as military personnel from Sydney would be unaware of small rural districts outside the city centre.
4. National Archives of Australia: B2455, First Australian Imperial Force Personnel Dossiers, 1914-1920; Lancaster Gordon William Horace.
5. Camden Museum.
6. National Archives of Australia: B2455, First Australian Imperial Force Personnel Dossiers, 1914-1920; Mcanene M M p. 8 & Macanene R pp.21-23.
7. National Archives of Australia: B2455, First Australian Imperial Force Personnel Dossiers, 1914-1920; Gallagher P, p. 6.
8. *Ibid.,* pp. 13-14.
9. *Ibid.,* pp. 13-14.
10. Australian War Memorial: Australian Imperial Force Nominal Roll; 1523 Moore, William Frederick and 17272 Moore, Henry James.' www.awm.gov.au
11. *Ibid.*
12. All service information for William Moore came from National Archives of Australia: B2455, Australian Imperial Force Personnel Dossiers, 1914-1920; Moore W F, pp.13-19.
13. *Ibid.,* p. 25.
14. National Archives of Australia: B2455, First Australian Imperial Force Personnel Dossiers, 1914-1920; Moore H J, p. 3.
15. 'Send-Off to Recruits' in *Camden News,* 1 June 1916, p. 1.
16. National Archives of Australia: B2455, First Australian Imperial Force Personnel Dossiers, 1914-1920; Moore H J, pp. 23-24.
17. *Ibid.,* p. 35.

Commander Frank Gardner RAN 1841 – 1927

Harry Stait-Gardner

My family moved to Camden in 1987. We have seen many changes since that time. Our street opposite the turf farm had very few houses. My trip to Sarah Redfern High School where I taught took only about thirty five minutes, there were no traffic hold-ups then except at the railway crossing into Campbelltown. My journey along the Narellan Road was through rural pasture and marshy swamps at Curran's Hill. It was about this time that the Native Garden at Mount Annan was opened. We could take the dirt track from River Road to the Nepean River where wooden stanchions marked where Little Sandy Bridge had once stood.

I first came to Australia from the UK in 1949 when I was 9 years old. We settled in Beverley Hills. I returned to the UK for a holiday in 1962 as a young man, met Janet, my wife, started a family and stayed in England for about twenty years. I grew restless to return to Australia and persuaded the family just to try Australia for a while. We arrived in Sydney in October 1986 and stayed with my parents before moving to Camden.

We chose Camden because it was the closest to an English country town we had seen despite its obvious differences of low rise shops with covered walkways and wide streets. My wife was feeling particularly homesick for green, albeit rainy Cheddar, in the West Country of England. The summer of 1986-1987 had been an extremely hot one. Estate agents drove us around some rather bleak estates. Rosemeadow was one. It was very new and there didn't seem to be a blade of grass or a tree in sight.

So when we came to Camden, St John's Church on the hill with its spire, the beautiful tree-lined streets and Camden's somewhat English atmosphere persuaded us to make it our home. It even had an English pub, The Camden Valley Inn. My parents thought Camden an excellent choice. They loved visiting Camden on days out since the early 1950s and had stopped regularly at Tildsleys, the butcher to buy their meat. My mother considered this to be the finest butcher in New South Wales.

There were other reasons for choosing this part of NSW. I had often spoken to Janet of my love for the countryside South West of Sydney. As a boy I lived in Australia and had attended boarding schools in Mittagong and Bowral. Journeys to the Southern Highlands took my family through Camden, where we stopped for lunch, and then along the old Razorback in our family Vanguard. It was common to pass cars pulled over to the side of the road steam pouring from their boiling radiators. Sometimes we were forced to join them.

I had been aware that my father's family had had a long association with Australia. My Grandfather was considered to be a headstrong young man who needed sorting out so he had been sent to a sheep station near Orange in the colony of NSW to learn how to manage sheep and cattle stations. During his time in Australia he stayed with his uncle, Commander Frank Gardner, a notable citizen of Newcastle. I was aware that this great uncle of mine had a very colourful history but knew very little about him. With a great deal of help from Newcastle Library and Newcastle Historical Society, I have pieced together Commander Gardner's story, which, I must say, begins a little like a "Boys' Own" adventure. Some of what he did and achieved follows.

Commander Frank Gardner RAN VD

Commander Frank Gardner, V.D.

Commander Frank Gardner, V.D. (Volunteer Division) was one of the oldest and most esteemed citizens of Newcastle. He was born in the Bell Hotel, Church Street, Tewkesbury, Gloucestershire, England in 1841. His father died when he was very young and he went to sea at the age of fourteen. His first voyage was to the Crimea on board the troop ship, Earl Eglinton, then engaged in transporting troops and assisting in the evacuation of the sick and wounded. He visited the battlefields of Sebastopol.

As a young man of about eighteen or nineteen years of age, Frank Gardner took part as a volunteer in The Second Opium War. In the taking of the Taku Forts, he lost his little finger in the fighting. It was during this time that he met Harry Rawson, later to become Sir Harry Rawson, Governor of New South Wales.

After the China Wars, Frank Gardner joined the mercantile service. He sailed to Savannah, where he arrived at the outbreak of the American Civil War. He joined the confederate forces and was present when the northern ships were burned in the river. After six weeks service in Fort Palaska, at the mouth of the river, he was drafted to Charleston. He found the service

Going on parade New South Wales Newcastle Naval Brigade (Newcastle Region Library)

uncongenial and joined the steamer, Sir Charles Napier. He spent some time in blockade running making two trips from Liverpool to the States on this risky business.

Frank Gardner came to Australia as a ship's mate aboard the famous Boston clipper, Lightning, one of the fastest clipper ships that ever sailed between England and the Antipodes. The vessel arrived in Melbourne in 1862, from where she took a crowd of gold-seekers to New Zealand where a "Gold Rush" had occurred. Frank Gardner took leave of his ship and stayed a year in Sydney before settling in Newcastle in 1862.

Frank Gardner's connection with the Newcastle Naval Brigade dated from 1863 when he joined the ranks and rose to the post of Commander. He retired after forty years of service and was presented by the men of the brigade with an illuminated address. His name is included as one of the Commanders of the Royal Australian Navy lists in 1911. On his retirement he was one of the oldest officers in the Australian Naval Reserves. Commander Gardner had been a member of the Naval and Military Association since its inception and was always a welcome figure.

Commander Frank Gardner on the right

Officers of New South Wales Newcastle Naval Brigade Cdr F Gardner VD (R) (Newcastle Region Library)

Apart from Commander Gardner's business life, his activities were many and varied and of a philanthropic nature. He was devoted to Newcastle Cathedral, which has benefited greatly from his generosity. He paid for the cost of the brick wall and entrances in front of the Cathedral and also for the marble altar in the Warriors' Chapel.

Commander Gardner's patriotism was intense. He subscribed liberally to every fund during the days of the Great War. As a fitting climax, he presented the City of Newcastle with its memorial monument and statue. This cenotaph is believed to be the first such one in Australia. It still stands in front of the Post Office.

With the late Mr. H. Contis, Commander Gardner was a founder of the Newcastle Sailors' Home. He was also instrumental, with others, in the formation of the Shipwreck Relief Society. During the period of the volunteer fire service, Commander Gardner was Honorary Superintendent of the Newcastle Brigades from 1882 and retired on the passing of the Fire Brigades Act in 1910, when the permanent system came into operation. He was one of the founders of the Newcastle School of Arts and occupied the position of Secretary in the Newcastle Hospital.

Commander Frank Gardner was keen on sport. He was a Secretary to the committee which conducted the New Year's Day regattas on Newcastle Harbour. He was an excellent rifle shot and a very good fisherman. It was, however, as a keen lawn bowler that he was best known. In the northern district around Newcastle, he was referred to as the "Father of Bowls". His interest in bowls came from the famous bowling green at the Bell Hotel in England, his place of birth. There is a lot more to say about this early settler to the Colony New South Wales and his contribution to building a nation but space does not permit the full story to be told.

Commander Gardner died at his home, Church Street, Newcastle on 2nd November 1927. He was 84 years old. An extract from his obituary reads:
"The late Commander Gardner was of a quiet disposition and was extremely liberal in cases of need. During his long and useful life he had made many true and lasting friends. His Funeral Service was held in Newcastle Cathedral."

Notes
Aldine Centennial History of N.S.W.   W.F Morrison 1888.
Commander Frank Gardner, Newcastle Morning Herald and Miners Advocate. 14 March 1898
Commander Gardner Dies, Newcastle Morning Herald and Miners Advocate. 3 November 1927
Impressive Funeral, Newcastle Morning Herald and Miners Advocate. 4 November 1927
Newcastle Regional Library Photograph Collection, photos Nos 001 000775 and 026 000191.
Nary List, 1 November 1911. Government Printers, Melbourne.

Acknowledgements
Newcastle Family History Society for research in 2002.

Memories of the Burragorang Valley

Ron Schofield

"The Burragorang Valley west of Sydney near the towns of Camden and The Oaks, was where I used to go camping years ago with my father and younger brother Geoff," writes Ron Schofield of Baulkham Hills, NSW.

"We enjoyed the peace and quiet, and the beauty of the valley with the fast-flowing Wollondilly River.

"The area was always teaming with wildlife, which made our camping trips most enjoyable.

"After completing my apprenticeship as a carpenter, father and I won a contract with the Sydney Water Board in 1959 to remove the farmhouse (in the photo above) and leave the site clean and tidy to make way for the catchment area of Warragamba Dam, which was nearing completion at the time.

"Our plan was to dismantle the seven-room timber-framed house, which was named Apple Grove, and rebuild it on a block of land in Vineyard Avenue,

Smithfield, an outer Sydney suburb.

'The house was very well built with high ceilings, timber weather boards, timber boxed frame windows and a high-pitched roof with corrugated iron roofing.

"Inside, the floorboards were wide with timber lining boards on the walls up to 1.2 metres fibro lining above that, with timber lining boards on the ceiling.

'The contracted time was six months and every weekend we would travel to the valley, work on the dismantling and transport the materials back to Smithfield on our three-ton tabletop truck.

"The dismantling work was very constant and after five and a half months we managed to leave the site clean and tidy. The house was rebuilt at Smithfield mainly by contractors and on completion was rented.

"It was a wonderful feeling to know that we were able to do our little bit to help keep the Sydney water supply clean.

[Originally published in The Senior March 2017 with the title 'They knew how to build 'em back when'. Reproduced with permission.]

Shirley Beaumont of Brisbane Queensland wrote in response to Ron Schofield's article saying that it brought back wonderful memories:

"They relate to my bushwalking days through the Burragorang Valley before it was flooded for the Warragamba Dam.

"Oh, how I wish I could see those places and walk them all again.

"Criss-crossing through the flooded river we walked, carrying our packs over our heads, sleeping in the old mines full of bats - the open campfires, sharing our tucker the stories we shared and the great social events.

"So many memories came flooding back when I read the article.

It also set happy memories in motion for Pat Allen who lives in at Springwood in the Blue Mountains.

"As a senior student at Burwood Girls High School together with six or seven other girls, we would travel by train to Camden, changing first at Campbelltown, and then taking the Nattai bus to the Burragorang Valley," she writes.

'It was 1954 and the residents of the valley were fast moving out, as required by the Sydney Water Board, and the timber-cutters were busy at work removing the trees below the expected water level.

"The valley was very quiet apart from the sound of axes felling trees. "We stayed with Mrs Waldron at the Hillside Guest House and daily rode horses from Ernie Pippin's stables - this same Ernie Pippin had gone to school with my mum at The Oaks during World War I.

"'The valley was ours and we rode to the deserted Wills Farm (a location in the film 'Bush Christmas') and to the ghost town to Yerranderie. The horses knew their way home, even after dark.

"In the summer we went swimming in the river or paddled the Wollondilly in canoes.

"Brown snakes were usually quickly disturbed when we arrived on a hot sandy beach.

"I remember a two-storey pine-log house we named the Artist's Cottage because there was a studio upstairs with a view of the valley and discarded works aplenty.

"My remembrance is of a most beautiful valley and fun times with school friends."

[Originally published in The Senior May 2017 with the title 'Bates, campfires in valley now lost'.]

A 1930 road trip from Sydney

Anne McIntosh

At the CHS meeting on 12 July, Roslyn Tildsley mentioned a reference to NRMA campsites at Narellan and Cobbitty in NRMA's magazine, Open Road.

Searching Trove, I came across this 1930 tour of the local countryside, which mentions a picnic ground near the junction of the Nepean River and Mount Hunter Rivulet. That reminded me that in the 1980s there was a roofed picnic table sitting on this small, flat block of cleared land.

The river's edge is today hidden by an overgrowth of woody weeds. I have copied the tour from page 8 of the Sun newspaper, 23 February 1935. Surprisingly, although there is now a freeway from the city, you could probably follow these directions today.

Picnic At Cobbitty, N.R.M.A. Tour, Historic Village

The old-world village of Cobbitty, with its historic buildings, famous polo grounds, and picturesque picnic areas along the banks of the Nepean, is visited today in the trip described by the N.R.M.A. touring department.

The drive from Camden through Douglas Park to Appin is off the beaten track, and, although the Nepean ford provides a doubtful point after rain, the attractive grazing and farming country makes for a pleasant drive.

From the city the motorist follows George Street west past Grace Bros, and continues on, passing the University on the left, to Summer Hill. Here Liverpool Road is taken to the left, passing through Ashfield and Bankstown before reaching Liverpool. At Crossroads Hotel take the Hume Highway to the right, and continue on to Narellan, where the Bringelly road is followed to the right.

Two miles further on, the tourist bears left along a road lending to Cobbitty village. The main road continues through the settlement and crosses the Nepean River by bridge.

Picnic Areas

Picnic areas are located along the river bank not far from Cobbitty village, and if the tourist travels across Cobbitty Bridge to the right of the road near the junction of the Mount Hunter Rivulet and the Nepean River.

Beyond the bridge the road to the left is taken, and the motorist runs south through undulating and hilly farming country to the Junction with The Oaks Road. At this point the way ahead is taken, and at the junction with the old Razorback road the tourist turns left and shortly afterwards enters Camden. At the southern end of the main street the main road to Picton is taken to the right, and it is then easy going over a moderately hilly road past a hospital to a point 4.7 miles [away], where the main Picton road bears to the right. The tour here described keeps ahead through farming country to Douglas Park, passing on the way turn-offs to Menangle and Maldon.

About a mile beyond Douglas Park the Nepean River is forded, and motorists are advised by the N.R.M.A. to take every care in ascertaining the depth of the water if heavy rain has fallen.

Bush Country

Then follows an interesting drive through mostly bush country to the Appin-Maldon road, which is joined near the turn-off to Cordeaux Dam. At this point a left turn is made, and shortly afterwards the road winds down through Broughton's Pass, at the bottom of which the Cataract River is crossed by bridge. After going up a moderate hill it is easy going to Appin, where the road from Bulli Pass comes in on the right.

The tourist keeps ahead at this town, and passes along a good road over undulating country to Campbelltown. The return trip to the city is then made by way of Denham Court and Liverpool.

The total distance of this round tour is 111.3 miles, and the most suitable place for a picnic lunch is on the banks of the Nepean River near Cobbitty village, which is about 41 miles from Sydney.

The CHS is interested to know whether anyone remembers the NRMA camping grounds located at Narellan and Cobbitty. Where were they? What facilities did they provide? Why did they close?

Memories of my first jobs in 1965 and 1966

Robert Wheeler

Last Friday (week before the society's August meeting) I visited Scots Church on the corner of York and Margaret Streets (fronting Wynyard Park) Sydney, with a small group of past Housing Commission architects. We meet regularly to explore Sydney's interesting buildings.

Scots Church was built in 1826 on what was known as Church Hill. It was demolished in 1929 for the construction of the Sydney Harbour Bridge roadworks, widening of York Street and construction of Wynyard Railway Station. The current building was commenced in 1929 is six storeys and of Gothic style. More recent additions of apartments have added another seven storeys to the building.

My first job, when 16 years old, after finishing the Leaving Certificate, was at 67 York Street with the architect Aaron Bolot. I remember my first job interview well, as sitting opposite Mr Bolot. I thought he must have been in his 70s, however on checking recently he was only 60, such is the perception of the young. The Royal Australian Institute of Architects have recognised his excellent work since the 1930s in an annual architecture award – the Aaron Bolot Residential Architecture Multiple Housing Award.

Young Robert looking dapper in a suit on his way to work in the city at 17 years of age. (Robert Wheeler)

Aaron Bolot's work was mostly in the Eastern Suburbs at Potts Point, Double Bay, Point Piper and Bondi Junction, as well as Hunters Hill. I remember working on some town houses in Rosemont Ave, Edgecliff. It was considered one of Sydney's most attractive streets in the 1960s. The proposed town houses were considerably ahead of their time. Locally, Aaron Bolot designed the 1936 addition to the Camden AH&I Society Hall.

Standing in Wynyard Park, which was only a half a block away from where I worked brought back same fond memories. I was one of three who worked in his office. Being the youngest I was the office boy who was sent on messages, which was good fun. The best being going to the Australia Hotel in Martin Place to have all the office typing done. Sadly, the hotel was demolished for the MLC building.

Waiting for the typing I was introduced to the National Trust as they had all the recent leaflets of the Trust's excursions by the Women's Committee of the National Trust. This led me to join the Junior Group of the National Trust and the many amazing trips that they organised, as well as meeting Margaret and getting married. The best trip was flying to Lord Howe Island on one of the last flights of the flying boats from Rose Bay.

One of Sydney's most significant landmarks was only a few buildings from

Camden Show Hall brick frontage designed by Sydney architect Aaron Bolot in 1936. 191-195 Argyle Street Camden in 2008 (Camden Images Past and Present/P Mylrea)

where I worked, ie the AWA tower. It was the tallest building in Sydney until the AMP building was built at Circular Quay. In my early teenage years when you came to Sydney the aim was to go up to its observation deck to view Sydney Harbour out to the Eastern Suburbs, without any obstructions.

Standing in Wynyard Park I noticed that there was a gap created by the demolition of the Menzies Hotel. Another Sydney landmark gone.

After a year of travelling on buses, an hour and quarter each way, plus travelling to UNSW (one afternoon and one night) I looked for a job closer to home. This turned out to be at Edgecliff with the architects, McConnell, Smith and Johnson Their offices were at the old Grammar School. Still the office boy. Now had a car so my travelling was all around Sydney. Travelling from home to university was under half an hour.

My first visit to Edgecliff by train was in early 2015, doing a National Trust Garden visit at Darling Point, the highlight being visiting Thomas Mitchell's 'Carthona' on the point. However, on returning to Edgecliff railway station I realised that my desk at McConnell, Smith and Johnson was probably where I was sitting on the railway platform, the old school being demolished for the railway and the station was where the school had been.

Another amazing memory, as well as finding another part of our heritage had been demolished.

Mother's Day at Belgenny Farm 2017

Anne McIntosh

Mother's Day was 14 May and Belgenny Farm welcomed more than 1500 visitors, including many children, to treat Mum with food and gift stores among the historic buildings. Despite threatening clouds, the rain held off until late afternoon. This year's most popular events and performers included an opportunity to milk a cow, the working dog show, a reptile demonstration and Gold Creek re-enactments who brought horses and riders kitted out as WW1 Australian Light Horse.

If you missed this opportunity to experience the magnificent setting and buildings of the Macarthur's historic property, there are other up coming events.

Replica Australian light horse waits in a Belgenny stable (Anne McIntosh)

Volunteers share a yarn in front of a milking machine display in a model dairy. (Anne McIntosh)

A visitor to Camden

Anne McIntosh

A presentation at the Camden Historical Society in Heritage Week May 2017

I moved to Elderslie in Nov 2015. Why did I choose Elderslie? Well, I didn't. My parents wanted me to move nearer to members of my family. My mother looked at many houses. My parents chose the house that I am currently living in. … Fortunately, I like it.

That might be the end of this presentation, but when I thought about my life, I realised that over a long period I have visited this area for many reasons. None are remarkable, but these recollections may remind people of how and when non-residents visit the area.

I grew up in Eastwood, a red brick, red roofed suburb, north of the city.
As a child, I know that we went to the Rotolactor at least once, and the family also had picnics at Warragamba Dam.

In early high school, I came to Teen Ranch, Cobbitty with a school friend. Apart from contempt for the horse that I was given – it was a plodder – my memories are vague. But we did have a good time. I also visited El Caballo Blanco at some stage, probably with a school friend.

In Year 10 history, my class was taken on an excursion that included a long bus trip to a private colonial home in a very traditional style - sandstone, with a veranda at the front, a cellar underground and two wings at the back for the kitchen, bathroom and servants' quarters. There was a railway line directly behind the back garden.

I did not think about that excursion again until a friend bought a Victorian Regency house near Menangle called 'the Pines'. He was eager to show it to me. When I visited, I was troubled by a familiarity that was inexplicable. This haunted me. It was a few weeks before I realised that my friends's new home was the house I'd been shown on that excursion about 30 years earlier.

In my last two years of high school, I went to James Ruse Agricultural School. My friends included a boy whose family was keen on rally driving. He would drive a few of us home in his red Renault, scrunched around the roll bar. When a school car rally was organised, David asked me to navigate and spot. It was a fabulous day with a number of picnic and pub stops.

There were drink driving regulations at that time, but I don't think there were on-street breathalysers. Many of the drivers, most still on their Ps had a beer at lunch, and another on the way home. We were more concerned about the 18 year old restrictions on pub entry and alcohol purchases than the blood alcohol limit. Among the locations on this trip were Bents Basin, the Caltex globe, and Thirlmere Lake, a busy picnic ground for families. The water lapped against a rock wall, children played in clear water on a sandy base and people launched boats from a ramp. I don't recall passing through Camden, so we must have circled around the town.

On an agriculture excursion we visited the university farm at Badgery's Creek, a large dairy on Northern Road and Roseneath Stud in Cobbitty, where we had the opportunity to watch as a mare dressed in her 'slippers' was 'teased' by a pony, before completion of the task by the chosen thoroughbred stallion. Fascinated and embarrassed, one of my class mates tapped me on the shoulder and whispered in my ear, "I've got one like that." He wasn't talking about slippers, and was amused by my expression as I moved away.

I loved agriculture and was relieved when I got the mark to do my first preference degree – veterinary science at the University of Sydney.
As a first year vet student, you were required to travel to the University Farms (Werombi Road) every Friday in third semester. We shared the driving. It was a long day, getting picked up around 6.30am and then driving out along the Hume Highway. There was no expressway; we passed through Rhodes, the 'meccano set', Liverpool and along Camden Valley Way. The boys were excited to pass Oran Park Raceway.

On these days 'in the country', we were introduced to animal husbandry and other rural trades – milking cows, dehorning cattle, looking at pastures, butchering a sheep, picking up horses' hooves, sexing chickens and a range of other farm tasks. We practised holding rabbits and guinea pigs. This experience was designed to fill knowledge gaps for those with only single industry knowledge, or no agricultural experience.

We ate with the fifth year students in the dining room at Nepean Hall, paying what we thought was an outrageous $4 for the hot midday meal. We watched the older students in their overalls and surgical greens, with awe. They seemed incredibly sophisticated and knowledgeable.

Every year during autumn, the final year students would organise BarBGrog on a Saturday. Students from agriculture and vet science travelled out from Sydney with copious quantities of beer and a swag in the car boot. In an

Aerial view of the Sydney University Farms at Cobbitty in 2008. Werombi Road centre right of image. (CIPP/P Mylrea)

open area behind some pine trees near the first bend on the road heading into Cobbitty from Werombi Road, a series of crazy and gross competitive events involving farm equipment, veterinary clothing, hay bales, offal, mud and faeces would be organised. Loud Cold Chisel and Midnight Oil music blared from a ute, and there were copious quantities of beer, frequently skulled.

The party went through the night at Nepean Hall on Werombi Road, with celebrations and fireworks around a bonfire beside the oval. I have limited memories of the evening events - that may relate to the passage of time, or perhaps the consumption of wine.

There was limited space in the three common rooms. Some students pitched tents, others slept in swags in the back of utes. You could shelter under cover on the road outside the library. It was cold, damp and uncomfortable at 3am. I do remember waking up covered in dew, taking a torch and heading for the residential building only to find it had been locked. It was very cold behind a tree on the edge of a foggy oval.

After four years on campus in Camperdown, it was time to spend a year at Nepean Hall. It was 1987 and Dr Liz Kernohan managed the university farms, Dr Tony English taught bovine practice and legends abounded about

Bob Love, who was an expert on pig husbandry. We studied in an inadequate and uncomfortable lecture theatre opposite the equine centre. There was so much to be learnt before final exams in surgery, clinical pathology and medicine.

On the university farms and around Camden, there were opportunities to develop and refine our practical skills - we practised pregnancy testing of cattle, repositioning calves in 'artificial uteruses', watched artificial insemination of sheep and cattle, and did post-mortems on animals otherwise destined for the knackers.

Students visited farms with resident vets and interns consulting with hobby farmers, pony clubbers, pacing trainers, and a few dairy farmers. We assisted in the small animal clinic. At that time, the university equine centre was a leading facility and horses were referred by vets across the state - we were able to watch top-line equine surgery on well-known racehorses. One very memorable day, the university anaesthetised a tiger for a travelling circus and cleaned its teeth, ears and eyes. Students also attended shows and race meetings to check animals before they competed.

A few years later, my father's workplace, the Plant Breeding Institute (PBI) at Castle Hill, sold their research farm for development. Because they work with cereal diseases such as rusts and smuts, they needed land in a non-grain growing area. As a research facility of the University of Sydney, the PBI was consolidated with other university farms and relocated to Camden. The "new PBI" was built on the site, where Bar-B-Grog had been held. A new complex with innovative and sophisticated glass houses was constructed on the site.

My parents searched for a house close to my father's workplace. It was almost a year before they settled on five acres at Theresa Park. They moved there in the early 1990s, a few years after I graduated, and have lived in the same house since that time. My youngest brother was still in primary school and from Cobbitty School, he went to Macarthur Anglican, then in Narellan. He still lives locally.

I moved house in early December 2015. In Woolworths late one evening during my first week, I heard a supervisor talking to another staff member. They were discussing how Camden was changing. The supervisor said, "It's not the same as it used to be. I cannot believe it, but more than five people came through the store today, and I'd swear I've never seen them before. I definitely didn't know their names." I am sure that in the past year, this has become increasingly common for everyone born and raised in Camden!

Sculptures, Monuments and Outdoor Cultural Material project

Sandra Dodds

In 1999 my father, Doug Dodds and I surveyed all of the monuments in the Camden area on behalf of the Camden Historical Society as part of the Sculptures, Monuments and Outdoor Cultural Material project.

The project was organised by the Australian Institute for the Conservation of Cultural Material in conjunction with the Art Gallery of NSW and the University of Western Sydney (now Western Sydney University). The project involved documenting the materials, dimensions, condition, significance, inscriptions and researching the history of each monument.

Photographs of the monuments were also part of the documentation process and they were enlarged and used for an exhibition at the Camden Museum. As part of the opening day events for the monuments exhibition I arranged for a local stone mason to provide a demonstration of various techniques.

The demonstration and talk proved to be of great interest to Museum visitors and complemented the exhibition. The information about the monuments has been made accessible on the National Library of Australia Trove website. Since the completion of the project, one of the drinking fountains has been repaired.

The completed reports about the monuments are in the Museum library.

Anderson Drinking Fountain 1976 located in Macarthur Park (S Dodds)

The Heath Years at Windamere, Cobbitty

Lenore Heath

This article was based on original notes written by Ella Heath and developed by Lenore Heath, daughter of Jeffrey and Ella Heath.

Ben Heath was born in England in 1887 and migrated to Australia in the early 1900s, marrying Alice Ward in Sydney in 1915. He served in the Australian Flying Corps in the First World War. On 3 December 1925 Ben and his wife Alice bought Cobbitty Park from the estate of Frederick Myers for £2050. It was a 200 acre farm extending from Cobbitty Bridge towards Cobbitty, and fronting the Nepean River. The sale of the estate had been advertised in the 'Camden News' and 'The Sydney Morning Herald' (SMH) in September and October 1925.

Windamere Guesthouse at Cobbitty (L Heath)

W Larkin has received instructions From the Executors of the Will of the late Mr F Myers to sell at his sale room, Camden on Tuesday, 8th October, at 1.30 *the above properties, namely: - 'Cobbitty Park' close to Cobbitty School, Post Office, etc, 4 miles from Camden. Area 199 acres, 3 rd, 3 per., with extensive frontage to Nepean River. All cleared, every acre arable land, above 140 now under cultivation, growing excellent maize, oats, wheat etc., above 10 acres orange and peach orchard. Comfortable cottage, barns, corn sheds, vehicle sheds and all necessary improvements.* ('Camden News', 17 September, 24 September and 1 October 1925, SMH 26 September 1925)

When they first arrived, Ben and Alice with their four children, Rodney (Rod), Jeffrey (Jeff), Joan and Dorothy and Ben's mother Susan Heath, lived in the old stone Cobbitty Park farmhouse. The Heaths had sold their business interests in Sydney, including a mechanical garage, Shell Oil Company agency, and private bus company. They had run the first daily bus service to the Blue Mountains using a 24-seater charabanc.

Ben was trained as an engineer's fitter and possessed mechanical skills, however he also had knowledge of, and experience in, the hospitality industry. His father had been publican in England and, prior to settling in Aus-

Relaxing on the verandah at Windamere Guesthouse at Cobbitty (L Heath)

tralia, Ben had worked for many years as a servant and steward on passenger ships.

The St Paul's Church journal of November 1925, welcomed the Heath family to Cobbitty. The school had been closed for a year because of insufficient numbers. The Heath children made up the required numbers for the school to reopen. From Jeff's memory the other children were: Doreen Malcolm; Lorna McIntosh; Dorcas McMinn, Tommy Holz; Keith and Kathleen Thorn; Eric and Ray Vicary and possibly Marjorie Vicary. Mrs Somers was the teacher and two of her children, Keith and Margaret, helped to swell the numbers. Miss Colty Wales followed Mrs Somers as teacher. Rod Heath later won the first bursary from Cobbitty School to Hurlstone Agricultural School, with the undoubted help of the wonderful Miss Wales.

The property deeds indicate Ben sold some of the property to Ernest Edgar Wyatt of Cobbitty in 1926. Ben's 1926 advertisements for the sale of farm animals, machinery and tools do not refer to "Windamere"; it is first mentioned in a 1927 advertisement.

Cobbitty. Saturday, May 22. Sale of cattle, poultry, machinery, seed wheat, tools and sundries. W LARKIN has received instructions from Mr B Heath to sell at Cobbitty, on Saturday, 22nd May, at 1.30pm, 5 Good Milking and Springing Cows; 45 Pairs Young W L Hens; 6 Hawkesbury College W L Roosters; 7 ½ Horse Power, Portable Meadowbank Engine; 2 Ton 4 speed International Truck, purchased new in January 1924 , and done very little running; 6 feet Reaper and Binder; Corn Sheller and Husker; Bentall Corn Grinder; Martin Corn Planter; w Disc Ploughs; Garden 1 horse Cultivator; 20 bags Florence Seed Wheat; Lot Sundry Tools and accessories. THE WHOLE of above plant is in first class order and is only being sold as the owner has disposed of part of his property. Sale: - Saturday, May 22, 1926. ('Camden News', 6 May 1926)

For Sale. – Good farm implements, practically new: - 4 disc Sunrise plough, suit team or tractor; Sunshine 10 disc harrower; Sunshine 5 ft harvester; Massey 11 disc seed drill; 3 HP Sunshine Engine; Ford late 1925 model. Inspection invited, any reasonable offer will be accepted. Apply Mr Ben Heath. 'Phone 132 Camden. 'Windamere', Cobbitty. ('Camden News', 7 July 1927)

Around 1927, the Windamere guest house was built and the whole estate advertised as a health and holiday resort. The house was built of weatherboard and fibro and had 28 rooms including bathrooms and a tiled kitchen.

A picnic at Windamere at Cobbitty. From left Jeff Heath, Ben Heath feeding a pet dog, a guest and Joan Heath patting dog, Nicky. (L Heath)

It had a telephone service with the number Camden 132. The property had one mile deep river frontage. Extensions were later added by Mark "One Nail" Jensen and Alva George. Extra buildings included a club house and kiosk.

Cobbitty. –Windamere, New Guest House, 100 acres, Nepean River Frontage, electric light throughout. Own golf links, tennis court, swimming, shooting, dance and lounge rooms. Cuisine unsurpassable. Tariff £2/12/6 weekly, 10/6 per day. Our cars meet trains Camden. Fare 3/-. 'Phone, Camden 132 or write B Heath. (SMH, 19 February, 16 and 27 April 1927)

Ben installed the first electricity plant in the Cobbitty/Camden area, buying the electric generator from the Kings Cross Theatre in Sydney. A 3½ horsepower engine drove the generator which was installed by electrician, Jeff Durant. Prior to this they used kerosene lights.

Ben also built the first tennis court in the area, fenced with fitted steel poles to house electric lights. Another first in the area was an American Maytag washing machine driven by a two-stroke engine. This was of course for the mountains of washing created by the guest house. There was a backyard toilet with the first sewerage system in the area. On the property were grazing paddocks, crops, flower and vegetable gardens, a small orchard, a 9-hole golf course and a polo ground. Light aircraft could land on the grounds. Animals included horses (for farm work, riding and polo) and half a dozen dairy cows. The Heaths used a horse drawn plough and Jeff broke in two Clydesdales named Darby and Joan.

During the late 1920s and the 1930s in the carefree days before the Second World War, hundreds of people had many happy holidays at Windamere. Guests were met at Camden Railway Station and transferred to Windamere by car. Visitors also came by bus or their own cars. Activities included, golf, tennis, table tennis, billiards, horse riding, polo, boating, swimming and fishing at the Nepean River, shooting, car trips and entertainment such as music (with an electric gramophone and a resident pianist) and dancing. Initially the Heaths employed a cook and an assistant. However Alice was an excellent cook and took over as cook and hostess. As the children got older, the running of Windamere became a family affair, with Jeff operating a horse riding school and all the Heath children assisting with various jobs. In their spare time the children particularly enjoyed horse riding and swimming at the river. When it was quiet Jeff would sit by the river and watch for platypuses.

Running a guesthouse involved purchasing large quantities of supplies. Every day, Jackie Noakes brought the mail to Cobbitty Post Office on his BSA motorcycle. Camden butcher Ray Boardman delivered meat, while Clifton Brothers and F C Whiteman & Son delivered groceries. In a very old truck, Charlie Fuller would supply fruit and vegetables. As a young adult Jeff used drive to Sydney to buy some supplies from the food markets.

Entries in a surviving visitors' book start in April 1930, the first name being that of renowned Australian artist George Lambert, who sadly died of a heart attack at Windamere in late May 1930. The visitors' comments highlight that Windamere provided a venue for an enjoyable holiday for a couple of days to many weeks. Some overseas competitive polo players stayed for months. For some guests it was a quiet relaxing time while others became involved in more exhilarating activities.

George Lambert: "A nice place and my horses like it too."
Margaret Jonson: "Days of sweet idleness."
Netta Stark: "Hectic time."
Mr & Mrs E H Horton: "Wonderful and exhilarating climate – beautiful scenery, free and happy home with all comforts – sorry to go."

Ben advertised the guest house in the Sydney Morning Herald from 1927 until 1941.

Cobbitty – Windamere. 100 acres, Nepean River frontage, tennis, boats,

Guests outside Windamere at Cobbitty ready for a swim in the Nepean River (L Heath)

swimming, riding shooting, dance, lounge rooms, billiards, excellent cuisine. Tariff £2/18/6 week, 12/6 day. Phone Camden 132; or write B Heath. Car meets trains, Camden. (SMH, 5 October 1929)

Cobbitty. Windamere for enjoyable holiday. Tennis, riding, polo, swimming, excellent table, lovely surroundings. Electric light, sewerage. £2/10/ weekly. 10/6 day. B Heath. Phone Camden 132. (SMH, 24 February 1940)

Cobbitty. Windamere. Excellent accommodation and cuisine. Sewerage, electric light, tennis, riding, swimming, farm produce. £2/10/ weekly, 10/6s a day. Phone Camden 132 B Heath. (SMH, 17 May 1941)

In the early 1930s, polo commenced at Windamere, with Curtis Skene, son of Bob Skene (world famous polo player of the time), and the Ashton brothers (from the circus family) being the instigators. Other players included Max Wheatley; John, David and Rupert Downes; and Lance Skewthorpe, a rough rider. Jeff Heath, who was an excellent horseman, played when they needed him to make up the numbers. The ground became the home of the Australian Polo Club.

Polo was attended by many VIPs from Sydney, amongst whom was Sir Philip Game, the Governor of NSW. George McLeod, Consul General of Siam (now Thailand), also attended. The prestigious Dudley Cup was held at Windamere.

Jeff's horse riding skills went up a notch when he received trick riding tuition from a Worth's Circus horse trainer. In 1932 there were insufficient numbers to form the Camden Light Horse troop of 1st/21st Light Horse. So, at the request of Captain Edward Macarthur Onslow, Jeff Heath joined at the age of 15.

Ben and Alice became involved in the Cobbitty/Camden community.

Cobbitty. On Saturday evening a dance and euchre party in aid of the local school tennis club, was given by Mr and Mrs B Heath, at their club house, "Windamere", Cobbitty. Despite the inclemency of the weather about one hundred people attended and spent an enjoyable evening dancing to music supplied by Mr Heath's electric gramophone. Mr W Chittick made an efficient MC. The euchre tournament was won by Miss Vicary and Mr W Moore. During supper, which was provided by the ladies of Cobbitty, and dispensed by Mrs Heath, assisted by Mesdames L Sommer and T Holz, Mr Sommer thanked Mr and Mrs Heath for the enjoyable evening they had spent at their new club house. ('Camden News', 16 October 1930).

About once a month in the 1930s, wonderful dances and suppers were held in Cobbitty Hall (called "the ballroom"), music being provided by Mrs Huthnance and her son Lionel. In 1932, amongst celebrations for the inauguration of the ABC radio station, an Australian song competition was held. It was won by the resident Windamere pianist Pat Dunlop, with the song "Croajing Along".

In order to bring in more income Ben and Alice expanded the business to include boarders. They also catered for day visitors from the local and surrounding areas.

'Windamere', Cobbitty. An enjoyable afternoon always assured. Golf, Tennis, Swimming, Lawn Games, Clock Gold etc, with an excellent Afternoon Tea provided on Wednesdays, Saturdays and Sundays, 2/- inclusive. Whole day with Luncheon, Afternoon Tea and Dinner, 6/-. Good riding Horses can be acquired at moderate rates. Entertain your friends at 'Windamere', Cobbitty, B Heath, Proprietor. ('Camden News', 25 March 1937)

In the late 1930s, prior to the outbreak of the Second World War, Ben made

Jeff Heath (second from left) at Windamere at Cobbitty conducting his riding school for his guests. (L Heath)

two trips to the Far East as Chief Purser on the SS Taiping of the Australian Oriental Line. Alice and Jeff were left in charge of Windamere.

On 14 February 1942 one of the last major events took place at Windamere. Jeffrey Heath married Ella Reid at St Paul's, Cobbitty and the reception was held at Windamere. Jeff and Ella had known each other since their childhood days in Sydney.

The Depression and the Second World War had an impact on visitor numbers and hence the prosperity of Windamere. In 1937 Ben had attempted to sell Windamere as a whole property. He was unsuccessful, and later subdivided the 100 acres into three properties and advertised them for sale.

Auction sale at Camden. Tuesday 30th March, 1937, at 1.30pm. 'Windamere', Cobbitty, On Account of Mr B Heath. The favourably known and well-established Guest House, 'Windamere', Cobbitty, on the Nepean River, with a beautiful parklike area of nearly 100 acres, including the Australian Polo Club's Ground, Tennis Courts, Golf Links and grazing paddocks, Small orchard, etc. The Guest House is built of weatherboard and fibro, and contains 28 rooms, inclusive of, bathrooms and tiled kitchen, hot and cold water. Wired throughout, Four Unit Septic System. Abundance of water laid on everywhere. Tastefully laid out grounds of ornamental trees and lawns. Continuous telephone service. Regulation dairy and cow bails, numerous garages, stables, and feed rooms. The property is in perfect order. The house contains every modern convenience. It is beautifully situated with long river frontage and close to the glorious Brownlow Hill Estate. This property should be inspected to be appreciated, and certainly is a wonderful opportunity to secure a most popular Guest House and Sports Ground. William Inglis & Son Pty Limited have received instructions to sell the above property by Auction, at their Camden rooms, as above. 28 O'Connell Street, Sydney, and Camden.* (Camden News, 18 March 1937 and SMH, 20 March 1937)

Camden. Tuesday, 20th February at 1 o'clock. To Guest House Proprietors, Market Gardeners, Agriculturists and Others. Important subdivision sale of Nepean River Frontage Property at Cobbitty. William Inglis & Son Pty Limited, have received instructions from MR B Heath to sell at Camden on the above date at 1 o'clock 3 choice Nepean River frontage blocks at Cobbitty comprising:- LOT 1 Area about 36 acres 16 per. All thoroughly cleared with Established Guest House of 28 Rooms, Electric Light, Telephone, Sewerage, Hot and Cold Water, Septic System, Garages, Stables, Bails, etc in perfect order. LOT 2 Area about 38 acres, 2 rds, 4 per. All cleared rich loamy soil and embraces The Australian Polo Grounds. Lot 3 Area 25 acres 1 rd. 20 per. All cleared and ideal Agricultural land. This Sales offer a wonderful opportunity to persons in search of Guest House and intense cultivation land with deep fresh water frontages. The owner is determined to sell as he is unable to manage the property. (Camden News, 8 February 1940; SMH 10 February 1940; SMH 17 February 1940)

Ben sold to Malcolm Robsart MacCulloch and Nellie Campbell MacCulloch in November 1941; to Edward Robert MacCulloch and Enid Rita MacCulloch in December 1941; and to Percy George Tait, in March 1942.

Jeff Heath had enlisted in the RAAF in December 1941 and Rod was working elsewhere in NSW as a veterinarian. Following the final sale of Windamere, Ben put his age down and enlisted as a private in the Australian Army in July 1942 but was discharged on 7 September 1942; he was actually 54 and in the First World War had been discharged due to an irritable heart. In October 1942 he was one of the many thousands of Australian civilians, from 15 years old to around 70, who joined the US Army Small Ships Section, South West Pacific Area. He served until August 1943 and twice met Jeff who was serving with No. 30 Squadron, once at Port Moresby and once at Milne Bay. Although it was at the height of the Japanese invasion, these were

Guests on the front steps of Windamere at Cobbitty (L Heath)

unusual and happy occasions for them both. Dorothy Heath and Joan Mason (nee Heath) both served in the Women's Auxiliary Australian Air Force (WAAAF).

Following the end of the Second World War, Ben and Alice Heath moved several times before settling at Erina on the Central Coast. In 1952, Jeff and Ella Heath and their family returned to the Camden area. They lived in Wilkinson Street, Elderslie, with Jeff working at the Camden Milk Depot, and Ella working at the Camden News office then later as a proof-reader for the Campbelltown Ingleburn News.

The Heath years at Cobbitty were a time of happiness, adventure and achievement.

"WINDAMERE"
COBBITTY, N.S.W.

The popular guest house farm, ideally situated in a charming and historic old District. Scenery and Climate Unrivalled. Forty Miles from Sydney.

B. HEATH, Proprietor.   'Phone: Camden 132.

100 Acres of Park Lands, One Mile Nepean River Frontage. Tennis, Golf Links, 9 Hole, Putting Green; Polo Ground; Riding School; Swimming. Lounge and Dance Rooms. Electric Light, Billiards, Player, Wireless, Gramophone. Lock-up Garages.
CUISINE UNSURPASSABLE.

TARIFF: From £2/10/- per week; 10/6 per Day.

Motorists and Tourists Specially Catered for.
Own Car Meets Trains at Camden.   Fare, 3/-.

Write or 'phone **B. HEATH, Camden 132.** Continuous Service.

CAMDEN HISTORY

Journal of the Camden Historical Society

March 2018 Volume 4 Number 5

CAMDEN HISTORY
Journal of the Camden Historical Society Inc.
ISSN 1445-1549
Editor: Dr Ian Willis

Management Committee
President: Dr Ian Willis
Vice Presidents: John Wrigley OAM, Cathey Shepherd
Secretary: Lee Stratton
Treasurer: Dawn Williams
Immediate Past President: Bob Lester
General Committee: Sharon Greene   Rene Rem
                   Julie Wrigley   Robert Wheeler
                   Cathey Shepherd Stephanie Trenfield
Honorary Solicitors: Vince Barrett

Society contact:
P.O. Box 566, Camden, NSW 2570.   Online <http://www.camdenhistory.org.au>

Meetings
Meetings are held at 7.30 p.m. on the second Wednesday of the month except in January. They are held in the Museum. Visitors are always welcome.

Museum
The Museum is located at 40 John Street, Camden, phone 4655 3400 or 46559210. It is open Thursday to Sunday 11 a.m. to 4 p.m., except at Christmas. Visits by schools and groups are encouraged. Please contact the Museum to make arrangements. Entry is free.

Camden History, Journal of the Camden Historical Society Inc
The Journal is published in March and September each year. The Editor would be pleased to receive articles broadly covering the history of the Camden district. Correspondence can be sent to the Society's postal address. The views expressed by authors in journal articles are solely those of the authors and not necessarily endorsed by the Camden Historical Society.

Donations
Donations made to the Society are tax deductible. The accredited value of objects donated to the Society are eligible for tax deduction.

Front Cover: Mid-20th century modernism shines through in Laura Jane's kitchen in the ever popular pink of the period. (LJA)

Back Cover: Some local identities at the Cobbitty 130 Anniversary Celebrations in 2016 at the St Pauls Anglican Church Hall LtoR Donald Howard, John Burge, Jill Lummis, Joyce Thorn OAM, Ngaire Thorn (Anne McIntosh, 2016)

CAMDEN HISTORY

Journal of the Camden Historical Society Inc.

Contents

Dr Peter Mylrea OAM	
Ian Willis	215
John Wrigley	218
Janice Johnson	222
John Wrigley	
A vintage girl in a modern world,	
why a 21st century girl loves living a 1950s life	226
Laura Jane Aulsebrook	
Archaeology and Elderslie Railway Station	232
Andrew Lundy	
John and Nona Souter, the story	235
Tony Souter	
Camden and Wollondilly LGA Rivalry, a view	242
Lynette Styles	

Dr Peter Mylrea OAM

Ian Willis

The founder of this journal and one of its most prolific authors was Dr Peter Mylrea. Peter was a stalwart of the Camden Historical Society over many years and initiated a number of firsts for the society.

Apart from starting this journal, he was instrumental in puting the society's photograph collection online, and archiving the society's map collection.

Peter wrote many articles for the society and amonst the titles were:

PJ Mylrea, Camden District, A History to the 1840s. Camden: CHS, 2002.

Peter Mylrea, Narellan, Two Centuries of Growth, 1810-2010. Camden: CHS, 2011.

Peter Mylrea, Belgenny Farm, Camden. Camden: BFT, 2000.

Peter Mylrea, Belgenny Farm, 1805-1835, The Early Years of the Macarthurs at Camden. Camden, BFT & CHS, 2001.

Pauline Downing, Peter Hayward, Peter Mylrea, Cathey Shepherd, Robert Wheeler, Camden School of Arts - a history : 1850s - 1930s. [Camden, New South Wales] : Camden Historical Society, 2016

Camden History Journal

Volume One
Dick Nixon & Peter Mylrea. 'The telephone comes to Camden', 104-115
Peter Mylrea, 'Bridges crossing the Nepean River at Camden', 183-192
Peter Mylrea, 'Camden Historical Society – Its first twenty five years', 3-11
Peter Mylrea, 'Military Activities in Camden in the late 1800s', 206-220
Peter Mylrea, 'Some photographers of Camden', 243-256
Peter Mylrea, 'Origin of the name Mount Annan', 123-124

Volume Two
Mylrea, Peter, 'Camden Fire Brigade', p. 313
Mylrea, Peter, 'Camden-Campbelltown Railway', p. 254
Mylrea, Peter, 'Henry Pollock Reeves, A Significant Camden Man', p.354
Mylrea, PJ, 'A History of Dairy Farming in the Camden District', p.144

Dr Peter Mylrea OAM (CHS)

Mylrea, PJ, 'A Revised Assessment of the Location of Mount Taurus', p.405
Mylrea, PJ, 'Gas and Electricity in Camden', p.139
Mylrea, PJ, 'The Birth, Growth and Demise of Picture Theatres in Camden', p.52
Mylrea, PJ, 'The Centenary of the Royal Foresters' Hall' , p.204
Mylrea, PJ, '125-147 Argyle Street, Camden', p.223
Mylrea, PJ, 'Swimming in the Nepean River at Camden', p.3

Volume Three
Mylrea, Peter, 'Local Government, Camden Municipality and Nepean Shire, p.118.
Mylrea, Peter, 'Advertisements in the Camden News 1896-1914', p.42.
Mylrea, Peter, 'An 1843 Map of Camden', p.61.
Mylrea, Peter, 'Development of Law Courts in Cawdor, Picton and Camden', p.139
Mylrea, Peter, 'European Explorers in the Camden Region', p.90.
Mylrea, Peter, 'Macarthurs Village of Camden', p. 23.
Mylrea, Peter, 'The Hassall Family as Land Owners in Cobbitty', p.248
Mylrea, Peter, 'The Original Village of Cawdor', p. 137
Mylrea, Peter, 'Water and Sewerage in Camden', p. 7
Mylrea, Peter, 'Crown Land and the Wild Cattle of the Cowpasture Plains', p.224

It would not be well known that Peter Mylrea also published other work associated with his employment as a veterinary pathologist. Some of these included:

PJ Mylrea & Division of Information Services, *Raising dairy calves*. Sydney: Dept of Agriculture, 1958.

G.L. McClymont and P.J. Mylrea, *Feeding for milk production* . Glenfield, Veterinary Research Station, Dept of Agriculture, 1958.

P.J. Mylrea and D.W. Dredge, *Glenfield Veterinary Research Station : the physical structure 1916-1990*. Campbelltown, NSW : Campbelltown and Airds Historical Society Inc., 2002.

H. Scott-Orr & P.J. Mylrea (eds), NSW exotic animal disease control manual. Sydney : Dept. of Agriculture, New South Wales, 1987.

M G Smeal, I K Hotson, P J Mylrea, A R Jackson, H C Kirton, 'Studies on nematode infections of beef cattle in New South Wales', Jan 1978, *Australian Veterinary Journal*.

P J Mylrea & I K Hotson, 'Serum pepsinogen and the diagnosis of bovine ostertagiasis', Sep 1969, *British Veterinary Journal*.

PJ Mylrea, RJT Hoare, P Colquhoun, IJ Links, RJ Richards, M Barton, 'The NSW Mastitis Control Program'. *Australian Veterinary Journal*, Nov 1977, Vol 53, Iss 11, 534-537.

Mylrea PJ. 'The laboratory diagnosis of diseases in livestock in New South Wales:1890 to 1947'. *Australian Veterinary Journal*, 66:114-117. 1989

Mylrea PJ. 'Professional activities at the Glenfield Veterinary Research Station 1929-1959'. *Australian Veterinary History Record* no. 33:14-19. 2002.

Mylrea PJ and Dredge D. 'Professional activities at the Glenfield Veterinary Research Station 1959-1990'. *Australian Veterinary History Record* no. 34:7-12. 2002.

PJ Mylrea, *NSW Department of Agriculture:* Veterinary Laboratory Service. (2002)Online @ http://sydney.edu.au/vetscience/avhs/milestones/NSW_labs.pdf .

Peter Mylrea OAM

John Wrigley

Dr Peter James Mylrea (1928 - 2018) passed away at Camden Hospital on 3 January 2018 after a short illness.

Peter had a distinguished career in agriculture. He graduated in Veterinary Science from Sydney University in 1951 and later obtained his MVSc from the University of Queensland and his PhD degree from Sydney University. He spent his professional career of 37 years in the NSW Department of Agriculture, serving in different parts of the State. His work covered many aspects of the investigation and control of animal disease, both in the field and in the laboratory.

He was at one time Director of Veterinary Research located at the Veterinary Research Station at Glenfield. Later he was appointed to the position of Chief of the Division of Animal Health, from which he retired in 1988. Upon his retirement Peter was asked to write a history of the Department of Agriculture. He completed this and the result was the book *In the Service of Agriculture. A Centennial History of the New South Wales Department of Agri-*

culture 1890 -1990 published by NSW Agriculture and Fisheries in 1990.

Peter left clear directions with his family regarding what he wanted to happen today and what he did not want. We expected no less of him. The only flaw in his customary careful planning was that in his speed of departure, he omitted to give me any such instructions.

So, accordingly I feel under no such restrictions regarding modesty or brevity. I will choose to be brief but there are a number of things that should be said about him at this celebration of his life. We all know what an intensely private person he was and it is typical that he would be uncomfortable with us recalling publicly all the amazing things he did for the town of Camden.

Peter joined the Historical Society in 1994 and became its archivist in 1996. He made it very clear to the society that he was not at all interested in taking office or attending committee meetings. He drew a clear line between work career and his retirement activities.

We were happy to have him on his terms because he then put in years of volunteer work on the history of our district. Peter developed his computer skills to greatly enhance the historical knowledge of the Camden district. He initiated the museum computer catalogue. This computer cataloguing involved many months of work and continued for years.

When he started with the society there were no computers in the museum and none of the catalogue was digitised. While not taking office beyond agreeing to be called the archivist, he had a skill in gathering like-minded people to his projects.

Peter always had to have a project and in fact he had many. I suspect that Margaret has had a lifetime of keeping up with and supporting Peter's projects. So I hope it has been interesting for you Margaret as Peter always had such an inquiring mind and a natural curiosity combined with a great energy to achieve things.

So there were numerous people who worked with him on these many projects and publications. Julie and I were his proof-readers and improvers. He also worked with Ian Willis, Cathey Shepherd, members of ADFAS, the people from here at Belgenny Farm, Robert Wheeler, Jo Oliver and Peter Hayward

His particular interest was in the photograph collection and under his management over 2,600 photos were digitised and made available on the internet for public research and use. In those early days this meant physically taking the originals of the photos to Penrith where a large high quality scanning machine was located.

Now this scanning can be done to a high quality in-house. He catalogued the Museum's Research Reference Library and the society's extensive historic map collection. He was always interested in maps and made excursions with Robert Wheeler to historic sites to verify map records.

Peter took many photos of rural areas which were being developed for new suburbs and – to the surprise of his family - even undertook aerial flights over Camden in order to take aerial photos of the district. You can see these on the website 'Camden Images Past and Present'.

Within the family Peter was known to have a tendency to discard to the recycling bin any paperwork he decided was no longer needed and sometimes with minimal consultation! So Margaret, you can now keep magazines and papers as long as you wish without wondering what happened to them!

In 2001 Peter was the Foundation Editor of the Journal of the Camden Historical Society for its first five years and continued to be a major contributor. For the Society he wrote and published three books: *Belgenny Farm 1805-1835 Early Years of the Macarthurs at Camden* (first edition 2001, second edition 2007); *Camden District to the 1840s* (2002); and *Narellan – Two Centuries of Growth* (2011). For these books Peter spent considerable time doing original research in the Lands and Title Office in Sydney.

Some of the more-than-twenty articles he contributed to the Journal of the Historical Society were about the wild cattle of the Cowpasture plains; the original village of Cawdor; the development of law courts in the Camden area; European explorers in the Camden region; the Macarthurs' village of Camden; heritage building in Argyle Street; military activities in the late 1800s; rabbit trapping and the Camden freezing works; Camden-Campbelltown Railway; the telephone comes to Camden; water, sewerage, gas and electricity in Camden; photographers in Camden; Camden Fire Brigade; the origin of the name Mount Annan; the location of Mount Taurus; bridges crossing the Nepean River in Camden; swimming in the Nepean River; dairy farming in the Camden district; picture theatres in Camden; advertisements in the Camden News 1896-1914; the centenary of the Royal Foresters' Hall; and the history of the first twenty-five years of the Camden Historical Society.

In 2006 Peter was made a Life Member of the Camden Historical Society in recognition of his substantial contribution to heritage conservation.

The Order of Australia Medal awarded to Peter in 2010 was in recognition of his extraordinary voluntary work within the community of Camden through the Camden Historical Society and for his services to the history of veterinary science in Australia.

Peter was an active member of Australian Decorative and Fine Arts Society and in 2016 was the coordinator of the group who researched and produced a book on the history of the Camden School of Arts.

Peter had a great enthusiasm for life and a great interest in nature. He was an honorary guide at the Botanic Gardens at Mount Annan for 10 years and co-wrote the official guide booklet for the gardens. He was a member of the Friends of Belgenny Farm and was also a volunteer guide here at Belgenny and wrote the first booklet for here.

He was a keen walker and joined walking groups over the years. He was also a keen birdwatcher and kept a close eye on the birds on the Camden bike track when he and Margaret lived at Sunset Avenue in Elderslie and on the water birds on the lake at Carrington in recent years. Peter was one of nature's gentlemen and will be sadly missed by all his family and friends.

The society extends deep sympathy to his wife Margaret, daughter Annette, son Anthony and his wife Mardie and their children Rosemary and Matthew, and daughter Jillian.

John Wrigley OAM
Vice President
Camden Historical Society
10 January 2018

Janice Johnson

17 October 2017

John Wrigley

Janice Johnson came to Camden for only the last nineteen years of her life but she certainly made up for any lost time by enthusiastically throwing herself into several local organisations and managing to achieve more in this time than many others achieve in a lifetime.

I will tell you something about her amazing output of original historical research on the Camden people. But I should also remind you of the variety of Janice's interests including her productivity in the realms of horse judging, dog-showing, and embroidery.

Janice was actively involved in a wide range of community activities. She was a member of the Camden Historical Society, Camden Area Family History Society, Camden St John's Anglican Church, Camden Country Wom-

Janice Johnson author and researcher (CNA, 2012)

en's Association and the Camden Show Society. She was a skilled calligrapher and actively exhibited at the Camden Show in floral arrangements and potted plants, winning prizes year after year.

She was a keen rose grower, but once she got hooked on the various history books that she published over several years, her garden became a sacrifice to the wonderful historical discoveries that she was making and was able to tell us about. So we should look at her overgrown garden and think that if she had had a beautiful neat well-kept garden then we would not have the six or so books that she wrote and published in the last ten years.

In 2007 Janice started researching the history of the historic St John's Church cemetery. She compiled a comprehensive data base and her book *If These Gravestones Could Talk* (2010) has been consulted by many family history enthusiasts. Once she became an expert on St John's cemetery she conducted guided tours of the graveyard for visiting groups.

Janice threw herself into the Camden Historical Society and was at various times a research officer, speakers co-ordinator, photo selection committee member and also secretary and treasurer for a period. For the Society she completed seven very comprehensive 'Statements of Significance' folders which are available at the Museum for visitors to read, about items to do with World War I and also the Museum's grand piano and the Onslow uniform.

She was able to, with Dr Ian Willis, obtain a grant for some of her books. She published *The Memoirs of Obed West* in 2011; *Reflections on Old Sydney & Colonial Days* in 2012; and *Reminiscences of Early Camden* in 2013.

She was a co-author of the fourth edition of *They Worked at Camden Park*. In April 2014 the Camden Historical Society launched her book *Camden World War I Diggers 1914 to 1918*. It was a proud moment when we had a book launch in the Museum for her book *Camden World War I Diggers* launched by our then Federal Member Russell Matheson. The book drew on published letters from Camden soldiers and nurses in World War I.

She was also a co-author with Brian Burnett of a CD *Camden Unlocking the Past* (2013) and a co-author with Joy Thorn and John Burge of a book on the St Pauls Graveyard at Cobbitty. Janice's books are popular and will be of long-term benefit to future researchers. She also has a couple more publications nearly ready to go so we will see if it is possible for these to be published in the future.

One of the things that Janice cared deeply about was St. John's. She loved its serenity as a place of worship, its history, the stained glass windows which she carefully photographed for her book, and the gravestones in the cemetery. And she could remember so much of the details of the people here in her head!

With Peter Hayward (who is unfortunately in Melbourne today) Janice was writing another book about the history of St John's and we hope that will proceed. But I like to think of Janice up on a ladder here taking the photographs of the beautiful windows which we can all enjoy seeing in her book.

Janice told me that she was hoping that you would be able to conduct this service for her today Tony Galea. I would like to acknowledge the excellent support which you and the parishioners have given to her during these difficult last months.

Since 2008 Janice has been a volunteer archivist at the historic Camden Park House. She typed the extensive card catalogue of the library, which is said to be the most important private library in Australia.

I am sure that John and Edwina Macarthur-Stanham would like me to acknowledge here what a wonderful and professional job that Janice did as a volunteer in improving the archives of the Camden Park library and collection.

Over the years Janice has been a prolific columnist in The District Reporter's *Back Then* history page, contributing many articles with excellent original research which revealed aspects of Camden's history not previously published. I know the editor Lee Abrahams was grateful for Janice's support. Janice's exceptional contribution to local heritage was recognised by a Heritage Volunteer Award in April 2014 by the Heritage Council of NSW. Janice was one of the 'heritage heroes' presented with awards during a ceremony at the Justice and Police Museum.

Janice was extremely capable and had very high standards in her research work and I must admit that not all of us were able to match her expectations. She was proud of her achievements and some of us received short shrift in conversations at times. But she was kind to many people and helped a large number with their family histories.

She had a very clever skill in the museum of quietly googling a subject while we were helping a museum visitor. The visitor would then be astonished to find that Janice already had the information available about their ancestors before our conversation was finished. She could also have several websites open at the same time and instantaneously cross reference subjects of interest.

I know of no other local person who combined such computer skills, with detective-like research curiosity and an inexhaustible capacity for hard work. We are all glad to have known Janice Johnson and Camden is a better place for her time as a resident. Peace be with you.

John Wrigley OAM
Vice President
Camden Historical Society

A vintage girl in a modern world, why a 21st century girl loves living a 1950s life

Laura Jane Aulsebrook

Laura is a new member of the Camden Historical Society and has a passion for mid-20th century modernism and its fashions. Here she tells the story of what drives her enthusiasm for this period of history. (Editor)

Pastel coloured petticoats, nipped waists, full skirts, seamed stockings, hat-boxes overflowing with gloves, hats, matching bags and shoes, pearls and screw on earrings... You would be forgiven for thinking that my wardrobe was straight out of the 1950s. Well it is.

My wardrobe doesn't just look like it belongs in the 1950s, it actually came from that time period. The only difference from my wardrobe and that of a typical 1950s girl is the *when*. The girls who originally wore my wardrobe were living in the 1950s...thirty-odd years before I was even born.

There are two questions that I seem to be asked more than anything else. "*Where* do you buy your clothes?" and, "*Why?*" To me these are frustrating questions that you think that I would have perfected an answer to by now, however the recipient never seems satisfied with my rather simple answers, conversely though, if I returned the questions, they too would struggle with an answer. "I just shop at places I like" is the response.

Well I do too! In short, excluding mainstream shopping centres, I shop like any other person who likes a particular style, at shops that cater for it. The vintage clothing stores I frequent just happen to be at vintage markets or fairs and online. I find clothes that I like, try them on and

Fun in a 50s ballgown at Camelot, Kirkham for A Place to Call Home Ball (LJA)

buy them, just like anyone else - I just cannot request another size if the dress I like is not in my size!

I also raid the wardrobes of my friends grandmothers who have hoarded items from their younger years and scour op shops, although out of the close to 200 dresses that I own, perhaps two have come from a an op shop, it is not as common as one might think – however they are my favourite place to pick up old linen, doilies and crockery.

The response to "Why?" is more complex. Why does anyone like a particular style or design? As humans we like to surround ourselves with beauty, style and objects that we admire and make us happy, this is really true of humankind in any time in history. For me this is no different, it just so happens that what I admire, and what makes me happy is a period in history that my parents don't even remember. I cannot quite pinpoint the exact moment that I began my 1950s obsession; I think it was a gradual evolvement. I grew up in a house of antiques and frequenting antique stores thanks to my parents love of turn of the century design.

Pink is the colour of choice for Laura Jane's 1950s styled home. (LJA)

As a child, it was commonplace for me to be able to identify vintage dolls, Bendigo Pottery, Shelley China and spot the difference between original and reproduction tin toys. Forget Ikea furniture like my friends, my bed was a cast iron bed from the late 1800s as was my marble top washstand. Raised on a diet of Shirley Temple and movie musicals from the Golden Age of Hollywood and devouring books such as Anne of Green Gables Frances Hodgson Burnett novels and Enid Blyton stories only solidified my appreciation of a bygone era. However it was always the mid century design that stood out to me. I loved the colour, the style and silhouette of the feminine clothes.

The design, cut and make far exceeded what I saw my peers being attracted to. I loved the daintiness of the china, the uniqueness of the furniture design and above all the history of the era and the fact that by embracing this time period in the 21st century meant that I was somehow preserving it and breathing new life into these clothes, crockery, linen, furniture and more. For when I really think of it, the true answer to "Why?" as in *why* the 50s, *why* the clothes, *why* this lifestyle comes down to this: I want to preserve history and heritage in all elements.

The thought of these beautiful clothes and everyday objects of a bygone era disappearing scares me and I adore the chance to be able to share this in a new era. I love being a bit different and standing out, I love wearing clothing that were once worn by someone sixty odd years ago and imagining what they got up to in those same clothes and most of all – and perhaps most simply - I love the way the fashions and styles of the 1950s feel so perfectly a part of my personality.

Fashion and Style of the 1950s

I may be entirely biased but there is no doubt that the fashion and style in the 1950s was a period like no other. A generation that had grown up during the depression and war years were finding their way in a new world, money was more readily available to be spent on entertainment and lifestyle and society were ready to embrace the abundance of new technology and modern conveniences.

From Tupperware to appliances, petticoats to kitchen gadgets, industry was well aware of this new found disposable income and a booming trade grew up. The key design elements of this era that set it apart was the abundance of colour that was used for everything- from dish drainers to dining room tables, shoes to undergarments, colour – particularly pastels - reigned supreme.

When it comes to clothing – it really was the era of the teenager and young women. Nipped waists with full skirts reigned supreme. Petticoats were derigueur – the bigger the better, with the fuller the skirt the more flattering the figure. Colour was constant and fun novelty prints were gaining popularity.

Whilst cottons and poplin were the fabric of choice for fun daywear, tulle, silk and chiffon dominated luxurious eveningwear. The highlight of both was of course, the accessories! No outfit was complete without a hat of course and matching bags and shoes. Novelty brooches, scarfs, strands of pearls and screw on earrings were the jewellery of choice and plastic and Lucite were the newest additions.

Above all what stood out as the utmost aesthetic was the sense of perfectionism and well grooming. Wet sets, pin-curls and weekly salon visits ensured that hair was perfectly set, the rise of the makeup industry saw red or bright pink lipstick and groomed eyebrows as the thing of beauty. Across all elements of life there was the opportunity for colour, for style and for beautiful aesthetics. This was not the disposable industry of today, everything was made to be beautiful and everything was made to last.

Embracing the 1950s in the 21st Century

So how does a 21st Century girl with an iphone, Instagram account and reliance on air-conditioning live a 1950s life? Well, for me it is about embracing the best of both worlds.

A snippet of Laura Jane's day wardrobe (note there is a separate wardrobe for ball gowns and petticoats!) Vintage hat boxes store everything from scarves, to gloves and of course, hats! (LJA)

When I bought my first home in 2017 – not only did I want it to be in the heart of Camden due to the history so alive in the town – I set about giving it a 1950s makeover.

Floorboards replaced the modern carpet, black and white checked lino was sourced to replace the tiles in the kitchen, along with pink handles for kitchen cupboards. An original pink and white kitchen dresser was sourced from Melbourne along with the matching laminate dining room table with chrome legs and coordinating pink and white vinyl chairs. I scoured ebay, estate sales and family and friends grandparents' homes for original 50s sideboards, glass display cabinets, cocktail cabinets and tri-mirror dressing table – complete with dovetail joints.

Thanks to an ongoing glory box I have been keeping since I was fourteen, and the afore mentioned key sources, these were all filled with crockery, glassware, linen and of course fashions that befitted the era. In all respects it looks like a house out of the 1950s – with the added benefit of 21st century air-conditioning. By surrounding myself with a house full of furniture and objects from the 1950s not only do I feel as though I am preserving and continuing to give life to elements of history, that sadly many of my generation would disregard, but I am also surrounding myself with things that make me happy and are aesthetically pleasing. Sometimes I wonder if my friends are as interested in filling their homes with items that make them happy as they are with the latest style and what society dictates their house should look like. In some ways, I suppose I do follow the same trends… just my trends were dictated by the fashion magazines more than sixty years ago!

In Laura Jane's favourite vintage dress at a night at the theatre – it is not unusual for strangers to approach and ask to take her photo. (LJA)

In living in a house that is a tribute to a bygone era and wearing clothing each day that was manufactured before my parents were even born I have built up a reputation as "the 50s" girl. In fact in the twelve months that I have been in Camden I have come to be known by the style of dress that I have, I know that it is because it stands out and is different to the norm. I would hope however if you met me you would soon realise that this lifestyle is more about who I am as a person – it is not a persona I adopt but a lifestyle I lead every day.

I am not alone in my 50s obsession, there is a growing community that are attracted to aesthetics of the era but what I find sets me apart is that it is not something that I turn on or off, my clothes are not a "costume" or special occasion clothes but something that I live every day, by combining the best parts of the past with the conveniences of a modern era to create a lifestyle that I absolutely adore. Instant access to sellers around the world has certainly made it easier to accumulate my collection and Instagram has opened up a world of likeminded people who share and appreciate the aesthetic.

I am often told I was born in the wrong era and was born too late, however I do not think that was the case. One of the best things about being a vintage girl in the modern world is just that – I get the best of both worlds and I get to share this appreciation with a new generation, hopefully continuing to share the love of the 1950s and saving items otherwise lost to history. And that's just the way I love it. Petticoats, gloves, full skirts, pin curls each night, dainty crockery and pink laminate dining room tables...with air-conditioning, the Internet and an Instagram following.

Laura Jane's pink dining room table is an original laminate pink table with chrome legs. The vintage chairs have been re-vinyled in a coordinating pink. The original kitchen dresser houses her collection of original glassware, china, linen and cookbooks. (LJA)

Archaeology and Elderslie Railway Station

Andrew Lundy

Some weeks ago I saw a photograph of Elderslie Railway Station, posted on The Camden Museum's Facebook page, and that image provoked two thoughts. These thoughts are not so much to do with Camden's history, which has been thoroughly researched and documented, but the archaeology of the region.

From 1986 to 2007 I was a history teacher at Elderslie High School. In the senior years I taught mainly Ancient History, and the introduction to that course is archaeology. Finding "hands on" activities for Australian history students, especially in the field of archaeology, can be a challenge, but after some research and a bit of simple observation of the local area, I came up

Camden Locomotive Pansy at Elderslie Railway Station 1950s (Camden Images)

with two "experiences" for the kids, both within walking distance to the school.

The first was the site of a house, built sometime in the early 20th century, in the field to the south of the then Anglican retirement home, *Hilsyde,* on Hilder St. The only clue to the site were 2 two metre high shrubs, 2 metres apart, right in the middle of a grass paddock.

These two shrubs once guarded the gate and path which led to the front door of the cottage. The students were able to uncover the brick path, and follow it to the site of the front door, then trace their way around the entire perimeter of the house by following the foundations. They even located 2 concrete pads, in the "backyard", presumably for the water tank and the dunny!

The second was a little more tangible. The Camden/Campbelltown rail line ran straight past the site of what was to become Elderslie high school, but the closest station to the school was actually Kirkham. The old station was about 20 metres to the west of the intersection of Camden Valley Way and Kirkham Lane, verified by old maps of the line.

I took many groups of Year 11 students over to the site, and there they sketched the site and recorded artefacts found. What remained there was the brick foundations of the platform, some weathered timberwork, rusted steel lines and a few sleepers. On the northern(Narellan) side of Kirkham Lane, the students could clearly see the raised rampart, stretching off to Narellan, which once carried the track and trains.

Nothing above ground remains of Elderslie station, but its site is still visible. Directly opposite the Macarthur Rd intersection, there is a flat piece of ground, amid surrounding undulating fields, and right beside Camden Valley Way.

Perhaps a little archaeology on this spot would yield up some artefacts which could be of immense interest to historians of the area and historians of transport?

Which leads me to a broader question.

How many historically significant sites have been lost or destroyed in this area over the years? The two sites mentioned earlier in this story are no more. The house is now buried under a housing estate and Kirkham Station's remains were bulldozed and covered up in 2014 when a massive water line was installed linking Cobbitty and Elderslie.

I'm also intrigued as to what ,if any, archaeological recovery is being done as Camden High School is demolished.

Archaeology can sometimes answer questions that historians cannot.

Maybe something worth considering, as more and more of our historical environment is swallowed by development.

Elderslie Railway Station in the 1960s after the line had closed. Elderslie was the first station out of Camden across the Nepean River near the Macarthur Road intersection. The next station on the line was Kirkham at Kirkham Lane (Camden Images)

John and Nona Souter, the story

Tony Souter

This is the story of a local family who owned a garage in Argyle Street Camden for many years. I asked their son Tony for the story after he posted an item on Facebook celebrating Nona's 95th birthday. (Editor).

John Souter was born in 1919 in Ashfield, Sydney, and had an older brother Ron. Nona was also born in Ashfield in 1923, and was the youngest of five girls and had a younger brother.

John went to Fort Street High School in Petersham, and with a couple of life long friends was a keen boy scout, graduating to rovers when in his mid-teens. He and 3 or 4 friends would plan 3 day hiking weekends away to the Blue Mountains.

Leaving on a Friday afternoon with all their camping gear, food and water in their backpacks, they would board the train at Strathfield for Blackheath.

The magnificent Burragorang Valley where the young Souters hiked as young men. Here the valley is shown in the 1950s before it was flooded for Warragamba Dam. (Camden Images)

From there they would hike south through the Megalong Valley, then onto the Burragorang Valley, a hike of nearly 100kms. The boys would call at a couple of farms and ask if they could stay overnight in a shed.

After a number of these trips, they would write letters to the owners of the farms, saying they expected to be on another hike in some weeks, and ask permission to stay overnight. After making an impression with these farmers, they would be greeted with a healthy baked dinner before retiring to the sheds to sleep.

After hiking through the Burragorang Valley, they would reach Nattai, where they would catch a bus to Camden, then train to Campbelltown, and another train back to Strathfield and home to Ashfield.

Having made this trip on a number of occasions, John came to realize what a wonderful country town Camden was. Predominantly supported by the dairy industry. Camden was surrounded by dairy farms. The Burragorang Valley had also served as the way for silver to be hauled from Yerranderie to Camden, using bullock teams, however, this industry had finished some years earlier.

After leaving school, John worked for John Sands, a well known greeting card manufacturer.

When war broke out in 1939, John like most of his friends signed up for the army as a 20 year old. After a short time he demobilized from the army to the airforce. When signing on to be a pilot at Waverton near North Sydney, he met a new friend Tom Young. They quickly were moved to Narrandera where they were to commence flying training. From then, John and Tom returned to Sydney, then onto Canada for further flying training, then onto England.

After arriving in England in 1941, the trainee pilots were re-assigned to the Middle East, and commenced a long sea journey down the west coast of Africa to round Cape of Good Hope and proceed to Egypt. Along the Atlantic coast, they received orders to proceed to Singapore which was then under grave threat from the Japanese. As they approached Singapore, word was received that the British stronghold has fallen, so John and Tom Young were among thousands of Allied troops who dropped off at Java, where the British shortly surrendered them to the Japanese.

From Java, John was a prisoner in the infamous Changi Prison, where he was grouped in a force under the command of Edward "Weary" Dunlop. After some time this group were transferred to the Thai-Burma railway construc-

The garage at 177-185 Argyle Street that was purchased by John Souter in the 1940s. Here the garage is owned by DJ Keane in the 1920s with the Crown Hotel next door and the Show Hall Pavilion in the distance without its current frontage. The forces of motoring and Interwar modernism combine with a frontage on the Hume Highway. (Camden Images)

tion where they worked mostly in the Hintok area near Hellfire Pass. On one occasion when John had horrific tropical sores on his legs and was confined to hospital, the Japanese were getting desperate to complete the railway, and were going to the jungle hospitals and selecting patients who they deemed were healthy enough to work. They approached John and ordered him to get out of bed. Doctor 'Weary" Dunlop then stood between the armed guards and John, saying "this man will not work today". After a standoff, the guards relented and John stayed in bed. This was typical of the way Dunlop looked after his men during the horrific conditions in the camps.

When the railway was completed, John and thousands of other prisoners were taken by train back to Singapore, where many returned to Changi. However, great numbers, including John and Tom Young, were transferred by broken down old ships to Japan to work as slave labour. These ships should have flown the Red Cross, but the Japanese refused, and many were torpedoed by American submarines, thinking they were carrying Japanese soldiers back to Japan. Hundreds of prisoners lost their lives to these attacks.

Souter's Garage at 177-185 Argyle Street in 1965 under renovation. The Crown Hotel on the left of the image. The former Interwar garage is being replaced by a new car showroom - mid-20th century modernism in Camden. (T Souter)

However, John and Tom made it to Japan where they worked at a town Saganaseki, at times in coal mines and steelworks. In 1945 when the atomic bombs were dropped, John was only 30 miles away from Nagasaki.

After repatriation, the Australians returned home by ship to Sydney in 1946. Before the war John had courted two sisters who lived nearby in Ashfield, but he found they had since married. However, their younger sister Nona was still living at home with her mother and younger brother. John and Nona married in 1948, and John also received a War Service Loan, which he intended to spend on buying a business.

John remembered his days as a scout travelling through Camden. There had been a garage in Argyle St next to the Crown Hotel that had always caught his interest, so he travelled to Camden with the intention of purchasing the garage, which he was able to do.

Renovation and rebuilding of the old Souter's Garage resulted in a modern car showroom in 1974 at 177-185 Argyle Street. The business was now operating as John Souter Pty Ltd and was the International and Toyota dealerships with a second-hand car division next door. The forces of mid-20th century modernism caught up with the former Interwar garage. (T Souter)

His next problem was convincing new bride Nona into moving from the city to the country, which she was reluctant to do. In 1948, they moved to Camden and purchased a small cottage at 1 Gilbulla Ave, just down from the Camden Hospital.

The garage at 177-185 Argyle St, had previously sold used cars and had a petrol bowser on the front footpath. The dairy industry was thriving around Camden, and John saw the opportunity to sell tractors and farm machinery to the farmers. He was able to establish an International Harvester dealership, which he later expanded to include trucks.

After the war, there was a huge demand for coal and although Ern Clinton and Stan Fox were creating their own fleets of trucks to haul coal out of the Kangaroo Valley, there was further demand for privately owned coal trucks. The garage, now known as John Souter Pty Ltd, was able to meet this demand and supplied International trucks to hundreds of contract drivers during the 1960s and 1970s.

There was also a huge demand for petrol and oil products, but rather than expand on the single bowser John had on the main street, he opened a fuel and oil distributorship at the back of the garage.

This became a burgeoning part of the business, as John was able to gain contracts supplying diesel fuel and oil to all of the coal mines at Nattai and Oakdale.

He also created Mobil petrol and diesel deliveries to the dairy farms and for many years, supplied products to farms from Bargo through Picton, Oakdale and Camden then north to Kemps Creek.

In 1965, the business was offered to take on a Japanese car franchise; some irony here considering the treatment John would have received as a Japanese POW. However, Camden gained a Toyota dealership, and a great number of local people purchased new and used Toyotas from John Souter.

By now, John and Nona had built a new family home in Luker St, Elderslie. With their three children, Anne, Tony and Penny, they moved into a quite large 4 bedroom home made of the new product Besser Brick. A swimming pool was installed in 1965 and many local Camden people enjoyed parties and a swim at the Souter home.

John was a founding member of the Camden Apex, Lions and Rotary clubs, quite an impressive feat, as these fine service clubs established themselves in the Camden Area. John was also a long term active member of the Camden Bowling Club.

However, he loved his business and family and devoted most of his time to them. In 1975, both International and Toyota were placing demands on John to expand the business, but he resisted and gave up both the franchises.

He sold the property in Argyle St, and it became Bryan's Furniture. John had retained the Mobil fuel distributorship and purchased a property in Narellan where he continued to serve the local coal and dairy industries, and also delivered the extremely popular heating oil in Camden and Campbelltown.

John retired in 1977 after serving the local community for nearly 30 years.

His wife Nona and children lived in the area, and they are survived by a very large number of grandchildren and great-grandchildren.

In February 2018, Nona turned 95, and celebrated with her late daughter Anne's children and families, son Tony, his children and families, and daughter Penny and her daughter.

Nona still lives independently in Elderslie and recently renewed her unrestricted driving licence.

The view today at 177-185 Argyle Street Camden on the former site of Souter's Garage with the Crown Hotel at the rear of the image. (GView)

Camden and Wollondilly LGA Rivalry, a view

Lynette Styles

When I was a councillor on Wollondilly Council in the nineties, a battle existed between the two organisations. Camden was seen as the greedy neighbour consorting with state government for a boundary variation of Wollondilly borders, and the sitting mayors were fiercely combative towards each other.

That Herculean mountain Razorback is the divide between Camden and Wollondilly. Protectionism abounds, but once over that mountain, there is a disparate ideology operating.

Residents at the foot of Razorback in Mt Hunter, Cawdor, Camden South may possess information about Camden outside the Shire in which they live. Once over the mountain, little to nothing is known of political issues in Camden and the same juxtaposition operates in Wollondilly.

Camden sought the inclusion of Cawdor within its local government area. Even though they did not obtain consent, the issue fermented quietly, like a tickle in the throat turning into a cough.

 The question is whether Cawdor should form part of Camden Council. The hierarchy on Wollondilly Shire Council would be rattled by the question, but let's look at the issue from an historical perspective.

 In 1805, John Macarthur was granted 5000 acres at the Cowpastures for sheep farming. He named the location Camden. In 1812, an area named Cawdor by Governor Lachlan Macquarie became a government cattle station on the Cowpastures Government Reserve

Incorporated into the Macarthur holdings, the Cawdor land was opened to tenant farmers by the time Camden was subdivided in 1840. Four decades later, a movement of Camden residents called for the creation of a municipal council and the first meeting was held in 1889.

In 1906, Wollondilly Shire Council was created and the boundary lines drawn up by the government incorporating a huge area from Yanderra, Appin, Menangle, Oakdale, Mt Hunter and all the land known as Cawdor at the foot of Razorback.

 From an historical viewpoint, the land belonged to Camden long before it was ever incorporated within the Wollondilly LGA.

CAMDEN HISTORY

Journal of the Camden Historical Society Inc.

September 2018 Volume 4 Number 6

CAMDEN HISTORY
Journal of the Camden Historical Society Inc.
ISSN 1445-1549
Editor: Dr Ian Willis

Management Committee
President: Dr Ian Willis
Vice Presidents: John Wrigley OAM, Cathey Shepherd
Secretary: Lee Stratton
Treasurer: Kathy Lester
Immediate Past President: Bob Lester
General Committee: Julie Wrigley, Robert Wheeler, Sharon Greene, Cathy Shepherd, Frances Warner, Warren Sims

Auditors: Amy Woodley, Start Fresh Accounting, Oran Park.

Society contact:
P.O. Box 566, Camden, NSW 2570.   Online <http://www.camdenhistory.org.au>

Meetings
Meetings are held at 7.30 p.m. on the second Wednesday of the month except in January. They are held in the Museum. Visitors are always welcome.

Museum
The Museum is located at 40 John Street, Camden, phone 4655 3400 or 46559210. It is open Thursday to Sunday 11 a.m. to 4 p.m., except at Christmas. Visits by schools and groups are encouraged. Please contact the Museum to make arrangements. Entry is free.

Camden History, Journal of the Camden Historical Society Inc
The Journal is published in March and September each year. The Editor would be pleased to receive articles broadly covering the history of the Camden district . Correspondence can be sent to the Society's postal address. The views expressed by authors in journal articles are solely those of the authors and not necessarily endorsed by the Camden Historical Society Inc.

Donations
Donations made to the Society are tax deductible. The accredited value of objects donated to the Society are eligible for tax deduction.

Image Cover: Alan Baker, White Roses, 1983, Oil. Donated to Camden Historical Society by Tegel Family, 2004. (Camden Museum)

CAMDEN HISTORY
Journal of the Camden Historical Society Inc.

Contents

Alan Baker, the artist — 242
Ian Willis

Alan Baker Art Classes — 248
Rizwana Ahmad, Patricia Johnson, Olive McAleer, Shirley Rorke, Nola Tegel, John Wrigley OAM

The Abusive Mr Chisholm, Part One — 258
Peter McCall

Please 'shed' light on Matavai — 267
Anne McIntosh

Ria and the story of the song, *Camden*. — 270
Ian Willis

Memories of Milton and Elaine Ray — 274
Gail Carroll (nee Ray)

A notable scientist from Camden — 276
Marilyn Willis

President Annual Report 2017-2018 — 278
Ian Willis

Changing environments for small charitable organisations — 282
Kathy Lester

Camden Item of Significance — 284
Kathryn Pesic

Alan Baker, the artist

Ian Willis

Alan Baker was an artist and local identity. With his wife Majorie they had a profound influence shaping the art scene in the Camden district by influencing the lives of a number of Camden artists including Patricia Johnson, Nola Tegel, and Olive McAleer. Baker contributed to the broader art world as vice-president of the Royal Art Society of New South Wales.

A collection of Baker's work has recently been installed at the new gallery in the Macaria building. The exhibition highlights the two identifiable periods in Alan's artistic career divided by the tragic drowning death of Alan and Marjorie's two sons in a Georges River boating accident in 1961. The collection, according to son Gary, 'tells the story of life…and the journey of the artist'.

After the family tragedy Baker's work had a more contemplative approach. The paintings have a 'zen' quality, according to Gary, and reflect the 'stories of love, family, community, war, beauty, darkness and tragedy'.

Gary Baker maintains that there is a 'purity' to Alan's work centred on his studio and the way the light played with it. Gary explains it this way:

My father's studio was located under his house at Belimba Park. It had one south window and it was cool dark and silent. There was a large sandstone rock over which dripped water. The water seeped from underground and was all around where he sat to work. The light was pure without any other sources and then went to total darkness further into the room, which was rather like a cellar.

In the morning he would pick fresh flowers that he grew with my mother's help. He would choose them from their extensive garden. Hundreds of camellias, roses, Japonica, peaches and all sorts blossom trees, annuals and perennials. He would arrange them with great care. Aware he only had time to paint them for the life of the flower. Sometimes one or two days.

The flowers would move to the light as the day passed. They were truly living. Some would fall to the table. They constantly changed. After arranging them he would cut a board that fitted the composition. Not being restricted to stock size he made his own frames.

During the process of painting, I felt he was in a state of meditation. He often painted with classical music playing. There was a rhythm to his work leading

Alan Baker Self Portrait in oil. The painting is part of the Alan Baker Art Collection at Macaria in Camden. (I Willis, 2018)

to this state of mind. His technical skill learned over decades enabled him to get to this heightened state.

He didn't have to focus on the difficulties of drawing colour tone, instead used his intuition. Sitting in an upright position close to his board he would spend hours or days completing the painting until done. He never over painted and rarely moved away from his easels to view his work during the painting stage.

The flowers had a stability and calmness. They are asymmetric in design. The reflections on the glass table show a sort of purity calmness. The delicate flowers capture a purity or truthfulness. The flowers were almost textured, the way the paint is applied.

His brush strokes are simplified. Directly confident. Almost abstract. I see a likeness to Chinese ink painting techniques. The designs with the vase in the middle. Most art teachers say that it should not be done this way.

I see some of his paintings as being perfect! I see how they are living, not still. I see the air flow around them. Even viewing at different angles the texture of the paint changes the look of each painting. They are so complex and yet so simple. The brush strokes are very pronounced on board enhancing a textured feel. He did not use canvas.

Flowers themselves are universal symbols of remembrance love. I feel that he was chasing perfection in beauty. His paintings of flowers seem to speak to people with this. Many a man has said to me that they do not look like flower paintings. His are different. You can appreciate that! His floral work is from the heart not intellectual. I feel it's spiritual.

Alan and Marjorie made The Oaks their home after the 1961 tragedy and maybe Baker was searching for the truth through the subject material he chose for his work. Certainly Alan's still-life paintings absorbed a large amount of his artistic effort and possibly account for Gary labelling his work as a form of 'realism'.

Alan Baker certainly did not pander to sentimentalism or heroic depiction of subjects as 19th century Romantic might have done. He was not a fan of modernist avant-garde styles and his commercial art commissions reflect a journeyman's approach to subject matter. Gary states:

This is the other side of his work. When you walk back and see his work from a distance. It comes into focus. You see a realist painting, the simple brush strokes disappear. He was so well trained in the art skills of tone, drawing

The Alan Baker Art Collection here showing the interior of the gallery at Macaria Camden (I Willis, 2018)

and colour. He found modern art to be "the refuse of the incompetent".

Alan learnt his trade at the J.S. Watkins Art School where he studied drawing at 13 years of age. Watkins had set up his art school after returning to Australia after studying in Paris in 1898 above the Julian Ashton's art school in King Street. By 1927 when Alan Baker was attending it had moved to 56 Margaret Street Sydney.

At the Watkins art school Alan was trained in tonal drawing in pencil charcoal, pen and washes and later oils, according to Gary's biography of his father. The art school provided a competitive environment and Alan thrived in it. His mentors included Henry Hanke, Normand Baker (his brother) and William Pidgen. Alan later became a teacher at the school.

In 1936 at 22 years of age Alan had a self-portrait accepted in the Archibald Prize at the Art Gallery of New South Wales. Alan's brother Normand won the Archibald prize in 1937 with his *Self Portrait* and the travelling scholarship in 1939. Between 1932 and 1972, according to Gary Baker, Alan entered the Archibald Prize with 35 separate paintings and made the finals 26 times. In 1969 he submitted a portrait of Camden surgeon Gordon Clowes which made the final selection that year.

The art collection at Macaria is representative of the art genres that Alan practised throughout his career and includes portraiture, still life, landscape, seascape, life drawing and life painting. The exhibitions has a number of examples of Baker's commercial hotel posters, pencil drawings and portraits.

Some of Alan's artwork was completed during his war service in New Guinea and the Pacific where he painted Papuans, fellow diggers and others. Alan enlisted in 1942 in the Australian Army with the rank of private and served in New Guinea. On discharge in 1945 he was with the 2 Australian Watercraft Workshop AEME (Australian Electrical and Mechanical Engineers).

After the war he met Marjorie Whitchurch (formerly Kingsell) who had taken up art classes at the Watkins art school. Alan worked an instructor at the school after he was demobbed from the army. Marjorie had fled Singapore in 1942 when the Japanese invaded the city, and in the process she lost her husband, who died on the Burma Railway, her home and her possessions.

Alan dated Marjorie for a year then married her in 1946. They lived in primitive accommodation at Moorebank with few facilities. Their first child was born in 1947. Alan's career started to prosper and he had a painting of his wife Marjorie accepted in the 1953 Archibald Prize at the Art Gallery of New South Wales and was a finalist with his *Artists Wife*.

The couple sought solace after the loss of their sons and moved to the isolation of The Oaks. Here they established their home, a garden, and Alan set up his studio in a bush setting. The garden provided inspiration and subject material for Still Life paintings. Gary Baker maintains that:

An artist must arrange his own composition by any means...the value of the shadow being thrown from one flower to the other...I spend hours arranging till I am satisfied the result will be successful.

Alan was a fan of *plein air* painting, a tradition which goes back to the French Impressionists in the mid-19th century. His landscapes reflect naturalism, the avoidance of stylisation and a 'commitment to the natural and man-made environment'.

Baker had a prolific work ethic, and had many exhibitions across Australia. The *Australian Art Sales Digest* lists 708 works, of which 77 are on display in Macaria and his artwork is exhibited in numerous galleries and private collections. He lived at The Oaks until his death in 1987.

Alan Baker's legacy is acknowledged by the foundation of the Alan Baker Art Gallery located in Macaria in John Street Camden in 2018.

The Alan Baker Art Collection is located in Macaria John Street Camden. Macaria is an impressive Picturesque Tudor Gothic town house built by merchant Henry Thompson in 1860 (I Willis, 2018).

Alan Baker Art Classes
Some memories by his students

In the 1970s Alan was asked to mentor and teach an art class at Camden Public School. These classes were instrumental in creating opportunities for a number of Camden locals to pursue careers as artists. The groundbreaking influence of these art classes is still evident today.

What follows are the memoirs of a number of these artists who tell their story in their own voice. These reminiscences are largely unedited and reflect the experience of these artists. This means that there is necessarily some repetition across the individual stories and the memories of the individuals who have written them. (The editor)

Rizwana Ahmad

My first encounter with the Alan Baker Art Group was in 1973. I had recently migrated to Australia after completing an MA in Fine Art from Punjab University, Lahore, Pakistan.

A patient of my husband's - who was then working as a physiotherapist - told me about the class and invited me along one evening. I was keen to meet other artists who were working in my newly adopted home. I accepted the invitation!

I noticed several things that evening. First, Alan was not obliged to instruct each student individually: his role was to be an inspiring and charismatic force for all the class. I recall his son, Gary (who was then a high school student) being trained and groomed under Alan's watchful eye.

Second, it was very interesting to compare and contrast Alan's techniques with those I had inherited from my European-South Asian training. For example, Alan kept his colour palette to several earth tones: he did not adopt the colour theory of the Impressionists. He was very much a Realist and had an excellent grasp of tonal values.

Third, he painted relatively quickly. Fourth, his studies of flowers were spot on and, in my view, were his most accomplished works.

Former members of the Alan Baker Art Group at Camden Public School Patricia Johnson, Nola Tegel, and Olive McAleer. (O McAleer)

Although I only attended a few classes with the art group I recall being asked to model for the class one evening in my South Asian wedding dress – a confection of shocking pink and gold brocade. Alan captured the shimmering golden hues brilliantly and the painting was sold in an exhibition shortly afterwards.

Patricia Johnston

Nobody crossed the room to meet me when I was an academic librarian, but I had some magical attraction as an artist.

My husband Ken, a Veterinary Pathologist and I had come to Camden in 1959. Ken pioneered the establishment of a clinical veterinary laboratory, while I set up a research library, for the new Veterinary Science and Agriculture campus of the University of Sydney. These facilities provided practical experience and education to the final year students of these facilities in Werombi Road, Camden.

I had always been interested in art and even gained admission to the East Sydney Technical College (now the National Art School) in 1949, but was discouraged from pursuing a professional artistic career as it was so difficult for women at that time to make a living from art alone.

It was only meeting the art teacher Ken Rorke in 1964, that encouraged me to join a new local art group, in which the professional artist Alan Baker would offer advice and criticism of our work.

But Alan did more than that, he changed my life and art became my passion. Each Wednesday for two hours a small group would meet and draw a model in charcoal or pencil under Alan's supervision. We weren't allowed to mess with colour until we understood thoroughly tonal variation and drawing techniques.

It was only after a year of drawing, we broke out the oils and the delicious application of buttery paint and the smell of linseed oil excites me still. In those two hours we were able to produce a portrait or a still life study.

As our skills progressed Alan took us to paint landscapes 'en plein air' and I can remember the first I attended was on the top of Razorback in the late afternoon. The experience combined all the complexities of technique and drawing we had learned, as well as how to cope with the flies, ants , dust and other hazards to produce a painting on the spot and capture the changing light.

By this time Alan's talented son Gary had joined the group. We noticed that he was encouraged to extend his art studies at the Royal Art Society of NSW, where Alan served as vice president. So Nola Tegel, Olive McAleer and I joined the class of Harry Hanke, former Archibald prize winner, and in the next 3 and 4 years studied to gain the Diploma of Fine Art showing proficiency in drawing, landscape, portrait and still life painting.

In 2003 I was made Fellow of the prestigious society, which proudly claims Tom Roberts and Margaret Preston as its former members, and my work is now part of the Society's collection.

My watercolour tutor there was Frederic Bates, who had begun to organize some of the earliest tours designed especially for artists, travelling to see wonderful museums and studios of famous artists and even painting on the sites , where they had painted famous works.

In 1994 following the serious illness of his wife Enid, he asked me to take over as tour leader, art and cultural teacher, interpreter and general trouble shooter on these tours. I enjoyed 15 years with the delightful companionship of Marjory Baker, then Alan's widow to visit France, Italy, Germany, Austria, Spain and Portugal, Czech Republic, Hungary, Poland, Russia Corsica and many others with Marjory alone in Asia.

I can thank Alan Baker for these wonderful adventures. He gave his knowledge and great experience of art so generously for 23 years in that little art group and inspired my own artistic journey.

Olive McAleer

[Part of address given at her exhibition on 14 April 2018 given by one of her daughters.]

Olive has always possessed an unaccountable urge to speak the language of art.

Dad [Geoff] recognized and encouraged Mum's talent. He met Alan Baker at Rotary in 1969 and asked him for a list of items for Mum to begin oil painting. I recall the day we all went to Parker's Art Supplies in George Street Sydney to buy Mum's easel and paints.

Alan began an art group at Camden Public School. Mum attended every Wednesday night and was delighted with her friends Nola Tegel, Patricia Johnston and Jack Dunn joined too. They formed the Camden Art Group and have continued to promote art and have successful careers in their own right.

Shirley Rorke

[Interview with Ian Willis, Camden, 5 May 2018]

Ken Rorke, a local school teacher who taught at Camden Public School, was a keen artist and was instrumental in setting up art classes at the school.

Shirley recalls that Ken initially asked artist Alan Baker would he be prepared to give advice to a group of budding local artists 'for a while so they might get started' and Alan agreed.

Ken was always interested in art and started the class in his classroom at the school where he was teaching at the time. Ken taught at Camden Public School from 1961 to his death in 1981.

Ken organised the classes for Wednesday nights. Shirley said that she felt Ken was keen to help others and had the advantage of having access to his classroom as a venue, which was used for the classes until 1981.

Ken, according to Shirley, loved painting in watercolours, doing black and white sketches and pencil drawings. He sold some of his work to local supporters and friends.

Margery
**Nola Tegel assisted by Alan Baker c. 1975. in oil.
(Supplied by N Tegel)**

Nola Tegel

Early 1970.

I was in my studio earlier today working on a painting of an Italian landscape; I was contemplating the area where the mountain meets the horizon. There is an almost indescribable tone, a penumbra of colour that is virtually impossible to capture. Is it orange, or lilac, or perhaps a rosy hue or even a mixture of those colours? Yes, impossible.

But I try.

And doing so I consider how I got here and the wonderful adventure of arriving at this place. It is in no small way due to Alan Baker, and his wonderful wife Margery moving to the Camden district.

When the local artist/teacher Ken Rourke discovered that Alan was a celebrated artist, he invited him to teach and…what pleasure…he accepted the invitation. Alan had his own ideas on teaching. Even though he had been employed as a teacher at the J S Watkins Art School. He stipulated that he would not teach, but if people were willing, he would attend an art group and paint along with us, encourage and direct us. There would not be any formal structure and definitely no money involved. We would just be a group of friends gathered together to learn from each other.

Alan suggested that we use the best materials. Always the finest archival paint, the top brushes, although there was not an enormous choice of artist quality paint available at that time. We were told to use tried and tested colours that would last many lifetimes. After forty plus years, I still use the same colours, in the same order. And so each Wednesday evening we would head to the primary school and sit on tiny seats and begin our evening project. The best seat in the house was behind Alan. One could watch each brush or pencil or charcoal stroke and hopefully, learn from it. After a while, even under his influence, we developed our own style.

Just watching Alan squeeze out oil paint onto his palette was a revelation for some. Great gobs of gooey paint, was mixed, back and forth with the brush, almost polishing it before it was applied to the board. Always the right colour, the right tone in the right place…what a skill. Although we started painting still life, we quickly moved on to portrait painting. As our master said, 'If you can paint a good portrait, you can paint anything'. That meant supplying a sitter or sitting for the group yourself.

Consequently, there would be no painting that week, so we tried hard to bring in members of our family. Olive McAleer had a bevvy of beautiful daughters,

The Master's Student. Alan Baker, c. 1975, oil painting. Completed in art class at Camden Public School. (Supplied by N Tegel)

Alan's wife Margery used to sit with exotic hats, but the prize for original sitters would have gone to Rita Bloomfield. Working for the Bullen Circus

Company, she brought in Beaver, an Indian Chief, who had a knife-throwing act. He would sit, resplendent in his feather headdress and leathers; his face was severe, long, grim and full of Indian character…He said nothing. This was a good idea, because if you heard him talk he sounded distinctly English! And I am also pleased to report that he left his knives at home.

We all worked hard. Alan would make a suggestion here or there. Sometimes and best of all, he would take our place, pick up our palette and with one or two brushstrokes he would bring the painting to life. I have such a painting of Margery …with corrections from Alan, an original Tegel/ Baker painting. Also, I have another painting by Alan. One evening he sat behind me and painted me painting Margery.

Although Alan did not often join us in the landscape, he organised one or two painting trips. On the top of Razorback Mountain with a simple view…a road…a house and a tree or two. One of our members came along with a "banana bed"…she had had a busy night, and she rested while everyone else struggled with the scene.

This gave many of us the confidence to venture further afield and the resulting paintings were shown on our evenings where Alan would gently criticize them. We found wonderful things to paint; indeed Camden was an art paradise. Of course, it has changed, as everything has, but it was and still is a great adventure.

As a result of our class, which lasted many years, numerous people started and made full time careers in the art world, and so many of them have their own stories.

I have travelled far and wide in the name of art, initially with my husband Max. While he would never hold a paintbrush, he has accompanied me following my favourite artists in many of the best galleries and museums at home and abroad. Also I have been on painting holidays with my dear friends, Margery, Patricia Johnston and Olive McAleer; we have truly experienced the world of art together.

There are many funny stories, sad and tragic stories, but as a result of Alan and Margery coming to Camden District, I can sincerely say it changed my life. It is a continuing joy to express myself in this medium.

And one more thing, I wonder if anyone could drop by help me decipher that elusive colour…

[Nola Tegel notes that one of the most important to us was Christine Parrish. She joined early and so importantly, started a commercial art gallery at Cobbitty. She did very well for all of us and made a living from its success]

John Wrigley

In 1972 I was invited to attend the regular art classes that were held on a Wednesday night at Camden Public School by Alan Baker. My work colleague, the American forester Arthur 'Red' Mitchell, was already an accomplished amateur artist and enjoyed the company of the various other people who attended.

For many years Ken Rorke, husband of Shirley Rorke, was a teacher at Camden Public School. In the early 1970s Ken was keen to start an art class in Camden and approached the artist Alan D. Baker and asked him to conduct weekly art classes and Alan very generously agreed. An advertisement was placed in the Camden News. The classes were informal, free, and open to anyone in the community who was interested. Ken acted as the host each night in his class room at Camden Public School. Alan Baker was the teacher but never asserted his position and just moved through the room stopping to assist or give advice. The evenings were held with a minimum of organisation and about 20 attended, varying each time. On any night people would be using a variety of media - pencil, pen, pastels, watercolour and oils.

It was expected that everyone would take a turn to either sit for the portraiture or bring a sitter friend or relative along. Sometimes a person would dress up or wear an unusual hat. One night my wife Julie, a teacher of English at Camden High School, came along, so that night everyone made a pencil sketch of her. Many years later, after Alan's death, his widow Marjorie, told us that she still had the pencil portrait of Julie drawn by Alan from that night in 1972 and would we like to have it? We enthusiastically said yes please. Gary Baker framed it and it is now a favourite work of art in our home.

Regular members ended up with piles of portrait drawings and could see how they had progressed over time (or not!) I believe that several of the other artists from the classes would still have similar piles of pencil sketches that they have kept from those days. I saw such a pile at the former home of Olive

McAleer in Elizabeth Macarthur Avenue about twenty years ago.

The classes inspired many successful local artists. Attendees that I can remember included Ken Rorke, Nola Tegel, Patricia Johnston, Olive McAleer, Red Mitchell, Rizwana Ahmad, Rita Bloomfield, Neville Clinton, Daphne Wilson and Alan's son Gary Baker, and some brought younger family members occasionally. Recently Daphne Wilson donated to the Camden Museum her collection of 14 portraits of local residents. Most of the portraits were started at Alan Baker's classes.

Ken Rorke was sadly missed when he died prematurely in 1981 but the classes continued. In 1987 Alan Baker died. For a time the group went on, but it finished when the Department of Education started being concerned about insurance, payment for electricity, and the filling in of appropriate forms. I have an interesting watercolour painting of a seaside scene which I had framed after one class. I can remember that I did all the washes and some of the details, beach, and trees but all the good parts of the painting were done by Alan, showing me how to do it! I chuckle every time that I look at it. After about a year of attending the class I realised that I was not a natural artist and was not progressing so I stopped attending. We had begun attending a local adult education discussion group which suited us both and which lasted for many years.

We were all very fortunate to have received Alan's kindly and thoughtful advice and tutoring in such a pleasant setting. We did not know that Alan and Ken would be leaving us so soon.

The Abusive Mr Chisholm (Part One)

Peter McCall

Calling someone "abusive" today is a fairly serious charge. I was therefore interested to find in the files of the Camden Historical Society an article headed "The Abusive Mr Chisholm in War Paint." It was dated 20 December 1897. What could it be about?

It emerged that it was a speech attacking the Camden Agricultural, Horticultural and Industrial Society (AH&I Society). The main role of the AH&I Society was the organisation of the annual Camden Show.

In 1897 the meetings of the AH&I Society were interrupted from their usual discussions of prizes for exhibits and dates for the next show by allegations of financial mismanagement, sale of sly grog and even corruption. The principal targets of these attacks were James K Chisholm, president of the society, Astley Onslow Thompson, the secretary, and William R Cowper, the treasurer. Considering the status of these people within Camden society, these were serious accusations.

James K Chisholm (1830-1912) was a wealthy landowner, founding president of the AH & I Society, having been in that role for eleven years. He was married to the first cousin of Elizabeth Macarthur-Onslow, owner of the pre-eminent local estate, Camden Park, and granddaughter of the founder of her family's fortunes, John Macarthur.

Astley Onslow Thompson (1865-1915) was a second cousin of Elizabeth Macarthur-Onslow's husband, Arthur Onslow. Thompson was the manager of the Camden Park estates and also was central to the Camden Mounted Rifles where he was a captain and as a result was often referred to in this matter as "the Captain".

William R Cowper (1858-1925) also came from a family of early settlers to the Camden district, being the grandson of the first Premier of New South Wales. He was the manager of the Commercial Bank in Camden from 1886 to 1906. He was involved in many committees and organisations in Camden, often in the capacity of treasurer. These included the School of Arts, Rifle Club, Dramatic Society and the Philharmonia.[1] He was praised for his role in establishing butter factories, a feature in the development of agriculture and industry in Camden at the time and specifically the Westbrook factory,[2] which was to become a source of controversy.

The person behind the allegations was Henry Willis (1860-1950), a politically minded man who worked his way from municipal office in South Australia and New South Wales up to state and federal levels, ending as Speaker of the New South Wales Legislative Assembly from 1911 to 1913.

He was an eloquent orator, and this made him popular as his speeches tended to be highly entertaining. He was a skilled debater, having much experience of this in Adelaide His eloquence often rested on debating skills rather than actual strength of his line of reasoning.

He was always determined to win an argument. In 1911 when Willis had been elected Speaker, an article written anonymously said this about him, "Under the guise of perfect peace he harbours the spirit of the warrior.

He takes delight in strife. ... he is the fortunate possessor of a supreme self-confidence ... which makes him regard opponents as weaklings, and raises him clear above any element of anxiety as to the outcome."[3] Willis's actions in Camden certainly fit with this estimation.

On 21 January 1897 Henry Willis announced his intention to stand for a position as alderman on Camden Council. He declared that his candidacy was based on his independence, experience and financial knowledge. Willis also was suppos-

Astley Onslow Thompson 1915
Sydney Mail **12 May 1915.**

edly expert in water supply technology, a matter of some import in Camden at that time.[4] He had already been the first mayor of Cabramatta and Canley Vale in 1893.[5] Willis was elected to Camden Council.[6] Willis's address at this time is sometimes referred to as "Hahndory", which was in Elizabeth St, but his connection with Camden came from his position as manager of the late EL Moore's estate[7] which had a number of properties to the south, west and north of Camden.[8] EL Moore was Willis's father-in-law.

The site of the show was Onslow Park. This land was part of the Camden Park Estate until donated by Elizabeth Macarthur-Onslow as a recreation ground in 1887. It was under a trust which leased the land to the AH&I Society for the annual show.

Henry Willis first attacked the leadership of the AH&I Society in a letter he wrote to the *Camden News* on 10 June, 1897. Willis stated that "if the Agricultural Society is to be used for personal aggrandisement and junketing of casual friends, it should be done at private expense." He estimated that two hundred people to the annual show were "regaled at the Society's expense," and that luncheons had cost £253.

It was true that at the show a free luncheon was held for show stewards and judges, donors of special prizes from outside the district, distinguished visitors and secretaries of kindred societies.[9] These luncheons may have been seen by some as extravagant. FWA Downes, at the April 1897 AH&I Society committee meeting, said "sometimes the feeling gets among members that we are a little too lavish in distributing tickets for our luncheons."[10] JK Chisholm said, "All the visitors regard[ed] their luncheons as banquets." He was applauded for this.[11] These statements predate Willis's accusations, but may indicate that there was some uneasiness about them even at that time.

Not surprisingly, at the AH&I Society Committee meeting of 24 June, this issue was addressed, although reference is made to an anonymous letter rather than the Willis' letter to the *Camden News*. Here the complaint was about £60 spent from the miscellaneous account. The Committee said that this had been spent on hospitality.

It was claimed that the prestige of the society was added to when it dispensed hospitality.[12] Further it stated that there was no "grog" on the account. The treasurer, WR Cowper did say that the accounts had been rushed, and he was supported in this by Mr Harris, the auditor. Committee member HP Reeves said that the letter on this issue showed envy, hatred and malice and that the matter should be dropped. It was.[13]

Or that is what the Committee hoped. Henry Willis had other ideas. In the

Portrait of Henry Willis, 1900s, The Swiss Studios (NLA)

next *Camden News* a letter appeared from him stating that the only prestige the AH&I Society had was from agriculture, not visitors.[14] He further suggested that the state government reductions in subsidies for agricultural societies throughout the state were, in the case of Camden, due to the AH & I Society's acceptance of £50 from a Mr Hennessy to open the refreshment booth. He questioned whether this meant that distinguished visitors got free whisky and soda. There is no evidence to show that the reduction of subsidies had anything to do with this. The AH&I Society minutes of 24 June 1897 give the actual reason- the state government had narrowed the scope of subsidies to a group of specific agricultural prizes. This applied to all agricultural societies, not just Camden.[15]

Two months later Willis wrote a further letter to the *Camden News*. Here he attacked the balance sheet of the AH&I Society as an "extraordinary document."[16] The balance sheet was not signed- the new treasurer, HP Reeves, admitted that this had been done inadvertently.[17] He also complained about a loan from a "resident" which smacked of patronage. The resident was Mrs Elizabeth Macarthur-Onslow, owner of Camden Park Estate.

In the 1930s, GV Sidman, recorded of the late 1800s that "it was generally a current topic that certain alderman have little love for Camden Park Estate and any excuse was a reason for an attack that made matters unpleasant."[18] As mentioned above, JK Chisholm and Astley Onslow Thompson were related to Elizabeth Macarthur-Onslow. Henry Willis was an alderman, and it is therefore likely that Kidman was thinking of him when he wrote this. The reasons for this dislike of Camden Park Estate will become clearer later.

Willis also enumerates the amounts paid for various miscellaneous expenses. Next to the £18 12s 6d for petty cash and postage, telegrams etc he wrote "Great Scott!" The editor of the *Camden News* suggested that Mr Willis in future must use a "temperate and courteous manner."[19]

At the AH&I Society Annual Meeting on 10 September the treasurer HP Reeves deprecated cheese-paring for judges' lunches and said that they had to be good to attract suitable judges. The meeting congratulated JK Chisholm for his twelve years as president and elected to him to life membership of the society. Chisholm said that Henry Willis "would have shown a more manly spirit ... if he attended this meeting."[20]

By the 28 October meeting Willis had threatened the Trustees of Onslow Park that he would take them to the Court of Equity on the grounds that they had not responded to his questions concerning the lease of land to the AH&I Society, the charging of admission to the grounds and the erection of unsightly buildings. He demanded to see the Trustee's account books.[21] Willis

J K Chisholm (Camden Images)

seemed to believe that original Deed of Trust prohibited the Trustees from charging for entrance. However, the deed for this quite specifically said "the said Trustee [may] charge for admission to the said land or any part thereof on any number of days not exceeding twelve days in the ... year,"[22] with the maximum amount being one shilling. This clause was designed to allow the charge of an entrance fee to the show. The AH&I Society did charge one shilling entrance to the show,[23] and collected rents from various stalls that were there. This was confirmed by the Trustees when they were interviewed by Camden Municipal Council on 5 January 1898.

Willis continued to raise the stakes in his attack on the AH&I Society. He called a public meeting at the School of Arts on the same day where he went over his charges. He suggested that the recreation grounds would be better used as a bowling green, quoit court, tennis court, children's playground and a band rotunda. He suggested that JK Chisholm had a conflict of interest as a trustee of Onslow Park which made a lease to the AH& I Society of which he was President. He called the 300 recipients of hospitality (later called sly grog) "deadheads" and that they would be made up of "very insignificant persons from the bye-ways and highways of Minto."

Chisholm lived in Minto. He stated that the show was run by a "little clique." He also attacked treasurer Reeves as a "toady." He complained that Onslow Thompson had sent him a "saucy letter."[24] This meeting seemed to prefigure much of the style of the speech Willis made on 20 December and which was the trigger for this article you are reading now.

Meanwhile, in the Camden Council Meeting of 10 November 1897, Alderman Willis gave notice of motion that a statement of claim be made against the Trustees of Onslow Park in the Court of Equity. The *Camden News* reported that several unpleasant expressions such as dog and pig were used at the meeting. Unfortunately these animals were not recorded in the council's minutes.[25] However, the *Camden News* of 18 November 1897 did give details; the animal terms referred to an altercation between Aldermen Griffiths and Coleman who were on opposing sides regarding Willis's motion. The matter was left there as it was felt there was an equivalence of insult in the terms "dog" and "pig".

At the same council meeting the trustees said that because of the motion to take the trustees before the Court of Equity, they could only respond to the council through solicitors. They were willing, however, to make their accounts available to any alderman except Alderman Willis "as the meeting would be unpleasant to both parties." The council however insisted that all alderman be able to see the accounts.[26]

A letter from "CRS" was published in the *Camden News* attacking Willis on 18 November 1897. It suggested that the accusations of toadyism and malversation[27] showed that Willis was ignorant about the matters he was commenting on. The success of the Camden Show in itself was sufficient evidence to show that he was wrong.

CRS believed that the attacks on Chisholm and Cowper had other motives. While he did not explain these, he did state that Cowper had done everything to benefit Camden and that of Chisholm it was difficult to speak a sufficient eulogy. He felt it wrong that Chisholm, in the evening of his life, should be troubled by "foul aspersions emanating from a black heart and an envenomed tongue."

Willis responded in the next issue of the *Camden News* with the claim that CRS is firing from behind a bush as in guerrilla warfare. This referred to the anonymity of the letter and the dishonourable nature of the attack he had made. He went as far as comparing CRS to Iago, the villain in Shakespeare's *Othello*.[28]

By this time, despite their earlier attempt to drop the matter, the AH&I Society felt the need to act. The matter had reached the stage where insults were being traded (although on the side of the AH&I Society the worst of these were left to acronyms like CRS) and legal action threatened. At the AH&I committee meeting of 22 November 1897, a motion for a Special General Meeting to be held on 6 December 1897 was made by the secretary, Astley Onslow Thompson.

Thompson said that Mr Willis's charges amounted practically to accusations of corruption and misappropriation of funds. The meeting would consider the proposed resignation of the President and some of the Committee. The Committee felt the need for 75% of membership support if they were to continue.

The motion for the Special General Meeting was carried unanimously.[29] Given its unanimous support, it would appear this motion was designed to demonstrate the complete support for the president and the Committee from the members of the AH&I Society and leave Henry Willis in a position of isolation. This manoeuvre might allow the society to overcome the problems Willis had created for them.

References
1. Chisholm, JK, *Speeches and Reminiscences,* Sydney 1907, p73.
2. 2*Ibid.*
3. 3 *Evening News,* 11.9.1911.
4. 3 *Camden News* 21.1.1897.

5. Spearitt, P & Stewart, E, *Australian Dictionary of Biography: Willis, Henry (1860-1950)* http://adb.anu.edu.au/biography/willis-henry-9124 Accessed 6.1.2016.
6. *Camden News* 4.2.1897.
7. Willis, Henry, *The Abusive Mr. Chisholm in War-Paint: Public Address by Alderman Willis at the School of Arts Hall, Camden, Monday, 20th December, 1897.* ND p18.
8. *Australian Town and Country Journal,* 6.5.1903; *Camden News,* 21.1.1897; Willis, Ian, *Oran Park,* http://dictionaryofsydney.org/entry/oran_park Accessed 6.1.2015.
9. *Camden News,* 1.7.1897.
10. *Camden Agricultural, Horticultural and Industrial Society Minutes,* 30.4.1897, p198.
11. *Ibid,* p197.
12. *Camden News,* 1.7.1897.
13. *Ibid.*
14. *Camden News,* 8.7.1897.
15. *Camden Agricultural, Horticultural and Industrial Society Minutes,* 24.6.1897, p202.
16. *Camden News,* 9.9.1897.
17. *Ibid,* 16.9.1897.
18. Kidman, GV, *The Town of Camden,* Camden 1995 (facsimile of 1930s publication) p44-45.
19. *Camden News,* 9.9.1897.
20. *Ibid,* 16.9.1897.
21. *Ibid,* 28.10.1897.
22. *Conveyance of land from the Wm Macarthur and Elizabeth Onslow to JK Chisholm and others,* 12.8.1882. 1897 copy held in Camden Museum.
23. Clissold N, *Camden Show 1886-2011: The People. The Story,* Camden 2011 p53.
24. *Camden News,* 4.11.1897.
25. *Ibid,* 11.11.1897.
26. *The Council of the Municipality of Camden Council Minutes 1896-1901,* p179-181.
27. Meaning corrupt governance.
28. *Camden News,* 25.11.1897.
29. *Ibid.*

Please 'shed' light on Matavai

Anne McIntosh

Above the barn door of a property near Cobbitty is a window plate that reads 'Matavai'.

Searches for 'Matavai' on Trove provide only limited information. The Tahitian origins of the name are well documented. Rev. Roland (or Rowland) Hassall ministered in outlying areas of Sydney, moving west and south as the population expanded and moved. He profited during the 'reign' of Samuel Marsden, gaining access to government supplies and acquiring significant land through grants and purchase, including 400 acres on the Nepean River. In 1814, he was appointed supervisor of government stock, the largest herd being in the Cowpastures.

After Rev Hassall died in 1834, three of his four sons maintained pastoral pursuits, and from 'Matavai', his youngest son James played a significant role in rural life at Cobbitty for many years. This illuminating article was published in the *Camden News* on Thursday 20 March, 1924:

The old Estate of Matavia (sic.) is about to pass into other hands. This was an original grant of 200 acres to Mr Roland Hassall on behalf of his third son, Johnathan – dated 8th October 1816. He called it Matavai after the residence of King Pomare (or Pomarre) of Tahiti where Mr Hassall had been a missionary for some two years in 1796-98. King Pomare had greatly befriended the Missionaries. Correspondence from King Pomare to Governor King at Sydney is addressed from 'Matavye'. There are many other spellings of the name by the clerks in the Parish registers here.

Mr Johnathan Hassall only lived a few years at Matavai. At his death, his next brother James, whose grant 'Bosworth' was adjacent, took up residence there and began great improvements. He soon had the show farm of the district. The spacious stable built of squared stones is a monument to the activities of his time. Mr Hassell (sic) was a most enterprising man. As a youth, he wrote splendid letters in a beautiful handwriting. At first, he managed the stock on the family grants at O'Connell and elsewhere. At Matavia (sic) he made great progress with farming on a handsome scale.

Mr Martin in 'Reminiscences' says Mr Hassall gave a harvest home every year which brought the whole neighbourhood together, and the eating and drinking and merry- making were something to remember. In those days, there were two cricket clubs; one at Kirkham and the other at Matavai. The late Mrs Hope, of Melbourne – a daughter of Mr James Hassall's eldest brother, the Rev. Thos. Hassall – used to say that all the young people loved to get to Matavai because her uncle's entertainment and hospitality were so grand. The ballroom floor was the whole length of the attic story under the great roof of the Bungalow cottage.

In the forties, Mr Hassall seems to have lived for a while at Freshfield, and in 1854, to have tracked in six weeks with all his belongings in bullock wagons to western Victoria.

But we can picture Matavai posed on a height between the Cobbitty rivulet and its junction with the beautiful waters of the Nepean, overlooking all the wonderful flats to Camden and the Razorback.. The grassy slopes running right down to the waters of the river and the wonderfully terraced garden over the banks of the rivulet, with its stone walls and steps and summer house, profuse with wines of all manner of fruits. We wonder whether Matavai will yet come back to its own pristine glory; its site deserves it.

In 1847, an ad for the lease of Matavai appeared on page 4 of the *Sydney Morning Herald*:

TO LET, a desirable farm on the Nepean River, near Cobbitty, in the district of Camden and Narellan, with an excellent cottage and offices, garden , &c., &c. The farm contains seven hundred acres. Rent extremely moderate. Apply to Mr Irving, Matavai.

On 18 January, Thomas Henry Skinner's youngest daughter, Mary, married Charles Egar Gregory of "Pleasant View", Narellan. The marriage was not held in Narellan or in Cobbitty; instead it took place at the large church, St Thomas' C of E in North Sydney and was ministered by Rev. H. H. Childe. (*SMH* 15 Feb 1913)

Thomas Henry Skinner was 73 years old when he died at 'Matavai' on 11 July 1923. He was buried at St Paul's in Cobbitty, eight days later.

On page 7 of the *Camden News* of 20 Nov 1952, there is an incidental item that includes "…In the neighbourhood [of Paddy Clark's Hill] is 'Matavai' – a holding to which Mr Hugh Gordon and family are coming, and 'Bosworth' …"

The sale by auction of the 310 acres of 'Matavai' was advertised in *The Land* on 22 May 1953 at which time, the property was described as:

SITUATION: 2 miles from Cobbitty; 6 miles from Camden

COUNTRY: From riverflat to low hill. 30 acres suitable for irrigation (15 acres under lucerne), 50 acres suitable for cultivation (20 acres sown with *oats, 8 acres barley, 8 acres saccaline (*Ed. = a forage sorghum), *8 acres subclover), 230 acres of grazing land.*

WATERED: *Half mile frontage Nepean River, Cobbitty*

Creek on northern end, which has permanent holes, 5 earth dams.

BUILDINGS: *Weatherboard homestead on brick foundation, louvred, iron roof, electric light, power connected in the home and dairy, garage and tool room, laundry. Weatherboard cottage with verandah. Dairy and milk room. Feed stalls and chaff shed. Feed shed – stone and brick. Large hayshed.*

CARRYING CAPACITY: *The owner considers this property, which has a Dairy Milk Board Licence would carry approximately 80 cattle or make an ideal horse or cattle stud, and could also be used for vegetable growing. ...*

The property did not sell and was re-advertised for auction by a rural Commission Agent on 5 June 1953.

Possible clue: In the registration of stock brands reference book, a brand registered in 1959 features a right pointing arrow over I-C. It is registered to: Haden Archie William and Craig Thomas Alexander of Matavai, Cut Hill, Cobbitty.

Does anyone remember 'Matavai' and its heritage, either as a show farm, a cricket ground, or a ballroom? Can anyone share insights into its incarnations since 1953?

Ria and the story of the song, *Camden*.

Ian Willis

Ria was the special invited guest at the 2018 Camden Shorts Program sponsored by Camden Council at the Camden Civic Centre where she performed her own song composition called *Camden*.

Ria is the stage name for Ria Brcic, a Camden local, who was inspired to write about her home town when she was working overseas. The story of the song *Camden* is told here in the first person by Ria and it goes like this:

Camden is a composition of mine that I hold very dearly to my heart. I wrote this song in 2016 when I embarked on an experience of a life time, moving to Spain on my own to learn a new language and culture. Lucky enough for me this experience gave me the opportunity to write more, through inspiration I founded whilst travelling.

In the midst of it all I found myself starting to feel a little homesick and on one particularly cold afternoon my emotions got the better of me, which somehow splattered out onto a page in under thirty minutes. I was purely inspired by the love for my home town and the people I missed. When I was writing this song that would later be called Camden, *I was reminiscing about all the great things this place had to offer. Camden is a beautiful town with a river that surrounds us and beautiful historic buildings and churches. It also wasn't until I was gone that I realised how lucky I was to live in this town, my home, Camden.*

Camden, the lyrics.
Ria Brcic

(Verse 1)
Ohh Camden is where I'm from
A place where I belong
With a home by the river
But it's just not that, some things go way back

(Verse 2)
Ohh Camden is on the map
South west in the old outback
With a home by the river
How could it be, it's still home for me

Ria Brcic 2018 at a performance in the Camden area (R Brcic)

(Chorus)
My home by the river
It's my safe keeping with a family
And we all have dreams
And mine starts right here so just keep listening
For the story, for the story

(Verse 3)
Oh I've travelled around the world

I've seen places that has got be curled
Landscapes of beauty pathways for life
But I didn't feel whole, I just wanted to cry

(Verse 4)
Oh my family they weren't there
Without my best friend nothing to share
Oh my home by the river
Could you please come back, lets have a chat

(Chorus)
My home by the river
It's my safe keeping with a family
And we all have dreams
And mine starts right here so just keep listening
For the story, for the story (X2)

(Chorus)
My home by the river
It's my safe keeping with a family
And we all have dreams
And mine starts right here so just keep listening
For the story, for the story (X3)
Oh Camden is where I'm from

Camden Shorts

Camden Shorts is part of the youth program of Camden Council and provides a venue for young performers to showcase their talent.

Camden Council website states:
The entertaining evening of short works provides young local musicians and performers an opportunity to showcase their talents in live music, dance and theatre by young local musicians and performers.

The 2018 Camden Shorts, on Friday 20 April, showcased 13 young performers ranging across dances, vocal, musical to performance art. There was an enthusiastic crowd of family and friends who cheered on the performers.

Ria says,
The first time I performed at Camden Shorts was in 2016 at the beginning of the year. It was a very surreal experience for me because it was run so professionally and there was such a big turn out on the night. I sang two songs that meant a lot to me and it was after that, my confidence levels boosted.

When I was invited by Cheryle Yin-Lo to come and perform as a special guest at the Camden Shorts 2018 I was very honoured. Honoured because she saw me as an inspiration and example for the younger performers to look up to. It's the performances like these where I am able to share and express my passion through music and the journey I've embarked with my community that I'll always remember.

Ria, a short biography

Ria tells her story so far trying to make her way in the music industry as a singer-songwriter and it goes like this:

I am Ria Brcic, an aspiring singer-songwriter immensely passionate for music. My constant hard work is put into building my repertoire and with that I focus on intertwining my influence of folk music with country.

My musical journey began at the tender age of five when I used to sing for my grandfather when we came down to Sydney to paint my house. He was the first person to recognise my musical talent and it was his encouragement that really sparked my passion. I then later went on and began lessons and have been vocally trained for the past six years and have taken guitar lessons for around four years. As well as this, I have been performing on stage since the age of seven, so I am no stranger to performing in front of crowds.

I currently have two song releases, one being an original called 'Shoot Me Down' and the other a rendition of the classic 'Can't Help Falling in Love'. In the likes of young artists such as Gabrielle Aplin and Birdy to the greats of Dolly Parton, Janis Joplin and Leonard Cohen, I hope to one-day forge a career in the music industry and with hard work and persistence believe it's possible.

Memories of Milton and Elaine Ray

Gail Carroll (ne Ray)

In June 2018 Gail Carroll responded to a Facebook post that Ian Willis's Linkedin blog article called Volunteering is a form of voluntary taxation'.

Gail recalls:

My father Milton Ray contributed many hundreds of hours as a volunteer Fireman and founding member of the Camden Historical Society. Volunteering was a very important part of his life and our upbringing. It enriched us all .

Both my mother and father were in the Camden Historical Society from the early 1960's and had regular bus trips to historical sites around Camden. I remember joining in when I was in Camden Primary School. Mr Nixon was president [and] my mother Elaine Ray was secretary.

My mother would have meticulously handwritten these minutes. My father was a keen movie photographer he put together The Passing of Pansy, segments of the last train trips from Camden to Campbelltown.

I remember being on those last Pansy trips hanging out the window waving madly. My father put on reel film all the bus excursions made by the historical society. My sister Lesley Anne Hoskin gave these to the society when my father passed away.

It was really something when the Camden Historical Society acquired their first display rooms at the back of the original Camden Library. My parents were there every weekend. Dad organised the wheel to commemorate the bullock drivers who brought the timber from Burragorang Valley. It still stands outside the old council chambers.

My father was a Camden volunteer fireman before I was born in 1952. I loved the Christmas Party at the fire station every year as I grew up. My father looked after the fire truck and would take us children on a loop of Camden Argyle Street., sitting on the side bench seats! The Camden Historical Society also has his fireman's uniform with the very distinctive brass helmet.

When Dad retired he joined Menangle Steam Museum again a founding member. He loved his Fordson and Whitehall tractors and would often lead procession on these at the Camden Show and Campbelltown Show. My father was also a dedicated volunteer of St Johns Anglican Church always joining clean up teams and regularly climbed the bell tower to wind the clock and provide maintenance. He was a church warden for many years.

My father loved Camden and helping out when ever he could was his way of life. My parents were on the Camden Primary [School] P&C as well as Camden High School P&C. My father would bring out his go kart for children to ride at school fetes! We were a part of a fantastic community of volunteers who made Camden an exceptionally great place to live.

Milton Ray (centre) at the 50th Anniversary Celebrations of the Camden Historical Society on 20 July 2007. The other Camden identities are Vic Boardman (left) and Dick Nixon (right). (R Herbert/Camden Images)

Dr Joan Mary Woodhill
A notable scientist from Camden

Marilyn Willis

A reserve at Gregory Hills in the Camden LGA has been named the "Woodhill Reserve" after a former notable Camden scientist Joan Mary Woodhill.

Joan was born in Camden on 5 May 1912 to New South Wales's born Frank Leslie Woodhill and Maria Louise, nee Pepper, born in Tasmania. She was the youngest of three siblings. Her father was a store keeper and ran his business out of the Whiteman building in Argyle Street Camden.

The family lived at 9 Menangle Road Camden in a house which was purchased in 1905. They lived in this house until her father died in 1918. After his death her mother sold the business and moved to Gordon in Sydney northern suburbs.

Joan had a successful career as a dietician although her first degree was in Agricultural Science where she graduated from University of Sydney in 1934. Being a male dominated area she was unable to find employment in the field of agricultural science so pursued employment in the field of dietetics. She travelled to United States of America where she worked, completed research and courses towards attaining a Masters Degree. Joan then returned to Australia to work at RPA and teach students and also to be involved in research.

Joan completed her Masters a number of years later back in the USA and then worked towards her doctorate (PhD) also in the USA. After completing her PhD she worked at Royal Newcastle Hospital and Prince Henry Hospital where she conducted many research projects.

She had many highlights in her career as a Dietician when she came back to Australia, being the first Australian to be given the title of Chief Dietician, a foundation member of the NSW Dietetic Association, a nutrition research officer in the Department of Medicine & also a biochemist in their Department of Biomedicine with the University of NSW.

According to a colleague she was a great mentor to dietetic students. She spent a lot of her time completing research projects in a variety of areas and wrote many articles for journals. In 1973 she was appointed an OBE & was made an honorary life member of the Dietetics Association in 1983.

She had a connection with the South Coast of New South Wales as she had a holiday house at Huskisson. She was also related to the Woodhills of Nowra who ran a general store situated in Berry Street Nowra.

Joan never married and died on 12 December 1990.

Reference:
Diana Brown, 'Woodhill, Joan Mary (1912–1990)', *Australian Dictionary of Biography*, National Centre of Biography, Australian National University, http://adb.anu.edu.au/biography/woodhill-joan-mary-15628/text26829 , published first in hardcopy 2012, accessed online 16 April 2018.

**Joan Mary Woodhill (on right) aged 21.
(Faculty of Agriculture, University of
Sydney, 1933)**

President Annual Report 2017-2018

Ian Willis

It is with pleasure that I present the annual report of the Camden Historical Society. It has been a busy and challenging year for the society.

The society continues to contribute to a number of roles in the community and including: acting as a centre of volunteering and construction of resilient communities; contributing to local tourism.

Advocacy
The society continues to tell the Camden story and support local heritage by contributing to:
- The Camden Town Centre Urban Design Framework.
- suggestions for street names in new suburbs
- Representation on Camden Council's Heritage Advisory Committee.
- Commenting on a number of development applications and the sale of land at St Johns Church, which have contributed to a drop in society membership.

Participation in the community
The society has attended at a number of community events including:
- In 2017: the Civic Centre Antique Fair; HCNSW History Week;
- In 2018: Australia Day parade; Camden Show; National Trust Heritage Week 'My Culture, My Story'; Camden Council Volunteers Night

Speakers at society meetings
Speakers at monthly meetings have included:
- Robert Wheeler on the history of the Camden Residents Action Group
- Peter Ryan on the history of The Pines at Menangle Park
- David Funnell on his memories of Camden
- Dr Harvey Broadbent on Gallipoli.
- Bradley Warner on an Aging Community
- Michelle Scott Tucker on her book on Elizabeth Macarthur
- Jeff McGill on his book 'Pictorial History of Campbelltown'.

Volunteers
Volunteers continue to do a great job in a range of capacities from staffing the front desk, research, attending functions, advocacy and other activities. The roster for the front desk in well managed by volunteer coordinator Rene Rem. He rounds up new volunteers and solves all myriad of issues that crop up. There are currently over 50 volunteers on the roster.

I conducted a brief survey of volunteer hours and preliminary findings indicated that in a notional week Camden Museum volunteers put in around 240 hours of voluntary unpaid effort.

Volunteers also attended:
>Volunteers Day in June where Laura Jane talked about her Shirley Temple collection and Frances Warner launched a new edition of *They Worked at Camden Park*.
>Glass Slide Conservation Workshop at The Oaks Historical Society

Museum
The museum attracted over 6000 visitors in the last year including a number of school visits and community groups. The society successfully obtained a grant from Camden Council for new display cabinets upstairs. The museum took possession of a convict love token that was given by Charles Green to his wife Sarah before he left England in 1831. The society has installed a new and improved CCTV system which was sponsored by Camden Rotary. The old photocopier was replaced with the lease on a new machine.

The Percival Wagon
In mid-2017 the Macarthur Anglican School announced to the society that it wanted the partially completed Percival wagon moved from the school premises. At the time the society was not in a position to restore the wagon or place the incomplete wagon in a suitable location.

After some negotiations the new custodian of the wagon is The Oaks Historical Society. Their members offered to move the wagon from the school and finish the restoration. The Camden Historical Society provided funds of $1000 towards the project.
By February this year The Oaks Historical Society had completed restoration of the chassis and tray. In March the Camden Historical Society wrote a letter of support for the The Oaks Historical Society as they sought grants for a blacksmith exhibit, with the restored wagon as the centre piece. By June two of the restored wheels from the wheelwright in Queensland arrived at The Oaks, and the cost of restoration of $4000 was met by Macarthur Anglican School (originally a grant from Camden Council in 2012).

Tim Cartwright, the Dean of Students at Macarthur Anglican School, organised the original offer to restore the wagon in 2012. He reports:

When the School took possession of the wagon, the entire sub structure was affected by white-ant and dry rot. This became evident when the front wheels folded under themselves unable to steer or take their own weight.

A small team of enthusiastic Year 7 and Year 9 boys with no practical carpentry experience gathered every Friday afternoon and sometimes through school holidays, with the intention of renovating and replacing all parts of the wagon to bring it to a point where it could be used rather than just as a display.

Over the four year period the boys learnt essential carpentry skills often producing work that demanded great attention to detail and a skill level that would be demanding even for modern practice.

The boys included: Adam Ebeling; Jack Jansen; Richard Cartwright; Henry Cartwright; Tom Oliver; Daniel Pearce

The boys took great pride in their work and were always concerned to replicate original parts instead of compromising on easier or more convenient solutions. This project has been rich in learning in many aspects and I am thrilled to have led the boys on this pathway of preserving our local heritage and introducing them to skills they will be able to revisit in years to come.

Trish Hill, the president of the The Oaks Historical Society, says 'the wagon is looking like new'. She also reports that:

A new shaft was needed to replace one that had rotted completely and under guidance from Jim Whyte, Kevin Wintle completed [this]. Others who worked on the wagon were Frank & Raymond Mackie and John Hyland.

The 2 smaller wheels were rebuilt by Nobby Forge in Queensland and we liaised with Raymond Mackie (who was working in Qld) to pick them up from Nobby for us.
We have been advised the 2 large wheels should arrive from Bungendore sometime in September and so will complete the wagon.

We now have our blacksmith facility/shed approved by [Wollondilly] Council and ready to commence building work (along with our extension). [The new building] will house the wagon under cover, which will be great.
If anyone wants to have a look please call in any time. When the last [2] wheels arrive and [the wagon] is fully finished we will organise an afternoon tea and invite your members.

Membership
Society membership is down by 20% in 2018 compared to 2017. The society will endeavour to improve this situation.

Administration

The society computer system was recently upgraded to Windows 10 and resulted in the accounting MYOB crashing. Accountant Kathy Lester has been working with treasurer Dawn to recover the accounting records. I would like to thank Kathy and Dawn for their considerable efforts in this area. In addition Kathy has prepared a detailed analysis of the society's financial position and highlighted a number of shortcomings which are being addressed by the committee.

Community Partnership
The society continues with the partnership with Camden Library and the Camden Area Family History Society. Joint activities have included: Heritage Week in April; History Week in September; and the collection of photographs in Camden Images Past and Present.

Communication
The society published a journal twice a year and a newsletter three times a year. Lee Stratton looks after the newsletter and I am the journal editor. A number of members provide stories to the Back Then page of *The District Reporter*.
The society has a strong online presence with its website, Camden History, managed by Steve Robinson. Rene Rem looks after the Camden Museum facebook page and I look after our presence on the Google business pages, where some visitors have uploaded their photos. The museum has received excellent ratings this year on TripAdvisor.

Welfare
Volunteer Sue Cross follows up members with messages of 'get well' and 'expression of sympathy'.

Financial assistance
The society has the continued support of Camden Council through a yearly subsidy covering insurances, the provision of two storage units at Narellan and the on-going maintenance of the museum. Camden Council has digitized a number of historic maps.

Final Thanks
In conclusion I wish to thank everyone on the committee, volunteers and others who have assisted the society over the past year. I wish to thank Dawn Williams for the sterling work as treasurer, particularly in the light of a recent tragic loss. The society remains in a strong financial position.
I look forward to 2019.

August 2018

Changing environments for small charitable organisations

Kathy Lester

The environment and legal responsibilities that small charities like Camden Historical Society Inc. operate within has dramatically changed within the last ten years.

Changes to various legislation means that the obligations and reporting responsibilities of small charitable organisations have increased from the days when all we had to do was hold an AGM, submit the annual return to the Office of Fair Trading and if required complete a quick and easy acquittals to funding bodies.

The introduction of the GST was only the beginning of many changes to follow. The advances in technologies and communication practices have made it easier for regulatory bodies to check and compare data provided to different government departments to ensure accuracy and avoid duplicated accounting.

The introduction of the Charities and Not-for-Profit Commission (ACNC) affords the government the ability to closely scrutinise the operations of Charities and NFPs. Reporting is no longer confined to financial reports and changes in constitutions or the Public Officer. The ACNC is streamlining the number of reports required while asking for more details from organisations.

Reports submitted are now used by more than one level of government and the Commission is attempting to adopt a report one use often approach. The ANCN is assisting charities understand their obligations by providing information and support, while assisting the public to understand how the sector works and that they can trust the legitimacy of registered charities and NFPs.

New regulations and responsibilities have filtered down to all aspects of the business in organisations such as ours. In running the society we are required to ensure that we provide good management that provides a safe environment for society members, volunteers and visitors to our museum.

Good management of the society's business practices that ensure the longevity of the organisation, needs to include a working knowledge and the application of best practices pertaining to, but not limited to:

- Privacy Act
- GST compliance
- Copyright
- Accounting Standards
- Provision of safe workplace practices (for volunteers)
- Child Protection measures
- Charitable practices
- Risk management

Together with best practice in museum management, the organisation's committee can ensure an ongoing opportunity for our volunteers and visitors to enjoy the society's promotion of Camden's history and heritage into the future.

Camden Item of Significance

WHAT IS THIS?

This activity could be used for grades 1-4 using the below outcomes. Lesson would be varied for the appropriate age group.

Outcomes:
HT1-2 identifies and describes significant people, events, places and sites in the local community over time

HT2-2 describes and explains how significant individuals, groups and events contributed to changes in the local community over time

Lesson Introduction
Present the above picture to your class. Using I See, I Think, I Wonder ask students to think about what they think the item is and what the purpose of it is.

Core Lesson
As a class, students will share their wonderings. Teacher explains to the class that the picture is of a spinning wheel. A spinning wheel is used to weave wool into cloth which is later turned into clothing.

Play students a video of a Spinning Wheel in operation such as: https://www.youtube.com/watch?v=ex1Atx1tQPk

Teacher explains to the class that this spinning wheel was made by Mr Domenico Brunero of Purcell Street, Camden. He made it for the Camden Red Cross Branch to spin wool for garments to be sent to the armed forces in World War One.

If teaching students in Years 1 to 4, students could then begin exploring Camden Red Cross. Teacher to provide material depending on the direction of the lesson/grade.

Resources
http://camdenhistorynotes.blogspot.com/2014/03/camden-museum.html
http://www.camdenhistory.org.au/cmrcmensbranch.pdf
Information from Camden Museum Object File.

Kathryn Pesic
Teacher
Macarthur Anglican School.

[This is a sample teaching resource for primary teachers of Stage 2 for the NSW K-12 History Syllabus. It was developed by Kathryn Pesic for the CHS Primary Teacher Programing Workshop held on Tuesday 28 August 2018.]

CAMDEN HISTORY

Journal of the Camden Historical Society

March 2019 Volume 4 Number 7

CAMDEN HISTORY
Journal of the Camden Historical Society Inc.
ISSN 1445-1549
Editor: Dr Ian Willis

Management Committee
President: Dr Ian Willis
Vice Presidents: John Wrigley OAM, Cathey Shepherd
Secretary: Lee Stratton
Treasurer: Kathy Lester
Immediate Past President: Bob Lester
General Committee: Julie Wrigley, Robert Wheeler, Sharon Greene, Cathy Shepherd, Frances Warner, Warren Sims

Honorary Solicitors: Warren & Warren

Society contact:
P.O. Box 566, Camden, NSW 2570. Online <http://www.camdenhistory.org.au>

Meetings
Meetings are held at 7.30 p.m. on the second Wednesday of the month except in January. They are held in the Museum. Visitors are always welcome.

Museum
The Museum is located at 40 John Street, Camden, phone 4655 3400. It is open Thursday to Sunday 11 a.m. to 4 p.m., except at Christmas. Visits by schools and groups are encouraged. Please contact the Museum to make arrangements. Entry is free.

Camden History, Journal of the Camden Historical Society Inc
The Journal is published in March and September each year. The Editor would be pleased to receive articles broadly covering the history of the Camden district . Correspondence can be sent to the Society's postal address. The views expressed by authors in journal articles are solely those of the authors and not necessarily endoresed by the Camden Historical Society.

Donations
Donations made to the Society are tax deductible. The accredited value of objects donated to the Society are eligible for tax deduction.

Front Cover William Macarthur brought in the "The Waratah Camellia" *anenomiflora (*The Camden Park Camellia*)* arrived in Port Jackson in 1831 on HMS Sovereign. (Engraving courtesy CPH) **Back Cover** New varieties of camellias were developed at Camden Park by nurseryman, William Macarthur, and promoted in his nursery catalogues. (A McIntosh, Camden Park Open Day 2017). Read more https://www.gardenclinic.com.au/how-to-grow-article/australia-s-first-camellia

CAMDEN HISTORY
Journal of the Camden Historical Society Inc.

Contents

The Camden District Hospital Nurses' Home   286
Ian Willis

Some Nursing Memories   290
Tricia Smith, Frances Warner, Trish Clark, Margaret Wheeler

Camden Museum Volunteer Project   298
Dianne Matterson

The Abusive Mr Chisholm (Part Two)   299
Peter McCall

***Baragal Ngurra darami* – Budbury and a paddock long ago**   307
Venessa Possum

My Story: The Tandem Team Launch Tourism, 1978-1988, Macarthur Country   314
Betty Yewen

A Picture Tells a Thousand Words. Fashion Speaks Just as Loud!   316
Laura Jane Aulsebrook

***William Macarthur and the Empire of Science*, presentation by Dr Julie McIntyre at State Library of NSW**   321
From notes taken by Anne McIntosh

The Camden District Hospital Nurses' Home

Ian Willis

Over 700 locals and visitors were present for the official opening of the Camden District Hospital nurses quarters, later known as the 'nurses' home', by the NSW Minister of Health WF Sheehan in June 1962. Official proceedings at the opening were led hospital-chairman FJ Sedgewick who said that the hospital-board had been working towards the addition of the new building for many years. (*Camden News* 27 June 1962)

Construction on the building had begun in mid-1961 and had cost £92,000. It was located on farmland purchased by the hospital-board in 1949 opposite the hospital in Menangle Road on Windmill Hill. The three-storey brick building had suspended concrete floors with a brick exterior. It was designed by architects Hobson and Boddington and influenced by mid-20th century modernism and International Functionalism. The nurses accommodation of 40 single rooms with separate bathrooms was a vast improvement on the wartime military barracks.

Adequate accommodation for nurses had been an issue for hospital administrators since the hospital opening in 1902. Originally Camden nurses were provided with two bedrooms within the hospital building which had soon proved to be inadequate. (*A Social History of Camden District Hospital*, by Doreen Lyon and Liz Vincent, 1998, p.17) Nurses were quartered within a hospital complex based on the presumption that this was necessary because of their 7-day 24-hour-shift roster that meant that they worked all hours. Added to this was the Nightingale philosophy that the respectability and morality of the nurses had to be protected at all costs. The all-male Camden hospital-board took their responsibility seriously and considered there was a moral imperative to protect the respectability of their young single female nurses.

Camden District Hospital was the major medical facility between Liverpool and Bowral and the booming Yerranderie silver field mines put pressure on the hospital. More patients meant a need for more staff. In 1907 a government grant allowed the hospital-board to purchase a four-room cottage next to the hospital for £340 and convert it to nurses' accommodation. (*Camden News*, 30 May 1907, 13 June 1907, 6 February 1908, 26 March 1908) Completed renovations in 1908 allowed the hospital-board to appoint a new probationary nurse, Miss Hattersley of Chatswood. (*Camden News*, 18 June 1908) The hospital's status increased in 1915 when the Australasian Trained Nurses Association (ATNA) approved the hospital as a registered training school. (*Camden News*, 28 January 1915) Continuing pressure on the

Camden District Hospital around 1930 in Menangle Road Camden. The nurses quarters built in 1928 are on the right hand side of image. The original hospital building has an additional floor constructed in 1916. The first matron of the Camden District Hospital was Josephine Hubbard assisted by Nurse Nelson with Senior Probationary Nurse Mary McNee. (Camden Images)

nurses accommodation stopped the hospital-board from appointing a new probationary nurse in 1916. (*Camden News*, 6 July 1916) While things were looking up in 1924 when electricity was connected to the hospital. (*Camden Crier*, 6 April 1983)

The hospital continued to grow as the new mines in the Burragorang coal-fields opened up and adequate on-site nurses' accommodation remained a constant headache for the hospital administration. In 1928 the hospital-board approved the construction of a handsome two-storey brick nurses' quarters at a cost of £2950 on the site of the existing timber cottage. (*Camden News*, 12 July 1928; *Sydney Morning Herald*, 20 July 1928) The building design was influenced by the Interwar functionalist style and was a proud addition to the town's growing stock of Interwar architecture with its outdoor verandahs, tiled roof and formal-hedged garden.

Temporary nurses' accommodation was added in December 1947 as each nurse was now entitled to a separate bedroom under the new Nurses Award. The hospital-board purchased a surplus hut from Camden Airfield as war-

This handsome Interwar building is the Camden Hospital Nurse Quarters built in 1928 on the site of the 1907 nurses cottage adjacent to the hospital in Menangle Road. The brick two-storey building has external verandahs and a formal hedged garden. The nurses' home is one of number of handsome Interwar buildings found in Camden town area. It was demolished for the construction of Hodge hospital building in 1971. (Camden Images)

related activities wound down and the airfield buildings were sold off by the defence authorities. The hut was formerly a British RAF workshop. It measured 71 by 18 feet, cost £175 and was relocated next to the hospital free of charge by Cleary Bros. RAF transport squadrons were located at Camden Airfield from 1944 and local girls swooned over the presence of the 'blue uniformed flyers' and even married some of them. Hut renovations were carried out to create eight bedrooms, two store cupboards and bathroom accommodation at a cost of £370. Furnishings cost £375 with expenses met by the NSW Hospital Commission. The new building was opened by local politician Jeff Bate MHR. (*Picton Post*, 22 December 1947. *Camden News*, 1 January 1948)

As the Burragorang coalfields ramped up, so did the demands on the hospital and the nurses' accommodation crisis persisted. The issue constrained hospital authorities from employing additional nursing staff (*Camden News*, 21

Camden Hospital Nurses Quarters opened in 1962 by the NSW Health Minister WF Sheehan. The building is influenced by 20th-century modernism International Functionalism and designed by architects Hobson and Boddington. The building is located in Menangle Road opposite the hospital complex. (I Willis, 2018)

September 1950) and the opening of the hospital's new maternity wing in 1951 did not help. (*Camden News*, 4 March 1954)

The new 1962 nurses' quarters did not solve the accommodation issue as the hospital grew from 74 beds in 1963 to 156 in 1983 (*Macarthur Advertiser*, 1 March 1983). Patient facilities improved with the opening of the 4-storey Hodge wing in 1971 on the site of the 1928 nurses' quarters. (*Camden News*, 3 March 1971)

The last intake of hospital-based training for nurses took place at Camden District Hospital in July 1984 and nurse education was transferred from hospitals to the colleges of advanced education in 1985. *(A Social History of Camden District Hospital,* by Doreen Lyon and Liz Vincent, 1998, p.58)

Some Nursing Memories

What follows are the memories of a number of local nurses who tell their story in their own voice. The reminiscences are largely unedited and reflect the lived experience of these nurses. This means that there is necessarily some repetition across the individual stories and the memories of the individuals who have written them independently (the editor).

Pat 'Tricia' Smith

I commenced my nurses training at Camden District Hospital in 1964. Back then it was four years training. I completed my training in 1968. Nursing was very different back then. You learnt on the job. Discipline was strict. You had to stand for anyone senior with your hands behind your back. So when you were a junior nurse, you never seemed to sit down, always up and down.

All nurses had to live in the nurses home. Junior nurses on the bottom floor, RNs (registered nurse) on the middle floor along with matron's flat. Senior nurses on the top floor. The nurses home was locked every night when evening shift finished and unlocked when the junior night nurse came over to call the day shift nurses. This was about 6.15am. No Workplace Health and Safety in those days. We were locked in.

We were allowed a late pass twice a month. This was 12 midnight. You had to go and find the night supervisor. She would come over and let you in. Of course, we had ways of getting in later. You would get one of the nurses on the bottom floor who had a balcony room and let her know you would be sneaking in. You had to be very quiet because our night supervisor Sister Kirby had acute hearing and could hear from the hospital, especially if a car stopped outside the nurses home. If you were caught, you were in big trouble.

We had visitors rooms at the nurses' home. It was a small room on the bottom floor. No male visitors passed this room. If you were off-duty or on days off, you had to go over to the hospital staff dining room for your meals. There was a kettle and a toaster in the little kitchenette of the recreation room on the bottom floor of the nurses' home. The RNs had a kitchen on their floor.

We nurses worked hard. We made lasting friendships. We had a lot of good times in the nurses' home because we were together for four years. We grew up together. Most of us were 17 years old when we came nursing and 21 years when we completed our training. We went on to further our training, got married and raised families.

I worked in nursing in Sydney Southwest Area Health until I retired in 2009. I have seen many changes. When I watch the television mini-series *Call The*

Midwife I did a lot of those procedures in the early 1960s. I had forgotten them until I saw it on the program.

Frances Warner

I came from Eastwood to start nursing training at Camden District Hospital aged 17 years in 1963. I lived in the nurses home opposite the hospital in a single room on the lower ground floor facing Menangle Road. There was plenty of room and a verandah. The rooms were cleaned by staff and linen given out each Monday.

We had a communal shower room and there were only females in the nurses home. There was a large community room, with lounges, table and chairs, TV, radio and a sunny verandah. There was a small kitchenette on the ground floor and a visitors' room, which was the only area for male visitors.

Rules. No going to Camden or out in uniform. No male company in the nurses' home, except for the visitors room. Nothing about cars at the back of nurses home. The front door to nurses home locked at 10.00pm. You were able to request a late pass for midnight and the night sister would unlock nurses home quarters.

Uniforms were supplied, washed and ironed and delivered upstairs to a store room. We wore a cotton dress, white full apron, wide white starched belt, with a starched white cap with Vs for every year of training. I extra starched my belt so it kept its shape longer.

Meals were supplied in the dining room at the hospital. There were large tables, white tablecloths and cloth serviettes. Mealtimes were breakfast, lunch and early dinner. There was a variety on the menu. Fish (battered flake) on Fridays. Tea, coffee and cool drinks whenever you wanted them.

Lectures were compulsory and held in a study room at the back of the hospital on the Old Hume Highway side. You might have to attend classes on your day off. There was a hospital kiosk outside the hospital. You were allowed to have 'tick', and pay account on pay day. We were paid in cash that we collected from the main hospital office near the left hand side of the main door. Now always locked. How much? Can't remember. I always had plenty of cash.

I mainly worked in male ward. There were two wards. The male public and an intermediate ward of four beds. The staff office was in the intermediate ward. There was an RN (registered nurse) office. The public male ward was L-shaped with 9-10 beds facing Menangle Road. The ward kitchen was off the public ward. The female ward KRAFT had 8 beds and verandah

A group of second year trainee nurses in uniform standing outside the Camden Hospital Nurses Quarters in 1965. Nurse Frances Fisher (later Warner) on right (S Roberts)

(Menangle Road side), and intermediate 4 beds. Children beds and cots. Isolation had a single bed. The emergency ward was in front on hospital facing Menangle Road. There was also the operating theater and maternity.

On duty. Starts were 6.00am, 9.00am, 2.30pm, 10.00pm. We had two days off and mostly had late shift after days off. Sometimes were had longer time off with three days together. Matron Harley's visit to the wards from 9.00am and you had to be ready! At change over there were oral reports and you needed a notebook. In the morning there was bathing and blanket bath. Tooth mug and bowl provided an oral toilet with glycerine swabs to clean mouth, lips and tongue, which also happened after each meal.

Nursing the pressure areas you would wash and dry and apply 'metho' or cream, or fish oil. This would apply to back, buttocks, elbows, feet and heels. Men were shaved by nurses if help was needed. The body was shaved for operations. Clean linen, hospital corners, bed spread. There was no lying on bedspread. There were wheels on the beds and they all faced inwards with a bed table at the end of the bed for a water jug and cup only.

Obs (observations) were done and noted on the chart at the end of the bed. You needed four coloured pen for recording pulse, respiration, B/P (blood pressure), temperature, urine and bowels. Patient meals for breakfast, lunch and dinner were in hot boxes. Nursing staff delivered meals to patients and also feed where necessary. Nurses made up morning and afternoon teas. There was a kitchen in the wards, with cake and biscuits coming from main kitchen. Tea, coffee, Bonox and Activate (chocolate) vitamins. There was egg flip and 1oz brandy for special diet. Trainee nurses cooked dinner for nurses in ward kitchen. It was mainly lamb chops, boiled potato, fresh greens and salad. I had never cooked in my life.

Visiting hours were 2.00-3.30pm, and 7.00-8.30pm. A bell rang to finish visiting hours. For visiting hours papers and magazines were out of sight, quilts on and wheels-in-line, then the RN checked and then the doors opened. The 2.30pm shift: rolled up washed bandages; organised dressing trays and wound cleaning; needles checked and steelwool along shaft to check for burs. Bedtime and lights out at 9.30pm. Night shift: one RN and 2-3 nurses on duty; RN – Sister Kirby, Sister Emms. Before going on night shift there were tasks that trainees could do unaided – temperature, B/P, and stitch removal.

PV swabs. For females warm water wash, cleaning with cotton wool swabs (per vagina cleaning). There were metal bedpans for both sexes. These were warmed, not hot, with tissue paper covers. Metal urinals also had covers. These were never allowed to stay in the wards. Some urinals were concealed under sheets. Bedpans and bottles (urinals) were shined up with Bon-Ami (powder cleaner). Urine was tested by boiling in glass tubes over 'metho' burners. I still have my training, practical experience booklet.

With a death nurses needed to care for the body and prepared it to be taken down a steep ramp at the back of the hospital, Old Hume Highway side. You had to wash and shave males and put a little make-up on females. Hair was groomed, body cavities sealed, jaw bandaged and the body dressed in a shroud. You would wrap round white cotton robe. In the daytime, 'Johnny' helped with the fridge at the mortuary (morg) while in the evening and at night there were nurses only. There were no male nurses in my time.

I travelled by steam or diesel train from Strathfield station. There was the local bus. The taxi was owned by Max Fuller and many times he did not charge. Max's wife, Mable, did her nurses' aid training course in maternity as a mature aged student.

Entertainment was watching TV and *Dr Ben Casey* was popular. There was tennis at the nurses quarters in the evening. There was the pictures at Browne St in Campbelltown and there was knitting. And going home to my family at Eastwood.

My nurses group included: Dossie Small (Blatch); Judy Pell (Appleton); Carol Dee (Carmagnola); Wendy Thompson; Monica Williams (Hall); Frances Fisher (Warner); Pat Dredge (Smith) ; … Scott; Matron Harley; kitchen – Elise Lord; wardsman – Bob Lavender; garden and odd job man – Johnny…

I did not finish my four year training course as I got married in January 1966.

Trish Clark

Although I am retired now, I often look back fondly on my nursing career and especially the time spent working in the Macarthur area at Campbelltown and Camden Hospitals and in Community Health. As I reflect on my time working in the Maternity Unit at Camden Hospital, one word to describe it was BUSY. In 1981, when I commenced midwifery training there, Camden was the only maternity unit between Liverpool and Bowral and the population in the area was already increasing.

As a pupil midwife a requirement for registration was to deliver at least 20 babies and attend and witness another 100 births. It did not take long to chalk up this tally as the labour wards were mostly always full, with overflow to 'prep' rooms. Postnatal mums often recovered in the adjoining female ward because the postnatal ward was full.

A prefabricated demountable building, which we nicknamed 'Fawlty Towers', was erected to accommodate the increasing numbers before the opening of Campbelltown Hospital Maternity Wing. At that time the original postnatal ward was located on the lower ground floor and the babies were trundled into the lift in their metal cots and taken back up to the nursery during visiting hours and at night. Many would remember displaying the pink or blue baby

Trish Clark (centre, back) at her 1982 nurses Midwifery Graduation at Camden District Hospital (T Clark)

name card at a large viewing window at visiting time and the midwife would wheel the cot with its precious cargo for friends and family to catch a glimpse of the new addition to the family. Rooming babies in with mums is now the order of the day.

There was often a baby for adoption in the nursery which was spoilt with lots of cuddles and affection by the nurses and midwives working there. I remember Matron J Harley who lived in the nurses home across the road doing her rounds with some old school methods ordering us to open up the windows to let in the fresh air, even in winter. We did so but closed them quickly when she had left.

I didn't ever live in the nurses home but there were still nurses residing there when I worked at Camden and we sometimes used the common room for meetings and study sessions. I stayed at Camden as a registered midwife after completing my training before moving into the Community Health sector.

Margaret Wheeler

We arrived in Camden in 1989, and in 1990 I applied at Camden Hospital as a Registered Nurse. It was the first time I had been interviewed by a male matron, or as they were then known, Director of Nursing.

The area was the beginning of change and I ended up working at the hospital for eight months. Many of the staff had been there for years. At first I worked in the surgical ward, where we were allocated a number of patients and were in charge of these patients until the end of the shift. Later I worked in the newly built rehabilitation unit. There was a great deal of settling in, and quite heavy nursing at times due to the type of patient to be looked after. There was a mix of geriatric care, palliative care, and rehabilitation for people recovering from injury or stroke.

Between 1963–1967 I trained at Sutherland Hospital and the matron was Miss B. B. Bonfield, an ex-army nursing sister. The hospital was fairly new to the area, and was set up with the wards on each floor set in wings – east and west— approximately 35 people per wing with 1 – 4 patients in each room. There was a Registered Nurse in charge of the ward, and each shift had a Registered Nurse and a junior and a senior nurse. The shifts were either 8 or 10 hours. (Some hospitals had split shifts and also 12 hour shifts).

Nursing training was made up of junior and senior terms. We worked in every section of the hospital, including operating theatres, recovery, casualty (as the emergency department was known then) . the sterilising department and out-patients. Of course there were the medical and surgical wards, where the

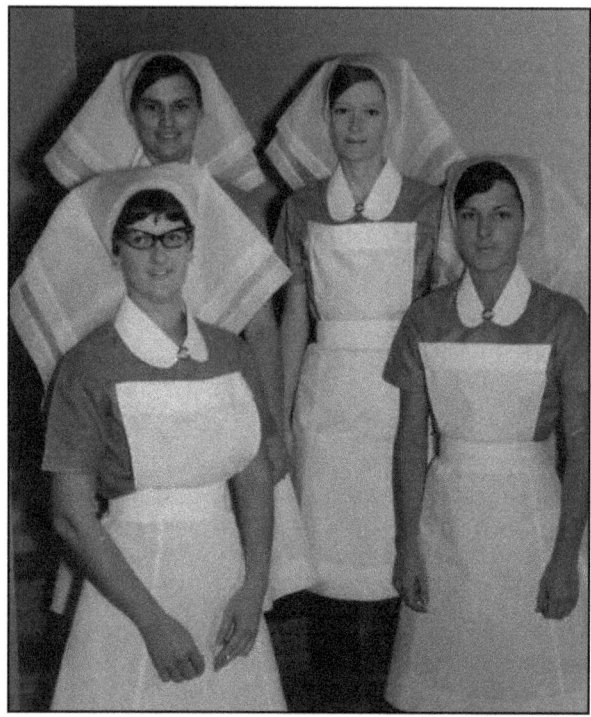

Margaret Wheeler (front left) with her nurses graduation group in 1967. (M Wheeler)

men and women were nursed in separate sections, and the children's ward.

Working for the New South Wales Health Department each trainee nurse in every hospital had a blue book to be filled as they went through their training. The first signatures were from the nursing tutors, and then later the ward sisters' as each procedure was attended. Each hospital that taught trainees in NSW had a curriculum, which was needed for the final exams. Each hospital had nursing tutors and at Sutherland Hospital there were two. Once a year we had a block of lectures, however I do remember having to get up in the middle of the day to do an exam, after I had been on night duty!

The final exams were held in The Great Hall at the University of NSW, and there were four groups that travelled over from Sutherland Hospital. Many trainee nurses were in that hall that day. Graduation ceremony was held on Friday 17 February 1967. We all read out the Nightingale Pledge (see below). We were given a hospital nurse's certificate in a bound cover with the signatures of the president of the board, the secretary, medical superintendent and the matron, B. B. Bonfield and my signature. Later, we paid annual fees to the Nurses Registration Board to remain registered.

Trainee nurses were not allowed to marry while they were training. After training many nurses married and have fond memories of their trainee days. We all lived in the nursing home while we were training. There were restrictions for lights out. The home sister would do her rounds to ensure that we were in bed if we were not working night duty. Some people knew how to get around the system! Each year we had six weeks holiday, which we had to take as allocated – no applying for holiday leave!

As a Registered Nurse we had a blue book 'Service Record in the Industry of Nursing New South Wales'. This was handed in to each hospital in NSW, and the record of service, payments of long service leave, sick leave, tuberculin reactions, and immunisation and vaccination The last section shows that I have had BCG, many chest X-Rays, quite a few Mantoux tests (for TB), also tetanus toxoid, typhoid and Hepatitis B injections.

I also trained in midwifery at St. George Hospital, and then later finished a 12-month Intensive Care course at Prince Alfred Hospital in Sydney. Later I worked at various Sydney hospitals and realised that different hospitals came to teach their nurses slightly differently. During the 1970s, nurses were first trained at the NSW College of Nursing and then later at university.

My experience of nursing over many years included working not only in Sydney, but Brisbane, Townsville, London and Bathurst. A very interesting time, which also included community nursing and 'specialling' (working through a nursing agency) and looking after patients who required extra care in their homes or hospital. My 12 months working at Sydney Hospital, in the Emergency department, gave me an insight into early nursing in Australia. The first Florence Nightingale nurses came to Sydney in 1868. I later found that Lucy Osburn, the superintendent of Sydney Infirmary and Dispensary, had connections with the Macarthur family in Camden.

Nightingale Pledge

I solemnly pledge myself before God and in the presence of this assembly to pass my life in purity and to practise my profession faithfully.
I will abstain from whatever is deleterious and mischievous, and will not take or knowingly administer any harmful drug.
I will do all in my power to maintain and elevate the standard of my profession and will hold in confidence all personal matters committed to my keeping and all family affairs coming to my knowledge in the practice of my calling.
With loyalty will I aid the physician in his work, and as a missioner of health, I will dedicate myself to devoted service for human welfare.

Camden Museum Volunteer Project

Dianne Matterson

It is 1855 and on the north-western corner of John and Argyle Streets, Camden, is a small, unassuming shoemaker's business that appears to be doing a good trade. Inside, John Viles can be seen tap, tap, tapping as he repairs the boots of a local farmer, pausing as a young woman enters to collect her new shoes; then pauses while another brings in a pair of child's shoes that are somewhat worse-for-wear and stops to bemoan the lack of rain in recent weeks. Now in his forties, John had worked in Sydney after emigrating with his wife and three young children from Somerset, England, in 1838. He moved to Camden where the sought-after Macarthur fleece was drawing business into town. John leased his site from John Lakeman who, at the time, owned considerable land fronting Argyle Street.

In 1878, and with a view to constructing a substantial building, the Commercial Banking Corporation purchased this corner site – taking in a 60' and 140' frontage along Argyle and John Streets respectively – for £500. This site (now the NAB) is still occupied today by the iconic building that was built by the bank between 1879-1880 at a cost of £3,480.

This history of the NAB bank site forms a small part of ongoing research that I am undertaking at the Camden Museum into each premises along both sides of Argyle Street from the former Milk Co-operative building in the east to the AH&I Hall in the west. The project aims to draw together different pieces of historical information currently held in various forms by the Museum, accompanied by contemporary newspaper articles and the memories of participants in local oral histories, as well as the resources of other agencies such as N.S.W. State Archives. It is anticipated that this historical resource – in the form of a timeline – will eventually be available to the public.

The Abusive Mr Chisholm (Part Two)

Peter McCall

In the last issue of the Camden History, *an 1897 published speech of Alderman Henry Willis was used as the starting point for an investigation of a quarrel between Willis and the leadership of the Camden Agricultural, Horticultural and Industrial Society (AH&I) over the Society's expenditure, with accusations of corruption and cronyism. Some of the AH&I Society's Committee had finally attempted to deal with this by offering to resign, expecting however that they would be fully vindicated by a vote of confidence. They hoped to stop Willis's allegations by doing this.*

Special General Meeting

But Henry Willis was not silenced. In another letter to the *Camden News*, Willis attempted to question the motives of James K Chisholm and Astley Thompson by suggesting that they were dragging the whole Committee of the AH&I to resignation without their knowledge. He felt that only the President and the treasurer had to refute the charges he had made, not the committee, stating that 'a few interested people have trumpted (sic) a letter and with unblushing effrontery, dragged in their train the whole of the committee without their knowledge or consent'.[1] This was a little unfair as the motion had called for the resignation of some of the committee, not all of them. It was now clear that the matter was moving to a climax.

The special general meeting was attended by some 85-90 members of the AH&I Society. Henry Willis was one of them. The motion discussed was not about the resignation of the president and committee, Instead, a motion was proposed expressing "continued confidence in the president, hon. secretary and committee...."

JK Chisholm's speech,

The *Camden News* gave a very long account of JK Chisholm's speech, and a detailed summary of WR Cowper's refutation of Willis. There were a few brief summaries of speeches in support of the president and committee. Henry Willis was given two opportunities to respond, which he did, according to the account 'at great length'. Chisholm's speech was largely a response to Willis's attacks from the public meeting he had called earlier. He now adopted stronger language than previously. He called Willis slanderous and said that he had employed a special reporter to take down all that Willis said at the meeting. To this intimation of possible legal action, he used such phrases as 'utterly beneath contempt', 'low bred sneer at myself', 'his malevolence', and asked 'what good has Mr Willis done for the district or this society? And the answer is nothing!' He then dug deeper into what he believed were the real motivations behind Willis's attacks. Chisholm believed he was trying to destroy the AH&I Society, 'sowing the seeds of dissension throughout the country, and trying to set one class of community against the other'. He asserted that he should be 'branded as the enemy of society'. Chisholm was basically accusing Willis of radicalism and even socialism. Willis's own principles were not so extreme, but it is easy to see why Chisholm was thinking this way. The future career of Willis would indicate that he had no firm commitment to radical ideologies. However, this speech helps explain the origin of the phrase 'The Abusive Mr Chisholm' which headed the pamphlet Willis later wrote.

Cowper's response was to compare the amounts spent by the AH&I Society on hospitality with other similar organisations and with earlier expenditure by the Society on these matters. He showed the Society was spending proportionately less than ten years before on hospitality and that it spent no more than other agricultural societies.

Standing in isolation

The vote was taken by asking those in favour of the motion to move to the right of the chair, those opposed to the left. Henry Willis was left standing alone to the left of the chair[2]. However, Willis reported that, 'my supporters, who were seated on the right, remained silent, but sent their congratulations [which] have reached me since'.[3]

Just above the report on the special general meeting, the editor of the *Camden News* stated that the paper would accept no more correspondence on the matters that Willis had raised. Both sides had been given an opportunity to present their viewpoints and that other news had had to be held over to leave space for this issue.[4]

The special general meeting of the Camden Agricultural, Horticultural and Industrial Society (AH&I Society) should have been conclusive. Henry Willis's attempt to show that there was incompetence/corruption in the Society had been defeated, leaving him in a minority of one. He may have had some supporters among the members of the Society. It is possible that they knew that Willis would be heavily defeated and did not wish to be publicly associated with this, especially as the victors included many of the social elite of Camden including members of the Macarthur-Onslow family and the rector of St Johns at Camden.

Willis did not acknowledge his defeat. Now that he had been blocked by the AH&I Society and the *Camden News*, he still hoped the viewing of the AH&I accounts by Camden Council aldermen might produce results. To bolster his case he called another public meeting, to be held in the Camden School of Arts on Monday, 20 December, 1897. Whether he was continuing the fight over issues where he knew he was in the right, or simply attempting to cancel out the humiliation of the Special General Meeting is not clear.

Willis had his speech from that meeting printed in a small booklet entitled 'The Abusive Mr Chisholm in War Paint'.[5] We see here Willis's great talent with language, even if expended here on a lost cause. Public lectures were an important form of entertainment in pre-cinema days. Famous figures could charge large sums for attendance (eg Mark Twain, Charles Dickens). Camden did not attract speakers of this stature, but Willis was well known in the district and entrance to the speech was free. Schools of Arts were often used for public lectures; the only other venues suitable were churches where divisive or sectarian issues were not appropriate. In the history of the Camden School of Arts,[6] between 1860 and 1908 33 lectures are recorded (including Willis's), but the list is known to be incomplete.

In the records of the School of Arts, the speech is described as a lecture by Alderman Henry Willis on 'The Agricultural Society and the Recreation Ground'.[7]

Poetry and debates

The speech demonstrates Willis's background in debating. He makes use of colourful and often colloquial metaphors, sarcastic and often literary insults, quotes poetry and perorates with reference to Shakespeare and comparison to Shakespearian heroes who, despite setbacks, triumph in the end. By quoting poetry, Willis at first gives the impression of a man of great erudition, but in fact it all comes from a single source, Charles Mackay (1812-1889), a Scottish poet popular at the time, who praised the virtues of liberty and the evils of tyranny. He quotes from four poems. Probably he could have got them from one book, *The Poetical Works of Charles Mackay.*[8] A sample follows which was used as the conclusion of the speech.

> We want no flag, no flaunting rag,
>   For Liberty to fight;
> We want no blaze of murderous guns,
>   To struggle for the right.
> Our spears and swords are printed words,
>   The mind our battle plain;
> We've won such victories before,
>   And so we shall again.[9]

Willis had some familiarity with United States political issues of the time, using such American terms as 'Boss Croker', 'Tammany Hall' and 'mugwumps' as terms of abuse for corruption. The phrases 'Doodlem-Buck'

Portrait of Henry Willis, 1900s, The Swiss Studios (NLA)

and 'Aunt Sally' are harder to work out, but probably came from the same source. He also compared his enemies to oriental potentates, seen at the time as examples of corruption and decadence. Thus we have Minto Pasha (Chisholm lived in Minto) and a clique of satraps mentioned. Other insults suggested that Chisholm behaved like a savage (a racist but acceptable form of abuse at the time), and included 'Mr Chisholm had bedaubed himself with war-paint for the occasion', and they watched him 'gnashing his teeth, his visage florid with war-paint'. Another attack said that Chisholm's arguments were 'the stringing together of grimy epithets like so many sausages'. These sorts of descriptions continue for the entire 20 pages of the speech and explain why, even if his sentiments received little support, the meeting was well attended. There can't have been too many places in Camden where you could hear the local elite being spoken about in such eloquent and sarcastic terms. This also helps explain Willis's electoral success at local, state and federal levels. The virulence of the language used may also make clear why his terms in office were invariably short. He certainly was entertaining, but naturally caused a great deal of resentment amongst the victims of his eloquence.

There are a number of issues brought up here which do not figure in the summaries of other speeches made at this time. Willis suggested that Chisholm planned to sue him for slander by having a transcript taken of his earlier speech,[10] he compared Chisholm to Boss Croker, the infamous and corrupt New York party boss,[11] he accused Cowper of taking over management of the failing Westbrook (Mount Hunter) Milk Factory knowing that the factory had no sinking fund to pay back investors.[12] The local historian Richard Nixon stated that, "'he [Mount Hunter Co-operative Butter Factory] got into financial difficulty and Wm Cowper, the CBC Bank Manager got them out of the problem'.[13] So Willis's accusation here was probably unfounded.

Willis attacked AH&I Society President Chisholm for hosting 'daily banquets',[14] with 'prodigal expenditure'.[15] He describes the luncheons as 'sly grog shops', suggesting that some of the guests were affected by alcohol and also as a 'hole in the wall',[16] a current term for a small dingy shop or bar with an implication of sleaziness or impropriety. He claimed the closure of the *Camden News* to discussion of the AH&I was due to the influence of Chisholm and John Kidd, the state MP at the time.[17]

A more substantial focus was revealed in his response to Chisholm's accusation that Willis was 'trying to set one class of the community against one another'. Here followed an attack on the Macarthur-Onslow family. He began by stating that the AH&I Society had borrowed £50 from Elizabeth Macarthur-Onslow. It had not been repaid, thereby the people of Camden were being patronised. Of course the Macarthur-Onslows would have seen themselves as patrons of many worthy causes. However, here it was used in the sense of being put under obligation to someone. Willis believed that this debt gave a certain power and influence to the Macarthur-Onslows. Willis believed that Mrs Macarthur-Onslow was in fact unpopular. She was puffed up (or self-important) but in fact had contributed nothing of real value.

His main target was Astley Onslow Thompson who had played a major if subsidiary role in defending the AH&I Society from Willis. Onslow Thompson was manager of Camden Park Estate. The 1890s were a period of readjustment for the estate as it was moved to a more efficient dairying scheme. Part of this involved the eviction of some of the tenants who were seen as not fitting into the new scheme. Willis claims the Macarthur-Onslow's unpopularity was due to evictions. I can find no evidence that this was the case, although such evidence may not have been written down or published at the time. Onslow Thompson was accused as the instigator of evictions and also the blocking of trade seen below.

Old Tenant

At one point Willis makes a fictionalised account of 'the Captain'[18] evicting an "Old Tenant" from land he had held and improved for many years. The account is heart rending-

> Old Tenant: ... but this is my home- the fireside where my children lisped at their mother's knee. It is a sacred place to me and mine.
> Captain: Enough! I will have this piece of land![19]

Evictions had occurred since 1876 as the Macarthur-Onslows attempted to keep their enterprises economically viable.[20] By 1899 there were twenty new share farms on the property. Astley Thompson had stated the type of man he wanted for these new farms.[21] This would imply that some of the current tenants may have been seen as unsuitable and that therefore evictions did take place. Whether they were as brutal as Willis suggests is unknown, but evictions, by their very nature are not likely to be pleasant. Willis's little dramatic piece here at least added to the entertainment value of his speech.

Blocking deliveries

As well, Willis claimed that the Macarthur-Onslows were forcing their tenants to use their company store at Menangle over stores in Camden. This was allegedly done by blocking deliveries from Camden whilst allowing those from Menangle. This led to lack of competition, higher prices and amounted to a virtual boycott of Camden. Once again, there is little evidence for this or the effects Willis alleged.

Willis's attack on the Macarthur-Onslows continued with a look at how the Macarthurs had come to be so influential in the first place. He suggested wrongly that John Macarthur received his initial 5,000 acre grant as a reward for helping get rid of Governor Bligh and that this was deserved because it removed tyranny. The land had now increased in value twenty times due to population growth, public funds, investment by private means and the labour of workers. And in return the Macarthur-Onslows had given ten acres of swampy ground for recreation which was now being used a showground. The implication was that the Macarthur-Onslows had done nothing of value and that Willis would fight the "boycott" of Camden, notwithstanding the abuse he had received from the 'family factotum' (probably Onslow Thompson, but maybe Chisholm).[22]

Pharisaical

Willis attacked Chisholm for dragging down the whole Committee by threatening that they all would resign, although the majority of the Committee were not involved with the issue. He called Chisholm and his associates 'a clique of interested satrapies'.[23] He described Chisholm as "pharisaical" for claiming that because other Agricultural Societies spent money for hospitality, it was acceptable for the AH&I Society.

Some of Willis allegations are obscure in detail, but their intent is clear. He claimed that many of the beneficiaries of the Society's hospitality were in fact locals and friends of Chisholm. The £18/12/6 spent on petty cash, postage, telegrams etc was in fact 'petty cash which is a new brand of whisky'.[24] He next attacked committee member FWA Downes who, together with Chisholm, had asked what good Willis had ever done for the district. He responded that whilst manager of EM Moore's estate (his deceased father-in-law) he had done what he could.[25] Downes on the other hand had been one of the first to stop sending milk to the Westbrook dairy. He thus associated him with Cowper for the failure of that factory. By 1896 the Westbrook dairy had been sold to the Macarthur-Onslows; it is not possible to tell whether Willis is referring to the period before or after the sale. The Macarthur-Onslows spent a good deal of money improving this facility.[26]

Tammany Hall

Willis concluded his speech by suggesting that the Society needed to be purged and that if Chisholm and Cowper were honourable men, they would resign. He said "I am not to be frightened by 'painted devils' nor the Boss and myrmidons of little Tammany. Never mind the odds: 'might is right,' so we are sure to conquer." Tammany Hall was the notorious centre of corruption in New York at the time which had effects on American politics.

His final flourish was to liken himself to Richmond who overwhelmed the evil Richard III in Shakespeare's play of the same name. 'Against our oppressors I will bend my bow till I have skewered every one of them'.[27]

In the printed version of the speech, Willis had included two newspaper 'reviews' of his speech at the conclusion from *The Camden News* and *The Picton Advocate*. They were hardly ringing endorsements; however *The*

Camden News stated that 'the hall was well filled', and that 'Mr Willis for over two hours delivered a spirited and sarcastic address'.[28]

Willis's public meeting had certainly allowed him to vent his opinion of the activities of the AH&I, but would his sarcasm and wit be sufficient to prove his charges?

References
1 *Camden News,* 2.12.1897.
2 *Camden News,* 9.12.1897.
3 H Willis, *The Abusive Mr Chisholm in War-Paint. Public Address by Alderman Willis in the School of Arts Hall, Camden Monday 20th December 1897. A reply to speeches delivered at the Special General Meeting of the Camden A.H. & I. Society,* Sydney, ND p1. The assumption is that Willis had it printed as there is no other attribution in the printed speech, and it is hard to think of anyone else who would have wanted to print it. This pamphlet is not an absolutely verbatim copy of Willis's speech, as he refers to some parts which he has italicised- he must have used some other method for emphasis when he was making the speech.
4 *Camden News,* 9.12.1897.
5 Willis, *Ibid.*
6 Downing P et al, *Camden School of Arts- A History,* Camden 2016.
7 ADFAS Camden et al, *Camden School of Arts,* Oct 2016 p21, https://adfas.org.au/what-we-do/adfas-in-the-community/school-of-arts-mechanic-institute/ .
8 C Mackay, *The Poetical Works of Charles Mackay,* London, 1876.
9 Willis, *Ibid,* p20.
10 *Ibid,* p3.
11 *Ibid,* p4.
12 *Ibid,* p5.
13 R Nixon, *Unpublished manuscript,* held in Camden Historical Society Files under Dairying General, p1.
14 Willis, *Ibid,* p12.
15 *Ibid,* p2.
16 *Ibid,* p16
17 *Ibid,* p6 & 7.
18 Astley Onslow Thompson.
19 Willis, *Ibid ,*p9.
20 Betteridge, C et al, *Elizabeth Macarthur Agricultural Insititute Conservation Management Plan,* Randwick, 2011, p27
21 Quoted in Walsh, Brian, *Milk and the Macarthurs- the dairy history of Camden Park* Camden, 2016, p26.
22 *Ibid,* p9-10.
23 *Ibid* p14.
24 *Ibid* p16.
25 *Ibid* p18.
26 Walsh, *Ibid,* p30.
27 *Ibid* p19.
28 *Ibid* p21.

[Part 3 will be in the next journal]

Baragal Ngurra darami – Budbury and a paddock long ago

Venessa Possum (Starzynski nee Williams)

Candidate in the Doctor of Philosophy in Fine Art. Queensland College of Art Griffith University. February 2019

During the winter of 2018, I was asked to write an article for the journal of the Camden Historical Society. At the time I was spending a week at the Camden Museum to immerse myself in the wonder of the collections. Writing this article is a great opportunity for me to discuss my research and upcoming exhibition at the Camden Library as 'Artist of the Month' in May. This happens to coincide with the National Trust Heritage Festival: 'Connecting People, Places and the Past'.

When I am researching in situation I am often asked about my PhD topic. In brief, my archival and literary research coincides with a site-specific art practice. I explore meaningful connections to my Dharug, Dharawal, Muringal-Baragal and Irish heritages in the Australian context. I work independently

Venessa Possum, collecting reeds for weaving 2018. (V Possum)

and collaboratively to explore these signs as well as European and Western colonisations that reveal interesting concepts of intergenerational times.

The title of my journal article and my exhibition emphasise my ancestry, particularly my paternal Aboriginal heritage to Budbury in the area that became known as 'The Cowpastures'.[1] In the early 1800s a renowned Aboriginal guide Gogy used the word 'Baragal' to direct non-Aboriginal peoples towards a 'belgeny.' This was an original waterhole at Baragal close to the Nepean River on the outskirts of the current town of Camden, New South Wales.[2]

Australian historian Alan Atkinson writes, 'There are so many doubts and difficulties in tracing the lives of individual Aborigines at Camden'.[3] This is true from an archival perspective, for example he found a baptism record for my Aboriginal ancestor John Budberry in 1842 at Camden and a death notice in 1860, whereas another prominent Australian historian Grace Karskens lists my ancestor as David Budbury (or Boothbarrie) born 1768 to 1833.[4] Additional archival spellings, Bootbarrie, Boodbury, Budberrah, Broadberry and Bradbury reveal a conundrum for early colonial transcribers. I choose to write 'Budbury' and I pronounce his name with a rolling of the tongue for 'd' and a forceful projection dissolving 'ie' or 'y' as in Boo-rdb-ere.[5]

The Lachlan Macquarie journal (1810-1822) contains the earliest reference to my ancestor as a Dharug, Dharawal guide. He once led the Governor from Stonequarry Creek to the Nattai River, however the relationship proved fragile over time. To reiterate a better-known early colonial history, an ex-convict pastoralist named John Warby and my Irish convict ancestor John Walsh, who was assigned to Warby, refused to take part in a plan to attack Dharawal Yura (Peoples). They allowed Budbury and Bundle to escape and warn neighboring bands prior to the shocking massacre at Appin on 17 April 1816.[6] As it happened, this allegiance led to the marriage of John Walsh and Budbury's daughter Mandagerry, my maternal ancestor.

My research reveals an original Dharug, Dharawal perspective of the past including intergenerational knowledges of places, peoples and languages. Dharug, Dharawal knowledges exist in continuity with guragal, darimi yuu yilabara, long ago, a long time and now. As a reflective experience of Baragal, I identify the 200 old oak tree on the grounds of the present day Belgenny Farm as a significant sign of continuity. Planted by William Macarthur from an English acorn seed, the majestic oak has embedded its roots in Baragal as a living presentation of people's coexistences dating back to Budbury's time.[7]

Dharug peoples axe carving of concentric circles on a rock platform along the Woodford Oaks Trail Blue Mountains National Park

The internal growth rings of the tree contain a plethora of experiences. The oak has shaded people from the harsh summer sun, felt the fluttering of birds' and bugs' wings, feet of animals and miniature creatures and seasonal cycles of the earth and cosmos. When picturing internal growth rings, I perceive the likeness to symbolic concentric circles, used globally as original signs for waterholes, places for ceremony and more.

My ancestor, Budbury, developed a lifelong relationship with the Macarthur family who were granted Baragal Ngurra, as land usurped by the English Crown. In a letter to his brother James in 1851 William, the youngest son of John Macarthur, speaks about his empathy for 'Johnny Budberry' and of his 'birth to this spot'. Perhaps without realising, William was acknowledging the first peoples of Muringal-Baragal Ngurra, a place with a belgeny (waterhole) and kirboowallie (a shallow area) used to cross durrubbin (the Nepean River) near Camden.[8]

On the Macarthur estate there was an area known as Budbury's paddock (c1840s). This is an irony, as I believe the paddock would have been the orchard. My study of a watercolour painting titled *View of the Government Hut at Cowpastures* 1804 helps me to picture the hut on the Macarthur estate.[9] I imagine Elizabeth Macarthur discussing the farm with Budbury while he is taking a break from shooting the birds that 'preyed' on the orchard. I also

View of the Government Hut at Cowpastures **1804, by an unknown artist, FL3143926, SLNSW.**

think about Budbury as 'Johnny' who slept in the supposedly 'miserable hut' with his beloved Nadaang also known as Black Nellie.[10]

For my exhibition at the Camden Library in May 2019 I have visualised site-specific experiences as Muringal-Baragal in conjunction with colonial historicisms. My collection of hand-made papers with drawings is a patchwork of compositions that resemble topographic maps I call 'farmscapes'. They are a blending of significant Indigenous plants collected as Baragal and human residues such as newsprint, packaging, old letters and junkmail.

On some of my surfaces I have made drawings of cultural signs and reproductions of early colonial art, graphic archives, photographs of the region and an unusual map by one Crown botanist named George Caley. In my research I have come to describe Caley as an 'accidental explorer.' By adding him to my story I acknowledge that he travelled with Aboriginal guides to document original languages for Indigenous plants and animals. Even after the first paper mill was built at Botany Bay raw materials for papermaking were scarce.

Venessa Possum, *View of the Government Hut at Cowpastures* **2019, detail of hand-made paper and drawing. (V Possum)**

Caley often made his own paper to store botanical specimens and like Caley my papers combine salvaged materials.

Hand-made paper can be fragile however I observe conservation strategies in Australian archives where paper is fortified with linen. I use Irish linen as a sign of my European heritage. In the penal colony of Sydney Irish convicts were jailed as criminals or political prisoners and even after their release they were marginalised. Meanwhile the linen of their homelands was an esteemed and essential material, regularly listed in supply requisitions to England.[11]

I suspend my paper with hand-made Casuarina, Eucalyptus and wire pegs, albeit a simplified version of antique wooden pegs. They are symbols of an Indigenous river-scape and the ingenuity of peoples to 'make do' by utilising materials in the environment.

As I bring my article to a close, I invite you to visit my exhibition at Camden and consider how my art presents ideas of connectedness between peoples and places in the past that continues today. Even though the works are fragile they speak of resilience and resourcefulness as well as a deep-rooted relationship as Baragal Ngurra and Camden country.

Venessa Possum *farmscape* 2019, hand-made Casuarina and metal peg, 42 x 62 cm. (Image: V Possum)

Acknowledgments
As a final note, I would like to thank Ian Willis for including me in this journal. I also extend my thanks to the wonderful people at the Camden Museum and Historical Society and Camden Library for sharing my delight for research and creativity.

References
1 Ian Willis, *Pictorial History Camden and District*. (Sydney NSW: Kingsclear Books, 2015), p. 4.
2 Alan Atkinson, citing William Macarthur 1862 in *Camden: Farm and Village Life in Early New South Wales*,(Canberra ACT: National library of Australia, $5^{3\,2\,2}$), pp. ^{2}, 64^1; Corroboree at Barragal: Peter Turbet, *First Frontier: The Occupation of the Sydney Region 1788-1816* (Kenthurst New South Wales: Rosenberg Publishers, 6455); Gogy indicated a belgeny (waterhole) during two surveys in 1805, pp. 11, 127.
3 Atkinson, p. 228.
4 Atkinson, p. 230; Grace Karskens, 'David Budbury', *Dictionary of Sydney*, 645^0, https://dictionaryofsydney.org/person/budbury_david.
5 The sounds and writing systems of Aboriginal languages: Aboriginal educational contexts 2010
6 Carol Liston, 'The Dharawal and Gandangara in Colonial Campbelltown, New South Wales, 1788-1830', *Aboriginal History* vol. 56, no. 5 ($5^{3\,2\,2}$), p.96.
7 Brian Walsh, 'Belgenny Walking Tour' (Belgenny Farm Trust, 2007, 2013).
8 Atkinson, 208, citing Isabel Bowman to Sir William Macarthur 10 May 1856; Peter Turbet, First Frontier. p. 88; Carol Liston, citing Ellis (1955) and L.Macquarie 1810-1822 in 'The Dharawal and Gandangara', p.55.
9 Dr. Edward Higginbotham., 'Archaeological Test Excavation, 2008: A Small Miserable Hut, Camden Estate' (Haberfield NSW: Belgenny Farm Trust, 2008).
10 Atkinson, p. 207.
11 Bladen, F. M and Britton, Alexander & Cook, James (1892), *Historical records of New South Wales*, NLA.obj-359771272, xxvi, p.16

Book Launch - *My Story: The Tandem Team Launch Tourism 1978-1988 Macarthur Country*

Betty Yewen

I believe my entire close family were relieved and proud of me finally completing *My Story*. A small book launch on Friday, 29 June 2018 with a number of my family and a few friends was arranged by my daughter Cheryl, who felt a great need to celebrate. Invitations from a variety of venues in the community to hold a more formal launch were proposed, however for personal reasons, I declined.

The book details the successful introduction of the tourism industry into local government areas that in the 1980s became known as **Macarthur Country**, (Liverpool, Campbelltown, Camden and Picton).

This book would not have eventuated without the dedicated work and expertise, over a long period of time, of my very good friend, Evan Lepherd. He was able to put my ideas and thoughts in order and arranged its publication. I always needed to write *My Story* to bring out all the work that my dear friend and work colleague, Jenny Eggins, achieved and wanted to achieve.

I also felt strongly the need to tell of the work that many people gave, both of their time and professional expertise, to attain the goal in the 1980's, of successfully introducing the major industry of tourism to Macarthur Country.
I received many kind words of congratulations on the quality and presentation of *My Story*. With Jenny's family's permission I include this very personal thank you:

Dear Betty,
I was moved to tears when Dad gave me a copy of your book. How hard you worked pulling it all together. I wish Delma* (who died 10 years ago) could have seen it – she would have loved it.
As I was away at boarding school, I missed a lot of what was happening at home. I knew a little but not the full extent of how long and frustrating was the road for the two of you. You were a formidable team. I had no idea you had so many matching jackets! How very smart you both looked. I loved looking at all the photos – such memories!
Mum would have been proud of you Betty, continuing on without her. You must have missed her so terribly as we did (and still do). She remains in my heart for ever. Thank you for being such a good friend to her, she did value your support. Thank you for this wonderful book, I'm sorry that the dream did not come to be.
Fondest regards, Astrid.   22 November 2018

*Delma was Jenny's mother, Astrid is Jenny's daughter.

The book has been well-received and continues to gain interest. Readers were delighted and surprised with the volume of not-seen-before coloured photos I hold in my personal collection. I also received comments from a variety of people who were involved with the Macarthur Country Tourist Association.

Self-publishing this 262 page colour coffee-table book has been a tremendous experience, one that with great relief, along divine intervention, I finally achieved in my lifetime!

Copies have been placed in the local study section of the libraries of Camden, Campbelltown, Liverpool and Picton as well as in the National Library of Australia, State Library of N.S.W. and the N.S.W. Parliamentary Library as requirements of the *Copyright Act*, 1968.

As a self-published author I chose a print run of 100 copies that have sold extremely well with an excellent article in *The District Reporter*, 30 November 2018. Editor, Lee Abrahams kindly gave her wide area of readers my telephone details. This contributed further to the sales leaving just a few copies. I personally believe *My Story* will become a collectible!

Author Betty Yewen holding her book *My Story* standing next to publisher Evan Lepherd (Image: B Yewen)

A picture tells a thousand words. Fashion speaks just as loud!

Laura Jane Aulsebook

It would come to no surprise to many that I have a great interest in fashion history. When looking at the photographs provided by Shirley Rorke for this issue, some might gravitate towards who is in the photographs, others reminisce about the setting or the long since updated technologies on display. For me it is the fashion and clothing choices that attract my eye. Far from being dismissed as superficial clothing, the fashion history of everyday photographs provides its own unique story, one that explores social mores, norms and cultural influences. Fashion is made to be photographed, and if a picture tells a thousand words, surely the fashion in the photo has a lot to say.

Poodle skirts, petticoats, and prom dresses; even for the least fashion conscious and non-history buffs among us, it is easy to call these to mind when picturing the fashion of the 1950s. Like any decade in history, the fashions of the 1950s were far more extensive than the stereotypical images we have constructed thanks to the revival culture that dominates the trends of main-

Shirley Dunk (Rorke) and Beth Jackman (left) both worked at the Clintons's Showroom in Argyle Street Camden in 1953. Clintons sold motor cars and a variety of electrical goods. (S Rorke)

stream media. Whilst the fashion magazines of the day, catwalk recordings and department store advertisements tell the tale of what was dictated as "on trend" it is the photographs of the everyday, ordinary Australians that show us just what it was that Australians wore and gives us an insight into how the fashion choices shaped who they were. Just as important as *what* and *who* is in the photograph, the fashion choices on display have their own story to tell.

To summarise an entire decade of fashion into a single style is far too simplistic. Yet there is a mainstay of 1950s fashion, it was overtly feminine and centred on the ideal hourglass figure, thanks largely to Dior's 1947 'New Look', which dominated the market until the early 1960s. Inspirations from the runways of Paris, the latest Hollywood films and film stars such as Audrey Hepburn, Grace Kelly and Marilyn Monroe, clearly influenced women's wardrobes all over the world. Into this market entered a new tour de force in the fashion world, one with their own marked style and fashion image – that of the teenager and young adult. Emerging from the Hollywood set of Mickey Rooney, Judy Garland and Dena Durbin in the mid 1940s, teenagers became defined as a subculture in the 1950s. They were the burgeoning market, recognised for their increasing influence and their embracing of freedom after a childhood spent in relative constraints during the Depression and war years.

This newly emerging consumer group was leading the trends with their youthful outlook, modern views and sunny disposition that was embracing of the new and youth directed opportunities that a post-war world welcomed. In light of this, it is easy to presume that Australia, due to its geographical location, would be behind the eight ball when it came to the latest fashions and overseas trends, and that this would be even more delayed in rural country towns such as Camden. Recent Australian films such as *Ladies in Black* dispute this theory in the hustle and bustle of Sydney and surrounding suburbs, where David Jones was a world leader in fashion trends, and TV shows such as *A Place to Call Home* depict the fashions of small country towns as still being up-to-date despite their rural location.

A country film set
Immortalised on screen as the fictional rural town of Inverness, one could argue that the onscreen town Camden portrays in *A Place to Call Home* is also a fairly accurate depiction of a town like Camden at the time, with fashion choices and sense of style differing from those that regularly visited the city and those that remained in the rural setting. (Although the fashion anachronisms of said characters are best discussed another day!) These fictional portrayals have brought about renewed interest in Australian fashion history of the 1950s, yet it is the photographs of everyday people that lived during this time that tell the true fashion story and illustrate just how style

conscious Australians were - and we need not look any further than Camden and its residents for inspiration.

In the fast-fashion, easy access world of fashion in today's society, it is hard to imagine a time not that long ago when fashion was not so mass produced and easily accessible. Whilst department stores like David Jones were flourishing in the city and small boutiques were popping up in towns around the country, the vast majority of women made their own clothing or used dressmakers, with haberdashery and material shops offering fabric inspired by prints from the catwalks and latest fashion magazines. The array of women's magazines flooding the publishing markets, such as *Australian Home Journal* and *Australian Women's Weekly*, always came with easy-to-follow patterns showing how to recreate the latest fashions for the women at home. Along with the fashion designs, there were reviews of the latest Hollywood films and plenty of advertisements of the latest household appliances and gadgets designed to make life easier. It was an era where spending was encouraged and consumerism rapidly growing.

These fashion magazines targeted young women, both career driven and housewives, and often came with dedicated teen or youth orientated lift-outs that directed teenagers to their own trends. With the country coming out of the Depression and war years, the economy was booming and a brighter disposition was welcomed by the newest consumer market, one with a growing influence and an increased awareness and appreciation of the independence and freedom that they wielded: the teenager.

A stylish teenager

Enter into this world a very stylish teenager from Camden. This article was inspired by photographs of long time Camden Historical Society member, Shirley Rorke, who shared some pictures of her stylish teenage self in Camden in the early 1950s. The picture of Shirley posing with a new model refrigerator was taken in 1953 at Camden Clintons sales office in Argyle Street and shows that Shirley was a teen very aware of being up-to-date with the trends.

Shirley's outfit is fashion forward for a teen living in country Australia in the early 1950s. Her crisp white shirt with the Peter Pan collar and thin black bow at the neck was typical teen styling, along with a very full striped circle skirt. Although not clearly visible in this picture, it is easy to see that this skirt would have been tea-length, that is, between the knee and ankle in length and a full circle in diameter, worn with a rope petticoat. It is reminiscent of the poodle skirt trend that dominated the diner scene for teenagers in America in the mid 1950s, yet with a slightly more sophisticated vibe, complete with swell cats-eye sunglasses and a wide patent leather belt which cinches the waist and provides the very definite 1950s fashion silhouette.

When questioning Shirley about the inspiration behind this particular outfit she could not quite recall, however she did mention that she and her mother made the majority of her clothing because of the lack of boutiques available. This certainly is a sentiment echoed by many who lived in Camden during the 1950s, that buying material and making clothing was much more commonplace than ready-to-wear, off the rack purchases. In today's mass produced world it is easy to acknowledge how this allowed for individual style and personal influences to be injected into one's wardrobe.

Whilst Shirley could not name a direct influence for this outfit, a certain famous 1950s fashion figure came to mind. Interestingly, this image was taken in 1953, not long before Shirley embarked on a European adventure, an experience far away from rural Camden. In the same way, a young woman clad in a similar outfit also experienced a European adventure in 1953, only this one was in Rome and played out on the big screen. *Roman Holiday* (1953 Paramount Pictures) staring Gregory Peck and a young Audrey Hepburn in her first American film role - one that earned her the accolade of being the first actress to win an Academy Award, a Golden Globe Award, and a BAFTA Award for a single performance - was a success around the world, and played at Camden Paramount Theatre.

The film depicts a young Princess who escapes royal protocol for a day and experiences a taste of freedom, much like the mainstream youth of the day. She symbolised an icon of a "free and easy" fun loving Roman spirit, in a country still recovering from the deprivation and stigma of World War II. The title outfit that Audrey wears throughout the film during the day long escapades, mirrors that of Camden's very own Shirley, a crisp white blouse with scarf at the neck, a mid-length circle skirt and wide

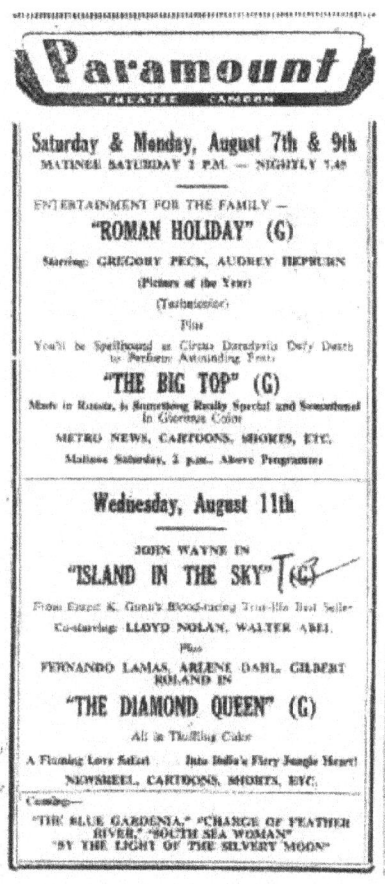

Camden News, 5 August 1954 (NLA)

belt, all in natural tonings. Short, neatly set hair and cats-eye sunglasses were to become an Audrey Hepburn trademark throughout the 1950s, showing Shirley was clearly on top of the trend!

Fashion trends, industry experts and fashionistas will tell you, come in cycles; and everything is created or influenced by a previous design in some way. Whether it be captured on film to display a character's emotional journey and characteristics, or footage of the catwalks of an international design house that influences a whole change in style, records from the fashion floor levels of an esteemed department store or evidence from the living room sewing machines of women and teenagers throughout the country, fashion and the clothing choices reflect the cultural and emotional stories of the time.

Private photographs provide an even more intimate glimpse into these choices. Whilst for many the 1950s was a period that was not that far in the past, as this mid-century period becomes more and more relevant in cultural history, it would be wonderful to see more private images appear of how the everyday citizens of all ages dressed and the stories behind them.

A picture may tell a thousand words but the clothing and fashion choices in the picture have just as much to say.

Audrey Hepburn's outfit in *Roman Holiday (Paramount Pictures 1953)* displays a striking resemblance to Shirley's outfit. (Wikimadia)

William Macarthur and the Empire of Science

Julie McIntyre, University of Newcastle, Scholarly Talk, State Library of New South Wales, 5 February 2019

Notes by Anne McIntosh

Julie McIntyre has been researching the development of the Australian wine industry, particularly focused on the Hunter Valley. She wrote *First Vintage Wine in Colonial New South Wales* and her research on the history of viticulture is ongoing. Her presentation on William Macarthur draws upon the same body of research, but looks at Australian agriculture, industry and science in Victorian times. William took a scientific approach when establishing his vineyard at Camden Park, yet, he had not attended university.

William Macarthur was born in 1800, and was the seventh of Elizabeth and John Macarthur's eight children. He and his older brother, James, were educated in England where they boarded with their tutor, Mr Lindsay, between 1809 and 1815. William's formal education was probably completed by the time he was 15 or 16 years old, after which John Macarthur set off with the two boys on a year-long agricultural tour through France and Switzerland.

Based on family letters, it is clear that from an early age, William was a very active and curious child. Despite having spent time in England and Europe, he returned willingly to his family in New South Wales, and he saw great potential for the 'new land'. James, two years his senior, found greater favour with his teacher, and was described in the *Australian Dictionary of Biography* as 'the more steady of the two'. Both boys were also educated in French, which almost certainly improved during their time in Switzerland, and James may have also had some capability in German.

At this time, a formal university education was not a prerequisite for participation in the global 'Empire of Science'. Information was exchanged through letters and many colonials subscribed to key journals and participated in the exchange of new knowledge. Taking into account communication and transport during early Victorian times, the shortest possible journey between England and Australia would have been three months. Access to recent information and a commitment to innovation enabled non-academics to make significant contributions in spite of their seeming isolation.

The idea that scientific thinking and knowledge should be secular, apolitical and accessible to all across the world, has underpinned scientific advances during the last 150 years. Through the application of scientific thinking and argument, it was believed that knowledge would be advanced to benefit man-

Camden Park House where William Macarthur lived during his lifetime. The house was completed in 1835 and is described as Georgian architecture and Regency in style. Architect John Verge was commissioned to design the house and it is built of sandstock brick and Australian Cedar has been used extensively on the interior for architraves and doors. (CPH)

kind.

In the areas of agriculture and botany, William Macarthur made a significant contribution. In addition to properties at Camden, James and William had major holdings on the Abercrombie River near Taralga. William fostered horse-breeding, assisted his family's wool business, introduced the camellia to Australia and then improved it, and grew many fruit trees, vegetables and flowers. From 1843, he published an annual catalogue of Camden Park plant offerings. Later he built a hothouse and imported valuable orchids.
He had connections to local aborigines, spoke the local indigenous dialect and considered information gained when evaluating the potential value for local timbers and garden plants.

William's contribution through advice and cuttings assisted wine growers establishing and experimenting in the Hunter Valley. He had brought out several families of German vignerons to aid vineyard development at Camden Park. By 1849, the 25 ac (10 ha) vineyard at Camden was producing

Camden Park Estate camelia developed during the lifetime of nurseryman, William Macarthur. (A McIntosh, 2017)

over 16,000 gallons (72,737 L) of red and white table wines and brandies, and large volumes were stored in the cellars.

The Macarthurs subscribed to a range of key journals and catalogues, so William had access to the latest thinking in horticulture. He was aware of, and supported, the efforts of Linnaeus to logically classify living organisms, and this highlighted the relationships between them. Also providing support was older brother, Edward Macarthur, who lived in England and was the 'agent' for family interests. Even at Camden Park, the Macarthurs had a committed person who could provide publications, contacts and plant materials.

Through correspondence and the sharing of plant materials with Hooker, a botanist in Glasgow, William's botanical knowledge and his passion grew. There were many collectors of botanical samples in Australia, but letters show that the relationship between these men was interactive. It was clearly a mutually beneficial relationship; when Hooker was appointed to manage Kew Gardens in 1842, William Macarthur became ever more connected to global leaders in horticulture. William was also a close friend of Ludwig Leichardt and even tried to lobby to overcome a possibly anti-German bias when the manager for the Sydney Botanic Gardens was appointed.

The sophistication of William's collecting is evident in the material that he provided for the Paris Exhibition of 1851, which raised awareness of Australia and promoted trade. William provided samples of native timbers for display (which can be seen on display whenever Camden Park has an Open Day), and had a 'handout' prepared for interested parties. Published in French and English, this tabulated information included Linnaean genus and species, common colonial plant name/s, and their applications, and aboriginal names and uses for the plants (as provided by the Dharawal man from the Illawarra, Dr Ellis, whose contribution was paid for by Macarthur). Samples of Queensland timber were also on display and included in the catalogue, however the same depth of information was not provided.

While in Paris, William visited vineyards in France and the Pyrenees, and later toured vineyards in Germany (Burgundy and Rhine Valleys) and visited Switzerland and Italy for the same purpose. He was always seeking ways to make his own enterprises more efficient and productive. William Macarthur was later appointed to a lead role for the World Trade Fair held in the Sydney Botanic Gardens in 1879.

It is evident that William was committed to the 'Empire of Science'. He respected knowledge for its own sake. He would source the information across boundaries of race and sought to communicate his learnings for both intellectual and commercial benefit. He corresponded widely with the leading scientific thinkers, and because his words demonstrated his knowledge, he was rewarded with respect.

In 1836, William joined a committee at the Australian Museum and from 1853 was a trustee. In 1870, William was made a trustee of the Free Public Library (which later became the State Library of NSW). He also held senior positions in the Agricultural Society of New South Wales for 20 years. From its establishment in 1860, William served on the Senate of the University of Sydney.

Julie McIntyre did point out that William was somewhat selective in those with whom he collaborated. In particular, she highlights that James King, a more traditional experimental scientist who made enormous contributions to the understanding of plant nutrition and soil science through work done in vineyard development on the Hunter, was not respected by Macarthur. Their ties to the wine industry through families such as that of Alexander Walker Scott in a big country with a tiny population, ensured that although the two men may not have collaborated, they were aware of one another.

William should not be regarded as a scientist. As a nurseryman and amateur botanist, and through his connections in Australia and overseas, he made a significant contribution in furthering scientific knowledge and this had big implications for the nation's agriculture. In fact, William was a lynchpin in the progress made in these areas during the mid-1800s. William's nephew, Edward Macarthur Bowman, continued his passion for science, collecting specimens in North Queensland and liaising with Ferdinand von Mueller from the Melbourne Botanic Gardens.

At the time of his death in 1882, five Linnaean plant names or groups referenced William Macarthur. He had been able to turn his passion to profit, with the horticulture business at Camden Park selling many plants, and particularly recognised for camellias and orchids. He provided grape vines to help start the wine business in South Australia. Through international exhibitions, he marketed Australia and expanded trade for his family and the nation.

[For more on William Macarthur see http://hortuscamden.com/]

Camden Park garden showing a Chilean wine palm (A McIntosh, 2017)

CAMDEN HISTORY

Journal of the Camden Historical Society

September 2019 Volume 4 Number 8

CAMDEN HISTORY
Journal of the Camden Historical Society Inc.
ISSN 1445-1549
Editor: Dr Ian Willis

Management Committee
President: Doug Barrett
Vice Presidents: John Wrigley OAM, Warren Sims
Secretary: Lee Stratton
Treasurer: Fletcher Joss
 Immediate Past President: Dr Ian Willis
General Committee: Rene Rem, Ian Ramsey, Frances Warner, Robert Wheeler, Dawn Williams, Julie Wrigley.

Honorary Solicitors: Warren & Warren

Society contact:
P.O. Box 566, Camden, NSW 2570. Online <http://www.camdenhistory.org.au>

Meetings
Meetings are held at 7.30 p.m. on the second Wednesday of the month except in January. They are held in the Museum. Visitors are always welcome.

Museum
The Museum is located at 40 John Street, Camden, phone 4655 3400 or 46559210. It is open Thursday to Sunday 11 a.m. to 4 p.m., except at Christmas. Visits by schools and groups are encouraged. Please contact the Museum to make arrangements. Entry is free.

Camden History, Journal of the Camden Historical Society Inc
The Journal is published in March and September each year. The Editor would be pleased to receive articles broadly covering the history of the Camden district . Correspondence can be sent to the Society's postal address. The views expressed by authors in journal articles are solely those of the authors and not necessarily endorsed by the Camden Historical Society.

Donations
Donations made to the Society are tax deductible. The accredited value of objects donated to the Society are eligible for tax deduction.

Cover Image: Ron Davies addressing Camden Historical Society 12 June 2019 (L Stratton)

Back cover: Painting of Abbotsford farm buildings c.mid-20th C. Owned by Ron Davies. (A McIntosh)

CAMDEN HISTORY
Journal of the Camden Historical Society Inc.

Contents

Disastrous Theatre Fire — 327
Dianne Matterson

Loyal Orange Lodges — 332
Brendan O'Farrell

The McMinn Royal Black Sash - Item No. 2017.73.4 — 333
Julie Wrigley, Anne McIntosh and Margaret Wheeler

An Independent Woman — 336
Jo O'Brien

Textiles, History and Smoking Caps — 342
Margaret Wheeler

U.S. Artist Exploring Seeds at the PlantBank — 344
Kaleigh Rusgrove

Memories of Ron Davies: Abbotsford — 350
Anne McIntosh

President's Annual Report 2018-2019 — 361
Ian Willis

The Abusive Mr Chisholm (Part 3) — 363
Peter McCall

Memories of Rob Shumack — 367
Anne McIntosh

Disastrous Theatre Fire

Dianne Matterson

I am researching the history of businesses that have operated in Argyle Street since the beginning of Camden as a township, and thought a 1st person, "eye witness" narrative would be an interesting way to approach this important historical event in Camden.

5 May 1933

As I walked along Murray Street through the early morning chill of late autumn, I had a feeling of both dread and anticipation. The events of last night had shocked the whole town, but as the weak sunshine began to warm my face, a faint hope crept into my mind that perhaps I had just dreamt the whole thing after all. But no, as I rounded the corner into Argyle Street, the black scar covering what remained of Phillip Fox's Empire Theatre came into full view. Not even the last remaining haze of early morning fog could disguise the devastation left by the fire that had started just after midnight.

After glowing red hot last night, part of the corrugated roof was now gone and streaks of blackened water were drying on the brick walls, while the footpath and roadway in Oxley and Argyle Streets still showed evidence of the

Foresters' Hall c. 1909 (later the location of P. Fox's picture theatre) (Coleman Postcard, Camden Museum Collection)

powerful streams of water directed onto and into the building from the fire hoses. Apparently, most of the interior, including the newly renovated seating and picture screen, is now just a chaotic ruin. Mr. Fox had spent a pretty penny on modernising his theatre just last spring and now it was no more than blackened, water-soaked debris. I wondered whether he would ever be able to reopen his doors after such a crushing blow.

Like me, there are several others just standing in Argyle and Oxley Streets and staring, almost in disbelief, while I can hear snatches of conversation as groups of onlookers speculate about the cause of the fire or relive the drama of the previous night. This end of the main street is a mess: muddy and uneven in front of the theatre where the water had pooled until it ran away down the hill towards the Crown Hotel, while the entire stock and shop fittings from the Misses Cahill's refreshment rooms (which had spent the night out in the open after being removed from the shop at the front of the theatre during the height of the fire) were now in the willing hands of many who were carrying the shop's contents across the road to the Cahill's other shop opposite the theatre. Somehow, the sisters, Agnes and Elizabeth, had provided refreshments for the fire fighters and other volunteers last night during the overwhelming confusion of noise, fumes and eye-watering smoke. In the cold light of day, it is very obvious how close the town had come to not only completely losing one of its landmark buildings, but also the office of the 'Camden News' (the western wall of which touches the theatre wall) as well as Nurse Taplin's residence at the rear, where only a narrow laneway separates the two buildings. Disastrous as it is, everyone in the town is only too well aware of how much worse it could have been were it not for the skill, quick thinking and persistence of Captain Poole and the other firemen.

It was Will Taplin (Snr) who'd first raised the alarm at about 12.30 a.m. after he was woken by voices that seemed to come from the nearby lane, while sleeping at his house in Oxley Street. As he looked through the window, he heard explosions in the vicinity and flames could be seen coming from the top and rear of the theatre. Will told his son, Ted, to phone the fire station, after which the fireman on duty rang the fire bell, a sound that quickly roused the townspeople from their beds. Mr. Fox came running along Argyle Street, and with one of his assistants, went inside to try and get the fire hydrant working, but the smoke and fumes were too much for them. They were, however, able to save the films from the storage area on their way out. So fierce was the fire, that even though the fire brigade arrived in a very short time, flames could already be seen through the ventilator in the roof, while other parts of the corrugated iron were glowing red.

Captain Poole and his men went in through the front doors to try to connect the fire hose to the hydrant inside, but, like the earlier attempt by Mr. Fox, they were forced back. As they retreated, they closed the front doors behind them, minimising any air draughts, in an effort to slow the progression of the fire. They turned their attention to the rear of the theatre, where the flames were edging closer to the Taplin residence with every passing moment. Persistence had its reward and after successfully dousing the fire here, the firemen focussed on the rear roof and were eventually able to enter the building from the Oxley Street entrance. What confronted them was catastrophic. The whole wooden ceiling of the theatre was on fire, but they were able to get a hose directed onto the stage where the flames were at their most ferocious, while other hoses pushed gallons of water upwards towards the centre of the hall. With three fire hoses attacking the flames, by 1.30 a.m., the inferno was under control, leaving only the dress circle, the operating room and the Misses Cahill's shop structurally untouched. With the exception of a small area near the stage, the floor was intact, but the seats were badly heat and smoke damaged. As the fire brigade packed away their equipment and returned to the station, one of the men remained behind to keep watch with the police until daylight.

This morning, the building was inspected by Mr. Fox, the police and the insurance representative; the word around town is that the fire started near the screen and the nearby stage curtains quickly fuelled the fire as the draught from the roof ventilator drew the flames towards the wooden ceiling. Apparently, the building and contents are insured for £5,000, and the damage bill is expected to come to more than £1,000. The insurance inspector has already authorised the repairs, commissioning Harry Furner to organise the work, so everyone is hoping it won't be long before the theatre is opening its doors again.

Mid-late May 1933
Tenders
BUILDERS desirous of tendering for the reinstatement of the Empire Theatre, Camden following fire, are invited to apply immediately to
HAROLD S. FURNER
Camden Timber Yards
Phone 40   Camden

───:─:───

Messrs. H. Willis & Sons have been entrusted with the contract for the reconstruction of the Empire Theatre. Work has already com-

---

There's been some speculation around the town about the nature of the fire earlier this month, so I'm hoping the inquiry that's coming up will give some answers and quieten the hearsay. I've heard that Campbelltown's Coroner, Mr. Payten, is going to act in place of our local Coroner, Mr. Baldock.

29 May 1933
There were few empty seats today in Camden Court House when the inquiry began into the theatre fire. Evidence was heard from W. and H. Taplin, Thomas Holbut, Sergeant Porteus, Captain Frank Poole, Moreton Stone and Phillip Fox, as well as Detective Sergeant Surridge who'd come from Parramatta to lead the investigation. Will Taplin told the court that despite hearing voices in the laneway, he hadn't heard anyone running away from the theatre and thought that Mr. Fox was a respected resident of Camden, and had a good character. Other witnesses echoed this, and added that they considered the theatre owner to be in a sound financial position as the business was doing well. Will Taplin heard explosions and this was corroborated by Moreton Stone, who heard something similar while he was on duty at the telephone exchange at the Post Office.

However, the two police officers and Captain Poole each gave evidence that fibro would make an audible crack under extreme heat, and testified to seeing a number of pieces of cracked fibro amongst the debris when they examined the scene later. These three witnesses stated they saw no evidence of forced entry into the theatre, and found nothing untoward to indicate arson, while

Rear of building in Oxley Street Camden (D Matterson, 2019)

each agreed the fire began in the stage area, quickly destroying the curtains, stage fittings and the talkie speaker. Phillip Fox and Thomas Holbut told the court the theatre was securely locked and all lights were off, while confirming there was a 'no smoking' policy for both staff and patrons. However, both Sergeant Porteus and Mr. Fox told of times when they'd needed to speak to patrons who were trying to 'steal' a smoke, and this was borne out by the fact that some cigarette butts were found behind the stage during the fire investigation. Detective Sergeant Surridge had the opinion the fire could've been caused by a wire shorting or fusing, or by a lit cigarette end being thrown down and smouldering until flammable material caught alight. He thought the cause of the fire was accidental.

Coroner's verdict: "The premises… [was] destroyed by fire, but how the fire originated the evidence adduced does not enable me to say."

Postscript:
While repairs were undertaken, Phillip Fox hired the A.H.&I. Hall and staged vaudeville shows. As part of the work, the building's walls were raised six feet – work that can still be clearly seen today when the building is viewed from Oxley Street. The theatre reopened on 30th August, and was a frequent venue for dances, fund-raisers, and school, community and church functions. In March 1934, the Empire and its opposition, the Paramount, came to an arrangement resulting in the Empire being used for 'public engagements and… dances' while the Paramount screened pictures.

This account is based on reports from the Camden News *dated 25 January 1917, 8 September 1932, 11 May 1933, 17 May 1933, 1 June 1933, 24 August 1933 and 22 March 1934.*

Loyal Orange Lodges

Brendan O'Farrell

Recent donations to the Camden Museum of Lodge regalia have led to research using *Trove* into the Loyal Orange Lodges in Cobbitty and Camden in the late nineteenth century.

It was not until a man named Henry James O'Farrell attempted to assassinate the Duke of Edinburgh at a Sydney beachside gathering in March 1868 that the Orange Order reached its zenith in Australia. O'Farrell was a Fenian sympathiser and following his failed attempt on the life of Prince Alfred (the first royal to visit Australia) the number of [protestant] *Orange Lodges in New South Wales increased enormously.*

By 1876 there were 19,000 Orangemen in over 120 lodges. Even in the small town of Kiama, in rural New South Wales, a concentrated burst of Ulster Protestant migration led to the establishment of no less than nine Orange Lodges and the naming of part of the local farming area as "Loyal Valley".
https://www.anphoblacht.com/contents/6550

The Loyal Orange Lodge No. 81 Camden started in 1873 but started advertising meetings in *The Protestant Standard* in 1874. On 9 May 1874 *The Protestant Standard* advertised the meetings in the Presbyterian Church on the Wednesday before the full moon in each month at 8 o'clock p.m. Monthly meetings continued in 1875. [This was the previous Presbyterian Church in Edward Street, Camden. The current Presbyterian Church was built in 1938.]

The Protestant Standard, Sat 23 Dec 1876, stated that No. 81 Lodge held its regular monthly meeting on Friday evening 1 Dec and officers for 1877 were elected and installed. *"The time of meeting was changed to the Friday on or before the full moon. The Lodge had been steadily increasing in numbers during the past year, and has a satisfactory balance to its credit."*

In 1879, *The Protestant Standard* reported that the anniversary of the formation of the Camden Loyal Orange Lodge, No. 81 was celebrated by a tea-meeting which was held in the Temperance Hall, followed by a public meeting in the School of Arts, Camden. Before the meeting, enthusiastic ladies and brethren who came from the surrounding districts, *"formed themselves into groups and paraded the town in their gorgeously coloured sashes. a noble exhibition of their spirit and their glory in Orangeism."*

In 1881, there were 180 Lodges in the colony of NSW, and Camden Lodge had a remarkable 400 members. There were Lodges at Cobbitty, Picton, as well as in Camden where there were both men's (No. 81) and ladies' Lodges (No. 403).

In 1883, the notice of the meeting states "*No. 81, Camden, meets in the Temperance Hall, Camden, on the Friday on or before the full moon in each month at 8 o'clock p.m.*"

By the time of World War I the political scene had changed. The items of Orange regalia are interesting for the community values of the times.

The McMinn Royal Black Sash - Item No. 2017.73.4

Julie Wrigley, Anne McIntosh and Margaret Wheeler

The item is a very ornate, heavy, black velvet sash backed with orange silk, featuring 25 silver-plated metal symbols, silver and silver-gilt bullion decoration with four tassel fringes of olive green, scarlet/ black, brilliant blue, and gold, at both ends of the sash. 235 x 15 x 2cm.

History and provenance

The object was owned and used by John Thomas McMinn, of "Freshfields", 229 Chittick Lane, Cobbitty. The obituary of John Thomas McMinn in 1913 stated that it was presented to him in the 1890s by his fellow Orangemen, the presentation being made by the Prince of Wales (later King Edward), when John Thomas sailed home to Ireland on a visit.

John Thomas was a Worshipful Master of Cobbitty Loyal Orange Lodge in 1872, and a founder of the Cobbitty Royal Black Preceptory, the senior branch of the Loyal Orange Order, in 1873. The term, 'preceptory' [order] is a designation borrowed from the Masonic Knights Templar. John Thomas McMinn was a member of the Camden Loyal Orange Lodge for about four years before his death in 1913.

The object was donated by Mr Peter Stone of Taynish Avenue, Camden. The sash was kept in the McMinn family after the death of John Thomas McMinn in 1913. Peter Stone said that it would have been given to his grandfather, Augustus Stone, sometime after John Thomas's death.

The McMinn Royal Black Sash

In 2018 and 2019 Mr. Brendan O'Farrell, a member of the Camden Historical Society, asked seamstress Mrs Nola Harris of Elderslie to restore the sash. She spent six months replacing the black velvet and orange silk on the sash, and sewing the metallic symbols back in place.

Statement of Significance

The McMinn sash is a good example of Royal Black Preceptory regalia. The engraved metal badges demonstrate the biblical allusions and symbolism of the Royal Black Order and its activities. The 'degrees of Orangeism' (Loyal Orange, Purple Arch, Royal Black) were highly regarded institutions attended by a large membership of Cobbitty and Camden Protestants from the 1870s.

The owner of the sash, Irish immigrant farmer, John Thomas McMinn, was a well-respected member of the local community and this ornate sash shows the high rank within the order that he held.

The sash has stirred the curiosity of researchers and led to investigation through *Trove* of the context of the Orange Order and the Royal Black in Ireland, Australia, and locally.

Created from velvet and silk, the sash fabric had degenerated over time. It has been restored using similar fabrics that convey its original colour and condition. The symbolism of the metal badges is intriguing; potentially being linked to special ceremonies which have remained largely secret. Taken at face value many of the symbols relate to Biblical themes, but online detractors suggest that the context has been distorted to support political agendas. For members of these societies, the rituals and their symbols teach moral and philosophical lessons.

The provenance of the sash is well documented. The chain of ownership passed from the McMinn family to the Stone family to the Camden Museum.

This is a very unusual object. Both velvet and silk are prone to damage over time and similar sashes were not located in similar NSW museums. Inquiries suggest that despite the widespread distribution of Orange Lodges and related Protestant orders across NSW, very few museums have memorabilia that represent their local Lodges. No objects related to the Royal Black were mentioned by any respondents from regional museums. The Powerhouse Museum (MAAS) has many Masonic items in its collection, but holds nothing relating to the Loyal Orange Lodge. As their collection is NSW-focused and extensive, it suggests that this ornate sash is a rare example of Royal Black regalia in a public collection.

The McMinn sash is a reminder of Camden's Loyal Orange Order and Cobbitty's Royal Black Preceptory. The sash is a reminder of the extreme Protestantism and sectarian values that were pervasive in the NSW community in the late 19th century and early 20th century.

An Independent Woman
My Mother Enid and her Travels

Jo O'Brien

Our family moved to Camden when our eldest children were young, seeking the space and lifestyle we wanted for our growing family. Part of the attraction of Camden was the sense of history, a place that felt like the home of my childhood and my mother's childhood. All the stages of its history co-exist, it is a living history of families, stories, places and locations, proud of its heritage without being frozen in the past. So much of Sydney is losing that, the suburbs we grew up in are changing so fast that they are losing their connection to their history.

I see a strong connection between Camden and the landscape of my mother's childhood in Bexley in the 1920s and 30s. Both close-knit communities of families and friends, villages with farms on their outskirts. And the starting points for two young women who travelled to the other side of the world.

A chance conversation with Dr Ian Willis about the story of Camden local Shirley Rorke and her travels has led me to reflect on my mother's life and the travels she made in the 1940s and 50s. Whereas Shirley travelled in the company of a friend for a year, my mother's journey lasted about 8 years, her voyages were solo, and she travelled literally around the world.

Enid joined the WAAAF (Women's Auxiliary Australian Air Force) aged 18 in 1942, serving until after the end of WW2 (J O'Brien)

****

My mother, Enid Wilmot, was born in 1923 in Bexley, and had a happy childhood, although the Depression made some aspects of life difficult. WWII started when Enid was 16, and her father immediately re-enlisted, and was in the army until 1947. When the Japanese bombed Pearl Harbour (7th December 1941), Enid felt like there was a direct threat to Australia. She wanted to enlist, aged 18, the army wasn't taking women recruits then, but the Air Force was, so she signed up with the WAAAF.

Enid wasn't called up until 4th April 1942. After a medical she was transported from Central to Robertson for a 3-week rookie course at Ranelagh House. It was uncomfortable and freezing cold, and as Mum was not fond of exercise, a difficult time, but she got used to it.

After a couple of days back home she was on a troop train to Melbourne, where she spent 4 months. For the rest of the war she was in Sydney and she was part of the celebrations in Martin Place when the war ended.

Enid said that if not for the war she would have likely married her then boyfriend, settled down and had children.

Fiji (mid 1948-mid 1949)
Restless after leaving the WAAAF, Enid worked in the city, and flatted with friends, not returning home to village life in Bexley, as she had become used to her independence. Then, in 1948 she took a one-year contract with the major store Morris Hedstrom in Fiji, to work in the office there.

Enid really enjoyed her time in Fiji, making friends, touring the island, and socialising. There is an album full of photos which she took with a box brownie camera, and

Enid loved her time living and working in Fiji, making friends and touring the island in 1948 (J O'Brien)

Enid on stage in New Zealand – Enid had a lead role in the show *Golden Boy* for the Wellington Repertory Theatre in 1951 (J O'Brien)

she loved the island and the native Fijian people.

While in Fiji she dated a New Zealander, following him to New Zealand when her one-year contract was finished.

New Zealand (Sep 1949-Dec 1953)
Not long after Enid arrived in New Zealand, the relationship was over. She returned to Australia for a short time, but then went back to New Zealand, and lived in Auckland and Wellington. While in Wellington she joined the Wellington Repertory Theatre and performed in plays, both acting and singing, and also did some radio work. She enjoyed the lifestyle - parties, dances and socials. She travelled a little, to Rotorua, and one time went for a flight in a Tiger Moth, but most of her photos are of her performances on the stage and attending balls with friends.

London (Feb – Nov 1954)
In late 1953 a couple of other girls and Enid planned to go to London – the other girls pulled out of the trip, but she continued the planned trip on her

own. She spent Christmas in Sydney with her family, then boarded the *Ontranto* on January 6, 1954. She would often mention the ports she visited on that trip, Colombo, Aden, Naples, Marseilles, travelling through the Suez Canal, and seeing Gibraltar. I believe she went ashore whenever she could and enjoyed the exotic nature of the places she saw.

She had saved up the money for a one-way ticket, but only had 25 pounds leftover, and no job to go to. She did however get an interesting job almost straight away, which she loved, at the fledgling BBC-TV, and met well-known people including Margaret Rutherford, and Margaret Lockwood. She shared a flat in Barnes with an Australian girl called Edna.[1]

Enid spent nearly a year in London in 1954, working for BBC-TV and living in Barnes, but money was tight, and she was unable do much sightseeing (J O'Brien)

She said that she didn't want to live with all the other Australian expats in places like Earls Court. Enid couldn't afford to travel much while she was there, which she would later regret as she would have loved to have done so. She was in fact hungry at times, food was still rationed, and the rent was higher because it was "a nice flat".

Canada (Dec 1954 – 1956)

After less than a year in London, Enid migrated to Canada – that was "the way to go then". It may have been the lack of money, the rationing, or restlessness that prompted that move. At the time she was an Australian born, NZ citizen, living in London and emigrating to Canada. She made the voyage on the *Empress of Australia*, saying that she sailed through a gale and it was the only time she was seasick. The ship arrived in Montreal, but Enid travelled by train on to Toronto as Montreal was French speaking and she didn't speak French.

In Toronto, she got a job at the bank, then worked for over a year as a legal secretary for a firm of solicitors. Here she was earning good money, able to

Enid in Canada in 1955 on holidays at Lake Catchacoma Ontario (J O'Brien)

live well, buy nice clothes, go out to dinner, and after sharing for a while able to rent a flat on her own. Enid said she was better off than she had been in her whole life. She went away with friends to Lake Catchacoma Ontario and had a holiday to New York and saw Niagara Falls.

Return home to Sydney

According to Enid, she reluctantly returned in the first half of 1956 [I have been unable to confirm the date of that voyage.] She caught a train across the US, visiting Chicago, the Grand Canyon, and Los Angeles, and then sailed home from San Francisco via Honolulu, Fiji, and Auckland – thus completing a circumnavigation of the globe, via some of the places she had lived in years earlier.

What was Enid looking for on her journey? I think she was looking for adventure, new experiences, variety, and wanting to discover more about the world. Possibly also an escape from a traditional home life, the confines of home, people's expectations or censure, and disappointment in love.

Was the travel bug/restlessness inherited? In my grandfather's memoir he says (after he returns from WWII service, escorting POWs back to Italy, and time serving in Britain):

"Had the wander lust left me? I am not quite sure, I don't think it ever will. I still gaze out over those great blue waters and long to feel the spray in my face and hear the wind howling through the rigging. My First born must have inherited the wander lust as she has seen and travelled many miles round the globe"[2]

Enid's life was forever changed, firstly by her war service, then by her travels and the experiences she had. The early independence from her years in the WAAAF made it hard for her to settle down into a traditional female role when the war ended. She loved playing a part, and perhaps moving about gave her the chance to redefine herself.

By the time Enid had journeyed to London, she was already an established traveller and a cosmopolitan lady. She lived in apartments in cities most of the time she was overseas. She was stylishly dressed, sophisticated, well-travelled, and had had many extraordinary experiences. In many ways she was a modern woman.

When she did finally marry and have children, she was more than ready to settle down, and was very happy, no longer restless, and content with family life.

I didn't realise how unique my mother was until I was grown up. She was ahead of her time in many ways. I knew many women of her era (including her sister) married, had children and followed a more traditional path, but I still thought of her as a typical Mum, just one who happened to have travelled the world on her own, lived overseas, and acted on stage.

*****

These notes are based on my memories, Mum's stories, stories from other family members, handwritten notes and a cassette tape Mum recorded in her 70s, and other items such as a 78rpm record recorded in 1952. I have some photographs but would dearly love a letter and memorabilia collection such as Shirley's, which would give so much more insight into her overseas travels.

Notes
1. I have located the flat in Church Rd, Barnes – it is still there, overlooking the Barnes Village pond
2. The Road we Travel by Bill Wilmot (Enid's father) typewritten in 1960s (age about 70)

Textiles, History and Smoking Caps

Margaret Wheeler

Understanding textiles and fashion is important in understanding the history of the times. People follow fashion designers and their designer labels, however it is the mundane in articles of textiles from all eras that gives insight to that period of time.

A little booklet printed in 1893, 'The Art of Living in Australia' by Phillip E. Musket, opened my eyes to the different way of

thinking at that time, and how as each generation changes, so do our textiles and the way we dress. The textiles mentioned were silk, wool, cotton, and linen. Flannel was used as an undergarment, thin in summer and thick in winter.

My favourite in the museum is in the drawers near the stairs, displaying men's smoking caps from the 1840s to 1880s. A set of three embroidered caps came from Miss Grace Moore "Ellensville", a Mount Hunter property. The crocheted cap came from Colin Clark: his grandfather James Sargeant wore the cap.

Smoking caps, also known as lounging caps, were popular in the 19th century, not only used to stop the hair smelling of smoke but also to keep the head

warm. A cap was often worn with a smoking jacket by men of some wealth. Their origin is probably of Chinese, Arabic or Turkish. Wives often made these caps for their husbands. Even in 1893, it was quoted 'that quite a serious amount of damage to health results from excessive smoking'. See https://www.victoriana.com/mens-clothing/mens-smokingcap

Conservation of Textiles

Old textiles may be easily damaged by poor storage and handling. The weight of the article may cause tearing and splitting and therefore support is necessary. The other big problems are dust, insects and light.

There are a number of good sites and references which explain the care of textiles.
- (1) Museum of Applied Arts and Sciences gives detailed information on conservation, storage, photography and documentation. https://maas.museum/research/conservation/conservation-resources/
- (2) Australian War Memorial, Canberra. For more information, telephone the conservation section (02)6243 4444 and ask for a Textile Conservator. https://www.awm.gov.au/our-work-/projects/conservation
- (3) Cavalcade of Fashion https://www.thecavalcade.org
- (4) YouTube has some interesting early film showing people in the streets of London, Paris and New York. These early films show what people wore in the streets. The early ones I most enjoy have been posted by Guy Jones. (Speed corrected and often sound added).
- **(4)** Peter McNeil (Australian) has written a number of books on the history of fashion.
- **(5)** (6) There was a 10 week lecture series in 2013 at the Art Gallery of NSW, "Fashion Matters: Fashion, Art and Society" which I found to be very interesting

Notes
Images shown are smoking caps at the Camden Museum, 2019 (M Wheeler).

U.S. Artist Exploring Seeds at the PlantBank
The Australian Botanic Garden, Mount Annan

Kaleigh Rusgrove

My name is Kaleigh Rusgrove and I am a postgraduate scholar visiting Australia from the United States through December 2019. I am a photographer and currently working to find ways to communicate the climate crisis through art. My research is funded by the Fulbright Program, which offers an opportunity for open research and study, while simultaneously forging bilateral relationships between the U.S. and partner countries. I am affiliated with both Western Sydney University as well as the Australian PlantBank, who have kindly allowed me to use their facilities and offered their support throughout the duration of my grant period. The Australian PlantBank, part of the Royal Botanic Gardens and Domain Trust, is a research facility which focuses on the conservation of native Australian plant species. PlantBank is located in Mount Annan and open to the public.

MoMA curator John Szarkowski once said, "one might compare the art of photography to the act of pointing". This quote was introduced to me while I was a student at the University of Connecticut, searching for a reason as to why I had spent so many years of my life behind a camera making pictures. Though I have always enjoyed the act of creating, and had been honing my craft for over a decade, I found myself at a standstill in my practice during a most critical time. While pursuing my master's degree, I had decided to turn my focus from images of fictional narratives to something very much based in reality – climate change. I was not simply interested in this field, but felt compelled to make work about it given the severity of the issue and the im-

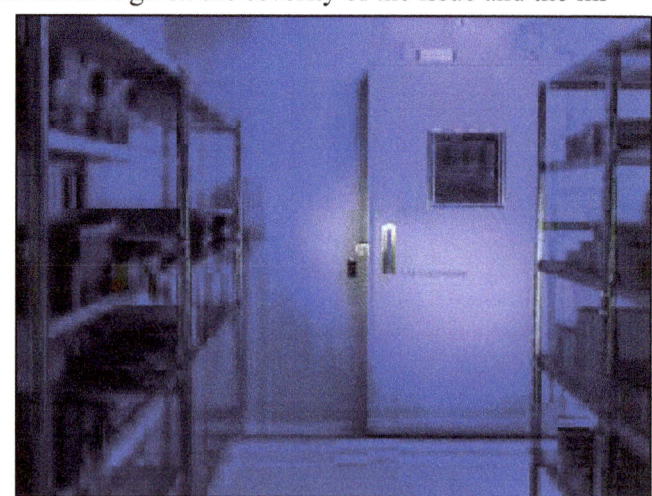

A door to one of the cold rooms in which seeds are stored long term. The collections are vacuum-sealed in aluminum packets and kept at a cool minus 20 C. (K Rusgrove)

Looking in on the seeds of Australian PlantBank. The facility houses 10,000 collections and over 100,000,000 individual seeds. (K Rusgrove)

pact I was learning it would have on my future. I had found something in the world that intrigued and concerned me, and I wanted to point to it.

Early on in my process I became overwhelmed at just how much there was to uncover about climate change. There were simply too many directions to turn and stories to be told. I decided to focus on just one element – seeds and seed banking – because it was something I was vaguely familiar with and often portrayed in the media in a very dark, science-fiction-like light. I began working with the Native Plant Trust in Massachusetts, and after successful shooting decided I wanted to seek out additional locations. It was around this same time that I first learned of the Fulbright Program, and decided to not only look for new locations in my own country but abroad as well.

I began researching seed vaults and bank programs, and came across the Ausralian PlantBank. After learning about the work being done at PlantBank and reading up on the astonishing variety of biodiversity in Australia, I knew I had to do everything I could to get here. Every step of the process felt as though it serendipitously fell into place, and though I knew the odds of actu-

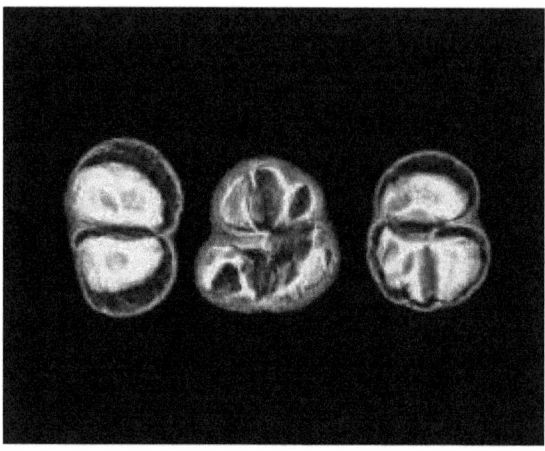

X-Ray of Unidentified Seeds (K Rusgrove)

ally receiving the award were slim, I felt I had crafted the best application possible. In May 2018 I received word that I had been selected, and a few short months later I was on a plane to Sydney.

As I prepared to come to Australia, I was wrapping up my previous body of work and contemplating what needed to change once I arrived. I knew that to get a better grasp on climate change as a major issue, I needed to gain a new perspective – and that's exactly what I have spent the last six months doing. I have been able to do what I pointed to in my application, but explore other avenues as well. I came to Australia with the mindset that science and art were two completely different fields, and that by making art about science I might help to communicate the research behind climate change.

It's not to say that I now have an advanced understanding of botany, or more than a rudimentary grasp of the scientific method. I sympathize with the general public, who often cite confusion as being in the way of taking a stronger stance on the climate crisis. Science can be incredibly confusing, and can often go above the heads of those of us who did not choose to walk down that particular career path. Because of this, I planned to spend my time here making allegorical imagery that would help a viewer better understand the facts. Yet I've pivoted from this mindset, and no longer aim to simplify these issues.

I've sought out new resources and talked to experts, and yet the first explanation I ever received regarding climate change is the same one repeated back to me in nearly every conversation. The science behind climate change is complicated, but the cause is not. We must stop mining fossil fuels. Humans are living beyond our means, and we must change these larger ways of operating if we want there to be a hospitable future for the human race on Earth. To make this change will be difficult. To restructure life as we know it is

Descending through the eucFACE experiement - Western Sydney University Hawkesbury Campus. The native trees within the experiment site are exposed to the same level of CO2 projected for 2050.
(K Rusgorve)

hard to imagine, and I'd venture to guess even harder to implement. But that does not mean we should not try.

To me the greater issue at hand seems to be a general lack of care, an overwhelming apathy that keeps us from progressing forward. It is easer to do nothing than to try and ultimately fail. We make small changes, forgoing plastic straws and buying reusable bags. We feel good about these motions, and they do add up to make a difference in the world. Yet we don't tackle the bigger issues, because they're often so deeply integrated into our lives, and feel out of reach of our everyday. On the farthest end of the spectrum, we are unaware that we as humans effect the planet at all.

Six months ago the Royal Botanic Garden and Australian PlantBank opened their doors for me to come inside and explore. They have asked nothing of me in return, and I have crept through the halls and into the labs to take pictures, remaining very much an outsider and quiet observer. For that I am incredibly grateful. At times I wonder if I should find a focus, go deeper into something of a particular interest. Yet the most transformative moments for me have been in the flux of working, offhand comments and simple questions answered. I've learned how difficult it is to store seeds and of the many variables that may keep them from germinating or propagating. For a field that I always believed to be so rooted in certainty, there is so much that is still unknown about our natural world and how it functions. As much as humans would like to believe we run this planet, there are still mysteries to be revealed.

What I've learned is in science, much like in an artistic practice, there are both the plans and then what actually happens. There are hypotheses and expectations, and unexpected results. Things don't always turn out the way we want them to, but we continue to try, and try again. We are always hoping for the best. But the greatest connection between science and art by far is persistent failure. Yet we return to the lab and the studio, day after day, searching for the answer. And just because we do not have one yet, does not mean that we are wrong.

While I started this journey wondering how I could make people believe that the world is changing and that climate change is real, I now think more often of what it would take just to gain any trust or interest of humans at all. It's easier to remain oblivious than to deal with these issues or to make a major change. We're living a time when so many people are dubious of facts and would rather believe self-proclaimed Internet experts. How can we rekindle trust of those who truly do know best? How can we get people to get off their phones and out of their cars and connected with the world around them again, to realize what is at stake?

My question and approach has changed. While I wanted to make things easier for people, I've done a quite dramatic turn to something more involved. I've

A Wollemi Pine, wrapped to keep in beneficial cryptolaemus montrouzieri (a type of ladybird beetle). These insects protect the rare plant from mealybugs. (K Rusgrove)

A vacant room at the Australian PlantBank. Empty chairs have become a recurring theme in my work, acting as a stand-in for humans. (K Rusgrove)

always enjoyed a good mystery, and I've started to make work that feels like clues to be uncovered and reassembled into a story. It feels the truest representation of my research thus far, still pointing to this issue, but not telling you what to do. If I leave people unsettled, I think I've done my job. If nothing else, I hope that this work provides a pause, a moment for contemplation and curiosity. I'll accept any emotion, so long as it's not apathy.

Memories of Ron Davies: Abbotsford
From Ron's talk at CHS Meeting, 12 June 2019

Anne McIntosh

Ron spent much of his life in Picton and grew up with his family, on the historically significant property Abbotsford located on the outskirts of Picton. Ron is now 90 years old and has moved to Carrington. Back in Picton, his family is not forgotten – Davies Place recalls his father, and Monds Lane is named after his brother-in-law, who managed dairying at Abbotsford for the Ziems family.

Abbotsford

Abbotsford was granted to George Harper who ran sheep on the land. Ron assumes that the financial difficulty he experienced occurred when NSW transportation ceased and management could not adapt from a reliance on cheap and readily available convict labour.

Major Antill, attaché to Gov Macquarie, subsequently purchased Abbotsford in 1865. It retained ties to Antill descendants until its sale in the 1950s. There were several other tenants before the Fresh Food and Ice Company took over the land in the 1930s.

Ron Davies addressing Camden Historical Society meeting 12 July 2019 (L Stratton)

This entrepreneurial company made Penguin ice-cream at a factory near Ultimo (1 Day St, Darling Harbour), and began exporting refrigerated goods. They sourced their cream from local dairies, including their own, the Byrnes dairy, which milked 40 cows on a 50 ac block at Rosebery. The Byrnes Company, owned by Jim Byrnes, needed a partner to facilitate their expansion, so Abbotsford was purchased by Deacons & Byrnes. Initially, it was a small enterprise that hand milked and transported the milk into the city to the factory (a three-hour trip each way), but expansion and further innovation had always been planned. Jim Byrnes also leased the Inglis property at Craigend. Ron distinctly recalls the sign on a building at the property as he corrects the spelling of the name 'Burns'. "When I was at school, Jim Byrnes reminded me of the spelling of that name. It seemed to matter a lot to him. It's B-Y-R-N-E-S, that's the Irish spelling, Okay."

During the 1930s, Ron Davies and his brother lived on the Rosebery property where their father managed the dairy. As the population grew, the government no longer wanted dairies close to the city.

Ron Davies' family (there would ultimately be seven children) moved to Picton in 1938, into a slab workers cottage on Abbotsford. Ron's father was foreman at the dairy. Later, when his father was promoted, the family relocated to the manager's homestead which was more spacious and comfortable.

The Byrnes Exhibition Dairy in the 1940s and 50s
The property is about a mile outside Picton, on the Barkers Lodge Road and was known as the Byrnes Exhibition Dairy. It milked 500 cows in winter, and around 460 during summer. The herd was a mix of Jerseys, AIS (Australian Illawarra Shorthorns) and Ayrshires – Ron remembers the Ayrshires for their tendency to kick – "If it wasn't the cups, it was the dairyman. Around 95% of the Ayrshires needed a leg rope. We almost never needed one for the Jerseys, which had a calmer temperament. Except the bull…" Ron recalled that the bull paddock was of post-and-rail construction (four rails), with a sliding wooden window that could be pulled aside to enable the bull to access the feed trough on the outside of the fence." The rule was that you never entered a bull paddock if you weren't on horseback," he recalled.

As 400 ac was insufficient land for such a big herd, the company leased the neighbouring two properties on the same side of the road, providing an additional 3000 ac. "As you travel down the hill into Picton, everything on the right side of the road was run from Abbotsford."

My father didn't believe in cross breeding, so the three herds of milking cows were kept separate, and milked in different batches.

Before milking, the cows would enter the feeders, 100 cows at a time, in four rows. A rail ran down an alleyway at the centre and a trolley was pushed by one man while another distributed the feed into the troughs. The cows were in a head lock to prevent the fastest eaters stealing from their neighbours' portions. The feed varied with the season and in different years. There might be biscuits of hay or other chaff, with concentrates such as hominy meal, beans, pollard and oats. At one stage, ensilage was produced and fed. "It was

Ruins of Abbotsford 2007 (WSC)

fermented and it really did stink," Ron recalled. "It sank into your skin, but the cattle loved it."

As an exhibition dairy, visitors would watch the feeding and the milking. It was a sophisticated set-up in the 1940s and 50s. When the rotolactor began operations, it was closer to the city, and impacted visitor numbers to the Abbotsford Dairy. It was drummed into Ron's head from an early age that the herd had to yield a gallon of milk per cow per day, to turn a profit. He laughs at this. recollection knowing that some Friesian breeders now average 7 gallons per cow per day.

The hours on the dairy farm were long, and even though dairy hands were not expected to do any additional farm work, for those who lived in town and walked to the farm, it was difficult to maintain the routine, seven days-a-week. Mal Travers, who lived down near the railway station (2 miles away), had to be up by 2am to be ready for milking at 4am. Between milkings, the exhausted men would bunk down near the boiler in the shed. Later, Edgar organised for his daughter, Gwen (later Monds), to set up a boarding house in the old homestead. It was popular among the workers who could now sleep in until 3.30 in the morning!

Arthur Hanley was responsible for raising the calves. The bull calves would be sent to Camden saleyards and sold on Tuesday mornings – they were destined to become the devon on his schoolmates' sandwiches. (Ron's sandwiches were invariably roast beef – a useful trading commodity in the playground!)

Unlike most local farmers who sent their milk to the factory in Menangle, Abbotsford's milk was piped, sieved using cheesecloth and stored on farm in a refrigerated 2,000 gallon vat at temperatures so low that ice crystals formed in the milk, but it would still pour. The tanker, was not refrigerated, and the milk would be transported to Sydney. The system was even more cost effective, because at the factory, they would skim off the cream, ensuring they could sell fresh milk for the Sydney market that met the minimum 3.2% butter fat requirement, while directing the additional high fat product into ice-cream. For the other farmers, testing at the milk factory could detect whether water was being added to dilute the milk. At Ultimo, nothing was added, but the cream was extracted!

Although there were milking machines in the 12-bail dairy, during the war, electricity supply was unreliable. When the power failed, a bell would be rung, for all hands to be on deck. On these days, all the wives, and sometimes people from the town, came to help. Hand milking would continue almost all day. Ron's memory is as much for the pea and ham soup served with chicory tea by one of the wives, as for the long hours.

Growing up on the farm
Life was very busy. Morning milking began at 4am and finished at 9.30; in the afternoon cows were milked between 2 and 7pm.

Although he attended school in town, there were lots of chores which tended to take priority when hands were short on the farm. Children were expected to pull their weight.

Like many boys, Ron hunted rabbits and skinned them. But by breeding ferrets for the other rabbit hunters, Ron was able to expand his business. Alongside his job as foreman, Ron's father was a draft horse fancier. There were 30 draft animals on Abbotsford during the war – all Clydesdales, except for one Suffolk Punch and a Shire. Twelve horses pulled the combine, and the harrow came behind. They also used a 12-disc plough, and in the heavy soils of their largest 55 ac paddock, they had to spell the horses at the end of each row.

Ron says that he learnt to harness the draft horses and drive the team from a young age. He recalls having his photo taken by some photographers after the

Abbotsford 2010 (Image by DarylH)

war. He had been instructed to plough up that big cultivation paddock which was one of the closest to Picton. (It was later sold to Wollondilly Council and was added to the town's sportsfields.) The sight of a large disc plough and such a significant team meant that the story was published on the cover of the Byrnes Exhibition Dairy Gazette.

Once a fortnight, he had to help with the muster. Cows were spelled on the steep hills of the adjacent property. Dry cows in calf would be taken out to be spelled, and the heavily pregnant cows and heifers would be brought nearer the dairy.

Ron had a lot of local friends. The town kids loved to visit the farm, and later, three of his friends would be recruited to assist in the dairy, a much sought-after gig.

He also got to know some of the children who were "exported" from England during the recession/war years. Many of these boys had limited prospects and so they sought to impress the farmers' sons in the hope of getting a job on their properties.

Ron had been handling horses all his life, and he regularly entered a horse that he trained in the Oaks Races which were held at the Airfield.

He also did some horse breaking, particularly for the owner. Jim Byrnes kept a number of ponies on the property which were used in the sulkies. One day, Ron jokingly asked him why he didn't invest in some 'decent' horses. Jim answered immediately, reminding Ron that although they might be small, the ponies did the same job, and they only ate half as much as a larger horse - fuel efficiency was a consideration, even then!

Through his friend, Edgar Downes, another local dairyman, Ron's father was recruited to assist at the Royal Easter Show as a 'green coat' ("… but I think they may have worn red coats, back then?"), one of the gentlemen who opened gates to facilitate the movement of stock to show areas and in the grand parade. This meant that his father would be away from the farm for a few days. For the dairy workers, it was a time for relative relaxation without the authoritarian discipline of his father. On one occasion, he recalls that two boys had been boasting their superior sprinting speed for several days. Ron turned off the milking machines, and they marked out a sprinting track in the paddock, and settled it in a 'head-to-head'. One of those boys went on to play first grade rugby.

Another time, in his father's absence, they had trialled riding a cow named Peggy. She was a crazy beast outside the yard, but very quiet while she was waiting to be milked. She tolerated having a boy on her back… and then, there was his father standing at the door to the yard. He was not amused. Ron is uncertain how or why he had returned early, but has not forgotten his reaction to their 'games'.

The job he hated most on the farm was dehorning the calves. The horn and the skin around the horns had to be removed – an awful, cruel and bloody procedure for the calves. However, he also saw the damage that could be done by horned cattle when they were packed into crowded dairy yards. It was awful, but necessary.

Innovations – many learnings
Abbotsford utilised ensilage/silage, a fermented pasture product for longterm storage of green feed. A deep hole would be dug into a sloping hillock, with steep sides and a sloping ramp at one end to enable access by horses. After the feed was cut using tractors it was dumped into the hole and covered by a deep layer of dirt so that air could not penetrate. The green cuttings would ferment over several months, and could be stored for several years. The ponies would then scrape away the dirt that covered a section of the silage pit.

They descended to the base of the pit where the feed was shovelled into their dray. Ron fondly recalls two of those ponies, Major and Dingo. "You only had to take them back to the shed two or three times, and they knew the routine. They'd work in tandem. It was very labour efficient – one guy to load the dray at the pit and another in the barn to unload. The dray had a tipping mechanism, and you'd just scoop the stuff out ready for feeding."

In winter, peas would be grown on the hills. Being legumes, they were a good crop for improving the soil. But picking and shelling peas as they ripened over several months is labour intensive. So farms in the area bought a new machine called a 'pea deviner' and housed it centrally in a special shed (which is still in use by the Picton Show Society). The machine was so efficient because it removed the peas and the vines in a single passage – which meant there was only one crop from the pea vines. This terrible loss in total productivity meant that the pea picker-viner was retired after only two years! Evelyn's and Crawford Creeks were the main water sources for the property, but they sometimes ran dry. At one stage, a bore was put in at the top of one of the hills. The water was red in colour, but plentiful, and easy to distribute downhill. Lucerne was planted and irrigated; it grew well, and then turned yellow... and did not flourish. A soil scientist was consulted. The bore water was very high in iron. Not only was it toxic for the crop, but it would accumulate in the soil, so that future crops could not grow. Unlike many local properties, Abbotsford abandoned irrigation from underground water.

After the war, there was a major campaign to eradicate tuberculosis (TB) from the cattle. It had been discovered that humans could catch TB from milk from infected cows. The campaign was organised by Dr Sydenham the local vet. All cows over 18 months old had to have a BCG test in the skin under their tails. At Abbotsford, 25% of the cattle were culled, which had a devastating impact on the farm and its management. As annual testing continued, the incidence of positive BCG tests fell dramatically.

For many years, there was no vet between Warwick Farm and Goulburn. Among the dairy farmers, Fred Watson was the 'unofficial vet' over Camden way, while Ron's father, Edgar, performed the same role in the Wollondilly area, assisting in difficult calvings (dystocia) and treating cows for milk fever (with calcium carbonate injections), grass tetany (with magnesium) and bloat (by puncturing the rumen with a trocar). It was a casual arrangement between the farmers, no money exchanged hands, but his father might come home with a box of apples or peaches. People had to cooperate and help was provided where people were able – they might loan a bull or a horse for a week, or help out during harvest.

The country around Picton is steep – Abbotsford was no exception. Farmers in the local area trialled aerial spreading of superphosphate. There was an airstrip on the Fairley place at Razorback and Clifton Bros provided the super. Many farms spread fertiliser by plane as frequently as six times per year. But Abbotsford could not – on the single occasion that they tried an aerial drop, shoppers in Picton complained when the white stuff fell out of the sky. In a recent conversation with Bobby Fairley, Ron learned that although Albert Baxter, Byrnes Dairy and Wonsons ceased the aerial drops in response to those complaints, the Fairleys had trialled the aerial fertilising for four years.

One advantage that Abbotsford had over the Rotolactor dairy at Menangle was that their relatively broadacre operations may have aided disease prevention. Abbotsford also washed udders in the traditional way using a bucket and cloth with disinfectant, which improved milk letdown and aimed to minimise mastitis. Infected milk could be detected in the vat using a white cell count, so udder infections had to be treated early. Antibiotics were administered into the teat along with a coloured dye. While treatment continued, the cow was milked, but was totally unproductive as her milk could not be sold. Mastitis was not absent at Abbotsford, but talk among local dairy farmers suggested that udder infections were a major issue for some farms in the district.

The war years
Ron may have been a child during the war years, but he has some very clear memories.

Picton responded enthusiastically to the aluminium drive donating their saucepans. Ron remembers that for years afterwards they were cooking their food in jam tins.

One time during the war, the army asked whether they could do some practice involving bren guns and their carriers. They arrived on trucks and went up the back of the property near Razorback. I don't know for sure, but I think they would test how they tipped over, and then practise righting them again.

He also remembers the Army marches that passed through Picton followed by an ambulance. The men would leave Holsworthy and walk up Razorback to Picton, then out to Menangle, Douglas Park and back to Holsworthy with full packs and weapons. Within a week, those men would be on a transport heading to a posting overseas. Friends who returned told Ron that they believed that the purpose of those gruelling marches was that when you were in a foreign land and the going got tough, you'd recall that dreadful march you did before you left home, and you would remind yourself that on the scale of hardships, things weren't really too bad.

An air raid siren went off on the night of the Japanese submarine raids on Sydney Harbour; the local warden, Mrs Picton, drove around the community reminding everyone to cover their windows and turn off their lights.

Ron was 15 years old when the war ended in 1945. At the end of the war, the army had a surplus of vegetables. These were shipped to Picton by train, to be fed to the cattle. Hundreds of cabbages would arrive to feed to the cows, who liked the leafy vegetables. Unfortunately, it gave the milk a cabbage-taint. Other uses for the cabbages were found.

The Army also sent root vegetables – turnips, swedes, beetroots. It was the bane of Ron's life, as it took too long to cut up the vegetables for feeding. Then it delayed milking as the cows took too long in the feeders eating their vegetables. So feeding was moved to the paddocks, where those vegetables had to be broken open for the cattle.

Ron Davies addressing Camden Historical Society meeting 12 July 2019 (L Stratton)

To break the tedium, the boys would throw the vegetables around. The beetroots were every mother's nightmare – stained clothes were not welcomed at a time of shortage. The problem was amplified when a competition in beetroot throwing between the Byrnes Dairy and the town kids developed. The mothers brought an end to those events.

The circus comes to town

It was probably 1941 when Wirth's circus arrived in Picton by train. The townsfolk turned out to watch the action. The four elephants were the first to be unloaded, and they then helped to get all the other items off the train and down to the showground. They even assisted in putting up the Big Top, lifting men up on their trunks as they hammered the poles into the soil.

During warm weather, Ron frequently went into town to the swimming pool – there were always nice girls down there. He would ride his pony, and tie it up while he went for a dip. This day, he was riding a young horse that had been recently broken in. The whole way the pony played up, challenging his horsemanship. When Ron got to the pool, there were four elephants in the water, and it was a muddy bog. He stayed and watched for a while, but his pony was very unsettled – "Until then, I did not know that ponies hate elephants," he said.

The circus stayed for two days, and left by train. There were huge piles of elephant poo that had been raked up. During the next week, townsfolk were seen at night moving around with wheelbarrows, and the piles shrank in size. That year, everyone said that their vegie patches were very productive, thanks to the circus.

Fresh Food and Ice Company sells Abbotsford

The factory in Ultimo was no longer 'state of the art', and as the city developed, its location was not strategic. The dairy at Abbotsford closed in 1955. Farming was changing, and the steep country, unreliable water supply and relatively unproductive, but high cream producing cattle, were not suited to the fresh milk market that most local farms were supplying.

For a while, Ron's brother-in-law (Billy Monds) managed the dairy farm, and continued in this role after it was bought by the Ziems family, who were butchers from Corrimal NSW. Billy became ill and left the farm – he was 62 years old when he passed away from a heart attack. Since then, the land has mainly been used to graze beef cattle.

Recalling that time, Ron said that he had been working in the mines and living near the railway station. During the 60s, he was walking up the road to visit his family, when some guys in a car pulled up and pointed to one of the highest hills on Abbotsford. They had recently imported a new 'human kite' from overseas, and were seeking somewhere to launch from to see how it would operate in Australian skies. Ron suspects their 'experiments' were the first time a hang glider was seen in the area, and perhaps among the earliest flights in the country.

After Ron's family, Max Dalton was a later manager on the property. Wally Greentree also lived in the manager's house at one time. At one stage, it was used as a rifle range with shots being fired across the valley.

The property clearly had a long history. There was an underground lock-up for housing convicts – this was knocked down in 1958. The carpentry in the feeding stalls was the finest, and the tallow-wood strong and long lasting.
A number of people recognised the value of the historic site, and suggested that it should be opened to the public. When heritage listing threatened in the 1970s, a fire ignited in the house. A passing car saw the flames and called for help. The fire was quenched before the buildings were destroyed. Soon after, there was another fire, and the buildings were destroyed. The roof was burnt and the old shingles were evident beneath the charred roof. This devalued the property from a heritage perspective.

On 2 April 1999, despite the damage, those historic farm buildings were added to the State of NSW Heritage Register, and in 2013, a report was completed to document their significance, and to guide their preservation. There is currently a DA with Wollondilly Council to stabilize the Abbotsford ruins on the site.

Painting Abbotsford farm Picton. Artist L Finlay. Owner Ron Davies (A McIntosh)

President's Annual Report 2018-2019

Ian Willis

It is with pleasure that I present the annual report of the Camden Historical Society. It has been a busy and challenging year for the society. The society continues to contribute to a number of roles in the community and including: acting as a centre of volunteering; elling the Camden story; and contributing to local tourism

Advocacy
The society continues to tell the Camden story and support local heritage by contributing to: the Camden Council Heritage Advisory Committee; public discussion in the media and elsewhere; and public submissions.

Participation in the community
The society has attended at a number of community events including:
- In 2018: the Civic Centre Antique Fair; HCNSW History Week; Camden Council Volunteers Night
- In 2019: Australia Day parade; Camden Show; National Trust Heritage Week;

Speakers at society meetings
Speakers at monthly meetings have included: Terry Gordon (Nov 2018); Cameron Archer (Feb 2019); Brian Walsh (Mar 2019), Doug Fulford (Apr 2019) and Ron Davies (June 2019)

Volunteers
Volunteers continue to do a great job in a range of capacities from staffing the front desk, research, attending functions, advocacy and other activities. The roster for the front desk in the last year was managed by volunteer coordinators Rene Rem and then Bob Lester. There are currently over 50 volunteers on the roster, and a Volunteers Day was held in July.

Museum
The museum attracted over 6000 visitors in the last year including a number of school visits and community groups.

The Percival Wagon
The Percival wagon has been completely restored by volunteers at The Oaks Historical Society and is the central part of a new blacksmithing display.

Membership
At the end of the financial year the membership of the society was 172.

Community Partnership
The society continues with the partnership with Camden Library and the Camden Area Family History Society. Joint activities have included: Heritage Week in April; History Week in September; and the collection of photographs in Camden Images Past and Present.

Communication
The society published a journal twice a year and a newsletter three times a year. Lee Stratton looks after the newsletter and I am the journal editor. A number of members provide stories to the Back Then page of *The District Reporter*. The society has a strong online presence particularly through with its website, Camden History, managed by Steve Robinson and other social media sites.

Welfare
Volunteer Sue Cross follows up members with 'get well' messages.

Financial assistance
The society has the continued support of Camden Council through a yearly subsidy covering insurances, the provision of two storage units at Narellan and the on-going maintenance of the museum.

Janice Johnson Bequest
Former society member Janice Johnson left the society a bequest in her will. Her instructions for the spending of the funds from her estate including plaques on a number of graves and publishing and re-publishing a number of her works.

Final Thanks
In conclusion I wish to thank everyone on the committee, volunteers and others who have assisted the society over the past year. I want to acknowledge the work done by four retiring members of the committee: Kathy Lester (Treasurer), Bob Lester (Volunteer Coordinator), Cathey Shepherd (Vice President), and Sharon Greene (Committee member). Everyone has done a sterling job in supporting the aims of the society.

The Abusive Mr Chisholm (Part 3)

Peter McCall

In the last issue of the Camden History, *an 1897 published speech of Alderman Henry Willis was used as the starting point for an investigation of a quarrel between Willis and the leadership of the Camden Agricultural, Horticultural and Industrial Society (AH&I) over the Society's expenditure, with accusations of corruption and cronyism. On the 20th December Willis held a public meeting. We have a copy of his speech where he attacks the leadership of the AH&I Society in strong terms. He was also working through Camden Council to bring the Society to book.*

On 22 December 1897 Willis was included in those allowed to see the trustee's deeds and books.[1] The council held an interview with the trustees on the 5 January 1898. Willis was not present. A Onslow Thompson was the main representative of the trustees. The trustees generally agreed that they were charging for use of the showground and that these charges fell within the rules of the Deed of Trust under which they had received the land from the Macarthur Onslows.[2]

Despite this, on 10 January, Willis gave notice that at the next Camden Council meeting a motion be considered to prevent the AH & I Society from charging admission to the grounds and that the Society's accounts be investigated.[3] At the next meeting, at which Willis was not present, Mayor Furner ruled the motion out of order.[4] On 16 March Willis then introduced a motion that the Mayor be sacked because of this action. The motion was lost on 30 March with Willis being the only vote in favour.[5] Willis's attempts to deal with the issue through Camden Council had therefore failed comprehensively. He seems to have abandoned the threat to take the Trustees of Onslow Park to the Court of Equity; presumably he realised that he had no case there.

Meanwhile, Alderman FWA Downes had described the 'Abusive Mr Chisholm in War Paint' in very strong terms - 'That pamphlet was in my humble opinion an insult to the intelligence of the people of the district'.[5] Willis now made Downes the target of his strongest invective- 'Now Mr Downes should not say that his opinion is "humble"- it is not. It is the quintessence of bombastic superfluity'.[6]

However, the AH&I Society had also finished with the issue, now ignoring it. As a coda, at its annual general meeting held on 24 June 1898 JK Chisholm said, '… it may be accepted as evidence that the committee throughout the adverse criticism which has been heaped upon its members, still retains the

Portrait of Henry Willis, 1900s, The Swiss Studios (NLA)

confidence and approval of those for whom it has worked.'[7] More specifically Downes said that '[Willis] now virtually admitted that his former censure was undeserved.... His only regret was that Mr Willis had not gone further and taken the honourable course of apologising to Mr Chisholm, ... for the grossly insulting attack he made upon him and other officers of the society'.[8] It is not clear how Willis had 'virtually admitted' that he was wrong, except to say that he seems to have stopped bringing up the issue of the finances of the AH & I Society after the defeat of his motion to dismiss the Mayor. In November 1898, Willis congratulated James W Macarthur Onslow on his election to council and said that there were no disagreements between the Onslow family and Camden.[9] This may have just been politeness, but indicates a change of attitude to that evinced in 'The Abusive Mr Chisholm in War Paint'.

Willis stood as an independent for the seat of Camden in the July 1898 July elections. He favoured federation. As a result, his attacks on Downes died away, his attentions being otherwise engaged. The sitting member, John Kidd, was re-elected. Willis then spent some time attacking Kidd in the *Camden Times*. However, by this time most of his correspondence was written from Kensington in Sydney. Of the thirty meetings Camden Council had held in the year prior to February 1899, Willis had attended eleven, making him one of the less frequent attenders[10]. He resigned from the council in July 1899[10] no longer living in the district. According to the author of a 1911 *Evening News* article, Willis said that, 'having "put things in order", he would resign and make way for somebody else'.[11]

Henry Willis seems to have been a man who attracted attention by his attitude and actions. Despite the apparent lack of support he received over the Camden AH&I Society, Willis was elected to Randwick Council in 1899,[12] reflecting his residence in that area. In 1901 he was elected to the new Federal House of Representatives as Member for Robertson (which was completely outside the Camden district). Defeated in 1909, he then successfully stood for election to the NSW Legislative Assembly in 1910 for the Upper Hunter. In The House of Representatives he supported Sir George Reid's Free Trade Party, and in the Legislative Assembly he was a Liberal. In both cases he was politically in the centre. At first this seems to clash with his seemingly radical views in Camden, but Willis seems to have been a person whose strong support for causes, backed by his undoubted eloquence, was not necessarily backed by any strong principles except a vague determination to help ordinary people and take down those who saw themselves as the "governing class" down a notch or two. On the other hand, he was associated with the estate of EL Moore, whose wealth must have placed him somewhere close to some of the people he attacked. It maybe that Moore's convict ancestry was still counted against him by the 'bluebloods' of Camden, or at least that Willis may have felt that this was the case.

His position outside the mainstream parties can be seen when he was elected Speaker of the Legislative Assembly in 1911 with the support of the Labor Party, which was thus assured a majority in the lower house. Not surprisingly, the Liberal Party was furious. Willis was an extremely pedantic Assembly Speaker, giving himself extra powers and privileges and arousing hostility from both parties. 'His overbearing presence and insensitive manner alienated support'.[13] He resigned in 1913 and was defeated in the next general election. He stood as an unsuccessful candidate for the Labor Party in the 1920 state elections. His later career had reflected his behaviour in Camden. He retired to a large house he had built at Middle Harbour in Sydney and supervised four properties that he owned, dying in 1950.[14]

Willis's attack on the Camden AH&I Society aroused tempers and concerns in Camden in 1897 to 1898, but apparently had no long term consequences. It does indicate that the seeming monopoly of power by wealthy landowners in Camden was open to challenge. In its accusation of brutal evictions from the Macarthur Onslow properties and an attempt to give Menangle commercial advantage over Camden, there are hints that there were some sources of discontent in the town. But they are only hints, and Willis's extravagant eloquence and failure to keep his focus on Camden did not mean that there was any proof for them. All that we are left with is the entertaining speech about the 'Abusive Mr Chisholm' which is worthy of reading as a diverting example of late nineteenth century rhetoric and sarcasm.

Notes
1 *Camden Council Minutes 1896-1901,* p188.
2 *Ibid,* p193-194.
3 *Ibid,* p198.
4 *Ibid,* p213.
5 *Ibid,* p215.
6 *Camden News,* 24 February 1897, p4,
7 *Ibid,* 3 March 1897, p1
8 *Camden Agricultural, Horticultural and Industrial Society Minutes,* 24 June 1897, p274.
9 *Ibid,* End Paper.
10 *Camden Council Minutes 1896-1901,* 1 February 1899, p287
11 *Evening News,* 11 September 1911, p10.
12 Spearitt, P & Stewart, E, *Australian Dictionary of Biography: Willis, Henry (1860-1950)* http://adb.anu.edu.au/biography/willis-henry-9124 Accessed 6 January 2016.
13 *Ibid*
14 *Ibid*

Memories of Rob Shumack
Camden Fire Brigade

In conversation with Anne McIntosh at the Camden Museum, 28 June 2019

In recent years, Rob has moved to the northern plains of NSW, but has retained ties to motor racing. He was visiting Camden before travelling with young competitors to race in Townsville.

Demonstrating the strength of his ties to Camden, Rob Schumack told me that he grew up on a horse stud, Lomar Park, and was born at Camden Hospital under Sister Hackworthy. He subsequently attended Camden Public School and later, Camden High School, at the 'in town' site.

After leaving school, he was living with his grandparents, Les and Helen Pluis, in Mitchell Street. Their house backed onto the high school. Through them, he knew Llewella Davies pretty well. Other young people thought she was a bit cranky, but whenever he and his friends asked for some fruit from her trees, she was generous. 'She expected people to be polite. She hated it when people just walked onto her place and didn't ask,' he said.

In those days, the Camden Fire Station was manned by 16 part-timers, referred to as 'retainers' who were on call. Each member of the brigade carried a pager, and there was a siren that would ring at the fire station. Available brigade members would leave their jobs and/or homes to go to the station. As volunteers, they were paid according to jobs attended, rather than a wage.

Key documents were the occurrence books for the fire brigade. 'The need to accurately record the details of the fires and who attended was drummed into us from the day we joined,' said Rob. He was excited to discover a copy of the handwritten records from the 1910 Occurrence Book in the museum's file. He said that the layout of the books that he had used in the 1980s and 90s was very similar. As his mind drifted, he queried what had happened to all those entries that he had made in the occurrence books.

He said that Llewella was a strong supporter of the firemen. Invariably, whenever the siren sounded, she would walk up the street with her dog, to see what was happening. When the truck returned, Llewella would join the firemen in the common room to share a cup of tea.

Rob was encouraged to join the fire brigade by Derrick Thorn and Kenny

Barrett and was still a member when the fire station moved in 1993.

The biggest fire he attended was probably at Camden High School. A search of Trove did not turn up the details of the fire, probably because it occurred too recently to be included in their collection of scanned newspapers. He said that the school had to close for a few days, so members may remember this.

Rob fondly remembers the parades that he participated in, using a historic fire engine that belonged to John Southwell, such as the Australia Day Parades and events associated with Camden Show. 'I remember running out of petrol one year on our way to the Fisher's Ghost Festival,' he recalled with a wry smile. Early in his time with the fire service, the firemen would throw lollies from the truck creating a scramble on the footpath. Eventually, the Council decided that this was too risky. During the 1990s, the Camden Fire Brigade celebrated its 100th anniversary – there were lots of celebrations at the Camden Show, and Rob was proud to have been there.

Rob remembers the role played by Liz Kernohan in finding the ground for a new fire station at Elderslie. 'Without her commitment and lobbying over quite a long time, I don't think it would have happened,' he said. 'With the council building opposite the fire station [in John Street], we knew the people who worked there, and Liz took a real interest.'

At the time of the move, Rob said that other members of Camden Fire Brigade included:
    Adam Smith (son of teachers who lived in Alpha Road)
    Tim Cooley
    John Cross (captain)
    Derrick Thorn (deputy captain)
    Ken Gooch (engine keeper)
    Dave Butler
    Danny Brooking
    Ken Barraet.

The NSW Fire Brigade organised the opening of the new fire station. Many dignitaries were there. At the last minute, the locals realised that ex-Alderman Liz Kernohan had been missed when the invitations were sent out. It was too late for an official correction. Knowing how hard the Mayor had lobbied to achieve the move to new premises and to assist with the relocation, the firemen took the initiative. Among the fire brigade members, one person didn't have a partner at that time. As a result, he had a spare ticket. A phone call was made, and Dr Kernohan sat proudly at the same table as the uniformed officers at the opening ceremony.

One of Rob's recollections of the time after the move was the terrible hailstorm that hit Sydney in 1999. 'We spent a few shifts putting tarps onto the houses with damaged rooves,' he said.

After the Olympics in 2000, Rob moved with his wife and three children to Cootamundra, where he has retained his interest in motor racing. 'As I walk through the glass rooved connection between the Library and the old Fire Station, it brings back a lot of memories,' he said. 'But I do miss the camaraderie – guys like Jonnie Cross, Kenny Thorn and Ken Barratt had a big influence on me.'

CAMDEN HISTORY

Journal of the Camden Historical Society

March 2020 Volume 4 Number 9

CAMDEN HISTORY
Journal of the Camden Historical Society Inc.
ISSN 1445-1549
Editor: Dr Ian Willis

Management Committee
President: Doug Barrett
Vice Presidents: John Wrigley OAM, Warren Sims
Secretary: Lee Stratton
Treasurer: Fletcher Joss
Immediate Past President: Dr Ian Willis
General Committee: Rene Rem, Ian Ramsay, Frances Warner, Robert Wheeler, Dawn Williams, Julie Wrigley.

Honorary Solicitors: Warren & Warren

Society contact:
P.O. Box 566, Camden, NSW 2570. Online <http://www.camdenhistory.org.au>

Meetings
Meetings are held at 7.30 p.m. on the second Wednesday of the month except in January. They are held in the Museum. Visitors are always welcome.

Museum
The Museum is located at 40 John Street, Camden, phone 4655 3400 or 46559210. It is open Thursday to Sunday 11 a.m. to 4 p.m., except at Christmas. Visits by schools and groups are encouraged. Please contact the Museum to make arrangements. Entry is free.

Camden History, Journal of the Camden Historical Society Inc
The Journal is published in March and September each year. The Editor would be pleased to receive articles broadly covering the history of the Camden district . Correspondence can be sent to the Society's postal address. The views expressed by authors in journal articles are solely those of the authors and not necessarily endorsed by the Camden Historical Society.

Donations
Donations made to the Society are tax deductible. The accredited value of objects donated to the Society are eligible for tax deduction.

Front Cover image: Burnham Grove homestead 2019 (Image courtesy Fortunate Fellow and Burnham Grove Estate)

Back Cover image: Burnham Grove homestead hallway 2019 (Image courtesy Fortunate Fellow and Burnham Grove Estate)

CAMDEN HISTORY
Journal of the Camden Historical Society Inc.

Contents

Recollections of Burnham Grove from Virginia Ghezzi
Anne McIntosh   371

The Quiet Achiever: Camden Post Office
Dianne Matterson   380

The Connections Between Local History and Family History
Jo O'Brien   388

St Johns GFS celebrates 50 years
Anne McIntosh   393

Trainee teachers Camden camp in 1924
Ian Willis   400

The Rise and Rise of the Camden Museum Celebrating Fifty Years!
John Wrigley   405

Recollections of childhood on Burnham Grove
Virginia Ghezzi (née Wheeler) and Anne McIntosh

"I grew up on 'Burnham Grove'. The property belonged to my grandparents, who I knew as Nan and Da. My father worked with my Da to manage the family farm. They both came from families, who'd lived in the area for several generations," explained Virginia.

Virginia's father (Frank) and Da (Raymond) were Wheelers; her Nan (Bertha Florence) was a Doust. They were married in 1917. Virginia's Nan inherited the property when her father passed away in 1936.

After her grandparents took responsibility for the farm, 'Burnham Grove' became known as the 'Wheeler place'. The Wheelers belonged to the congregation at St John's, and Da would attend occasionally. Yet even after her marriage, Virginia's nan remained a devout Methodist attending church regularly in Cawdor.

Burnham Grove homestead and Virginia as a young child in the driveway (V Ghezzi/CAFHS)

Virginia's grandfather, Frank Wheeler, and her Nan, Bertha, at Burnham Grove (V Ghezzi/CAFHS)

Virginia always knew that she was Anglican. Her parents had been married by Rev Kirk at St John's without much family ado. Her mother grew up in 'the city' - Nan would have preferred that her son had chosen a local girl. Virginia and her siblings were christened at St John's and raised in the Church of England.

First home

She recalls a happy and adventure-filled childhood on the farm. "There were more than 50 acres of land and we were free to roam across it all." As they grew older the children would venture further from home. Wild blackberries grew beside the road and were delicious. Smart's farm was next door, and he grew watermelons. Sometimes the children would sneak onto his place and treat themselves.

The neighbouring farms of the Smarts and the Dousts had access to the creek. Approaching the water was forbidden but, in summer, irresistible. The children would play and swim in the waterholes.

The cottage. "It was built as a workman's cottage, and had been there for a long time." (V Ghezzi/CAFHS)

The farm was next to where Camden High School stands today; back then it was mid-way between the schools in Camden and Cawdor, and more than two miles from both. "My father went to school in Camden – so we did, too. There was no bus – we rode our bikes. Mine was a Malvern Star. You had to be careful – there were some big coal trucks on that road!" It would be many years before the school bus service operated along Cawdor Road, "though whenever Mum was going into town, she would drive us," said Virginia.

"Our family lived in a timber slab cottage behind the main house." She pauses, and moves on to the realities: "You had to walk along a path to the bathroom. There were two bedrooms, a kitchen and a lounge room – it wasn't large. When I look back, I remember the love, not the lack of space.

"When my sister was born, three kids and our parents were living there. There were electric lights, but Mum cooked on a metallic black fuel stove. Dad made sure she had plenty of wood. Our cottage had been built as a workman's cottage, and had been there for a long time."

Virginia, Michael (cousin) and Greg Wheeler c1950s (V Ghezzi/ CAFHS)

Mixed farming around a dairy

Horses played a prominent role on the farm and all the children learnt to ride – mostly bareback. When Virginia was very young, her father used a draft horse to plough the paddocks. He also had an ex-racehorse, a big stallion called Duke – "it was ridden by no-one but my father". There was also one very cranky pony. "The bigger kids would ride him, and he kicked and bucked. Luckily, my pony was smaller and friendlier," Virginia recalled.

Her father had a German Shepherd called Prince who was with him constantly. After many years, the dog became slow and sick. "When Prince was dying, Dad spent several nights sleeping out with him in the hayshed."

As a child, Virginia often went to the dairy with her father. Before milking, the cows would be fed in a separate shed. A rail track ran beside the trough and was used for distributing the feed. The farm produced hay and stored it in a shed. She recalls that all the cows had names, and she conscientiously learnt those names and the characteristics of the cows. She struggles to recall the colours of the cows, but describes a mixed herd with a dominance of Ayrshires and Friesians.

Alan and Doreen Marshall, Virginia and Greg Wheeler, Michael Wheeler (V Ghezzi/CAFHS)

It was only a small dairy – probably six bails and the cows were milked by hand. Virginia believes the milking machine must have been installed when she was a teenager, by which time, her own family was no longer living on the farm. In addition to her father and grandfather, her nan was actively involved in dairying. Virginia clearly remembers feeding the poddy calves with her.

Later, the milk would be picked up from the tank at the dairy, but, Virginia does recall the men loading milk cans onto a truck and leaving them at the side gate. There were a number of dairies nearby – the Smarts, the Dousts and others – they all shared a 'tanker run' back to the depot in Camden.

Back then, most dairy farms raised pigs, and there were always ducks and chickens for meat and eggs. "I loved collecting eggs and in primary school, I had to feed the chooks. We butchered our own birds for Christmas and Easter, and whenever family came to stay," Virginia says.

Yet, of all the husbandry activities on the farm, branding calves is the one that Virginia recalls with particular distaste. "The calves would cry, but even worse I think, was the burning hair and flesh. It's years since I was around at branding, but I will never forget that smell."

At the main house, the gardens were large with hedges and roses, and scope for fabulous games. For family use, Virginia's grandparents grew vegetables, so the food served was almost always fresh. Virginia fondly recalls the corn which was very sweet. Her nan also had some fruit trees – in season, there were peaches, pears, apples, oranges, apricots, figs and pomegranates.

At the big house

'Burnham Grove' was one of the earliest farms on the Cawdor Road. The land had been one of four clearing leases offered by the Macarthurs along the road.

Virginia remembers her nan and two aunts fondly. For her, the house was a place of community, comfort and love. "Lola and Edna taught me to cook and sew." Virginia laughs as she recollects her early attempts on the black treadle sewing machine. "It took coordination. My aunts were very patient with me.

BURNHAM GROVE Alan Marshall with Greg and Virginia Wheeler c1951 (V Ghezzi/ CAFHS)

"My aunts and grandmother all sewed; they had their own specific interests and skills. They would embroider designs onto homemade objects. They did a lot of their own dressmaking and gifts were always handmade – stitched or knitted. Auntie Lola also did leatherwork – she made bags and belts."

As a child, Virginia was rarely invited into her grandparents' bedroom where there was a four-poster bed with a fabric 'roof'. However, on the rare occasions that she had access (sometimes invited, occasionally in secret), she would sink into the feather mattress. "It was so deep and soft that there would be an impression of your body when you moved away," she recalled.

Every bedroom had a fireplace with a screen; in winter, a fire would be lit in every room that was occupied. Each bed had its own handmade quilt.

BURNHAM GROVE Frank and brother Arthur Wheeler playing tennis (V Ghezzi/CAFHS)

Monday was washing day and the laundry with its wood burning copper would be busy. When they were washed, the clothes would be taken to the back of the yard where there was a frame with parallel wires to which the clothes were pegged. A forked pole was then pushed under the wires to lift them and the clothes would hang high to catch the wind.

Her grandparents were very 'hospitable'. Virginia would hear stories about how, during the depression when cash was short and supplies limited, every itinerate swaggie that passed through Camden would learn of the abundance at 'Burnham Grove'; there was no work on offer, and the men would be sent on their way, but they never departed empty-handed.

There was a grass tennis court near the house. This area now houses the marquee used for events at Burnham Grove. The court was used regularly, both socially and by local comp teams. "Because of that court, we and our cousins all learnt to play tennis and became competent and enthusiastic players. Michael Wheeler went on to win tournaments around Sydney."

Virginia remembers that there were always people visiting 'Burnham Grove'.

All the girls were great cooks. A dairy farmer's days were long, and breakfast

BURNHAM GROVE Bertha Wheeler and Deirdre Wheeler (daughter-in-law) playing tennis (V Ghezzi/CAFHS)

would be eaten at the dairy.

However, the men always returned to the main house for morning and afternoon tea. Approaching from the paddocks, they would be greeted by the smell of baking from the wood-burning oven – it might be scones or a cake, or biscuits. Family, workers and guests would gather around the table in the centre of the kitchen. Over the years, Virginia's nan and her two aunts won many prizes at Camden Show for their cooking and their preserves. Food was always served with tea; "everyone drank tea". The tea was poured from a teapot into a cup on its matching saucer; most people drank white tea, but the quantity of milk and sugar could vary greatly.

Relatives from Sydney frequently spent the weekends at the main house. Locals dropped in for a cup of tea, filled up on cake, and always left with a swathe of seasonal fruit and vegetables.

Fresh bread was delivered daily by Stuckey Bros. "Sometimes when you picked it up at the front gate, it would still be warm," says Virginia.

Once a month, the Methodist Minister would come for Sunday roast. The family would gather together in the dining room, sitting around the big rectangular table. "It must have seated 14! I know we played a game called bobs on it." There would be a range of vegetables on offer with the traditional accompaniments such as gravy, and apple or mint sauce. Dessert was much anticipated – hearty treats that used the fruits from the orchard, home-grown eggs and cream from the dairy. Virginia recalled fruit pies with custard, bread and butter puddings, rice and tapioca puddings. Occasionally her grandmother made ice-cream – "it didn't taste like ice-cream from the supermarket," Virginia recalled. "Nan's ice-cream was very rich and filling."

Her nan, Bertha, had a pantry/office that was accessed from the dining room. It was small and narrow with a desk filling the space near the window at the end. There were shelves along the walls and they were filled with preserved fruits, jams and chutneys. There was a trapdoor in the floor that led to the cellar, which "was always cooler than in the house".

Nan hated storms. When she heard the thunder, Virginia recalls her going to the pantry and sitting in the dark beside the window.

The end of small-scale dairying in Camden

As the years went by, mixed farming enterprises that included dairying became more marginal. "Burnham Grove was too small to maintain two families," said Virginia.

Bertha Wheeler passed away in 1973, leaving the house and an acre of gardens to her two living daughters; the farmland was left to her sons, Virginia's father, Frank, and his brother, Arthur. The house and land were sold separately, however today, much of the property has been reunited as a wedding and function venue. The gardens were restored to their Victorian magnificence and subsequently extended, and a large carpark has been built. There have been a series of owners of the venue, and the interior of the house has been renovated several times.

(In 2008, Jenny Akers recorded a conversation with Edna Marshall (Virginia's aunt) which described her knowledge of 'Burnham Grove'. That article was published in the Jul/Aug edition of this journal.)

The Quiet Achiever: Camden Post Office

Dianne Matterson

In 1828, seven country post offices were established outside Sydney, the closest to Camden being Campbelltown. However, when the Goulburn mail coach began to stop at Cawdor courthouse in 1836, the Clerk of Petty Sessions, James Pearson, was authorised to also act as postmaster, assisted by his wife, Eliza. Two years later, the Colonial Secretary established a post office near the Cowpasture Bridge and John Pettingale, followed by George Skinner, were appointed as postmasters. By January 1839, this early post office, located midway between Macarthur Road and Wilkinson Street on the southern side of Camden Valley Way, was open for business.[1]

As the Macarthurs began to sell more ½ acre lots on the western side of the river, it wasn't long before the post office was moved to Camden. The timber courthouse at Cawdor was dismantled and rebuilt at 55 Argyle Street (Argyle Gourmet Delicatessen), opening its doors as Camden Post Office on 1 May 1841. James Pearson was once again the postmaster, but when he died shortly afterwards, his wife took over as postmistress and filled this role for nearly 40 years. As well as providing a postal service, Eliza Pearson also sold drapery, lollies, cabbage-tree hats and took in laundry.[2]

By the 1870s, telegraph lines were spreading out from Sydney using Morse Code to transmit messages. In December 1877, a telegraph office was opened in Camden in the two front rooms of a cottage rented from James Bocking for 10 shillings a week, while the back was rented to a baker. However, just a year later, the postal authorities proposed combining the post and telegraph offices into one building[3] as an amalgamation of the two services would reduce the costs to the public purse. The new telegraph office was considered unsuitable as a combined office, and despite the possibility of renting Dr.Moreton's house or Mr.Waterworth's cottage, the amalgamation of the two services didn't actually happen for another two years.[4]

In May 1879, the colonial government advertised for a telegraph and post office site 'between Oxley and Elizabeth Streets'.[5] Two sites were recommended by the postal inspector: one owned by the Bank of N.S.W. (Westpac) or one of John Lakeman's vacant lots from the corner of Argyle and Oxley Streets to Charlie Smith's Saddlery, which was adjacent to the Commercial Bank (NAB).

Camden Post Office, 1841-1882 (Source: Camden Images)

Although land had not yet been secured, tenders were called for the construction of the new post office in June 1879. After offers of land from the Bank of N.S.W. and William Macarthur, the postal authorities purchased Lot 15 from John Lakeman in January 1880 for £330 (£5 per foot of frontage).[6]

While the plans for the new post and telegraph office were considered, William Macarthur rented 61 Argyle Street (Barry Smith Dental on Argyle) to the government for £40 as a temporary post and telegraph office. The fit-out of the combined office cost about £14 and included the addition of a 'few panes of glass', a stove (as there was no fireplace) and an office table. In April 1880, the plans for the new building were completed, but the £2,000 price tag was considered too high; the Postal Inspector also thought the plan lacked merit and recommended that a building like that at Cooranbong be erected. The Cooranbong Post Office was located on a corner and the design included a corner verandah over the main entry, a design feature that became part of the Camden Post Office plans despite the building site being in the middle of the street block.

In October, amended plans for the Camden Post Office were again forwarded to the Postmaster General. The estimated cost of £1,800 was still £600 more than the amount approved in the budget. It was considered a large sum to spend on a 'small office' such as Camden, so the plans were again altered to reduce the cost and tenders were again called. The plans at this stage included an office, sorting room, sitting room, dining room, two bedrooms, kitchen and a pantry.

On 23 December 1880, the Dept. of Public Works accepted a tender of £1,070 from local builders, J. & W. Packenham.[7] Work was to be completed within 6 months, however, in April 1881, Thomas Garrett M.P. drew the attention of the Minister for Works to the advisability of erecting the whole of the building as originally planned. The architect forwarded a tender of £487 from the building contractors for the additional work and the following month the extra funds were obtained from the Colonial Treasurer.

On 1 April 1882, the telegraph and post office was opened. There were verandahs on each side of the building that were accessible from Argyle Street: the left-hand one gave access to the telegraph office while the right-hand verandah led to the postal boxes. The single-storey telegraph and post office was in the Late Victorian style and sections of the original construction are visible from the rear of the existing building where a darker brick to that used during later construction can still be seen. A different sub-floor/wall vent style to that used later, is still in place in this older section. The 'seam' between this building and the later addition can be seen immediately above the current postal boxes on the eastern side of the building.[8] The verandah protecting the entrance was supported by timber posts decorated with fretwork.

In December 1895, Ald. Frier raised the issue of the lack of privacy for customers using the telegraphic, postal, money order and banking services. Ald. Whiteman suggested that as the foundations of the present building were laid with a 'view of future enlargement', it could easily be extended 'for the convenience of the public'.[9] After the mayor's unsuccessful representation to the Postmaster General on the matter, it was referred to the local member, Mr. C. Bull M.P.[10] In July 1896, £150 was allocated in the government budget for the construction of a 'servant's room' and a 2nd-floor addition to the existing building[11] that would then include a "Post Office room, Postmaster's room, public lobby, porch and store room, on the ground floor extending 40 feet along the building alignment, with a depth of 29' feet. On the first floor there will be two bedrooms, a bathroom and balcony. A laundry will also be erected, as well as a new fence and gates, extending from the building along the

Camden Post Office, 1882-1898 (Source: Camden Images)

front alignment."[12] The rear and first floor accommodation was for the postmaster. The estimated cost of £475 was far in excess of the allocated funds.

Ald. Willis had another idea, and proposed Camden Council "urge upon [the Postmaster General] the advisability of erecting an imposing building on the street corner adjoining the present post office, and that the building of the present office be vested in [the] council for a fire brigade station".[13] A new building was considered unnecessary by the Postmaster General, and instead he increased the £150 already allocated to the upgrade to £750.[14]

The upgraded building was built in the Federation Free style with a terracotta tiled roof, a balcony and a slat work timber frieze over the front step supported by a sandstone column.[15] The original front elevation was brought some feet closer to the footpath. The sides of the new building were extended to the width of the verandah on the old building, and the main entrance was constructed on the south-eastern corner. The western side of the building where 'letters and newspapers' used to be deposited became part of the larger office space for the dispatch and receipt of mail. The main office was 'considerably enlarged and made more commodious' to accommodate the diverse functions undertaken by the post and telegraph office at this time, which included the registration of all births, deaths and marriages.[16]

The successful tenderer for the upgrade was the local firm of Cleveland and Peters; Mr. Peters was the builder.[17] James Stuckey, a bootmaker, agreed to lease his premises at 95 Argyle Street (Crèmè Della Crèmè) to the postal authorities for £1 a week during the work on the post office.[18]

The official opening of the post office on 30 September 1898, was to be done by the Postmaster General, the Hon. V. Parkes. No officials from the government or the postal department turned up on the day and the Mayor, Ald. W.C. Furner took over, and opened the Post Office before the gathered crowd.[19] The upgraded post office had a main hall, "whilst the accommodation for the general public, outside the counter is 12' by 9', and in this open space is the desk for writing out telegrams, etc., and a lobby screen for entrance to the main hall, for the use of the officials... the delivery of letters may be obtained from a window in the portico, without entrance to the main building. The telegraphic operating department is on the left of the main office, the table or counter for the various instruments, telegraphic and telephonic, being some 24' in length, and such a distance from the public counter that the telephonic communications will not be audible. The telephone instrument is not so far enclosed or cased, and will be used by the operators only to the various existing stations, The Oaks, Narellan, the Carrington Convalescent Hospital and two local private telephones. The mail bag is at the farther side of the building with a separate roadway and entrance, the public will not therefore be incommoded by the arrival and dispatch of the various mails; adjoining this entrance are the various store rooms for the use of the post officials and the quick dispatch in sorting, etc. The main office is well lighted (sic) by three windows on the left facing Argyle Street, and between the telegraphic, etc., tables and the main office are three arches, supporting the rooms over the building proper. The various fire-places (sic) are adorned with tiled hearths, with mantel-pieces (sic) to match. In the interior of the office stands the various tables for the working of the very many requisite duties. The whole of the fittings throughout are of polished cedar, the counter is some 12' long by 3'4" wide. The residence of the postmaster has been substantially altered and improved, adding more essential requirements as a residence. Over a portion of the office building with entrance from the chambers of the postmaster, is a spacious balcony some 26' long by 10' in width, facing Argyle Street. The painting or colouring of the various walls are of a light green, with brown dado, dark green dividing."[20] This description places the telegraphic office on the western side of the building, while the 'separate roadway' referred to is now the laneway on the eastern side of the post office.

Camden Post Office, from 1898 to date (Source: Camden Images)

With Federation, came a national system of mail collection and delivery, and the Postmaster General's Department (P.M.G.) was established. All colonial post office authorities no longer existed. In 1902, unsuccessful requests for a direct telephone connection to Sydney were made to the P.M.G. by Camden Council. Another unsuccessful request was also made for a telephone or telegraph service to be available on Sundays during certain hours. On this occasion, the P.M.G. advised Camden residents to go to Campbelltown where "any urgent messages would be accepted at the Post Office there between the hours of 12 noon and 1 p.m.".[21] It would be another 3 years before the telephone line was extended from Campbelltown to Camden.[22]

In August 1905, the P.M.G. replied to another Camden Council request for the establishment of a telephone exchange at Camden Post Office, pointing out that this would cost £240, but if the council could 'get fifteen subscribers with an average payment of £16 each per annum', the P.M.G. would agree to the establishment of a local exchange. The aldermen thought this would only work if the 'trunk-line' charges to Sydney were abolished, a suggestion the P.M.G. refused to countenance.[23]

At last, in 1910, Camden Telephone Exchange was constructed in the south-western corner of the main postal hall within the existing building footprint in a small room immediately opposite the entrance door,[24] and opened in November with 17 subscribers[25] who received a service at stipulated times of day.

In 1913, Postal Department revenue from the Camden Telephone Exchange was £27 in calls and £120/19/4 in 'ground' rentals. Camden Council was informed that once the total revenue reached £150, the exchange would be entitled to a 'continuous' service that wouldn't be limited to certain times of day.[26] By 1916, the phone service was still not 'continuous' and the P.M.G. informed subscribers that a minimum revenue of £250 was now required before such a service could be provided. Subscribers could choose to either make up the shortfall by paying an additional annual charge that would equal the required amount, or, pay an amount equivalent to the additional wages that would be paid to exchange staff while working the extra hours.[27]

In 1920, a public phone booth was placed inside the post office. This once again created concerns about the privacy of calls being made within earshot of members of the public who were using the Post Offices' other services at the same time. By November 1948, at least one public phone booth was in place outside Camden Post Office.[28] The cement foundations of two boxes can still be seen today adjacent to the south-eastern corner of the post office. People who wanted to make a trunk (long-distance) call from the public phone box rang a bell on the nearby wall. One of the staff from the exchange opened a window, took the booking, advised the caller how much the call would be for 3 minutes, and took the payment in cash. It was a challenge sometimes to be heard when making a call here, especially during the day when the coal trucks from the mines at Burragorang went through the main street. Even at night the noise from interstate freight trucks was a problem, as in those days Argyle Street was part of the Hume Highway. The last shift for female exchange workers ended at 10 p.m. at which time, the male employees took over until the morning shift began.[29]

By 1953, as the number of phone subscribers in the district grew, the exchange within the post office footprint was no longer adequate, so W.C. Peters sold his old sawmill land at 40 Argyle Street (now Liv For Beauty & Soul) to the Commonwealth of Australia for the construction of a new telephone exchange. In 2020, the area within the Post Office footprint that was vacated by the exchange after 1953, is now occupied by the small office/ storage area opposite the main entrance.

Camden Post Office sits quietly on our main street, having evolved from what were humble beginnings at Cawdor courthouse, followed by the occupation of the front rooms of a cottage at Elderslie and a small building at 55 Argyle Street, through to its development during two major construction phases at 135 Argyle Street. In 2002, Camden Post Office was included on the N.S.W. Government's heritage items list as part of Camden Council's Local Environmental Plan and, a decade later, joined the Commonwealth Heritage List.[30]

Notes
[1] An 1840 map held by Camden Museum shows the Post Office marked at this location. Martin, J.B. et al, *Reminiscences of Early Camden,* Ed. J. Johnson, Camden Historical Society Inc., 2012, pp. 29, 91
[2] Martin, J.B. et al, *Reminiscences of Early Camden,* Ed. J. Johnson, Camden Historical Society Inc., 2012, pp. 28, 49. Atkinson, Alan, Camden – *Farm and Village Life in Early New South Wales*, Oxford University Press, Melbourne, 1988, p. 48
[3] Australian Government Dept. of Agriculture, Water & the Environment: Commonwealth Heritage List – Camden Post Office
[4] National Archives of Australia: Camden Post Office file – Box 139, Series SP32/1: Camden Part 1, barcode 315495, pages 105-106, 109
[5] N.S.W. Government Gazette, 13.5.1879, p. 2129 [Issue 166]
[6] Land Sales: Book 198, Number 554 (Camden Museum Archives)
[7] N.S.W. Government Gazette, 21.1.1881, p. 403 [Issue 28]
[8] Observation by Dianne Matterson in 2018
[9] Camden News, 19 December 1895, p. 6
[10] Camden News, 12 March 1896, p. 2
[11] Camden News, 2 July 1896, p. 5
[12] Camden News, 27 January 1898, p. 4
[13] Camden News, 22 April 1897, p. 2
[14] Camden News, 6 October 1898, p. 1
[15] Australian Government Dept. of Agriculture, Water & the Environment: Commonwealth Heritage List – Camden Post Office
[16] Camden News, 2 September 1897, p. 4
[17] Camden News, 23 December 1897, p. 4
[18] Camden News, 16 December 1897, p. 4
[19] Camden News, 6 October 1898, p. 1
[20] Camden News, 6 October 1898, p. 1
[21] Sidman, G.V., *The Town of Camden*, Camden Public Library & Liz Vincent, 1995, p. 52
[22] Sidman, G.V., *The Town of Camden*, Camden Public Library & Liz Vincent, 1995, p. 53
[23] Sidman, G.V., *The Town of Camden*, Camden Public Library & Liz Vincent, 1995, p. 54
[24] Australian Government Dept. of Agriculture, Water & the Environment: Commonwealth Heritage List – Camden Post Office. Nixon, D. & Mylrea, P., *The Telephone Comes to Camden*, Camden History – Journal of the Camden Historical Society, Vol. 1, No. 5, p. 104
[25] Sidman, G.V., *The Town of Camden*, Camden Public Library & Liz Vincent, 1995, p. p. 60
[26] Camden News, 28 August 1913, p. 8
[27] Camden News, 8 June 1916, p. 4
[28] Camden News, 11 November 1948, p. 6
[29] Memories of Charles Dunk, a former Camden resident
[30] N.S.W. Government Department of Planning, Industry and Environment: Heritage Places and Items – Camden Council's Local Environmental Plan. Australian Government Dept. of Agriculture, Water & the Environment: Commonwealth Heritage List – Camden Post Office

Other general references:
Camden Museum archives, particularly the 'Post Office' file.
We Deliver: A Brief History of Mail Delivery and The Oaks Post Office, 1858-2008: Australia Post publication

The Connections Between Local History and Family History

Jo O'Brien

As secretary of Camden Area Family History Society I have been asked several times recently "What is the difference between history and family history?", "What does your Society do?" or "Which society should I join – Family History or Historical Society?" (for many of us the answer is both of course!). But what are the differences between studying the history of an area and family history?

I grew up with stories of family, and I have always found them fascinating, who my ancestors were, where they lived, and what they did. But I must admit - at school I found history, especially Australian history, a bit boring. Lots of dates and journeys of explorers, and the machinations of government, and wars. The emphasis was on the big picture and the famous people, and I didn't feel a personal connection. However, I did feel connected to the places in my family stories – Bundeena, Bexley, Liverpool - and interested in what they looked like then and now, and what everyday life was like for my ancestors.

I have been doing family history research most of my adult life and have been able to add significantly to the stories and research I inherited. Through my research, I became increasingly interested in the times in which my ancestors lived. Now those once boring historical events fascinate me, mostly because of the family connections - the details of my grandfather's war service, the ancestors who were the early settlers that followed the explorers, the convicts and their journey to freedom in the new colony. Knowing where my ancestors were and knowing the events that happened while they were there, the well-known people they may have met, the places they saw with their own eyes – it all adds to the story and brings it to life. Knowing that my ancestor's family lived in Ballarat is one thing, reading that my ancestor's sister witnessed the Eureka stockade is much more exciting.

 One of the obvious differences is that with family history the focus is on your family and your ancestors. You follow their journey wherever they go, so unless they spent their whole lives in the one place, your research will include places from all around the world, and the travel between the two. In Australia we all have ancestors that have travelled, some multiple times and great distances from the other side of the world, as well as throughout Australia. Over the course of his life my great-grandfather John Torpey, born in

> **EUREKA STOCKADE BATTLE**
>
> A message from Stawell (V.) states that Mrs. Caroline Tauschke, 87 years of age, one of the few remaining eye-witnesses of the Eureka stockade battle fought at Ballarat between the miners and the soldiers, died at Eltham (V.) on Monday. Mrs. Tauschke had lived at Stawell for nearly half a century.

In 1854 Caroline Hanney (aged 8) witnessed the Eureka Stockade battle, presumably her sister Ann (my great great-grandmother, then aged 12) was also there.

Bungonia, travelled south probably as far as Wagga Wagga, then north via Condobolin, and Bourke to outback Queensland and Toowoomba before he ended his days in Dunwich on North Stradbroke Island. Quite a journey over the span of his life, and many places whose history is of interest to me as I pursue my family history research.

With local history, the focus is on place, including the people, but also events, objects, buildings, and the environment. The focus stays in the area as the people come and go. The stories of buildings, archaeology, events, historic items and local features are all fascinating in themselves. Yet people are an essential ingredient of any study of history - who lived there, who was at the event, how people used an item. Although, in the past the focus has often been on those who are more notable, this is changing as we recognise everyday people and their contribution to the history of a place. The provenance of an item, who owned it and how it was passed on, adds significantly to its value and to its story.

So, family history is a powerful way in which we can connect with the histo-

This historic building in Camden is known as Dr. Crookston's House, the connection with its well-known owner being a key part of its history. (www.camdenhistory.org.au)

ry of a place and vice versa. The history of the area, the story of the buildings, the key events, all these can explain why our ancestors moved to a place, where and how they lived, and why they may have moved on. For example, many people from the mid-1850s onwards, including several of my ancestors, went in search of gold, moving on as prospects became more attractive elsewhere. My great great-grandfather William Glover, recruited from England as an engineer for the new railway lines, worked his way from Sydney to Bourke via Picton, so the history of railway construction is part of his story too.

Other families have mostly resided in the same place for many generations. Camden is one of those places were this is still happening for many local families. The local history is then much more closely intertwined with family history. If you listen to people's reactions to local history, they will often say, "one of my relatives worked there", "they lived in that building" or explain their family connection to an event, object, or place. History is more personal and accessible when it connects to your own family story.

Books on history can be brought to life if they are told from the perspective of a person or a family. Diaries, memoirs, and historical biographies illustrate how everyday people felt about the events of their lives. Even if the stories are not about your family, following the fortunes of real people who lived through major historical events connects us to that time in a more personal way.

History and family history go together, the study of each compliments the other. In some places, Family History Societies combine with Historical Societies and become one organisation. In other cases, they start as one and move apart. Sometimes both roles are within the local studies section of the library. In any case there is logic in keeping the different disciplines connect-

Camden Museum and Camden Area Family History Society side by side in the Camden Library complex – John St Camden   (Camden Area Family History Society Facebook page)

ed but separate, something that I think we have achieved with the partnership between Camden Library, Camden Historical Society and Camden Area Family History Society.

I hesitated before I joined both the local societies as I don't have that local connection, none of my family ever lived in Camden before I did. I wondered if it would be relevant to me. It turned out that joining both Societies has been very rewarding. The Family History Society, while holding records on local families also has plenty of resources for those researching across Australia and around the world. And the stories of Camden's history and people are fascinating, often encompass broader issues, and are relevant to where I live now – a place I have come to love.

Tony Jackson from the Camden Area Family History Society at the 35th Annual Conference of Family History Societies, at Knox Grammar School, Wahroonga, 11 October 2019 (CAFHS)

So, if you are at all interested in where you came from, who your ancestors were, why your ancestors did what they did and how the world and their local community impacted their lives – come and visit us at family history. If you are interested in the heritage of this beautiful area, the buildings and places, the events and people visit the Museum and attend a meeting of the Historical Society. Or do what I have done and get involved with both!

St John's GFS celebrates 50 years

Anne McIntosh

On Saturday 7 September 2019, Camden GFS (formerly Girls' Friendly Society) celebrated 50 years in Camden with a Thanksgiving Service and meal attended by around 200 people. Many girls who attended GFS continue to live nearby, but there were also a number of travellers from as far away as Tasmania.

What is GFS?

The Girls' Friendly Society was founded in England in 1875 by Mary Townsend. This Anglican Church group aimed to give "maids and female domestic staff spiritual guidance and social activities for their days off". In this early period, GFS was for girls over 14 years, but later this was extended to girls from eight years old.

All GFS attendees 50th anniversary celebration, St Johns' Church Hall, September 2019 (N Hill)

Early GFS leaders – Betty Annabel, Lesley-Ann Hoskin (LHS) with original members – Vicki Shepard and Roslyn Tildsley (RHS) (N Hill)

The aim was for young ladies of the upper and middle classes to reach out and provide role models for working class girls. The contacts and activities were particularly valuable to young servants who worked in smaller houses, where they were often away from their home towns and had no social ties. The Society also functioned in part as an employment agency. (To read more about GFS founding in England, see http://anglicanhistory.org/women/money_gfs1911/)

The first local Australian branch was formed in Adelaide in 1879. The next year, Sydney's first branch was established at St Paul's in Redfern, then at St John's in Parramatta, and by 1901, there were branches in all states. In Australia, GFS aimed to facilitate friendship between ladies (Associates) and working girls (Members). The Associates would help find jobs for members and encourage them in 'Christian behaviour'. The organisation's motto was drawn from the Bible: *Bear one another's burdens and so fulfil the law of Christ* (Galatians 6:2).

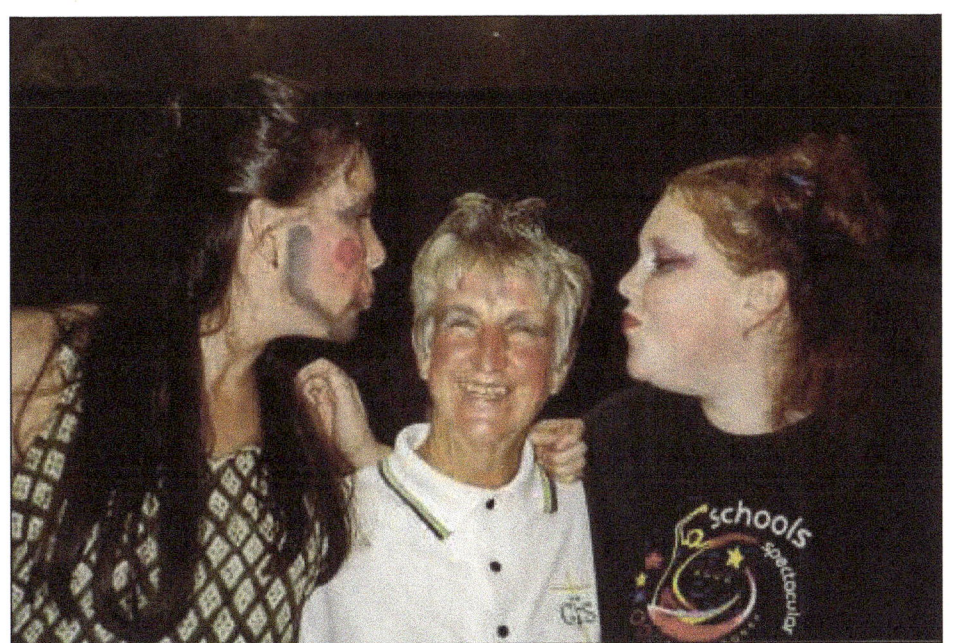

Mother and daughter makeup night, 1990s. Lisa Briggs, Neidra Hill, Fiona Bailliss. (N Hill)

By 1886, there were 61 branches in the Sydney diocese, with a membership of 1018, which included 350 associates. The activities of local groups varied depending on the needs in that area. In those early days, branches generally held weekly meetings for working girls and several also ran hostels to provide them with accommodation. There was a GFS hostel close to the University of Sydney in Arundel Street.

Over the years, the focus for GFS changed, and membership was extended to younger girls. It remained a local outreach that linked girls who had strong ties to the church, with families that had limited links to their community. The organisation continued to expand and during the 1970s, most Anglican churches in Sydney had youth outreaches based around GFS and CEBS (Church of England Boys' Society).

GFS no longer focuses solely on girls. Since 2004, its stated aims have been 'to minister to children, youth and their families'. The strict uniform policy has evolved into a more casual organisational 'style', however over the years, GFS clothing has always been blue and white.

Despite the changes, the structure of the weekly meetings continues to draw

Group photo 1983
(back row, L->R) Neidra Hill, Cheryl Hunt, Rebekah Davis, Julia Mullen
(Middle row/s) Kerry Sidman, Jodie Davis, Eleanor Flett, ?, ?, Alison Newport, Jacqui Richards, Kelly ?, Kelly ?
(front) Renee Wilson, Kirsty Miln, Katrina Sorenson, ?, Bronwyn Richards, Kim Edwards, Jemima Flett
[Please assist to name the unknown children (?), and alert us to any names that are incorrect.] (N Hill)

upon the goals and vision of Mary Townsend. The GFS motto and prayer are unchanged. There is an emphasis on broad Christian teaching, and the group welcomes girls irrespective of their faith background, helping to build confidence, contacts, self-esteem, independence and a broader vision of the world and its opportunities. The aim has always been to cement a welcoming peer group founded on kindness, peace and love.

GFS leadership in Camden

GFS began in Camden in 1969 under the ministry of Rev. Barry Burgess. The first leader was his wife, Marcia, who was supported by Mrs Stewart. Later Betty Annabel, Betty Doran (now McKay), Doreen Thornton and Lesley-Ann Hoskin were leaders. Meetings were held in the church hall at the top of Hill

Street. Among those who attended on the first night were Vicki Shepard and Roslyn Tildsley. (who remains involved with GFS in the local area and nationally.)

In 1980, Neidra Hill, joined the team as branch leader. With her strong faith and love of sport and camping, she has played a significant (and ongoing role) over many years. Other leaders in the 1980s were Sue Owen, Barbara Hend and Roslyn Tildsley. Membership peaked during the 1980s, with around 60 girls attending each week.

Efforts were ongoing during the late 1980s to expand the leadership group, with GFS welcoming Debbie Bannister, Loraine Ryder, Corinna Edgar and Sue Storey. Ex-members who later became leaders included Renae Sharpe (now Copas) and Nicole Semler.

Allan Hughes instructs Renae Sharpe. Abseiling at Cataract River Ranch, late 1980s (N Hill)

Although this list is not comprehensive, others who have played a significant role in GFS at Camden include Sylvia Hansen, Jenny Goodhew, Kate Stevenson, Kay Hudson, Sharon Crocker, Colleen Jeffcott, Lauren Giles and Fiona Bailiss (now Drury).

Members

Since the 1970s, GFS has met in the new church hall. Over the years, membership has fluctuated, but weekly attendance has been fairly consistent at around 30-40. Looking at surnames, members include many multi-generational Camden families, supplemented by a very international mix as later immigrants have joined the community. From its origins reaching out to

Tegan Hudson (left) coordinates shepherds, St John's Nativity Play, 2000s (N Hill)

the working class, GFS in Camden now looks towards its expanding multicultural community.

The girls are divided into three groups (Teddies, Juniors and Seniors) with age-appropriate activities, that might include crafts, games, cooking and adventure. As weekend commitments of children have grown, it has become a challenge to organise overnight adventures. In the 1970s and 1980s, GFS girls were exposed to bushwalking, caving at Bungonia National Park, hiking, abseiling, orienteering, bush cookery and camping. Singing around a campfire was always a highlight.

In the local area, there were also opportunities for canoeing and bike riding. These small group adventures would build teamwork and independence. At larger gatherings such as district and diocesan camps, the girls and leaders had opportunities to meet new people and share ideas.

GFS also contributed to church and community fundraising. At the AHI Flower Show in the 1980s, the group would enter flowers in the competitions and raise money by making and selling jams and chutneys. On another occasion, they raised money so that Rosie Benn, a church missionary based in

Mongolia, could establish art classes for the kids in her overseas community. The Camden community was very proud when Tegan Hudson was chosen to represent Australia as a Junior Delegate to the GFS World Council. Her selection came after a nationwide search and led her to a two-year commitment during which she travelled around the country visiting church groups. Tegan now lives in Tasmania and remains active in the church.

Amazing people

Talking with Neidra Hill who does not have a daughter, but remains enthusiastic about GFS at 85yo, you understand the close relationship she has shared with "her girls" over many years. She speaks about the satisfaction of seeing girls develop in their Christian faith and become leaders, both within and beyond GFS.

The original idea of providing a safe environment where girls could be around other Christian women is evident today. Over time, the girls grow in self-awareness and build friendships beyond their school. GFS also provides opportunities for them to develop specific interests and skills, and professional contacts.

Neidra laughs aloud recalling a recent episode on camp. At the campsite, the leaders selected suitable sites and assisted the girls to raise their tents. The senior girls chose an alternative, 'better' position – "It's flat, has no rocks and is closer to the toilets." They raised their own tent, separate from the main group.

It wasn't until they retired that those older girls realised that their carefully selected campsite was also beloved by bull ants. There were screams as the girls evacuated. Seeking assistance, they learnt that others were tired or too busy, and were told to "deal with it". The girls had to deconstruct and move to a new site. According to Neidra, sometimes independence has a price! Those girls (and onlookers from the 'poorly-sited' tents) now have a great story to recount.

Trainee teachers Camden camp in 1924

Ian Willis

Recently Rene at the Camden Museum posted an intriguing photograph taken at the Camden Showground on the Camden Museum Facebook page. It showed a large group of young men and women who were identified at trainee teachers from Sydney Teachers College.

Camden resident Peter Hammond asked on the Camden Museum Facebook page: Any idea why they were in Camden? The photograph is a bit of a mystery.

The photograph was contributed to the Camden Museum by John Donaldson and was taken in May 1924. The photograph shows 48 women, 34 men and 2 children.

The group photograph of the trainee teachers from Sydney Teachers College at Onslow Park adjacent to the Show Hall in 1924. This is the image that prompted the original question by Peter Hammond on the Camden Museum's Facebook page. (John Donaldson/CIPP)

The photograph reveals more. You can see the spire of St Johns Church in the background and the absence of the 1938 brick front on the show hall. There are no brick and iron gates on the showground. The brick building at the corner of Argyle and Murray is yet to be built.

Photographs can tell so much about the past. They are a wonderful resource and this image provides much information about this mystery. So I set off on a journey to solve the mystery of the question about the photograph.

A quick search of the *Camden News* on Trove revealed that in May 1924 there was indeed a camp of trainee teachers who stayed at the Camden Agricultural Hall in Onslow Park. The report in the Camden News revealed more information.

There are 109 students and some ten lecturers and authorities gathering, from the University Teachers' College. The students are obtaining practical

Trainee teachers from Sydney Teachers College at the 1924 Camden camp have a game of tennis in the local area on their recreation time (SLNSW)

knowledge by attending the different schools in the district, and much good should be the result. Those in charge are to be complimented on the excellent arrangements at the camp. (*Camden News,* 15 May 1924)

So was this a one-off or is there more to the story?

Further digging reveals that the first camp was in 1921, there were two camps per year one in May and the second around August. There were between 70 and 100 trainee teachers at each camp and they attended a number of local schools during their stay. The camps seem to have been for about three weeks each. There appears to have lots of interaction between locals and the visitors with sporting events, dances, lectures, and lots of other activities.

The first camp in May 1921 seems to have been a big deal not only for the town but also for the AH&I Society. Following the First World War the finances of the AH&I Society were in a parlous state and the hall hire was a welcome boost to finances.

Camden was first graced with the presence of these bright eyed and bushy tailed budding young teachers in 1921 when 64 of them settled in for a week at the show hall. The Camden camp provided for them an opportunity to practise their teaching theory and practice of the New South Wales New Syllabus that they learnt in the classroom at Sydney Teacher's College. The 1921 trainees were all single and were made up of 49 women and 15 men and four weeks after the Camden camp were to be placed in schools. (*Camden News,* 12 May 1921)

The Sydney Teachers College trainees were allocated to schools across the local region and the list included: Camden, Campbelltown, Campbelltown South, Cawdor, Cobbitty, Glenfield, Ingleburn, Minto, Mount Hunter, Narellan and The Oaks. (*Camden News,* 12 May 1921)

The teaching practice visits were organised on a group basis and transport was either by train or bus. By end of their training course the students had had at least three weeks of practice teaching in teaching at rural schools. (*Sydney Mail,* 8 June 1921)

In 1920 the STC students had been based at Glenbrook and the success of the experiment encouraged the college to extend it to Camden. The venture, according to the Sydney press, was a first in Australia for teacher training and it was believed at the time to be a world first for such a camp. During the week

Source: *Sydney Mail,* **8 June 1921**

in Camden the camp was visited by the New South Wales Director of Education Peter Board and the chief inspector HD McLelland. (*Sydney Mail*, 8 June 1921)

In 1921 the party of 89, made up of students and lectures and their families, had arrived by train at Camden the previous Saturday afternoon. The group were put up the show hall with conversion to a dormitory and the construction of cubicles to accommodate the mixed sexes. The show pavilion was converted to a kitchen and dining area from 6am to 9am, and then again after 4pm. The Camden press reports stated that at these times 'the show ground was a scene of great activity'. (*Camden News*, 12 May 1921)

The Sydney Teachers College trainees had some time for recreation and in the evenings singing and games were organised between 7pm and 8pm by the music lecturer Miss Atkins, and the education lecturer Miss Wyse. Games and singing were held at the St Johns Parish Hall and sometimes the students organised tennis games. (*Camden News*, 12 May 1921)

Do you have any mysterious photographs that tell a great story about our local area?

The Rise and Rise of the Camden Museum Celebrating Fifty Years!

John Wrigley

As the Camden Museum celebrates its first fifty years on June 20th this year, members and supporters might be interested to learn something of the story of the museum. The Museum is owned and operated by the Camden Historical Society and is located at 40 John Street, Camden, in a building owned by Camden Council as part of the Camden Library complex.

The Camden Historical Society was formed by a small group of local enthusiasts in 1957. The Society started with the support of several teachers from Camden High School and began holding its regular monthly meetings in a classroom at the High School. The meetings were held there for forty-three years until 2000.

At first the society had no collection of material or historic items but as the years progressed and the members became active in protecting the history of the area, documents, photographs and objects were collected and donated. The Camden High School kindly allowed one of its broom cupboards to be used initially to store such items and a number of Society members also kept things at their homes in storerooms and garages. Through the 1960s there was a rising call for there to be a place where the Society could have a small museum for visitors to come and see the growing collection of items from Camden's past.

In the late 1960s, thanks to a group of forward thinking volunteers, a plan was made for a Museum. The society's president, local pharmacist Colin Clark, was active in the Camden Rotary Club and worked with Alderman Bruce Ferguson to identify a room at the rear of the then Camden School of Arts (now the Camden Library) which council could make available for such a use. The council agreed and the Rotary Club adopted the establishment of the Camden Museum as its major project for 1969-70. This was under the Presidency of Noel Riordan, with Geoff McAleer as its hard working Community Services Director, supported by the entire membership of the Club. Other stalwarts of the Historical Society at that time included Owen and Nan Blattman, Miss Llewella Davies and Miss Nancy Freestone, among others. The new Museum was opened before a large assembled crowd on 20 June 1970 by Major General Sir Denzil Macarthur-Onslow as Patron of the Historical Society. As the new museum neared its opening the word went out that items were needed for the Museum. Many items that are in the collection were donated at that time, including some of the "treasures' of the Museum. Camden artist and Rotary Club member Alan D. Baker donated a beautiful oil painting "Camden From the Grove" which has pride of place in the Museum reception area today. Many families made donations of beautiful china, trophies, Edison phonographs, furniture, tools and household equipment.

In 1970 Mr Owen Blattman became president and with his wife Nan, began twenty years of dedicated commitment and leadership to the Society and Museum. Owen had grown up in the Burragorang Valley and along with many people in the Camden area had been required to move out of the Valley for the building and filling of the Warragamba Dam. He came from an agricultural background and worked for many years in the field for Southwell Engineering, particularly with agricultural equipment.

Owen knew many people in the district and so was an effective gatherer of donations for the museum. These were significant years for the museum and many of the agricultural and domestic items came in at that time. The result of this success was predictable and in 1980 the museum, with council support, was extended to include the upstairs chamber of the old School of Arts building. Again the Camden Rotary Club worked hard to bring this about, led by president Ian Clifton and directors Fred Skinner and Leon Young.

In the 1990s with the rising interest in Australian heritage the museum continued to develop. The NSW Government Ministry for the Arts assisted museums to improve their level of professionalism and curating standards. The society obtained a large capital works grant and tripled the size of the museum with a large contribution from Camden Council and help from local donors and service clubs. Presidents John Wrigley and Peter Hayward worked with an enthusiastic committee to bring this development to completion in 1999. The voluntary contribution of honorary architect Richard Stringer was enormous and ensured a high standard for the project.

The redevelopment of the Camden Library and the former Camden Fire Station took place in 2007. About $2.5 million was spent by Camden Council and the State Library of NSW to create a beautifully integrated library and heritage complex by joining the library, museum and former fire station with an elegant and light-filled galleria. The museum now has much higher standard of fire-safety than previously, and also has a lift to give access to its upper floor for disabled visitors. The Camden Area Family History Society now has a room adjacent to the museum. The redevelopment of the library has resulted in an excellent partnership and shared usage of the building. Co-operation between the library, the historical society and the family history society is very productive. The galleria is able to be used for book launches and visiting speakers by all three groups.

Two enthusiastic Camden Historical Society members, Frances Warner and husband Harry, outside the Camden Museum after a recent Australia Day parade in 2018. They were both dressed for the occasion. Both of these local identities have engaging and interesting tales to tell of the local area that are all part of the Camden Story. (CHS)

The earliest written record of the arrival of donated items is in a small red-covered exercise book which is still in the collection along with other early catalogue records. A card catalogue was prepared by Nancy Freestone, Frank Hammond and Reg Cole in the 1970s. In the 1990s the first computer catalogue was keyboarded by Rhonda Reynolds, Julie Wrigley and Peter Mylrea. The Mosaic system was adopted in 2000 and the earlier data was transferred across to the new system. In the 2000s-2010s John and Julie Wrigley extended the Mosaic catalogue information on collection items and their donors. As much provenance as possible has been gathered during that time.

Through the active seeking of relevant items for the museum, some very interesting personal collections have been gathered into the collection over the years. The development of a collecting policy in the 1980s has guided collection activities since that time and a number of items have been deaccessioned according to the policy. The following is a listing of the major personal or themed sub-collections in the overall collection. The listing is alphabetical and therefore not in order of importance or significance.

Blattman Collection
Owen Blattman OAM and his wife Nan Blattman nee Daniels, were the public face of the Camden Historical Society and its museum for many years in the 1970s and 1980s. Owen was president for 21 years and Nan was secretary for a lot of that time.

Clark Collection
This collection of letters home and souvenirs from World War One by Private Cecil Clark was donated by his niece in 2009. It is a very complete set of correspondence from Clark in which reference is made to various items of poignant war battle souvenirs sent home by him and now in the collection.

Crookston Collection
These 30 items relate to the Camden medical doctor Dr Robert Melville Crookston, his wife Zoe and daughters Suzanne and Jacqueline. Almost all the items were donated by Jacqueline Crookston or came to the museum from her estate after her death. Significant items are Dr Crookston's OBE medal, the De Groot-made casket and two letters, the Charles I silver spoon, Miss Crookston's set of 5 World War Two medals and 2 silk World War Two maps, several items of quality jewellery and a scrapbook.

Davies Collection
Miss Llewella Davies OAM was an enthusiastic foundation member of both Camden Historical Society and its museum and was a great advocate for heritage conservation in the Camden area. Her collecting and donations led to over 160 items coming into the collection, making her the most prolific single donor for the museum. Significant items are her OAM medal, extensive badge collection, silver and pewter collection, photographs, telescope and Chinese abacus. Many other items were donated by others at the encouragement of Llewella.

Feld Collection
Barry Feld OAM was a very popular Camden Council employee and later alderman. He was the editor of an independent local newspaper 'The Crier' for some years and also played the voluntary role of Camden's Town Crier complete with tricorn hat, green coat, white breeches, black shoes and white

The interior of the Camden Museum on a recent Australia Day. The many exhibits and artefacts on display all have tales to tell that make up the patina of the Camden Story. These all contribute to place making, the construction of community identity and a sense of place. (CHS)

horse. He loved sports, story-telling and good company. His widow Gaylene generously donated all his medals and awards to the museum. Items include his OAM medal, National Medal and his participant's medal from the 1956 Olympic Games when he carried the Olympic torch through Camden.

Ferguson Collection
Alderman Bruce Ferguson OAM was a highly respected Camden citizen. He was an elected alderman on Camden Council for over 20 years and its mayor for many terms. He was a member and Patron of the Camden Historical Society. As mayor he was instrumental in the establishment of the museum with the assistance of Camden Council.

Hodge Collection
Ben Hodge was a watchmaker and jeweller in Argyle Street Camden and was secretary of the Camden Hospital for several decades. He held numerous other public offices in Camden. He donated 29 items and a number of significant early photos of the area and its people. Items include his wife's

wedding dress, baby's sterling silver rattle, sovereign case, seven pocket watches, spectacles, telescope, binoculars, optometrist's kit of test lenses, hospital collection boxes, Show Society ballot box and the Camden Show wall clock.

Indigenous Collection
The collection of over 80 indigenous items in the Camden Museum is thought to be the largest in south west Sydney. It consists of mainly stone axes, cutting tools, flakes, boomerangs, woomeras, shields, photos, a message stick and a brass breastplate.

Johnson Collection
Miss Janice Johnson was an active member of the Camden Historical Society from the 1990s to her death in 2017. In her will she left a number of items for the museum and research papers and a generous amount of money to the Society for specific purposes. These included the placement of plaques on nominated graves and the publishing of her unpublished draft manuscripts on Camden history.

Kernohan Collection
The former mayor and local state Member of Parliament, Dr. Liz Kernohan, was one of the district's best known and most popular citizens when she died suddenly in 2004. She had associated herself with a huge number of local organisations during her life. After her death her close friend and estate executor, Nance Cottle, agreed to donate all of Liz's medals, awards and many personal items to the museum to honour her remarkable contribution to public life in Camden.

Library
An important feature of the museum is the reference library which is computer-catalogued and can be used by visitors to the museum. It is a specialist library which contains only material which is relevant to the history of the Camden district. The rarer and more valuable books are kept in the locked book cabinet.

Macarthur-Onslow Collection
The history of the Macarthur-Onslow family is a major integral part of the history of the Camden district. At one time the Macarthur family owned most of the district and employed most of the people. The family members have associated themselves with all aspects of the district's development. The family provided a lot of interest for the newspapers and social magazines. As a consequence the collection of the museum includes lots of books, photos, documents, souvenirs of events, speeches, plans, newspaper and magazine articles, Camden Park House items and uniforms relating to the

family. The family have supported the museum from when it opened and made donations to assist the museum to advance.

Mariott Collection
Lou and Marion Mariott were a popular Camden/Catherine Fields couple who supported the museum, donating 31 items including a small but choice decorative collection of English sterling silver domestic items which had come from Marion's side of the family.

McCrae Collection
The well known bohemian poet, artist and writer Hugh McCrae OBE came from Melbourne but married a Camden woman, Annie 'Nancy' Adams. From time to time in the 1930s-50s Hugh lived in River Road Elderslie and his writings include references to Elderslie grape vines, St John's spire, Camden hotelkeepers and fellow hotel patrons. He often illustrated his letters to relatives and friends. The museum holds several letters from him to Camden identities Colin Clark and Llewella Davies.

Medal Collection
The museum has encouraged the donation of various medals by local families where there are no obvious family descendants to care for them and where the items will help to tell 'the story of Camden'. The museum now has an extensive collection of medals for war, peace, honours, coronations, royal jubilees, schools, agricultural shows, religions, royal visits, fire brigade, bi-centennial and other anniversaries, from many separate donors.
The medal holdings of the museum are extraordinarily fine for a small museum and are a measure of the community spirit of the district that so many have been donated.

Nixon Collection
Richard Nixon OAM was a lifelong resident of Camden who acquired a vast knowledge of the history of the district. He was renowned for his guided tours, history talks, radio talks, and newspaper columns. He was the director of the Camden museum and president of the Camden Historical Society in the 1990s. The upper exhibition chamber is named the Nixon Room in his honour.

O'Farrell Collection
Brendan O'Farrell is a local history teacher and collector who has taken a keen interest in improving the museum collection. In the 1990s-2010s he collected and then generously donated over 100 items to the collection. These included original documents relating to Lord Camden and Evan Nepean, many Camden souvenirs, medals relevant to Camden and other collectables. With his knowledge he has been able to give advice on the significance of

other items in the collection.

Ray Collection

Milton Ray was a Camden motor mower businessman and a long-time worker for the museum. He was a volunteer fireman with the Camden town fire brigade. He was on the management committee and a vice-president of the Society for several decades. He was a very practical person and a man of few words. He used his skills to build things, mend things and gather donations of photos, aircraft equipment, fire fighting equipment, tools and metal toys for the museum. His wife Elaine supported Milton in all these activities and was herself the secretary and treasurer of the Camden Historical Society at times in the 1960s.

Red Cross Collection

The Camden Branch of the Australian Red Cross was formed when World War One began. It quickly became the most effective charity in Camden and continued as a strong force for philanthropy and caring for people in need. At times it had hundreds of members and was at its most active during the two world wars. It celebrated its centenary in 2014 and the Camden Historical Society used a Federal Government grant to mount an exhibition to demonstrate the great local commitment to the cause over those hundred years.

Sidman Coin Collection

The Sidman family came to Camden in the 1890s when William Sidman purchased the Camden News newspaper and the family has lived here for several generations. George Sidman was the editor in the 1930s and was also a keen coin collector. After his death his executors and the family decided to donate his coin collection to the museum.

Smith Collection

The poignant story of Reginald Sydney 'Rex' Smith, his wife Amelia and daughter Ida and son Rex, is one of the most powerful in the history of Camden. It involves happiness, tragedy, suicide, Gallipoli, war battle death and the story of two orphans raised by two different families. The photo of the handsome, confident Australian Light Horseman is a haunting one, being taken in South Africa before the family tragedies came to pass. The collection includes a set of original hand-written letters from the Boer War from Rex to his brother Archie describing in detail the army exploits. His important medals from both wars and his Memorial Plaque are significant items in the museum collection.

Tools Collection

One of the strongest collections in the museum is of practical tools donated by a wide range of donors. These are to do with agriculture, carpentry, plumbing, bricklaying, cutting, sharpening, gardening, mining, masonry, blacksmithing, leatherworking and boot-making. Some of the tools are from the German vignerons of Elderslie and from the Chinese market gardeners along the Nepean River.

West Collection
This collection is a crucial one for the museum. From 1901 until his sudden death in 1932 Dr. Francis West and his family were at the centre of the Camden community. They literally lived at the centre of town in the historic home Macaria 37 John Street. Dr West was the highly regarded and much-loved general practitioner who died in his prime at the age of 58. The upper-middle class family was involved in the full range of local activities: medical, hospital, church, social, sport, and the show. The family left Camden soon after his death but retained an interest in the town and contact with their friends. When his two elderly unmarried daughters died in the 2000s Dr West's granddaughter, Virginia West, offered the museum their extensive archive of objects, documents, photos, and a scrapbook. The archive provides a good understanding of the social structure of Camden over those years.

World Banknote Collection
The Museum has an anonymous donor and generous citizen of Camden to thank for this collection. For many years his hobby was collecting banknotes and studying their history. In 2016 he donated his extensive world banknote collection to the Camden Historical Society saying that Camden had been very good to him and that he wished to support the Camden Museum with this gift.

Conclusion
As well as the collections described above there are many sub-collections of items. These can be found in the 'Mosaic' computer catalogue by calling them up by classifications. There are at present about 4000 items in the museum catalogued collection. The museum is strong in the areas of photographs, coins and banknotes, vertical subject files, books, maps, plans, artworks, tools, bottles, badges, domestic equipment, geological specimens, health and medical equipment, irons, smoking equipment, clothing, recreational/sports equipment, photographic equipment, dairying equipment, phonographs/record playing equipment, communications equipment and commemorative ware.

All are invited to come to the Camden Museum on Saturday 20th June for an Afternoon Tea from 2 to 5 p.m. to join in the celebrations of the fiftieth anniversary.

CAMDEN HISTORY

Journal of the Camden Historical Society

September 2020 Volume 4 Number 10

CAMDEN HISTORY
Journal of the Camden Historical Society Inc.
ISSN 1445-1549
Editor: Dr Ian Willis OAM

MaManagement Committee
President: Doug Barrett
Vice Presidents: John Wrigley OAM, Warren Sims
Secretary: Lee Stratton
Treasurer: Fletcher Joss
Immediate Past President: Dr Ian Willis OAM
General Committee: Rene Rem, Ian Ramsay, Frances Warner, Robert Wheeler, Dawn Williams, Julie Wrigley.

Honorary Solicitors: Warren & Warren

Society contact:
P.O. Box 566, Camden, NSW 2570.   Online <http://www.camdenhistory.org.au>

Meetings
Meetings are held at 7.30 p.m. on the second Wednesday of the month except in January. They are held in the museum. Visitors are always welcome.

Museum
The Museum is located at 40 John Street, Camden, phone 4655 3400 or 46559210. It is open Thursday to Sunday 11 a.m. to 4 p.m., except at Christmas. Visits by schools and groups are encouraged. Please contact the museum to make arrangements. Entry is free.

Camden History, Journal of the Camden Historical Society Inc
The Journal is published in March and September each year. The editor would be pleased to receive articles broadly covering the history of the Camden district . Correspondence can be sent to the society's postal address. The views expressed by authors in journal articles are solely those of the authors and not necessarily endorsed by the Camden Historical Society.

Donations
Donations made to the Society are tax deductible. The accredited value of objects donated to the Society are eligible for tax deduction.

Cover: Tildsley Butcher Shop, 155 Argyle Street, Camden in 2016 (I Willis)

CAMDEN HISTORY
Journal of the Camden Historical Society Inc.

Contents

From the Editors Desk	415
Camden's Heritage and the Impact of the 2020 Pandemic Jo O'Brien	417
Covid19 and the 1919 Spanish Influenza pandemic Ian Willis	421
Camden Covid comments Ian Willis	424
COVID has grounded my travel plans for now Genevieve Lowry	426
Old Photographs Ian Willis	431
Digitizing The Roy Dowle Photographic Collection Trish Hill and Allen Seymour	431
Unlocking Camden's History with the Camden Council Heritage Advisory Committee Laura Jane Aulsebrook	436
Community Recognition Statement given to the NSW Parliament by Peter Sidgreaves MP, Member for Camden, on 6 August 2020	440
A Familiar Face: Tildsley's Butchery Dianne Matterson	441

From the Editor's Desk

In these times of Covid-19 it is a useful exercise to reflect on what these usual times mean for the historical society and the remainder of the Camden community. Our local community has suffered as have many communities around the globe in the pandemic. Covid-19 is a once in a generation event and has been life-changing many local people. Some immediate effects are quite obvious while others are more subtle and will only be apparent when the pandemic has gone,.

Covid19 is not the first pandemic to effect the local community and it will not be the last. Apart from the Spanish Influenza Pandemic of 1919, which I have written about in this issue, the community has been effected by a host of notifiable diseases in the past.

A quick search of Trove and the pages of the *Camden News* and *Picton Post* reveals the extent of notifiable disease within our community in the past. There were a host of outbreaks in the early 20th century and late 19th century reported by these newspapers. They have included: scarlet fever (1914, 1927, 1948); measles (1914); cholera (1899, 1900, 1902, 1911, 1914); infantile paralysis or polio (1932, 1946); typhoid fever (1914, 1916, 1921); consumption or tuberculosis (1912, 1913, 1916); diphtheria (1896, 1898, 1907, 1922, 1948); and others.

The content of this issue of the journal has a Covid-19 flavour. Jo O'Brien has reflected on the current impacts, while I have drawn observations from a number of other local residents. There is a contribution by a young member of the Camden community, Genevieve Lowry, who was on her life-time adventure overseas as many other young Camden girls have done in previous generations. Her journey was cut short in Turkey by Covid-19 and she had to make a hurried trip back to Australia. Major institution around Australia, including the National Library of Australia and the State Library of New South Wales have been collecting Covid stories from people as the pandemic progresses.

The workings of the Camden Council Heritage Advisory Committee, on which the society has a permanent presence, are covered by Laura Jane Aulesbrook. The committee has made an important contribution to History Week in 2019 and 2020 with Unlock Camden. Members of the society who are interested in the workings of the committee should consult the minutes on the council website.

The Oaks Historical Society has done a sterling job digitizing the collection of glass photographic plates of Camden photographer Roy Dowle. Interested members should have a look at the images and help The Oaks Historical Society identify pictures. Our society has a number Dowle images on Camden Images Past and Present and former member Peter Mylrea has documented Camden photographers in a story in 2005 in *Camden History*.

The activities of the society were recognised recently in the New South Wales Parliament by Mr Peter Sidgreaves MP, Member for Camden. The society is appreciative for the recognition.

To round out his issue regular contributor Dianne Matterson has written an interesting and detailed account of a local business, Tildsley's Butcher. Stories of local businesses are not common and this is a valuable contribution about a local institution which has made an important contribution to the construction of place in Camden.

This is the last issue in the current series of Camden History. Volume 5 will commence in 2021 with a new cover colour and more exciting stories about out local area.

Ian Willis
Editor

Camden's Heritage and the Impact of the 2020 Pandemic

Jo O'Brien

A person's 20/20 vision implies clarity, but 2020 so far has been anything but straightforward. In the awful summer of bushfires and drought, we prayed for rain - and then there were floods. Finally, the sense of emergency passed. Not forgetting that even now some are still suffering from the problematic aftereffects of that summer, most of us could look ahead. Then a once in a lifetime event emerged – the coronavirus pandemic – and 2020 and our path to the future changed.

There was so much to look forward to for Camden's heritage groups. The family history Society calendar was packed with events. I was also looking forward to attending all the events planned for the historical society. I was particularly pleased that the family history society would have a table at the Camden Show for the first time, next to the historical society in the hall, an excellent opportunity to interact with many Camden locals and celebrate Camden's history and heritage.

And then came the pandemic. Slowly at first, distant, affecting those that travelled. Then it was here, and suddenly the situation changed every day. It felt like the ground was sliding under our feet like I imagine it feels in an earthquake. When I heard that the Easter Show was cancelled, I knew how serious this would be, and that everything was going to change. Soon after, the Camden Show was cancelled, along with all the other planned events, one by one.

The impact on historical and family history societies has been profound. Our regular contact and meetings have gone, our rooms have been closed for extended periods. All the events planned for the year ahead, the Camden Show, the heritage festival, book launches, speakers, meetings, all cancelled. Access to our rooms and resources was severely limited, and stopped altogether much of the time, hampering our efforts to keep things going. Opportunities to connect with new people have been lost, and we may lose existing connections as some members and volunteers may not return. It may be some time yet before we can resume our regular meetings and activities.

The loss of volunteer work is not as stressful and impactful as losing income, but it is a loss of meaningful work and the social connection and a sense of purpose it brings. We do these jobs. After all, we are passionate about history because we want to contribute to our community, and for many of us, it was an essential part of our lives.

Camden's Argyle Street precinct where people stop and have a chat or just catch up on the latest gossip. These types of social interaction have been part of the Argyle Street precinct for decades of local residents. (I Willis)

Societies like ours provide important social contact - the cuppa at the end was sometimes the most important part! We miss sharing information, ideas, and stories, and talking about our common interests and our love for Camden and its history.

We are also missing most of our other social interactions, both with friends and casual conversations with people in Camden. It was common to meet someone you knew in the street, and sometimes have quite a lengthy discussion, now lingering to chat is discouraged. Conversations have moved online or on the phone, but it is not the same without the personal connection, the greeting kiss, handshake, or hug (will this still be how we greet each other after this?). I miss sitting with friends, having lunch or coffee, and having an in-depth discussion and sharing a laugh with a group and talking through a topic, going to a seminar, and learning something new.

The Camden Library Museum building is part of the John Street historic precinct where the Camden Historical Society manages the Camden Museum and the Camden Area Family History Society has their research room. (I Willis)

All we can do is keep in touch online, on social media, and by emailed newsletters, although it is noticeable that not everyone likes to stay in touch this way. Luckily, many historians and family historians are independent researchers, can work online, and love to read - we have plenty of files to sort, and research to write about, so at least we have something to do at home.

Camden has always been a friendly place, with a country town atmosphere and a local focus. Even as Sydney grew and the town became part of the Greater Sydney metropolitan area, the locals still felt they had their community. Many live and work in the area, their families live here, and they have their continuous heritage here. The country town atmosphere has been challenged of late by the expansion of the urban area, new families moving to the district. The government plans to expand infrastructure building, encourage developers, and cut red tape, and this may speed up the pace of change. Will heritage, tradition, open space, and the environment be casualties of the quest to revive the economy?

The future of Camden township was already challenged with shops closing and so many people going to shopping malls and more significant centres for goods and services. In previous downturns and challenging times, locals needed the Camden shops and services, and Camden had a full range available then. Many essential services have already moved, and it is hard to see how all of the local shops, services, restaurants, and cafes will survive this challenge. People are increasingly shopping online. Without a critical mass, shopping in Camden could progressively close down until there are stretches of empty shops. And that all-important social connection that gives the town its identity – its sense of community - will it continue if most people are shopping elsewhere? Camden businesses must be supported throughout the restrictions, and when the pandemic is over, a plan developed to promote opportunities for new businesses and shops in Camden.

There is a consensus that we should protect and promote Camden's remarkably well-preserved history and heritage, and encourage heritage tourism, art and culture, fresh and gourmet food. There will be a delay in these plans - as arts, heritage and culture facilities were amongst the first to be shut and are likely to be the last to open. Their role in the economy is less prominent, they are considered optional, and funding may become hard to get. Tourism and events that involve crowds and meetings will not return for some time, and we will lose the opportunity to connect with people and share Camden's stories.

We need our heritage, art and culture more than ever, to learn from the past, to come together positively with a focus on something wonderful and fascinating – things of beauty and history that inspire us, and make us think. We can learn a lot from studying our history, to see how our ancestors coped under challenging times. Perhaps, as the restrictions and pandemic continue, people will turn towards the arts and escapism as they did in the past – during the Depression and War. Those events lasted for years, and people survived and came out the other side, and moved on, and I expect we will as well.

I look forward to the time when we can all meet again, share a cuppa, and talk about Camden and its history.

*****

As I finish writing this, times have changed again, and we watch the worrying changes in Victoria. There are still so many questions and so much uncertainty about the future, but people need to do whatever they can to live their lives as naturally as possible. Words such as social distance, self-isolate, no touching, no hugging, stay home, keep apart are joined by a call to wear masks. While there is an apparent medical requirement for these measures, these increasing barriers to human contact will contribute to the sense of isolation that so many are feeling. I hope we can support each together and make an effort to stay connected and look after each other in these disconnected times.

Covid19 and the 1919 Spanish Influenza pandemic

Ian Willis

Corvid-19 has caused the introduction of washing hand and social distancing of 1.5 metres for the first time. Or is it the first time?

Well no, it is not the first time. It is an exciting proposition to note that the past is bound to repeat itself. The past has undoubtedly come to revisit us with this pandemic.

The Covid-19 pandemic has brought a new normal to our lives. What parts will outlast the pandemic?

Historian Frank Bongiorno reminds us that Spanish influenza pandemic was not all bad. The failure of the states to cooperate led to the formation of a federal Department of Health in 1921.

During the 1919 Spanish Influenza pandemic, people had to wear masks, wash hands and avoid crowds. Very similar to recommended health practices in the current Corona outbreak.

In Camden, the first case occurred in April 1919, and the patient had a speedy recovery. There was a more severe outbreak with nine patients in May 1919, and the emergency hospital was re-opened at Camden Public School for six weeks.

The Methodist School Hall became the site for the hospital kitchen. Matron McAnane from Camden Hospital provided supervision, and she was assisted by Nurses Burk, Smart and Mackay, and the local Voluntary Aid Detachment.

The Camden Red Cross opened a centre to distribute clothing, food and kitchen utensils.

Out at Mount Hunter, there were no nurses for the six beds that were made available in local homes. In April the Camden mayor reported that 'the people out here are ready to assist in any practical way'. (Camden News 10 April 1919)

At Narellan, there were 12 beds made available in several local homes. Local people volunteered as ambulance transport, stretcher-bearers, nurses, cooks, laundry workers and housekeepers. (Camden News, 10 April 1919)

The northern end of Argyle Street Camden in the early 1920s. The town would have changed little from the days of the Spanish influenza pandemic. (Camden Images)

There were many patients in local homes and both Dr West and Dr Crookston became ill, along with two nurses and one voluntary aid. The highest daily intake at the Camden emergency hospital was 36 patients with an average stay of 21 days. There were four deaths.

Kissing at Camden railway station broke social distancing rules.
The habit of some railway passengers kissing and breaking social distancing rules caused consternation at the local council.

The matter was raised in April 1919 by the Camden Nuisance Inspector. He was worried that people would 'insist on kissing' in a report to council.
He complained that 'residents met the trains at the [Camden] railway station and hugged and kissed passengers'.

The inspector recommended to the all-male council that 'council should take steps to prevent kissing altogether during the crisis'.

On discussion, the aldermen decided that they 'did not favour framing a by-law to prevent kissing' and that Mayor Furner 'should visit the railway station' to stop this type of fraternisation.

Council aldermen were quite amused by the discussion. They finally agreed that they would leave the supervision of kissing on Camden railway station to the Nuisance Inspector. (Camden News, 24 April 1919)

Camden Covid comments

Ian Willis

In these days of Covid19, we are all experiencing a new normal. In the Camden area, more people are walking and exercising in a time of social isolation.

Camden South resident Cathey Shepherd says, 'I have used this time to walk all over Camden.'

'This town has a distinctive country feel about it. I know we are always being told this, but becomes noticeable when you don't go beyond the town', says Cathey.

The Corvid19 crisis and forced isolation have given some people a time to reflect on their past.

Elderslie resident Fiona Woods says, 'The current isolation has given me more time to think about my past and the people that came before me.

'I have developed a fascination for their stories, especially discovering how they overcame challenges', she says.

'The extra time I now have has seen me reading through our family book, soaking up as much as I can about their lives,' said Fiona.

Fiona recounts the story of her great-grandmother, who had 15 children. She says, 'Suddenly I had a connection with an ancestor I've never met'.

'Everyone has a story', says Fiona. 'In years to come, I want to be remembered for more than my name on a page'.

Fiona thinks that love and kindness can triumph over many challenges in the current situation.

'If my ancestors could survive wars, depressions and the untimely loss of children, I can get through this pandemic thing. I may need a little more wine', she says.

'One thing I'm learning from this is we all have a story to tell. Maybe we should use this time to write stories down so our future descendants can read them', she says.

Elderslie resident Marilyn Willis says, 'More cards, less cash'. Cashless transactions had been gaining momentum before the current crisis. This trend is likely to continue. Maybe cash is ultimately doomed.

What will be the shape of the local economy? Online usage has increased for consumption, business, entertainment and learning. These practices are destined to continue and may re-shape our lives even more.

Recent bushfires have created community trauma. The Covid19 crisis has added to this anxiety. Together these events have created much uncertainty in people's lives. People are going to be cautious during the recovery phase of the current crisis.

South Camden resident Cathey Shepherd says, 'Covid19 makes our communities stronger and makes you think of the welfare of your community members'.

The Camden Town Farm Miss Llewella Davies Pioneer Walkway has proved a popular spot to take an exercise break and go for a walk during this Covid-19 period. Check it out. (I Willis 2020)

COVID has grounded my travel plans for now

Genevieve Lowry

With trepidation I moved forward along the line at the check-in at Singapore Airlines terminal at Istanbul Airport, I stifled a cough, glad at this moment I was wearing a mask. The words my family and friends from Camden said to me rang in my ears as I approached check-in – "Don't cough and look relaxed." I could hear every single word that was uttered down the phone when my family were beckoning me back home from what was supposed to be my year away overseas.

The trip is what I had wanted for so long, but university and the recent death of my much-loved grandmother saw me delaying my trip. At age 23, I finally did it. My friend Veronica and I finally took the plunge one-night booking one-way tickets. We booked three tickets to Paris to be precise without a return date; one for myself, one for her and one for my sister- although she wasn't aware at the time. The price was right. Admittedly, the reason it was cheap was the fact it was right in the middle of winter.

My sister was surprised but excited. She is also the down to earth one, who without doubt booked a return ticket for February. She was starting an honours degree and had many different priorities to me.

For me, it was working at Shoe Talk, which I did from the age of 15. A stint in hospitality at Back Galley in Camden and administration work at a local Camden law firm, far removed from my International Studies degree that saw me save the money and a strong determination to spread my wings. As much as I love the relaxed setting of Australia, I wanted to be one of the many to make their rite of passage overseas. For years I had heard people of different ages tell of their experiences; I wanted to have my own.

The travellers going ended up including two other friends – we were now on our way to Paris – all beloved school friends from Magdalene Catholic High School at Camden; people I could not wait to share my excitement with. Paris was to be our first stop in a long itinerary – followed by Amsterdam, Switzerland and then the Alps of Chamonix. The rest of the journey was a solo mission, just myself and I.

We left Camden, 24 January with temperatures in the high 30s heading to a climate with single digits and with little sunshine.

I was so looking forward to finally being away. The world as people say "was my oyster" not sure if that's the appropriate expression for a vegan, anyway, I

Genevieve Lowry in Monaco (2020)

had so many plans, and adventures in store and I thought I could dodge this virus.

We had arrived in Paris and were taking in the city and cafes; little concerned about what was happening at home. We headed off to the famous Louvre to see the works of art we had only read about and seen in photos, finally up close and personal. Admittedly, the Mona Lisa wasn't all that awe-inspiring – a small dark painting with long queues. On the other hand, the Moulin Rouge was just something else. We roamed the city taking in the different points of interest, and the numerous café delighting in vegan croissants – which are non-existent in Camden.

At this point we had heard stories of the coronavirus spreading across Europe, we shook our heads thinking "no way will it affect our trip".

Now a group of four, we went onto the ski field of the Alps; it was the highlight of my entire trip. The mountains of Kosciusko, whilst beautiful, are minuscule compared to the Alpine ranges of Chamonix, a skiers version of Disneyland. After a long day of skiing, there was nothing more rewarding than going to have a drink with other fellow snowboarders and skiers, all foreigners who were able to share their experiences whilst having a laugh.

At this point, the group of four then became two as my friend Veronica and I headed live in the South of France for four weeks before heading to Germany, Munich and Berlin to be exact and soaked up the atmosphere wholeheartedly. We are not beer drinkers by any stretch of the imagination but managed to enjoy one in the beer halls along with the beautiful vibrancy of the local people who were very welcoming and enjoyed a sing-a-long. I couldn't imagine doing the same thing in Camden.

Each city we visited had its unique flare. There were highlights of this short trip, which made me crave more adventures for the future. From cycling the congested pedestrian streets of Amsterdam, having a 'vin chaud' (mulled wine) and roasted chestnuts on the streets of Strasbourg, to hiking to the top of Pic- Saint loop in the South of France, a day trip which quickly taught us the valuable lesson of hitch-hiking to make it back to our temporary home in Montpellier. Everywhere we went, we were greeted warmly by locals; making friends in the most bizarre situations, friends I am still in contact with today.

In the background, the spectre of the virus was following us.

It was 11 March 2020, the last night together for Veronica and I before we went our separate ways, she was heading to England, while I was off on my own. We celebrated by going to a famous Berlin nightclub – where we were warmly greeted by the locals who shared with us their uncertainty, that possibly this would be the last night Berlin would be able to party. We laughed again with the stranger and thought nothing of it.

The next morning, on the 12 March 2020, I ventured alone to the airport, Turkey was my next stop– a country rich in history, art and culture with food I could appreciate.

It was this day that all the globetrotters were starting to feel grounded. I had just landed in Istanbul, Turkey, feeling both a sense of uneasiness and excitement. Turkey was the part of the trip I was anticipating the most, to test myself and see how I would be travelling solo. I accepted the challenge with open arms and was ready for whatever came my way, or so I thought.

After settling in comfortably in my new accommodation, it was seven stars, minus five – what more did I expect on my budget. I switched on my phone to hear the tragic news, my dear friend Veronica, had just informed me that all her travel plans were abruptly cancelled. A day before her trip was to start.

The city of Istanbul. (Genevieve Lowry 2020)

Feeling exhausted and distraught, she had booked a flight home.

The world had started to close up overnight. In response I reached out to my own family back home in Camden only to be notified the situation was getting much worse – all Australian travellers were being encouraged to book flights home. Ignoring the advice, I decided to travel to Cappadocia in Turkey and ride out the rest of this adventure, and no way was I heading home. Cappadocia was another world in already unfamiliar territory. With a small group of newly made companions, we explored the underground caves. We were travelling into the valley of Göreme, exploring the homes of 'cave dwellers' whilst enjoying the sunsets over the valleys. It was perfect, but a nervous sensation was washing over me, conversations of borders closing were becoming too apparent.

I began questioning everything I was doing. So my sister Ally did what any sister would do, thinking I was an idiot, and maybe I was, she booked my ticket home. It dawned on at that point I couldn't go on.

My heart broke at the thought of leaving this adventure behind. But I accepted the reality; nothing was improving.

There were too many experiences in the short two months to put into words, but none more so than the exact moment when I decided to go home finally. I was utterly heartbroken and in disbelief over the reality. I valued my eight weeks away because I was lucky enough to have been able to experience an adventure in 2020, and it's left me hungry for more.

It became a race against time. This was not how I wanted to leave Turkey. I didn't want to let the sadness I felt effect my mind-frame in such a beautiful part of the world. So with another group of soon to depart travellers, we set out onto the streets of Istanbul once more, to enjoy one last sunset across the waters of the city. I decided it's a place I will come back to one day.

As I arrived at the airport I was dreading the lady at the check-in, after hearing her ask passengers before me if they had been to any of the red zone countries during the last 14 days – I had and there was clear proof in my passport.

I don't know whether at this moment she felt sorry for me, realizing I was on my own or if it was simply luck, she told me to place my bags on the coveter belt and printed my boarding pass.

A final indication that I was on the way to Camden.

Old Photographs

Ian Willis

Old photographs provide an entry to a world that was more authentic than the present. The viewer of an old photograph is a time traveller into another world. A snapshot of a moment frozen in time. The observer has a glimpse of a world before the present. For the viewer, it as a form of nostalgia, where they create a romanticized version of the past accompanied by feelings that the present is not quite as good as an earlier period (Willis (2020).

Peter Mylrea wrote an article about Camden photographers in 2005 for the Camden History Journal. He lists some of the districts photographers from the 1860s, and they have included: W Macarthur; JB Mummery; HP Reeves; HT Lock; W Norton; J Donnellan; C Kerry; W Jackson; W Thwaites; CA Sibert; OV Coleman; AE Cash; R Cash; HE Perkins; R Dowle; and J Driscoll (Mylrea (2005). More recent photographers have included: J Burge; R Herbert; J Kooyman; P Mylrea; J Wrigley; B Atkins and others.

The work of some of these Camden photographers can be viewed on the photographic database Camden Images Past and Present. (http://www.library.camden.nsw.gov.au/camden-images)

Photographer Roy Dowle created a series of glass plates during his photographic work. The collection of slides has recently found it way to The Oaks Historical Society where its digistisation was organised by members.

Digitizing The Roy Dowle Photographic Collection

Trish Hill and Allen Seymour

Roy William Dowle was born in 1893, the first child to Charles and Madeline Dowle (nee Dominish) and his siblings were Frank (1896), Edgar (1898) and Leonard (1904). Charles Dowle purchased their "Collingwood" property in Quarry Road, at The Oaks around the time of Roy's birth. It is presumed that Roy lived there until his marriage to Emily J Smith in 1915.

Roy & Emily's home was in Camden at the top of Barsden Street. Roy was a photographer and the Camden News of 26 March 1914 records that he received an award for photography in the amateur section at the Camden show. In 1937 he supplied photographs of Camden to the Council for use by the railways in their passenger carriages. Roy worked for Whitemans, and in 1943 he was called on to make a presentation to Charles Whiteman when the

Portrait of Roy and Emily Dowle in the 1920s. Roy was a keen photographer in the Camden district, and his collection of glass plate negatives is now with The Oaks Historical Society at the Wollondilly Heritage Centre. (TOHS)

latter retired. The Dowle's also had a holiday home at Erowal Bay – St

George's Basin.

Roy died in 1955, but fortunately, a large number of his glass and film negatives survived. These were donated to the Wollondilly Heritage Centre in 2016 by Roy's grand-daughter. An index book came with the collection, but unfortunately, a lot of the negatives were not in their original boxes, making identification of the people difficult. The photographs range in age from around 1910 to the 1940s.

The Wollondilly Heritage Centre was successful in obtaining a New South Wales Community Heritage grant in 2019 to digitize the collection which consists of 1100 glass plate negatives and a further 120 plastic film negatives. There was considerable work in preparing the negatives for digitizing, as they all had to be cleaned and numbered. Volunteers from the centre did this work from the centre over several weeks, and they were then transported in batches to Digital Masters at Balgowlah for digitizing. Most were still in excellent condition, and the quality of the scanned images is superb.

Roy photographed a lot of people, with weddings, babies and young children being popular subjects. He also photographed local buildings and houses, views, animals, local events such as parades or sporting events.

Buildings photographed include St Johns church (inside also), Camden Hospital (even inside shots), Camden Inn, Plough & Harrow Hotel, Narellan Hotel, Oakdale wine shop, Maloney's store, Narellan school, Mt Hunter school, Camden railway station, Camden Milk Depot, Mater Dei and others.

The unveiling of the Mt Hunter war memorial (pictured) was also covered by Roy, along with Mt Hunter School and some beautiful interior shots which show honour boards with photos of local soldiers.

Some fascinating photos are of children in fancy dress, and two that stand out, are of the same girl dressed firstly as a wedding cake, and then as a lampshade!! A number of the houses have been identified as still being in Camden, and other more easily identified homes include "Edithville" in Mitchell street, the former Methodist parsonage in Menangle Road and Harrington Park house.

Among the groups photographed is St John's Choir, returned servicemen, cricket teams, football teams, Masonic dinner, the Royal Forrester's, staff and children from Macquarie House, visiting school teachers and Sunday school groups. One photograph of a group of three male cyclists picnicking may be one of the first selfies, as we believe the centre one is Roy himself, holding a

The opening of the Mount Hunter Soldier's War Memorial, opposite the public school took place on Saturday, 24 September 1921, at 2.30 pm. Brigadier-General GM Macarthur Onslow carried out the official unveiling ceremony. The memorial listed 40 names of local servicemen. Afternoon tea was provided by 'the ladies' at 1/- with all money going to the memorial fund. (*Camden News*, 15 September 1921, 22 September 1921. Image Roy Dowle Collection)

string which runs to the camera. Soldiers were another popular subject, and there are also some women dressed as soldiers. Roy also copied photos. This process was done by photographing it, and a lot of the soldier photos have been copied this way.

Some of the views are of Wollongong, Bulli, Burragorang, Douglas Park, Theresa Park, Chellaston Street and some great shots taken from St Johns steeple. There are also numerous flood scenes around Camden. Animals didn't escape Roy's camera, and there are shots of cattle, horses, poultry, dogs. Even a camel. Some other remarkable photos are of a shop window display featuring Persil washing powder. Some of these have been dated to 1910.

A lot of the film negatives show his holidays, with some taken at their holiday home, while others are taken whilst on a trip to the north, and scenes have been identified as Cessnock, Dungog, Taree, Kew & Paterson. There are some photos of Warragamba Dam in the very early stages before any concrete was poured, and a magnificent shot of the winding drums of the overhead cableway.

Several of Roy's photos have already appeared on the Back Page and in numerous publications on local history because his subjects were local and numerous copies of them have survived in private collections.

The bullock team of Davy Nolan at Mount Hunter with a load of produce. (Roy Dowle Collection)

The scanned photos can be viewed either on a computer or in albums at the Wollondilly Heritage Centre & Museum, open on Saturdays, Sundays & public holidays.

Check out old photographs from the Roy Dowle Collection at the Wollondilly Heritage Centre Website. http://www.wollondillymuseum.org.au/archives/photographic-archives/

References.

Ian Willis (2020), 'How the mysteries of a pretty picture from yesteryear allows you to peel back the layers of the past'. *Camden History Notes blog.* Online @ https://camdenhistorynotes.wordpress.com/2020/04/03/mystery-of-a-photograph/ Accessed 14 September 2020

Peter Mylrea (2005), 'Some Photographers of Camden'. *Camden History Journal.* Vol. 1, No. 10, September 2005. Pp243-259.

Unlocking Camden's History with the Camden Council Heritage Advisory Committee

Laura Jane Aulsebrook

The Camden Council Local Government Area is repeatedly referenced as the fastest growing LGA in the country with a focus on contemporary lifestyle and an abundance of new residents. Despite this rapid growth, it remains an area that is proud of, and eager to promote, the rich heritage of the community and celebrate the contributions the community had to the "birthplace of Australia's Agricultural wealth". To create a *continued vision to help inform strategic heritage directions and community education around the importance of Camden's heritage to the unique identity of the Camden LGA*, Camden Council resolved in 2018 to establish the inaugural Camden Council Heritage Advisory Committee [1].

Who's who on the Committee?
The Committee consists of three community representatives who were appointed through an application process; two Camden Councillors and an alternate Councillor as nominated by their fellow Councillors, a Camden Historical Society representative and an Indigenous representative for the area. The Committee, along with key personnel from Camden Council meets bi-monthly, working to promote and educate the broader community about the heritage of the area.

Camden Council Heritage Advisory Committee Members:

Chairperson
    Councillor Cindy Cagney

Councillor Members
    Councillor Eva Campbell - Primary
    Councillor Paul Farrow - Alternate

Community Members
    Ian McIntosh – North Ward
    Michael Kennedy – Central Ward
    Laura Jane Aulsebrook – South Ward
    Glenda Chalker – Cubbitch Barta Native Title Claimants Corporation
    Dr Ian Willis – Camden Historical Society

Unlock Camden - The start of an annual event.
Celebrating Camden's community and heritage in an accessible way that coordinates with national History Week, was the focus of the inaugural Commit-

Camden Council Heritage Advisory Committee 2020 (with permission Camden Council)

tee event in September of 2019. The theme of "Unlock Camden" was established as a way to celebrate what residents love about the Camden community and "unlock" something new about the history that surrounds the community and town in which they live. The celebration was designed to be a way for older residents, those that grew up in the area, and newer residents, to celebrate and share their experiences. The day also promoted a heritage education, by allowing residents to learn more about the buildings they walk by on a regular basis, along with the history of the many community groups and how each contribute to the fabric of the town. The event allowed the community to learn more about infamous buildings, the history of groups of the town and why they are so crucial to the fabric of the community.

Despite gale-force winds forcing the closure of other community events in town, the 2019 celebration in the foregrounds of the Macaria Building in John Street went ahead with more than a dozen community groups showcasing their heritage and contribution to the Camden community. The day was a celebration of the people and organisations that make up the Camden community. From Girl Guides in historical uniforms, CWA selling homemade jams and chutneys, to family history research with the Camden Family History Society and the Camden Scouts showcasing their role in the community for over 100 years. The Camden Heritage Walking tour and brochure were relaunched, and members of the Camden Historical Society were there to provide more information. The self guided tours are year round activities and the relaunch encouraged residents far and wide to take up a tour for the first time. The Camden Community Band and local duo The Honey Sippers provided entertainment on the day along with the recently launched Alan Baker

This is a stall at the Unlock Camden street fair in 2019 on the front lawn outside Macaria Alan Baker Art Gallery (Brett Atkins 2019)

Spring Exhibition which welcomed visitors inside Macaria.

Of particular excitement was the reveal of the #mycamdenstory artwork. The hitching post outside Macaria was revealed to have over 100 images of Camden residents. Local places made up from anyone who had used the hashtag #mycamdenstory over the weeks leading up to the event. It was a way of sharing the people and stories that make up the Camden history and community today, combining the modern-day social media phenomena with Camden heritage made the event accessible to all.

Unlock Camden Online
By the time of print, the Unlock Camden Online event should be in full force. This year the Covid-19 Pandemic that forced the cancellation of all community gatherings and events for the year. The Heritage Advisory Committee decided to take the event online for 2020, by filming a "virtual walking tour" that allows residents and those further afield the opportunity to explore Camden and some of its iconic buildings from the comfort of their home. This virtual tour follows the Camden Walking Tour brochure, to provide an accessible tourism resource for residents and visitors to Camden alike, to explore the heritage the community has to offer. The virtual walking tour is being

published online via Camden Council's website and social media accounts and provides a global audience with the chance to tour Camden and learn more about the significant heritage buildings from the comfort of their home! Coinciding with History Week 2020, the virtual tour launch is alongside many other online resources to celebrate Camden's History that will be accessible year round. Of particular interest is the armchair time travel experience. Highlighting pictures from "Camden Images" and the Museum's database, the Camden Library's website is launching a series of "then and now" digital puzzles allowing for a visual time travel experience on our screens. It is hoped that these online resources will encourage an increased interest in the heritage of the Camden region.

#mycamdenstory - Accessing heritage in the Social Media Age
Love it or loathe it, understand it or be confused by it, there is no denying that we live in the social media age and that it is here to stay. Social media and heritage promotion do not necessarily spring to mind as being complimentary; however, it is surprising how well they align as a platform with instant and widespread access. Social media is a powerful tool in the digital age, with a mainstream audience that allows greater accessibility to heritage. Hashtags are a mode of gathering like-minded viewers by combining similar images in a connected and easily searched way. The #mycamdenstory hashtag, first promoted in the lead up to the Unlock Camden event in 2019, allows social media users with the platform to share their "Camden Story" and connect to their heritage, sense of belonging to the Camden community and their personal experiences with iconic Camden locations.

In the isolated world that 2020 has become due to Covid19, this sense of shared connection and community outreach on a digital platform has allowed residents to take the time to connect to their lived heritage and find out more about the stories and histories that community members share within the region. Once again, these images will be collated to create an artwork for display on the hitching post outside Macaria. They are thus creating a piece of art history that celebrates residents' connection to heritage in 2020.

The Future of the Committee
As Camden LGA continues to grow and develop, sharing the heritage of the Camden region with newer residents presents new and challenging ways to communicate this knowledge in an accessible way. The Camden Council Heritage Advisory Committee looks forward to being able to promote all elements of Camden's heritage and reach new and old Camdinites alike!

Notes
1. CCHAC Website - Camden Council's Heritage Advisory Committee -https://www.camden.nsw.gov.au/planning/heritage-conservation/heritage-advisory-committee/

Community Recognition Statement given to the NSW Parliament by Peter Sidgreaves MP, Member for Camden, on 6 August 2020

CAMDEN MUSEUM 50TH ANNIVERSARY

Mr PETER SIDGREAVES (Camden)—The Camden Museum has long been an integral part of cataloguing and displaying Camden's rich history. This historical museum was established by the Rotary Club of Camden and
The Camden Historical Society. It was opened on the 20th of June 1970 by Major General Sir Denzil Macarthur Onslow CBE, DSO, ED who was an Australian Army Officer, businessman and grazier and whose family the iconic
Onslow Park in Camden was named after. On the 20th of June 2020, the Camden Historical Society celebrated 50 years since the museum's opening. The Society met and held a celebration for this important milestone of one of
Camden's great historic centres. I'd like to note the efforts of the Camden Historical Society's committee members Ian Ramsay, Rene Rem, Frances Warner, Robert Wheeler, Dawn Williams and Julie Wrigley as well as President Doug Barrett, Vice Presidents Warren Sims and John Wrigley OAM, Treasurer Fletcher Joss and Secretary Lee Stratton for all the work they do recording, maintaining and displaying Camden's rich and important history for our future generations.

Notes
Legislative Assembly Hansard – 06 August 2020 https://www.parliament.nsw.gov.au/Hansard/Pages/HansardResult.aspx#/docid/HANSARD-1323879322-112208

Peter Sidgreaves MP, Member for Camden (with permission)

A Familiar Face: Tildsley's Butchery
Dianne Matterson

When Edward Griffiths leased the small shop on the corner of Argyle and Oxley Streets for his butcher's business in 1894, he would never have dreamed that the site would be continuously occupied by a series of butchers during the next 126 years, eventually culminating in the familiar Tildsley's Butchery at 151-155 Argyle Street. Before Edward's lease, and as early as 1840, the man who did much of the work on the font and stone flagging of St. John's Church, William Buchan, had his stonemason's business here.[1]

In the early 1850s, William left his family in Camden and joined the crowds trying to make their fortunes on the Victorian goldfields. In 1854, having not heard from him for some time, and believing he was at the Port Phillip diggings, his family appealed for information. They asked anyone who knew his whereabouts to contact his wife, Margaret, or his son, Alexander.[2] The outcome of this appeal is unknown although it is possible it revealed that William was deceased. In December, Alexander purchased the corner site for £60, possibly from his father's estate. When Alexander died in 1859, ownership of the land passed to Margaret Buchan.[3]

By the end of the 1850s, Richard Potter, a harness maker, was open for business on the Buchan corner,[4] followed by Charles Whiteman. The latter began his commercial activity in Camden in 1878 when he brought produce to the town to sell. He occupied the single-storey premises on the corner of Argyle and Oxley Streets and ran the store from here. However, before the end of the year, Charles' produce store had burnt down.[5] A former resident of Camden, PC Furner, recalled that Charles Whiteman subsequently rebuilt a wooden shop and residence on this same site.

In 1889, the newly incorporated Camden Municipal Council valued all properties within the municipality based on their rental values. As a result, owners were liable for council rates based on a levy of one shilling in the pound, revenue that was matched pound for pound by the New South Wales government.[6] At around this time, Charles Whiteman vacated the building.[7]

Edward Griffiths' tenure on the small Whiteman building began about 5 years later.[8] In 1895, he advertised in the *Camden News* for 'good condition' hides, telling the public he had negotiated a commission with a firm of exporters and could offer the 'highest possible price' to anyone able to supply him with quality hides.[9]

In March 1896, a public meeting was held to discuss the issue of land tax and to determine the unimproved value of land within Camden township. A year earlier, the New South Wales government had legislated for land taxes centred on the unimproved value of the land. This value was based on one penny in the pound of the capital value of a property.

Land Tax

All landowners had to submit their land tax returns by 27 March 1896, but this was not possible until the unimproved value of their land was resolved. As there was no centralised land valuation agency, a meeting of local landowners was called to arrive at a 'fair and honest' land assessment. After some discussion, various values were agreed upon depending on their location within the town; the land from Oxley Street to the drill hall had an unimproved value of £1/10/- per foot.[10] Margaret Buchan's land had a frontage of 66 feet, requiring a land tax payment of £99 per annum.

Small debts court

Edward Griffiths was the plaintiff in action he took against AJ Doust in the Small Debts Court in 1896 for the amount of £16/9/2, asserting he had supplied meat to Mr Doust going back to 1893 and some of those accounts were included in the current claim. He admitted he owed Mr Doust £11/18/- and just wanted to get the 'account settled and off his books'. However, Mr Doust said the meat 'was not sound' and was 'short in weight'. He also told the court that according to his records, he only owed £15/0/2.

Edward Griffiths responded, saying that his meat was sound when it was delivered and that he could account for the difference in weight as it was 'usual to charge for the bone taken out of meat for rolling roast meat.' The plaintiff and defendant were told by the solicitors present that the 1893 accounts were beyond the statute of limitations. After some discussion, the bench decided they had no jurisdiction to make a ruling on the case.[11]

In February 1897, Edward again appeared in the Small Debts Court, this time as the defendant. Mr Hamilton said he was employed by Mr Griffiths for a fortnight's tuition in preparation for the defendant's inspector of stock examination, at £2/2/- per week. The defendant had paid him £3/10/-, but this didn't include two days of tuition, leaving a deficit of 14 shillings.

Travelling expenses

The plaintiff also claimed 5/11d. for travelling expenses, making a total claim of 19/11d. Mr Hamilton said he'd arrived in Camden at 7 p.m. on 2 December and began his tuition of Mr Griffiths the next day and continued – including working on the Sundays - until 14 December when Mr Griffiths' exam was held. Edward asserted that Mr Hamilton should have arrived on 30 November as agreed, but then telegrams were produced showing the court the plaintiff was unable to reach Camden on the arranged date.

The defendant said Mr Hamilton had worked on Sunday, but some of the day was spent sightseeing, as he had taken the plaintiff for a drive around the area. The Bench's verdict favoured the plaintiff (14/10d) as they thought Mr Griffiths 'should have varied the agreement after the arrival of Mr Hamilton'. The plaintiff's application for expenses was disallowed.[12]

By 1897, Edward Griffiths had two assistants working for him, namely Jack Parker and Dave Wilson, the latter being the slaughterman.[13] Around this time, their employer met with an accident while feeding his horses in the stables. One of the horses attempted to bite the neighbouring horse, and when the harassed horse moved quickly out of the way, it struck Edward on the side of the head, knocking him unconscious for a time and resulting in severe bruising.[14]

Nepean River floods

When the Nepean River flooded land and businesses in and around Camden in February 1898, Edward lost several sheep, who either drowned or were washed away from his slaughter yard. However, in a fortunate turn of events, his pigs escaped to higher ground.[15]

In September, nearly two years after falling out with Mr Hamilton over the training for the inspector's exam, Edward was offered a position with the Department of Health as a meat inspector, an opportunity he accepted and quickly made preparations to leave Camden.[16] He sold his business to Albert Dunk (Bert) who wasted no time advising the public he would buy hides, tallow, sheepskins, horsehair and 'every kind of produce' at the 'highest pric-

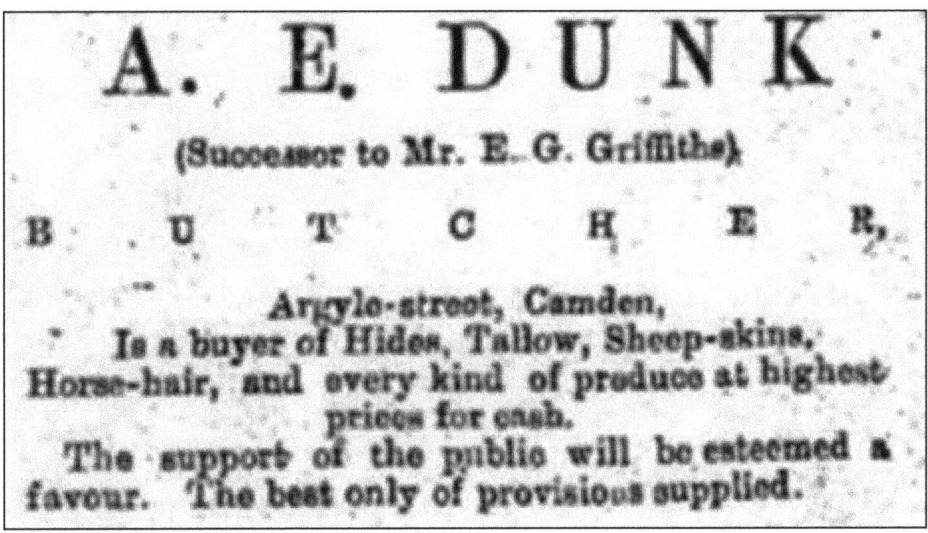

Bert Dunk's advertisement (*Camden News*, 27 October 1898)

es'.[17]

Since 1897, when Margaret Buchan died, the corner site had been managed by her executors. In April 1899 this was about to change. The *Camden News* advised readers that the shop and cottage, with a frontage of 66 feet and a depth of 330 feet, were for sale by auction by the local auctioneer, R. Inglis.[18]

Overlaying these measurements on the buildings near this intersection in 2020, the extent of the Buchan land becomes apparent. It takes in the current Tildsley's Butchery, Camden Photo Centre and Queen's Charcoal Chicken in Argyle Street, as well as the Camden Dental Centre, the adjacent Oxley Street laneway giving access to Woolworths' carpark and about ¼ of Woolworths' store up to a point approximately level with the bus stop. In 1899, this was a most desirable site in a developing main street; bidding began at an eye-watering £250, before the hammer fell at £425, selling to brothers, Alfred and Frederick Little.[19]

In August 1902, Bert Dunk ceased delivering meat to his customers owing to the costs involved,[20] but just six months later was preparing to move into the new building constructed for the Littles on the site of the old shop by local builders, Hindes & Farindon. The two-storey building was considered an enhancement and a 'credit to the town', particularly when, a month later, a balcony was added that curved around the corner into Oxley Street; the location soon became known locally as 'Dunk's Corner'.[21]

Winter shop fire

On a winter's night in 1907, Bert's shop could easily have been destroyed by fire if not for the skill of the Camden Volunteer Fire Brigade. The flames took hold in the shops of his neighbours, Horace Doust and H. Rafter, and were so fierce that by morning both premises were just smouldering ruins. Miraculously, Bert's shop and Mrs Wilkinson's boarding house were saved. The Littles had insurance on the two devastated properties and soon began rebuilding, this time constructing a two-shop premises with a residence above. At this stage, it is possible they subdivided the land, so the butcher shop and the new building each had separate land titles. Certainly by 1929 it had been subdivided, by which time the land on which the butcher's shop stood had a frontage of 26 feet.[22]

For two decades, Bert successfully supplied meat to the Camden public. However, in 1921 the Board of Health reported to Camden Council that the "improvement [previously] recommended was carried out, but upon inspection, I found the shop walls, particularly around benches, the interior of cool room and walls of salt room, dirty. The sausage filling machine was in a very dirty state. The plunger and cylinder were most dirty and encrusted thick with stale meat, grease and dirt. Outside the mincing room door was a tin dish containing scraps of mince-meat which was offensive and swarming

Laurie Dunk's advertisement (*Camden News*, 13 December 1923)

with flies, and which the butcher admitted, had been there several days."[23]

At the same time, stormwater and sullage from the Dunk premises and the adjoining two businesses were carried by a system of pipes, and open brick drains through the rear yards before discharging into an old garden at the Crown Hotel, creating a 'nuisance'. The 'nuisance inspector' suggested mitigating the problem by breaking up the ground in the garden and 'properly' distributing the drainage water through the area.[24]

Bert Dunk died in October 1921 and his widow, Hilda, advertised the business for sale four months later. The sale notice stated that it was a 'first-class family butchering business'. The sale included goodwill, cattle, sheep, horses, carts, harness, saddles, fixtures, utensils, sausage machine (horsepower), ice house and Drayton scales. All were in good condition.[25] By June 1922, Frank Paine occupied the shop and successfully applied to Camden Council for a slaughterman's license.[26]

Town improvement levy

In 1923, Camden Council introduced a 'Town Improvement' levy for all properties within the town's boundary. The rate was one penny in the pound on the unimproved value of each allotment. It raised £251/10/3 for the improvement of Macarthur Park and extensive tree planting for street beautification.[27] It is unknown what the unimproved value of the butcher's shop was in 1923, but in 1929 it was £286. Using this as a guide, the Town Improvement levy payable by the Littles for this site, would have been something less than £1/3/9.

Board of Health

Like Bert Dunk before him, Frank Paine also came to the notice of the Health Inspector when the Board of Health's Inspector Curry, charged him with failing to keep his premises clean, a charge to which Frank pled not guilty. Inspector Curry said he found a wooden box used for the storage of bones in a dirty condition in the shop; the box had not been cleaned for several days and contained grease, blood and fat. Behind the ice chest, there were floor sweepings, the needle attached to the brine pump was in a dirty condition and a number of stale bones and waste was giving off an offensive smell and was covered with flies.

In the same room was a tin of waste fruit and vegetable matter, along with cooked meat and kitchen offal. The nozzle of the sausage filling machine was dirty and contaminated with mince and fat, while the mincing machine was also dirty. At the rear of the 'closet' was a heap of ashes, tins, kitchen waste, sawdust and shop sweepings. The cart used to transfer carcasses from the slaughter yard to the shop was dirty as was a piece of hessian used to cover the carcasses. In his defence, Frank said he was absent from his shop on the day the inspector arrived.

Frank asserted: the box used for bones was emptied daily and limed every Saturday; the sawdust at the back of the ice chest was placed there to prevent the sawdust in the chest running out through a hole near the floor of the chest that had been made during a recent removal; the bag of bones in the room adjacent to the shop would have been emptied that day and contained no stale bones or waste; the sausage machine had not been used for 3 or 4 months, was clean and could have been used immediately; the heap of rubbish at the rear of the 'closet' was harmless; the cart was washed twice a week with hot water; and there was no hessian used to cover the carcasses as he used a waterproof sheet instead, which was kept on the back veranda when not in use. Despite his protestations, Frank was fined £2 and 18/- costs. On a further charge of allowing his stable yard to become littered with manure, he was fined £1 and 18/- costs.[28] After this, he ceased business.

Quality Corner

In December 1923, a Dunk once again occupied the butcher shop when Laurie Dunk opened for business, advertising his shop on 'Quality Corner'. He had previously owned a fruit and vegetable business before becoming the proprietor of a butcher shop next to Betts & Co in 1922.[29] Once he was settled in the former Paine shop, Laurie Dunk made 'vast' improvements to his butcher's premises. He enhanced the method by which meat was handled and rid his business of the difficulties of keeping meat cold using the ice storage he had used in the past. Laurie refitted the front of the shop with the latest appliances and installed a modern refrigerating plant powered by a five hp Hornsby gas engine fuelled by town gas.

Refrigeration

The refrigerator, which maintained a temperature of 30°F, operated through two specially built rooms that were capable of storing the carcasses of ten bullocks and 25 sheep at one time, while also allowing for meat to be cut up. The refrigerator also chilled the brine tanks that cured and stored corn meat. The gas engine powering the refrigeration unit also provided electric light and fans for the premises.[30] However, the introduction of such modern technology was not all smooth sailing.

In June 1925, Les Marden, an employee in the Dunk butchery, was injured when his right hand was caught in a power-driven mincing machine. He lost a portion of three fingers in the accident and spent a few days in Camden District Hospital. Just a couple of months later, a number of residents living nearby complained to Camden Council about the noise from the gas engine, resulting in Laurie having to fit a silencer to the motor.[31]

By 1926, the drains from the butcher shop and its immediate neighbours fronting Argyle Street were once again cause for concern and were in such a bad state of repair that Alfred Little, the owner of both the butcher's shop and its neighbour, had no choice but to submit a sketch, plans and specifications of the proposed improved drainage work to Camden Council, ready for the Board of Health's consideration.[32]

Supplying meat to Camden Hospital

In February 1927 as Camden Show approached, Laurie offered a 'beast' to the organisers of the weight judging competition and donated £2/2/- towards the prize for the competition winner. By December, he had successfully tendered to supply meat to Camden District Hospital, but in early 1928 found himself on the wrong side of the Board of Health when he was fined 30/- and 8/- costs for selling adulterated sausages containing more sulphur oxide than was allowed.[33] However, an inspection by the Health Department in August 1928 brought good news: his premises were reported to be in good condition, although a few minor improvements were required.

Laurie's slaughter yard also received a tick of approval, but he soon found life as a businessman involved more than selling to the public, and in 1929, an oversight cost him another 10/- and 8/- in costs when he failed to pay the Department of Labour and Industry the required registration fee for his premises by 1 December 1928.[34]

In 1926, the New South Wales government had established a centralised Valuer General's Department, so the self-determined values settled on by the Camden landowners back in 1896 were now superseded by the assessments of the government agency. The rates of the Council were based on these new valuations. Consequently, in 1929, the unimproved value of the two-storey butcher shop and residence was determined to be £286 with an improved value of £1,100.[35]

In 1929, Laurie Dunk's butcher and slaughter yard licenses were transferred to J. & E. Smith (Smith Brothers) although Laurie still maintained ownership of the slaughter yard.[36] His business versatility came to the fore again, when he took up a living as a real estate agent and auctioneer after disposing of the butcher shop. The Smith brothers weren't in the shop for long, however, when an employee, Sid Dunk, was involved in an accident on the Hume Highway near Hilder Street, Elderslie in February 1930.

Truck accident

Sid was driving the butcher's lorry when he was hit from behind by another vehicle. The lorry overturned and landed in a ditch, trapping Sid inside. His two passengers were slightly hurt, but, through good fortune, Sid escaped injury.[37] However, the death of the Smith brothers' father in the United Kingdom soon after, heralded another change to the proprietorship of the butcher shop. One of the brothers had to travel to the United Kingdom to attend to his father's affairs, so the partnership was dissolved in 1930 and the business sold to G. L. Chapman.[38] Within four months, Mr Chapman had sold to Fred and Glenroy Dunk, two well-known local men. "Thus, the corner...revert[ed] back to the old name of Dunk's Corner, which was established when the building was erected."[39]

Three years later, the shop was about to receive a facelift. Alfred Little called for tenders to paint the shop and residence occupied by Dunk's Butchery and the two adjoining businesses. However, before the month ended, Alfred died, and it seems the building was sold, and although the transfer date is unknown, the Dunks were certainly the owners by 1936.[40]

In 1936, Fred and Glenroy Dunk received approval – subject to the 'conditions' of the Board of Health - from Camden Council for a new slaughterhouse in Dunk's Road just off The Oaks Road. The site had received pre-

Tildsley's Butchery c. 1948: (l to r) Reg Tildsley, Kevin Sinclair, Frank Tildsley [Camden Images]

vious approval from the inspector, Sergeant Porteus.[41] Glenroy also had a slaughter yard at Cawdor, which now forms part of the garden of a home in the village. He did his own slaughtering and regularly attended the stock sales at the sale yards at the rear of the Plough and Harrow Hotel and Camden Hotel and, after 1940, in the new yards in Edward Street.[42]

Business was good for Fred and Glenroy and another local butcher, R. S. Boardman, if the number of animals passing through the Dunk slaughter yard is any indication. During the six months from 1 January to 30 June 1936, 308 cattle, 1,677 sheep and 78 pigs met their end at the hands of the slaughterman.[43] Although the exact time is unknown, Freida Dunk was employed as a cashier in the butcher shop, and two other employees were Peter and George Watson. At one stage, Glenroy Dunk had the motto, "Try our famous sausages" painted on a side wall.[44]

Balconies and verandas

October saw Camden Council pass a controversial ordinance requiring that all balconies and verandahs built over the footpath be demolished within two years of the date of the order. Individual notices were sent to all the affected building owners, including Glenroy Dunk. Any replacement structures had to cantilever from the building's façade.[45]

By March 1937, the Cleary brothers, John, Patrick and Daniel, had purchased the building two doors down, which had been the Royal Oak Inn before Mrs Wilkinson took it over as a boarding house followed in later years by Mrs Skinner. Soon after, the Clearys wanted to purchase 2 roods (about half an acre) of the adjoining Dunk land fronting onto Oxley Street.

The land in question was part of the backyard of Dunk's butcher shop, as well as the adjoining premises at 157-163 Argyle Street, which were also owned by Glenroy Dunk. Ownership of this piece of land would give the Clearys rear access to their newly acquired property at 165 Argyle Street. The subdivision was approved[46,] and with the sale, the depth of the Dunk land (151-163 Argyle Street) was reduced from 330 feet to 225 feet. The access to the rear of the Clearys' property at 165 Argyle Street had a 105 foot frontage to Oxley Street, taking in the current Oxley Street lane access to Woolworths' car park, along with a portion of the land occupied by the Woolworths' building, up to approximately the existing bus shelter.

In April 1937, the Dunk butcher shop was remodelled, perhaps using the money received for the land sold to the Cleary brothers. As part of the renovation, the verandahs of the two shops at 157-163 Argyle Street, as well as Dunk's Butchery, were removed following the 1936 Camden Council order. However, as the order only applied to verandahs in Argyle Street, the portion of the Dunk veranda in Oxley Street was not demolished and still stands today. Cantilever awnings were erected in the place of the balconies. Brickwork was added above the residence to strengthen the butcher shop and form a parapet to screen the roof.[47]

In 1945, Council permission was given for the construction of a fibro cement garage and storeroom at the rear of Dunk's butchery, although the Council said they would prefer the building to be constructed from brick, or at the very least, to have a brick frontage.[48] Once more known as 'Quality Corner' – a legacy from Laurie Dunk's day - in 1946 the shop was leased from Glenroy Dunk (now sole owner) by Reg Tildsley, a butcher who'd worked in the family shops in Campbelltown and Narellan.

Reg opens butcher shop in Camden

After these businesses were sold, Reg opened the butcher shop in Camden, along with his sons, Frank and Les, and by 1948, also employed Kevin Sinclair. Reg, his wife, Grace, and their three children, Frank, Jean and Les, lived in the residence. There were bedrooms and bathroom upstairs, lounge room and kitchen downstairs in what is now the tobacco shop – while the backyard held a garage and fruit trees.[49] After the 1937 subdivision, the rear fence was directly in line with the northern wall of the current Camden Den-

Tildsley Butcher Shop at 155 Argyle Street Camden in 2016. (I Willis)

tal Centre. In 1950, Reg Tildsley successfully applied for registration of his slaughter yard in Westbrook Lane (Mount Hunter) and over the next two years supplied meat to Camden District Hospital.[50]

Between 1950 and 1953, Glenroy Dunk sold another 60 feet of his backyard leaving a property depth of 165 feet, bringing the back fence to a line approximately level with the southern wall of the Camden Dental Centre. It had an unimproved value of £1,690 and an improved vale of £3,900.[51] In 1956, Glenroy sold the property to Reg, Frank and Les Tildsley, and it stayed in the family for the next 38 years. Reg and Grace's granddaughter, Roslyn, recalls her grandmother sitting at the kitchen window talking to passers-by and keeping an eye on the comings and goings in the street.

The double garage in the backyard housed the 'famous green Bedford meat truck', along with the family's Holden car. During these years, like the Dunks before them, Tildsley sausages were famous in the area and highly sought after by locals. Roslyn recalls sausages even going interstate when the family went on holidays, and today she still hears people remark that Tildsley's is the only place they will purchase sausages. In the late 1960s, Keith Weatherburn began to work in the shop, followed in 1976 by his son, Mark. In the early 1990s, the residence's downstairs kitchen and lounge room were converted into a small shop that was occupied by the ladies' wear business, 'Aussie Casuals'.[52]

In 1990, the size and style of the 87-year-old Tildsley building were duplicated by Les Tildsley on the land fronting Oxley Street that had previously been what remained of the backyard of Reg and Grace Tildsley. The new building (55 Oxley Street) had five shops on the ground floor with two residences above. During these years Mark Weatherburn continued to work in the butcher shop, and although the length of their employment is unknown, was a colleague of both Barry Harper and Wayne Wells.

Sale of butchery

In 1994, the butchery was sold to Mark Weatherburn and his wife, Sonya, who continued to trade under the name "Tildsley's Butchery". To the Tildsley family, the sale of the business to Mark and Sonya Weatherburn felt like it was being kept 'in the family' as there had been a Weatherburn working for them for almost 30 years.[53] In 1998, Camden Tobacconist moved from premises at 167 Argyle Street into the small shop that had previously been the kitchen of the butcher's residence and continues to trade from this location today.[54]

And so, after decades of butchers on this site, Tildsley's Butchery continues to present a familiar and affable face to the shoppers of the town. The occupants of the shop have earnt their place in the history of a main street that is filled with a collage of stories and characters. In 2010, the significance of the 117-year-old building was acknowledged when it was added to Camden Council's Local Environmental Plan, giving formal recognition to the comforting presence of an established part of the streetscape and the town's history.[55]

Notes

[1] John Burge's 1993 Argyle Street index. Martin, J.B. et al., *Reminiscences of Early Camden*, Ed. J. Johnson, Camden Historical Society Inc., 2012, p. 26. *Camden News*, 7 October 1897; 7 November 1940
[2] *Sydney Morning Herald*, 24 October 1854
[3] John Burge's 1993 Argyle Street index. N.S.W. Government Gazette, 9 August 1859, Issue 153, p. 1740. *Camden News*, 7 October 1897
[4] Atkinson, Alan, *Camden – Farm and Village Life in Early New South Wales*, Oxford University Press, Melbourne, 1988, p. 54, 56. Hand-drawn map in John Burge's research papers.
[5] Willis, Ian, 'Whiteman's Commercial Building', *Camden History Notes Blog*, pub. 25 December 2017
[6] Sidman, G. V., *The Town of Camden*, Camden Public Library & Liz Vincent, 1995, p. 36
[7] Willis, Ian, 'Whiteman's Commercial Building', *Camden History Notes Blog*: pub. 25 December 2017
[8] Camden Council Municipal List: Rates Book 1894-1907
[9] *Camden News*, 20 June 1895
[10] *Camden News*, 19 March 1896

[11] *Camden News*, 6 August 1896
[12] *Camden News*, 11th February 1897
[13] Recollections of the former resident, Ben Hodge
[14] *Camden News*, 11 March 1897
[15] *Camden News*, 17 February 1898
[16] *Camden News*, 29 September 1898; 13 October 1898
[17] *Camden News*, 13 October 1898; 27 October 1898
[18] *Camden News*, 13 April 1899
[19] *Camden News*, 27 April 1899
[20] *Camden News* 7 August 1902
[21] Martin, J.B. et al., *Reminiscences of Early Camden,* Ed. J. Johnson, Camden Historical Society Inc., 2012, p. 51. Camden News, 30 April 1903; 7 May 1903; 6 August 1903
[22] *Camden News*, 18 July 1907; 25 July 1907. N.S.W. Valuer General's Assessment Book: 1929
[23] *Camden News*, 5 May 1921
[24] *Camden News*, 5 May 1921
[25] *Camden News*, 6 October 1921; 9 February 1922; 23 March 1922
[26] *Camden News*, 11 May 1922; 1 June 1922
[27] Sidman, G. V., *The Town of Camden*, Camden Public Library & Liz Vincent, 1995, p. 72
[28] *Camden News*, 19 April 1923
[29] *Camden News*, 12 January 1922; 13 December 1923
[30] *Camden News*, 16 October 1924
[31] *Camden News*, 18 June 1925; 20 August 1925
[32] *Camden News*, 2 December 1926; 10 February 1927
[33] *Camden News*, 24 February 1927; 29 December 1927; 22 March 1928
[34] *Camden News*, 23 August 1928; 28 March 1929; 16 May 1929
[35] N.S.W. Valuer General's Assessment Book: 1929
[36] *Camden News*, 21 November 1929; 27 November 1930
[37] *Camden News*, 20 February 1930
[38] *Camden News*, 27 March 1930
[39] *Camden News*, 31 July 1930
[40] *Camden News*, 2 February 1933; 2 March 1933
[41] *Camden News*, 27 February 1936
[42] Recollections of the former resident, Charles Dunk
[43] *Camden News*, 16 July 1936
[44] Recollections of the former resident, Charles Dunk
[45] *Camden News*, 15 October 1936
[46] *Camden News*, 4 March 1937
[47] *Camden News*, 15 April 1937
[48] *Camden News*, 15 February 1945
[49] *Camden News*, 2 July 1936; 11 July 1946; 25 July 1946. Recollections of Roslyn Tildsley – Reg & Grace's granddaughter
[50] *Camden News*, 15 June 1950; 28 June 1951; 17 July 1952
[51] N.S.W. Valuer General's Assessment Book: 1953
[52] Recollections of Roslyn Tildsley and Sonya Weatherburn
[53] Recollections of Roslyn Tildsley; 'Joe', owner of J.P.'s Hairdressing Salon; Sonya Weatherburn.
[54] Camden Telephone Directories 1968-2019, Camden Museum.
[55] Local Environmental Plan – Schedule 5 'Environmental Heritage' Camden Council.

www.ingramcontent.com/pod-product-compliance
Lightning Source LLC
Chambersburg PA
CBHW051533010526
44107CB00064B/2712